# THE COMPLETE CRUMB

# THE COMPLETE CRUMB

## VOLUME 4

## MR. SIXTIES!

### R. CRUMB

Edited by Gary Groth
with Robert Fiore

**FANTAGRAPHICS BOOKS**

**EDITOR'S NOTE:**
In editing this series we have attempted to place material insofar as possible in its original context and chronological order. Consequently, the reader may notice differences in the material as it appears in the *Complete Crumb* and as it appeared in the most common underground comics. Differences are particularly notable in *Zap* #0 and #1. As drawn in 1967, these two comics were to be 24 pages each. Between the first and second printings of *Zap* #1 and before the first printing of *Zap* #0 the publisher, Don Donahue, obtained a larger press that would accommodate 14-page signatures, and four pages were added to each issue. In this volume we are reprinting the 24-page comics as drawn in October and November of 1967.
The following pages were added in 1968:

*ZAP #0:*
"Sky-Hi Comics" from *East Village Other* January 12-17, 1968 (appears in *Complete Crumb* Volume Five);
"Itzy and Bitzy in 'Cause and Effect,' " from *Yarrowstalks #3* (appears in *Complete Crumb* Volume Four);
"Kozmic Kapers," sketchbook strip reprinted in *Yellow Dog #6* (appears in *Complete Crumb* Volume Four);
"Freak Out Funnies Presents Those Cute Little Bearzie Wearzies," from *EVO* January 26-February 1, 1968 (appears in *Complete Crumb* Volume Five).

*ZAP #1:*
"Mr. Natural Encounters Flakey Foont," from *Yarrowstalks #3* (appears in *Complete Crumb* Volume Four);
"Nuttin' But Nuttin'," from *EVO* January 19-25, 1968 (appears in *Complete Crumb* Volume Five);
"Har Har Page," sketchbook strip (appears in *Complete Crumb* Volume Four);
"Flakey Foont Encounters Fatback," from *Yarrowstalks #3* (appears in *Complete Crumb* Volume Four);
Various short strips from *EVO* pages (all appear in *Complete Crumb* Volume Five).

FANTAGRAPHICS BOOKS
7563 Lake City Way NE
Seattle, WA 98115

Editorial coordination by Robert Fiore.
Design and art direction by Dale Crain.
Consulting editor: Donald Fiene.
Typesetting by Gil Jordan & R. Fiore.
Color separations through Palace Press.
Gary Groth and Kim Thompson, Publishers.
Special Thanks to Donald Ault, Glenn Bray, Mark Burbey,
Brian Cleary, Al Davoren, Donald Fiene, Caroline Kennemuth
and the American Greetings Corporation, the Mad Peck
Archives, Victor Moscoso, Eric Sack, Anthony F. Smith,
Fred Vigeant, and Mark Wistinghausen.

Strips on pages 18 to 31 and 49 to 58 were first
published in *Yellow Dog* #1-10 and *R. Crumb
Sketchbook, 1966-67*; "Let's Get Outa Here"
was first published in *Print Project Amerika*, December 1970.

First Fantagraphics Books edition: September, 1989
Second Fantagraphics Books edition: July, 1995
(There is no second hardcover edition.)

ISBN (soft) : 0-930193-79-2
ISBN (hard): 0-930193-80-6

Printed in Singapore by SNP Printing Pte Ltd

# CONTENTS

# INTRODUCTION
## BY R·CRUMB

So, uh, Marty Pahls died... it looks like I'll have to write these @✱!!! introductions myself now — for the time being anyway. I was afraid this would happen... @✱!!! Marty... there's only a couple other people I'd trust to write them, and they're not interested. Maybe Fantagraphics can find somebody eventually... except who's a decent writer who knows my history as well as Marty did?

So, what the hell happened to old Martle, you ask? What'd he DIE of?? Good question, dear reader... nobody knows for certain. He was found dead in his apartment by the custodian. I can't figure it out... to me he seemed to be in a slow state of decline practically since I first knew him. It's amazing to think how different he was thirty years ago, in 1958. The brash, crew-cut college freshman from Kent, Ohio, trim... athletic, even... brimming with charm, optimistic, rambunctiously enthusiastic about his cultural interests, his corny midwestern sense of humor... it was all sorta irritating to the morbid, introverted Crumb family sensibility, but we developed a strong relationship based on mutual interests, we wrote long letters to each other for years, and occasionally Marty would come east and stay at the Crumb house for a few days. He was the first "outsider" to appreciate the great Crumb artistic genius.

He was very popular with the intellectual-folknik-literary crowd at Kent State, and had lots of girlfriends. People who met him in the later period of his life would shake their heads in disbelief when I described this early Marty to them. He certainly came down in the world — WAY, WAY DOWN... I've never been able to figure it out — nor could HE! The last time I talked to him he said, "I wonder what's wrong with me".. maybe it was genetic or something. It's a mystery. Ironically, I was the one who was depressed back then, when I first knew Marty. He would give me pep talks; don't let the thick-skulled idiots get you down! He was a big help to my morale. He was the first real "intellectual" I'd ever seen. I thought he was REALLY SMART, and must know what he's talking about. I listened to him.

Man, he could really lay down a line of talk-very articulate... I stood by and watched with amazement his easy way with women — oh, he had the gift of gab! He talked those girls into a hypnotic stupor of submission — he had them coming and going — it made me sick with envy — I, who was helplessly tongue-tied in the presence of any attractive woman.

It seemed like he just threw it all away-all the opportunities to do something with his life. He gradually retreated from the world — he shucked a potential career in academia. He threw away his writing talent on shitty low level jobs, like writing ad copy for employment agencies. For awhile he talked about writing the great American novel, but he never got around to it. He spent more and more of his time alone in his apartment. He collected books, comics, old records, magazines, newspaper pages — the stuff piled up, stacked to the ceiling. His cultural interests enveloped him, engulfed him! He had to have EVERYTHING on tape! He amassed a huge collection of reel-to-reel tapes — every jazz, blues, country, R.&B., rockabilly & irish record ever made — he occupied his time with busy work. He made lists, catalogues of all his stuff. He was a vast encyclopedia of information on his favorite subjects. He used to bend my ear for HOURS about bygone street railway systems, which type of cars ran in which cities during a given period and what lines they ran on. He knew the geographical layout and history of the growth of most of America's larger cities. He would lament the decline of the great cities. Cleveland, his birthplace, was his favorite emblem of the downfall and destruction of American culture by blood-sucking capitalist greed. He took it to heart, that was his trouble. But he was right about these things. He was a sharp, astute observer — and though it was hard to take his hours and hours of talk, it was always interesting, he knew his stuff. I'd be falling asleep on the couch at five in the morning, and he'd still be going on about some esoteric point about the Nazis... my brain had

long since become numb. I could only take in so much.

Too bad he never was able to put his mental abilities to any good use. The flower of his creativity was squandered on a cheap Chicago tabloid called CANDID PRESS. He worked for this bunch of gangsters for about five years in the 'seventies. Marty's attitude about writing for this sleazy rag was very cynical, but within the formula of titilation he had to work with, he did some funny writing... lots of enema humor and fake expose's about Jackie. The paper folded and the owners threw everybody out into the street. It was Marty's last steady job.

Then he came down with a bad case of diabetes and was forced to deal with the welfare system. Out of this experience he developed a deep hatred of bureaucracy and further retreated from the world. His biggest mistake, though, was falling in love with my sister Sandra. That didn't help his situation at ALL! He always had a powerful attraction to this nasty little female ever since he first started coming around the Crumb house. He courted her for years, the poor sap. He would come to Philadelphia and hang around the house, mooning after her, trying to charm her. It was a joke to her. She was bitterly sarcastic to him and completely unimpressed by his erudite rap. What were Marty's powers compared to the mind-control techniques of older brother Charles, twisted wizard of the Crumb children? He kept Sandra in a mental vise-grip for her entire late adolescence. I guess her indifference inflamed Marty's passion for the black-clad, chain-smoking, giggling, sarcastic, self-absorbed twerp. She basically hated all men and used the good-natured slob to get away from home, out from under our psychotic parents and the tyranny of the Charles regime. They lived together for two or three years in Chicago, maybe longer. They had a kid, a son named Avery. Sandra drank heavily and visciously insulted Marty constantly. His self-esteem went down several more notches, then she left him. She went to San Francisco and shortly "came out" —— a radical separatist lesbian. She moved into a lesbian "collective". I saw her occasionally during this period, the early 'seventies. She and her lesbian sisters believed that heterosexuality was soon, to become obsolete. They worked themselves into a state! Giving birth was considered "barbaric". Babies in the future would all be born in glass containers. Included in this program was the idea that I, Sandra's famous chauvinist-pig brother, should pay her 400 dollars a month "reparations". We didn't speak to each other for years over that one. She has since modified her views somewhat. At my father's funeral in '82 she admitted to me that women can play the same asshole power games that men are reknowned for, and she was disgusted with the lezbo "community."

After Sandra left, Marty had a series of girlfriends. A couple of these were amazingly high-quality items; young, fresh, cute AND intelligent! They all eventually gave up on him and moved on. He was on his way down, a slow but sure losing streak. I don't know what happened. When he moved to San Francisco in the late 'seventies we all thought it would be a good change for him - a fresh start in a nice town would revive his sagging, decaying life, get him out more, something. Instead, his nice clean San Francisco apartment quickly became the reincarnation of the filthy pack-rat hovel he'd left behind in Chicago, roaches included. The books, papers, records began again to pile up everywhere. The oppressive claustrophobia became worse, if anything.

His health, as well as his attitude, continued to deteriorate. He went out less and less. His nerves were completely shot. The last few times he visited at friends' houses terrible, embarrassing things happened. He projectile-vomited all over the dinner table in the middle of polite conversation... he lost control of his bowels in the living room. The wives of his friends stopped allowing him to come back. He started having dizzy spells. The last year of his life he never once left the apartment. He had the groceries delivered. He had work sent to him — what work he could get. He was always in need of money. Naturally, the I.R.S. began picking on him. He sold off a few valuable collectibles. He fretted and worried but wouldn't do anything, wouldn't make a move to save himself. It was horrible to watch, but impossible to help him. He died broke, completely penniless.

But, you know what? Even in the grimmest last days of his decline, the women still came around! I dunno what

IT WAS HE HAD — MAYBE HE WAS AN EXPERT PUSSY LAPPER OR SOMETHING. HE STILL HAD HIS RAP.... THERE WERE NICE, ATTRACTIVE YOUNG WOMEN STILL HANGING AROUND IN THAT FOUL, FETID DEN OF HIS. ONE OF THEM EVEN ASKED IF SHE COULD MOVE IN AND LIVE WITH HIM! THIS WAS NOT SOME DRIED-UP HAG WE'RE TALKING ABOUT. I MET HER. SHE WAS A FINE-LOOKIN' ITEM! I HAD THE HOTS FOR HER MYSELF. I TRIED TO LOCATE HER AFTER MARTY DIED BUT HAD NO LUCK...

MY LAST VISIT TO MARTY'S RAT-HOLE WAS IN OCTOBER, '88. HE WANTED TO INTERVIEW ME FOR THE NEXT INSTALLMENT OF THE COMPLETE CRUMB SERIES — THIS VERY ONE, IN FACT. WHEN I SHOWED UP AT THE DOOR HE WOULDN'T OPEN IT. INSTEAD, HE BEGGED ME URGENTLY TO COME BACK IN FIFTEEN MINUTES. SO, I TOOK A WALK. WHEN I CAME BACK THE DOOR WAS AJAR. I WENT IN. MARTY HAD POSITIONED HIMSELF PROPPED UP ON HIS BED. HE WAS SHOCKINGLY EMACIATED. HE HAD THE LOOK OF DEATH ABOUT HIM. I PUT THE TAPE RECORDER NEXT TO HIM ON THE NIGHT STAND, AND SAT ON A CHAIR NEXT TO THE BED. HE NEVER MOVED WHILE WE TALKED. HIS BODY WAS LIFELESS, EXCEPT THAT WHENEVER A TAPE CLICKED OFF AT THE END, A JOLT WOULD GO THROUGH HIM AS IF HE'D GOTTEN A VIOLENT ELECTRIC SHOCK. BUT HIS MIND WAS STILL SHARP AS EVER. EVEN HIS CORNY MIDWESTERN SENSE OF HUMOR WAS STILL IN TACT. NATURALLY, I LECTURED HIM ON THE URGENT NECESSITY OF DOING SOMETHING IMMEDIATELY ABOUT HIS RAPIDLY DETERIORATING CONDITION. EVERYONE WHO STILL SAW HIM GAVE HIM THE SAME LECTURE. IT'S OBVIOUS ON HINDSIGHT THAT HE WAS ALREADY WAY PAST THE POINT OF BEING ABLE TO TAKE ANY ACTION ON HIS OWN BEHALF. "YEAH, I KNOW, I SHOULD....." HE'D WHINE. IT WAS EXASPERATING... HE WAS A BULL-HEADED FUCKER.

HE DIED IN FEBRUARY, '89. A BUNCH OF US WENT OVER THERE WITH HIS BROTHER AND FATHER TO DEAL WITH ALL HIS STUFF. HIS SON AVERY, NOW NINETEEN, CAME DOWN FROM SEATTLE. IT WAS AN ENORMOUS TASK. IT TOOK SEVERAL DAYS OF SOLID WORK TO SORT IT ALL OUT. ALOT OF IT WAS BAGGED UP TO THROW AWAY. THE REST WAS SOLD OFF TO OTHER PACK-RAT COLLECTORS AND DEALERS. AVERY GOT THE MONEY, SEVERAL THOUSAND DOLLARS, TO HELP HIM THROUGH COLLEGE. I TOOK A FEW BOOKS AND RECORDS FOR MYSELF, SOME OLD LETTERS AND SNAPSHOTS FROM THE OLD DAYS. SOME COMPULSIVE COLLECTOR LUNATIC EVEN PAID GOOD MONEY FOR THE REEL-TO-REEL TAPES, ALL 2,183 OF THEM! I THOUGHT FOR SURE THOSE THINGS WOULD END UP IN THE TRASH HEAP. THAT AMAZED ME! EVERYTHING OF VALUE WAS EVENTUALLY SOLD OUT OF THE APARTMENT, THE JUNK WAS HAULED TO THE DUMP, AND THE BOOK WAS OFFICIALLY CLOSED ON MARTIN L. PAHLS.

I GOTTA SAY, AS IRRITATING AS HE WAS TO DEAL WITH, MARTY WAS A GREAT HELP TO ME AT DIFFERENT TIMES IN MY LIFE. HE HAD A GENEROUS HEART TO HIS FRIENDS, THOUGH, LIKE JONATHAN SWIFT, HE DESPISED THE WORLD IN GENERAL, AND WHO CAN BLAME HIM? HE WAS MY BIGGEST FAN IN MY "EARLY YEARS OF BITTER STRUGGLE" AND GAVE ME A HAND UP WHEN I WAS A QUIVERING, SUICIDAL CULL BARELY ABLE TO TALK TO PEOPLE. I WASN'T MUCH HELP TO HIM IN HIS DECLINING YEARS, I DIDNT KNOW WHAT TO DO EXCEPT LECTURE THE GUY, WHICH DID NO GOOD AT ALL. I USED TO RANT TO HIM ALL THE TIME ABOUT HIS DIET, HE ALWAYS ATE THE ABSOLUTELY WORST SHIT. HE LIVED ON OSCAR MYER WEINERS AND CHEERIOS. THE LAST TIME I ATE OUT WITH HIM, HE INSISTED ON GOING TO A NEAR-BY COLONEL SANDERS. I GOT A BAD CASE OF INDIGESTION BUT HE LOVED IT! HE WOLFED DOWN A BIG OL' BUCKET!

WHEN I CAME HOME FROM HELPING SORT THROUGH HIS STUFF I IMMEDIATELY BEGAN GOING THROUGH MY OWN PILES OF OLD PAPER GOODS. I SPENT A WEEK OBSESSIVELY SORTING AND ELIMINATING. IT WAS INCREDIBLE HOW MUCH STUFF I PURGED OUT! I WAS DRIVEN BY AN ACUTE SENSE OF URGENCY BORDERING ON PANIC! I DIDNT WANT TO LEAVE A LEGACY LIKE OL' MARTY HAD LEFT FOR HIS FRIENDS. I PUT MY THINGS IN ORDER. IT WAS VERY SATISFYING. MARTY'S DEATH WAS A GREAT UNEXPECTED LESSON THAT WAY.

NOW, BACK TO MY LIFE... LET'S SEE, WHERE DID MARTY LEAVE OFF IN THE LAST VOLUME? YEAH, SO IT'S EARLY IN THE YEAR 1966. I'M 22 YEARS OLD, AND I HAVE NO IDEA WHAT I'M DOING. I'VE JUST BROKEN UP WITH MY WIFE DANA. SHE WENT BACK TO CLEVELAND, AND I STAYED IN NEW YORK. MY BIG CAREER AS A COMMERCIAL ARTIST WAS JUST ONE MORE CARDBOARD CUT-OUT DREAM FORGOTTEN IN THE DUST AFTER MANY HEAVY TRIPS TAKEN ON LSD. I FEEL LIKE I'M BACK IN KINDERGARTEN. IT'S ALL NEW TO ME... I'VE BEEN STUMBLING AROUND IN A DELIRIUM SINCE I TOOK SOME WEIRD PSYCHEDELIC DRUG... THE STUFF CAME ON LIKE NORMAL ACID... THE USUAL TRIPPY SENSATIONS, THE VISUAL EFFECTS, THE EXPANDING CONSCIOUSNESS INTO INFINITY — LIKE, WOW — THEN ALL OF A SUDDEN EVERYTHING WENT, LIKE, FUZZY — LIKE, THE RECEPTION WENT BAD — I LOST THE PICTURE, THE SOUND, EVERYTHING — IT WAS SO WEIRD, BUT NOT PARTICULARLY FRIGHTENING. FOR THE NEXT COUPLE OF MONTHS I FELT LIKE THE GUY IN ERASERHEAD... EVERYTHING WAS DREAM-LIKE AND UNREAL. IT WAS RATHER PLEASANT IN A CERTAIN WAY EXCEPT THAT I WAS HELPLESS AND BARELY ABLE TO COPE,

ONE MORNING AFTER BEING UP ALL NIGHT TRIPPING ON A MILD DOSE OF LSD WITH THIS GIRL BOBBI FOX AT HER PLACE (ALL I REMEMBER ABOUT IT IS SITTING ON HER ASS WHILE SHE WRITHED ON THE BED, AND HOLDING HER BY HER MOP OF CURLY HAIR AND FLOPPING HER HEAD AROUND, AND LATER HER TALKING TO MY BARE FEET LIKE THEY WERE TWO LITTLE CRITTERS.) I WENT INTO THE SUBWAY AND SAW AN ATTRACTIVE YOUNG GIRL LYING DEAD ON THE PLATFORM. A CROWD HAD GATHERED, POLICE WERE THERE. I TOOK THIS AS AN OMEN THAT I MUST LEAVE NEW YORK. I DECIDED I'D GO TO CHICAGO, STAY WITH OL' MARTY. HE'D GIVE ME SHELTER FROM THIS HARSH WORLD. HE HAD A JOB, HE WAS STABLE, HE DIDN'T TAKE MIND-ALTERING SUBSTANCES. SO I ABANDONED THE APARTMENT ON EAST 11TH STREET IN MY YOUTHFUL, IRRESPONSIBLE WAY, AND TOOK THE GREYHOUND TO CHICAGO. MARTY WAS A LITTLE BEWILDERED BY THE SICKLY GREEN PSYCHEDELIC AURA THAT BUZZED AND CRACKLED AROUND MY HEAD, BUT HE WAS FASCINATED BY THE STRANGE IMAGES THAT BEGAN TO APPEAR IN MY SKETCHBOOK.

A WHOLE NEW THING WAS EMERGING IN MY DRAWINGS, A SORT OF HARKENING BACK, A CALLING UP OF WHAT G. LEGMAN HAD CALLED THE "HORROR-SQUINKY" FORCES LURKING IN AMERICAN COMICS OF THE 1940s. I HAD NO CONTROL OVER IT, THE WHOLE TIME I WAS IN THIS FUZZY STATE OF MIND, THE SEPARATION, THE BARRIER BETWIXT THE CONSCIOUS AND THE SUBCONSCIOUS WAS BROKEN OPEN SOMEHOW. A GROTESQUE KALEIDOSCOPE, A TAWDRY CARNIVAL OF DISASSOCIATED IMAGES KEPT SPUTTERING TO THE SURFACE... ESPECIALLY IF I WAS SITTING AND STARING, WHICH I OFTEN DID. IT WAS DIFFICULT TO FUNCTION IN THIS CONDITION. I WAS CERTIFIABLY CRAZY. I SAT STARING ON THE COUCH AT MARTY'S APARTMENT, OR ON LONG AIMLESS BUSRIDES AROUND CHICAGO. THESE JERKY ANIMATED CARTOONS IN MY MIND WERE NOT BEAUTIFUL, POETIC OR SPIRITUAL, THEY WERE LIKE AN OUT-OF-TUNE PLAYER PIANO THAT YOU COULDN'T SHUT OFF.... PRETTY DISTURBING... THIS STRANGE INTERLUDE ENDED AS ABRUPTLY AS IT HAD BEGUN THE NEXT TIME I TOOK A POWERFUL DOSE OF LSD IN APRIL, '66. MY MIND SUDDENLY CLEARED. THE FUZZINESS WAS GONE, THE FOG LIFTED. IT WAS A GREAT RELIEF... A WEIRD DRUG THAT WAS. BUT WHAT THE HECK — "MINDS ARE MADE TO BE BLOWN."

AND WHAT A BOON TO MY ART! IT WAS DURING THAT FUZZY PERIOD THAT I RECORDED IN MY SKETCHBOOK ALL THE MAIN CHARACTERS I WOULD BE USING IN MY COMICS FOR THE NEXT TEN YEARS; MR. NATURAL, FLAKEY FOONT, SCHUMAN THE HUMAN, THE SNOID, EGGS ACKLEY, THE VULTURE DEMONESSES, SHABNO THE SHOE-HORN DOG, THIS ONE, THAT ONE... WHICH IS INTERESTING. IT WAS A ONCE-IN-A-LIFETIME EXPERIENCE, LIKE A RELIGIOUS VISION THAT CHANGES SOMEONE'S LIFE, BUT IN MY CASE IT WAS THE PSYCHOTIC MANIFESTATION OF SOME GRIMY PART OF AMERICA'S COLLECTIVE UNCONSCIOUS.

ON THOSE COLD DAYS IN CHICAGO MARTY AND I WANDERED THE STREETS TALKING AND LOOKING. WE FOUND A DRAB, UNNAMED STORE FRONT WHICH WAS FILLED WITH REMAINDERED OLD MAGAZINES AND COMICS WITH THE COVERS TORN OFF. THE COMICS WERE ALL BRAND X, LOW-GRADE STUFF FROM THE POST-WAR ERA... A NICKEL APIECE. WE PURCHASED A BIG STACK AND LUGGED THEM BACK TO THE APARTMENT. I STUDIED THESE FUNNY BOOKS CLOSELY... I GOT INTO THEM... LURID FUNNY ANIMALS THAT TRIED TO LOOK CUTE BUT WEREN'T LIVED IN A CALLOUS, SAVAGE WORLD OF COLD VIOLENCE AND BAD JOKES, EXACTLY AS FREDRIC WERTHAM AND G. LEGMAN HAD SAID. THEY WERE VERY MUCH AKIN TO THE NIGHTMARE VISIONS SPUMING UP OUT OF MY FEVERED BRAIN. MARTY OBSERVED THIS PHENOMENON WITH DETACHED FASCINATION. HE ENCOURAGED ME TO CONTINUE WITH THIS LINE OF EXPLORATION.

I BEGAN TO MISS DANA MORE AND MORE. I SAW HER WEEPING FACE IN MY DREAMS. I WAS LONELY. I HAD TERRIBLE CRAVINGS TO KISS HER OVAL KRISHNA FACE, TO CLIMB ON HER ROBUST YOUNG BODY — YOUNG LOVE, FIRST LOVE. THE PULL WAS TOO STRONG. GOOD SENSE GAVE WAY. I NEEDED HER LIKE THE ADDICT NEEDS HIS FIX. I BID FAREWELL TO MARTY AND GOT ON THE GREYHOUND BACK TO CLEVELAND. OH MY GOD, CLEVELAND AGAIN! I WAS OVERJOYED TO SEE THE WIFE.... SHE LOOKED GREAT — THE BEST SHE EVER LOOKED. I COULDN'T BELIEVE I WAS REALLY THERE AS I STOOD TRANSFIXED BEFORE THAT KRISHNA FACE. SHE'D LOST SOME WEIGHT. HER LONG DARK HAIR WAS IN BRAIDS. SHE WORE TIGHT-FITTING BLUE JEANS ON HER BIG SHAPELY LEGS, AND COWBOY BOOTS. MY WHOLE BEING LUSTED FOR THE BIG JEWISH GODDESS (THIS AWE WORE OFF QUICKLY AFTER A COUPLE OF GOOD SHTUPPINGS — AINT I AWFUL?). IRONICALLY, SHE WASN'T ALL THAT EAGER TO TAKE ME BACK AT FIRST. SHE WAS DOING JUST FINE WITHOUT ME. SHE HAD A LITTLE APARTMENT, A LITTLE SCENE GOING. SHE EVEN HAD CUTE BOYS MOONING AROUND AFTER HER. SHE'D GOTTEN A JOB AT A HOSPITAL PHARMACY AND WAS PASSING OUT METHEDRINE TABLETS LIKE CANDY TO ALL HER FRIENDS. THIS ENDEARED HER TO A HOST OF

MARTY PAHLS, CLEVELAND, 1958.
ON THE BACK OF THIS PHOTO HE WROTE:
"INTRUDER ADJUSTS POLE ON OLD 450, RECALLING DAYS WHEN DECK-ROOFED JOBS WERE KING."

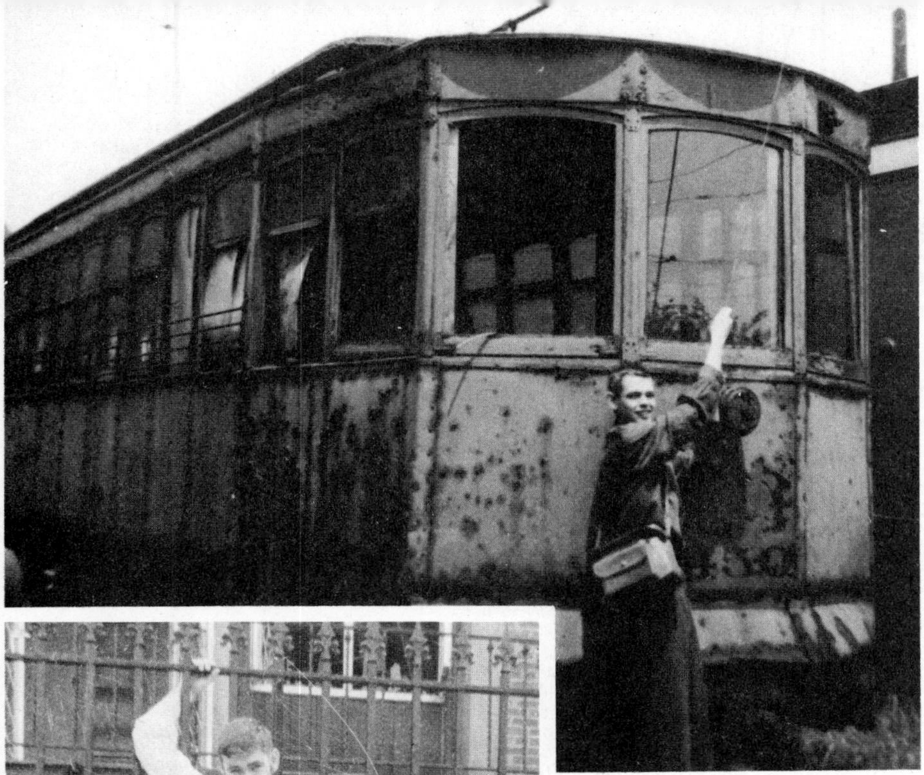

R. CRUMB & MARTY PAHLS IN BACK OF BASEMENT APARTMENT, CARNEGIE AVE., CLEVELAND, 1963.

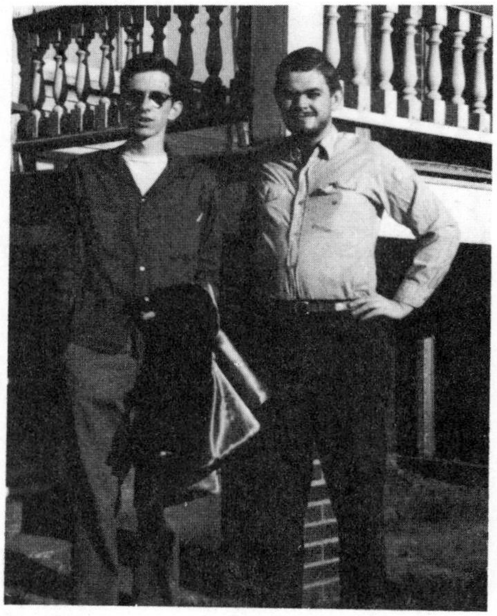

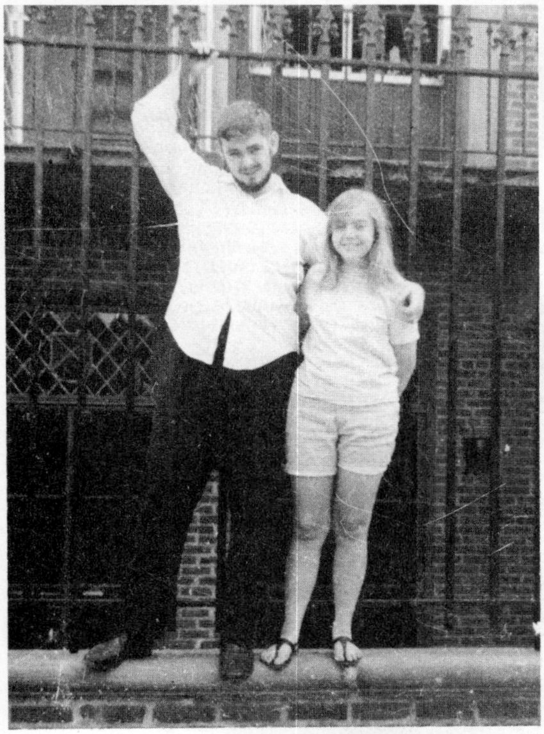

MARTY WITH THE ANGEL-FACED BARBY BROCK, HIS GIRLFRIEND IN THE EARLY '60S.

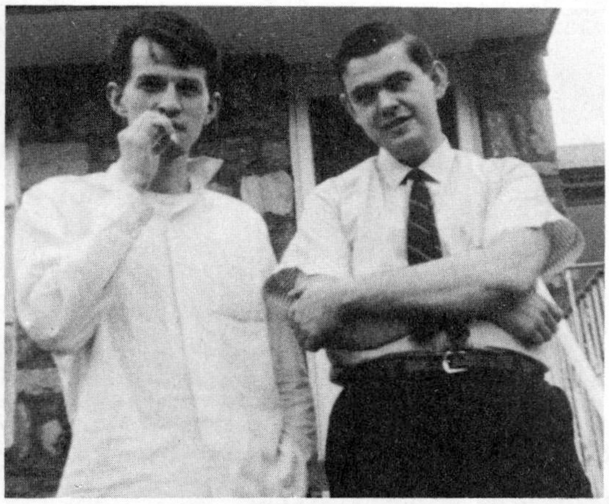

CHARLES CRUMB & MARTY IN FRONT OF CRUMB FAMILY HOUSE, PHILADELPHIA, FALL, '65.

MARTY WITH THE DIABOLICAL SANDRA CRUMB, TAKEN IN PHOTO BOOTH, MID '60S, BEFORE THEY WERE MARRIED.

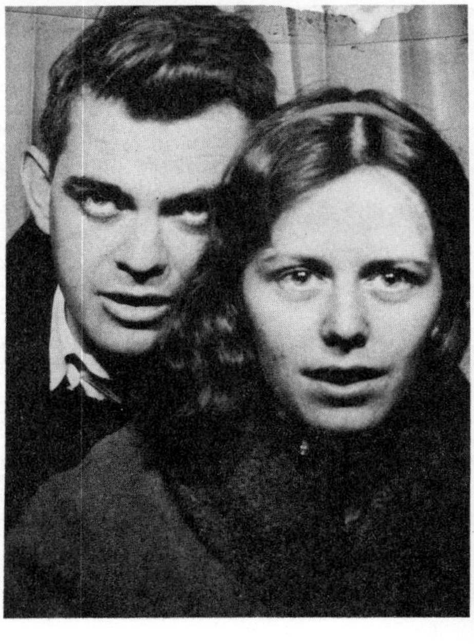

ALINE KOMINSKY, R. CRUMB & MARTY, HIGHLAND PARK, ILL., CIRCA 1975.

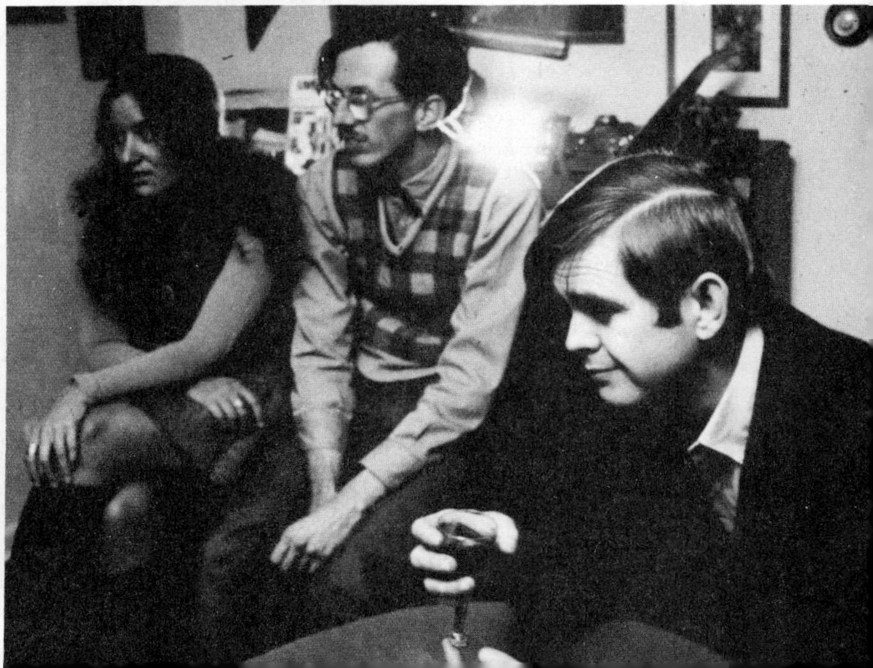

YOUNG NE'ER-DO-WELLS WHO WERE ALWAYS HANGING AROUND. I MOVED IN WITH HER AND WE IMMEDIATELY FELL BACK INTO OUR OLD PATTERN. I WENT BACK TO WORK IN THE "HI-BROW" DEPARTMENT AT AMERICAN GREETINGS FOR ANOTHER STINT OF EIGHT MONTHS. IT WAS THE LAST TIME I EVER HELD DOWN A NINE-TO-FIVE JOB... I'VE BEEN LUCKY. SECURE IN THE MARRIAGE SITUATION, DANA SUNK BACK INTO HER ROLE AS THE FAT HOUSE-WIFE. SHE STOPPED MESSING WITH PILLS. HER LITTLE FAN-CLUB DRIFTED AWAY. WE CONTINUED TAKING LSD AND POPPING THOSE HIGH-QUALITY METH TABS OCCASIONALLY. MORE AND MORE PEOPLE WERE TAKING PSYCHEDELIC DRUGS. EVEN SOME OF THE LESS CONSERVATIVE ARTISTS AND WRITERS AT THE CARD COMPANY EXPERIMENTED WITH IT. THE WAVE OF THE '60S WAS BEGINNING TO HAVE ITS EFFECT ON EVERYONE.

I BEGAN SERIOUSLY REGRETTING MY RETURN TO CLEVELAND. IT WAS A BIG MISTAKE. I WAS A COWARD... I'D OPTED FOR SECURITY— THE WIFE, THE JOB... NOW I WAS RESTLESS AGAIN, ITCHING TO ESCAPE. I FELT AS IF I WAS LIVING IN THE PAST. THERE'S GOT TO BE MORE TO LIFE THAN THIS, I KEPT THINKING. I WAS DRAWING ALL THE TIME, STILL FILLING UP THOSE SKETCHBOOKS. I MADE SEVERAL ATTEMPTS TO START SOME KIND OF COMICBOOK BUT COULDN'T GET IT OFF THE GROUND. I SAW SHELTON'S WONDER WART HOG IN THE TEXAS RANGER, A COLLEGE HUMOR 'ZINE, HILARIOUS, HIP STUFF, SOMEONE BROUGHT SOME PSYCHEDELIC DANCE POSTERS BACK FROM SAN FRANCISCO. YOU COULD TELL RIGHT AWAY THOSE CALIFORNIA ARTISTS WERE INSPIRED BY LSD! CLEVELANDERS WHO'D BEEN OUT THERE SAID SAN FRANCISCO WAS THE HAPPENING PLACE.

DANA'S MOTHER KNEW THIS GUY WHO WAS THE CURATOR FOR THE ART MUSEUM IN PEORIA, ILLINOIS. HE SAID HE'D GIVE ME A SHOW IF I'D DO A BUNCH OF LARGE PEN-AND-INK DRAWINGS. I QUICKLY TURNED OUT SIXTY-SOME DRAWINGS OF VARYING SUBJECT MATTER. THE GUY IN PEORIA HAD THEM ALL NICELY MATTED UNDER GLASS. WE DROVE TO PEORIA TO ATTEND THE OPENING. A VERY IMPRESSIVE SHOW, I THOUGHT... I WAS IN FOR A RUDE AWAKENING. THE CROWD AT THE AFFAIR WAS MADE UP ENTIRELY OF OLDER PEORIA BUSINESSMEN AND THEIR WIVES. IT WAS UNBELIEVABLE. THERE WASN'T A SINGLE YOUNG OR "HIP" LOOKING PERSON IN THE ROOM! BY THE TIME WE GOT THERE THE PEORIA BOOSHWAHZEE WERE ALL HUDDLED TOGETHER IN THE MIDDLE OF THE ROOM WITH THEIR BACKS TO THE ART, TALKING AND SIPPING THEIR DRINKS. THE CURATOR TRIED HIS BEST TO MAKE ME FEEL AT HOME. HE INTRODUCED ME TO A FEW PEOPLE. THEY REMAINED DISTANT, COLD. ONE MARGARET DUMONT-TYPE MATRON IN A FUR STOLE MADE A BRAVE ATTEMPT TO COMMUNICATE. "WHY DO YOU HATE US SO MUCH?" SHE ASKED WITH A POLITE SMILE ON HER ROSY, MIDWESTERN FACE. INTERESTING QUESTION. I'LL NEVER FORGET HER... I SAID NOTHING, I LOOKED DOWN, CHUCKLING NERVOUSLY. SHE WAS RIGHT. I WANTED TO MARCH HER TO THE WALL AND SQUASH HER SMUG, ROSY FACE AGAINST ONE OF MY PSYCHOTIC DRAWINGS. IT'S COMPLICATED— ATTRACTION AND REPULSION AT THE SAME TIME... THE "BOHO DANCE", AS TOM WOLFE CALLED IT.

THEN IN JANUARY, '67 I RAN AWAY AGAIN. I'D GOTTEN IN THE HABIT OF GOING TO BARS AFTER WORK. ONE HAPPY HOUR EVENING I RAN INTO A COUPLE OF CHARACTERS I KNEW, TIM AND SKIP, IN ADELE'S BAR. THEY TOLD ME THEY WERE ABOUT TO SET OUT FOR SAN FRANCISCO. SKIP HAD AN OLD BROKEN DOWN FIAT. I ASKED THEM IF THEY HAD ROOM FOR ONE MORE. THEY SAID SURE, COME ON ALONG. I ASKED ANOTHER FRIEND IF HE'D DO ME A FAVOR AND TELL DANA I'D LEFT. I DREADED ANOTHER TRAUMATIC SCENE WITH HER.

BY SOME MIRACLE THE OLD FIAT MADE IT ACROSS... IT WAS A COLD, COLD JOURNEY BUT WE GOT TO THE LAND OF MILK AND HONEY AT LONG LAST. THREE WEEKS LATER I CALLED THE WIFE FROM SAN FRANCISCO AND INVITED HER TO COME OUT AND JOIN ME. I WAS LONELY AND GUILT-RIDDEN AGAIN. HEY, THIS PATTERN OF BEHAVIOR STILL HAD SEVERAL MORE YEARS TO PLAY ITSELF OUT... SHE CAME, OF COURSE, AND THERE WE WERE, NEUROTIC BAG AND BAGGAGE, IN A NICE APARTMENT IN THE "HAIGHT-ASHBURY" SMACK DAB IN THE MIDDLE OF THE WILD AND WACKY '60S-SAN FRANCISCO HIPPY SCENE AT ITS HIGH-NOON OF ACID-INDUCED EUPHORIA! EVERYBODY IN SAN FRANCISCO SEEMED TO BELIEVE THAT THE WORLD HAD BEEN PERMANENTLY TRANSFORMED! AS SOON AS ALL THOSE NASTY UP-TIGHT OLD FARTS OVER THIRTY DIED OFF WE'D TURN THIS PLANET BACK INTO A GARDEN OF EDEN, NOTHING TO IT! SKEPTICAL THOUGH I WAS OF SOME OF THE EXCESSES OF HIPPY BEHAVIOR, I, TOO, WAS SWEPT UP IN THE INCREDIBLE OPTIMISM. IT WAS A BREATH OF FRESH AIR IN THE WEARY WORLD, NO TELLING WHEN WE'LL SEE THE LIKE AGAIN....

IT'S HARD TO HAVE A CLEAR MEMORY OF EVENTS FROM THAT PERIOD. EVERYBODY WAS STONED, HIGH ALL THE TIME. LIFE WAS UNSTRUCTURED. "IF YOU CAN REMEMBER THE '60S, YOU WEREN'T THERE" AN OLD HIPPY SAID RECENTLY. MISTY MEMORIES OF CLUSTERS OF PEOPLE HANGING OUT— ALWAYS HANGING OUT— SMOKING DOPE IN LIVING ROOMS— GURGLING WATER PIPES— ROACH HOLDERS— PIPES MADE OF STONE— PIPES MADE OF BRASS— LISTENING TO THE LATEST BEATLES OR STONES ALBUM— THESE RECORDS WERE VERY IMPORTANT. HANGING OUT IN THE WOODS SMOKING DOPE— ON HAIGHT STREET, AT THE BEACH— MOST PEOPLE HAD NO MONEY TO SPEAK OF, BUT

RENTS WERE CHEAP AND NECESSITIES CAME EASY— IT WAS CONSIDERED UNENLIGHTENED TO FUSS AND FRET ABOUT A LITTLE MATTER LIKE SURVIVAL.

IT WAS ACTUALLY A LITTLE NERVE-WRACKING... NOBODY EVER KNEW WHAT TO DO NEXT— WELL, HERE WE ARE, WE'RE BEAUTIFUL, NOW WHAT?? TOO MUCH FREEDOM? I DUNNO... SOME PEOPLE MADE BETTER HIPPIES THAN OTHERS... THEY LIVED IN A MAGIC KINGDOM, THESE GOLDEN ONES. WE LOOKED AT THEM, TRYING TO FIGURE OUT WHAT IT WAS THEY KNEW AND WE DIDN'T. I THINK THEY WERE ALL TAKEN UP IN SPACESHIPS TO SOME MORE HIGHLY EVOLVED PLANET AROUND 1970. PERSONALLY, I COULDN'T PULL IT OFF, I HAD TOO MANY HANG-UPS..... I WAS CURSED IN SOME WAY, BANISHED FROM THE MAGIC KINGDOM.

DANA GOT A JOB AS A COUNSELOR IN AN UNWED MOTHER'S HOME, UNTIL SHE CAUGHT THE BUG AND GOT PREGNANT HERSELF. I DID A LITTLE FREE-LANCE WORK. I WAS FREE AS A BIRD, GENERALLY SPEAKING. THIS WAS THE SUMMER I WENT "ON THE ROAD", ATTEMPTING TO HITCH-HIKE 'CROSS COUNTRY. I HAD A LOT OF INTERESTING ADVENTURES. THE TIMES WERE VERY LOOSE. WE HAD A SUCCESSION OF PEOPLE STAYING WITH US, REFUGEES FROM CLEVELAND, MOSTLY. THEY ATE OUR FOOD AND LOUNGED AROUND, NOODLING ON THEIR RECORDERS AND WRITING POETRY. THEY WERE NURSING THEIR NEUROSES, RECOVERING FROM A CRUEL UPBRINGING IN THE UPPER-MIDDLE CLASS CLEVELAND SUBURBS. DANA ALWAYS KICKED THEM OUT EVENTUALLY. THEY WOULD'VE STAYED FOREVER OTHERWISE.

ONE SET OF VISITORS WHO NEVER LEFT UNTIL DANA GAVE THEM THE BOOT WAS JOEL DEUTSCH AND HIS WIFE JANE. JOEL AND I SPENT ALOT OF TIME HANGING OUT TOGETHER DISCUSSING SPIRITUAL AND ARTISTIC MATTERS, A COUPLA DREAMERS. JOEL WAS A PRETTY FUNNY GUY, ONE A'THESE SENSITIVE JEWISH BOYS WHO WAS TRYING TO FIND HIMSELF... DANA FOUND HIM VERY IRRITATING. JANE WAS A BEAUTIFUL, STATUESQUE "SHIKSA" FROM OAK RIDGE, TENNESSEE, RATHER DISTANT AND REPRESSED. SHE WAS AN INDOLENT CREATURE WHO LAID AROUND ALL DAY. I'D COME HOME AND SEE HER SPRAWLED ON THE BED ON HER STOMACH READING. DANA WAS AT WORK. JOEL WAS OUT SOMEWHERE. SHE ALWAYS WORE TIGHT-FITTING PANTS AND THESE HIGH-HEELED BLACK BOOTS. HER BIG, PERT BUTT JUTTED BOLDLY UP INTO THE AIR. OH MAN, IT WAS ALL I COULD DO TO STOP MYSELF FROM GOING OVER THERE AND LEAPING ON TOP OF THAT NUBILE, ANGEL-FACED THING! BUT SHE WAS OUT OF MY REACH. SHE MIGHT AS WELL HAVE BEEN A THOUSAND MILES AWAY. "FREE LOVE" SEEMED TO BE HAPPENING EVERYWHERE EXCEPT OUR HOUSE. BOO HOO...

HIPPY GUYS I KNEW WOULD COME OVER AND TAKE ME ALONG ON THEIR WANDERINGS. THEY'D GO UP TO GIRLS IN THE PARK AND THE NEXT THING I KNEW THEY'RE TRIPPING OFF TOGETHER. IT WAS A WONDER TO ME. I HAVE NO IDEA HOW THEY DID IT. I GUESS YOU HAD TO HAVE THE RIGHT LOOK, THE RIGHT LINE OF TALK. ONE OF THESE GUYS, ALAN, ONCE LOOKED AT ME SERIOUSLY AND ASKED, "CRUMB, DON'T YOU LIKE GIRLS?" I LAUGHED NERVOUSLY. "SURE I LIKE GIRLS", I ANSWERED MEEKLY. "THEN WHY DO YOU STAY WITH THAT FAT WOMAN WHEN THERE'S THOUSANDS OF BEAUTIFUL GIRLS OUT HERE??" IT'S TRUE... THERE WERE, IT WAS UNFATHOMABLE TO HIM THAT ANY RED-BLOODED MALE WOULDN'T BE OUT THERE TAKING FULL ADVANTAGE OF A VERY UNIQUE OPPORTUNITY. EASY FOR HIM TO TALK, WITH HIS BAMBOO FLUTE AND CHRIST-LIKE APPEARANCE, HE COULD HAVE ALL THE HIPPY-CHICKS HIS HEART DESIRED. EVERY DAY WAS FILLED WITH NEW BEAUTIFUL EXPERIENCES FOR ALAN. DANA, JOEL AND JANE DIDN'T LIKE HIM VERY MUCH. I DIDN'T EITHER, FOR THAT MATTER. HE WAS A COCKY, SWAGGERING LITTLE SHMUCK, BASICALLY, BUT WE WERE ALL A LITTLE INTIMIDATED BY HIM. HE WAS SUCH A PERFECT HIPPY. HE LIVED THE DREAM. ONCE AT OUR HOUSE HE SAID TO JANE, "YOU SHOULD FUCK ROBERT...," HEAVY... WE ALL STOOD THERE AWKWARDLY, NOT TALKING, WHILE ALAN TURNED AND WENT HIS MERRY WAY, PLAYING HIS BAMBOO FLUTE.

MY COMIC THING FLOWERED IN THIS FERTILE ENVIRONMENT. I FIGURED IT OUT SOMEHOW— THE WAY TO PUT THE STONED EXPERIENCE INTO A SERIES OF CARTOON PANELS. I BEGAN TO SUBMIT LSD-INSPIRED STRIPS TO UNDERGROUND PAPERS... NOT FOR PAY, NEVER GAVE IT A THOUGHT... BUT THEY LOVED THEM. THESE 1967 STRIPS OF MINE CONTAINED THE HOPEFUL SPIRIT OF THE TIMES, DRAWN IN A LOVEABLE "BIG FOOT" STYLE. THE STUFF CAUGHT ON. THEY WANTED MORE. SUDDENLY I WAS ABLE TO CHURN IT OUT. JOEL GAVE ME ALOT OF ENCOURAGEMENT. HE WAS ALWAYS KNOCKED OUT BY THE STRIPS I WAS DOING IN MY SKETCHBOOK. HE WALKED AROUND QUOTING THEM.

LATE THAT SUMMER ONE OF THE UNDERGROUND PAPER PUBLISHERS ASKED ME TO DO AN ENTIRE ISSUE OF HIS PAPER YARROWSTALKS.... (CORNY HIPPY SPIRITUAL STUFF-"YARROWSTALKS" ARE WHAT THEY USED TO USE TO THROW THE 'I CHING') THIS WENT OVER SO WELL THAT HE SUGGESTED I DRAW COMIC BOOKS AND HE WOULD PUBLISH THEM. THIS WAS A THRILLING IDEA TO ME— A DREAM COME TRUE. I COMPLETED TWO 24-PAGE ISSUES OF ZAP COMIX IN TWO MONTHS (I WORKED FASTER AND MORE SPONTANEOUSLY IN THOSE DAYS— HEY, I WISH I COULD STILL DO IT, COMIC FANS! YOU KNOW, YOU GET OLDER, THINGS GET MORE COMPLICATED— IT CAN'T BE HELPED). I SENT THE ARTWORK FOR THE FIRST ISSUE TO MY WOULD-BE PUBLISHER, BUT NEVER HEARD FROM HIM AGAIN. MONTHS LATER, IN A STATE OF FRUSTRATION, I CALLED AND WAS TOLD, "OH, HE'S GONE OFF TO INDIA, MAN." LUCKY FOR ME I'D

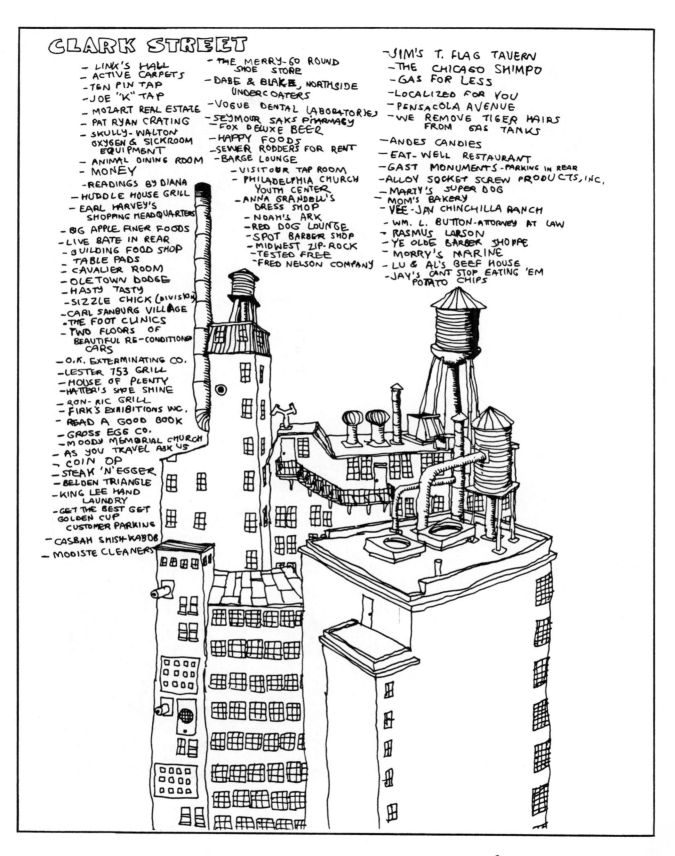

# CLARK STREET

- LINK'S HALL
- ACTIVE CARPETS
- TEN PIN TAP
- JOE "K" TAP
- MOZART REAL ESTATE
- PAT RYAN CRATING
- SKULLY-WALTON OXYGEN & SICKROOM EQUIPMENT
- ANIMAL DINING ROOM
- MONEY
- READINGS BY DIANA
- HUDDLE HOUSE GRILL
- EARL HARVEY'S SHOPPING HEADQUARTERS
- BG APPLE FINER FOODS
- LIVE BATE IN REAR
- BUILDING FOOD SHOP
- TABLE PADS
- CAVALIER ROOM
- OLETOWN DODGE
- HASTY TASTY
- SIZZLE CHICK (DIVISION)
- CARL SANBURG VILLAGE
- THE FOOT CLINICS
- TWO FLOORS OF BEAUTIFUL RE-CONDITIONED CARS
- O.K. EXTERMINATING CO.
- LESTER 753 GRILL
- HOUSE OF PLENTY
- HATTER'S SHOE SHINE
- RON-RIC GRILL
- FIRK'S EXHIBITIONS INC.
- READ A GOOD BOOK
- GROSS EGG CO.
- MOODY MEMORIAL CHURCH
- AS YOU TRAVEL ASK US
- COIN OP
- STEAK 'N' EGGER
- BELDEN TRIANGLE
- KING LEE HAND LAUNDRY
- GET THE BEST GET GOLDEN CUP CUSTOMER PARKING
- CASBAH SHISH-KABOB
- MODISTE CLEANERS

- THE MERRY-GO ROUND SHOE STORE
- DABE & BLAKE, NORTHSIDE UNDERCOATERS
- VOGUE DENTAL LABORATORIES
- SEYMOUR SAKS PHARMACY
- FOX DELUXE BEER
- HAPPY FOODS
- SEWER RODDERS FOR RENT
- BARGE LOUNGE
  - VISIT OUR TAP ROOM
  - PHILADELPHIA CHURCH YOUTH CENTER
  - ANNA GRANDELL'S DRESS SHOP
  - NOAH'S ARK
  - RED DOG LOUNGE
  - SPOT BARBER SHOP
  - MIDWEST ZIP-ROCK
  - TESTED FREE
  - FRED NELSON COMPANY

- JIM'S T. FLAG TAVERN
- THE CHICAGO SHIMPO
- GAS FOR LESS
- LOCALIZED FOR YOU
- PENSACOLA AVENUE
- WE REMOVE TIGER HAIRS FROM GAS TANKS

- ANDES CANDIES
- EAT-WELL RESTAURANT
- GAST MONUMENTS - PARKING IN REAR
- ALLOY SOCKET SCREW PRODUCTS, INC.
- MARTY'S SUPER DOG
- MOM'S BAKERY
- VEE-JAY CHINCHILLA RANCH
- WM. L. BUTTON - ATTORNEY AT LAW
- RASMUS LARSON
- YE OLDE BARBER SHOPPE
- MORRY'S MARINE
- LU & AL'S BEEF HOUSE
- JAY'S CAN'T STOP EATING 'EM POTATO CHIPS

CHICAGO, EARLY '66, "FUZZY" PERIOD...
RIDING THE CLARK STREET BUS AND
WRITING DOWN THE NAMES OF BUSINESS
PLACES AS THEY PASSED.... AN ATTEMPT
TO STAY IN TOUCH WITH REALITY.

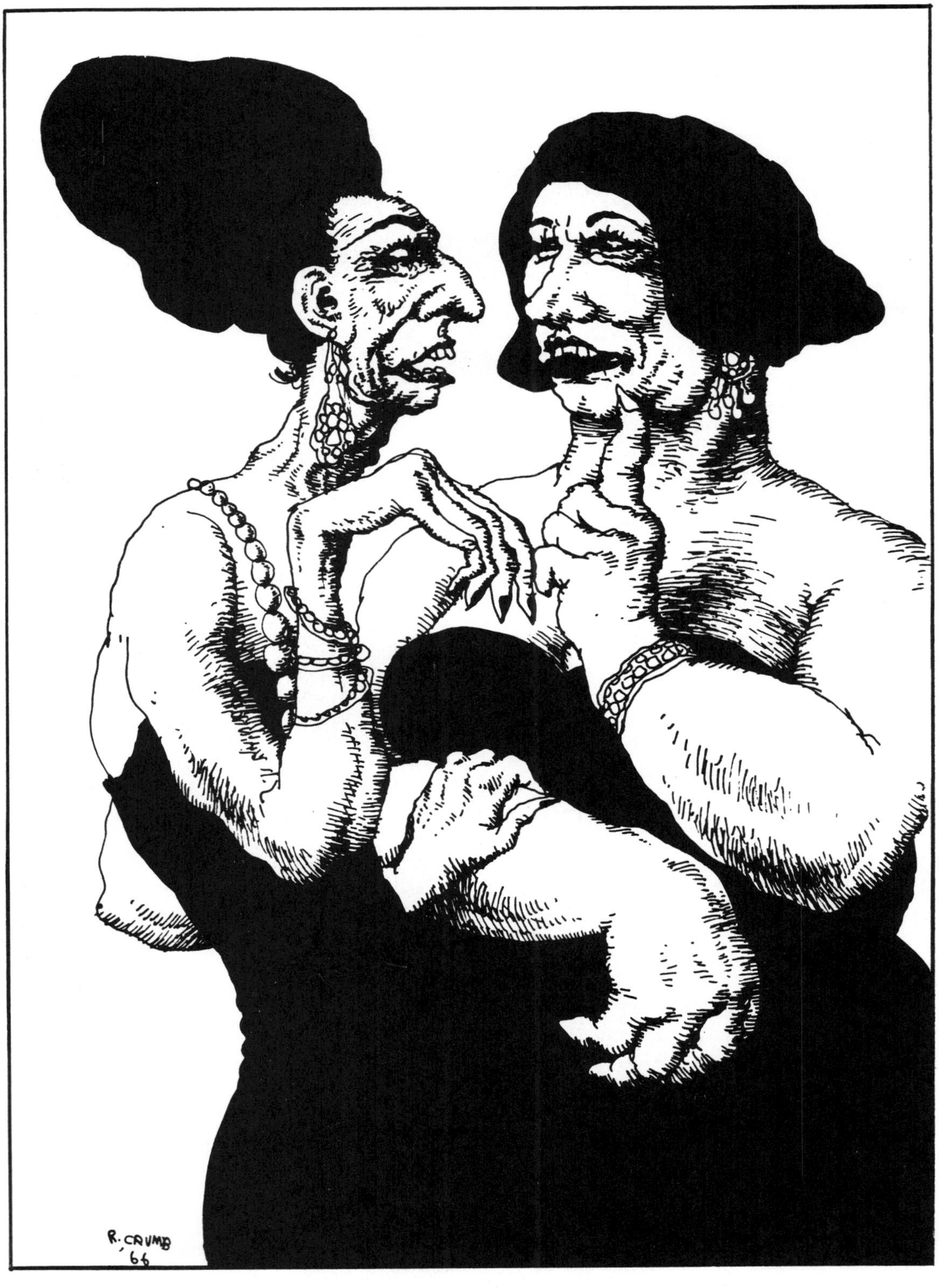
R. CRUMB
'66

ONE OF THE DRAWINGS
THAT OFFENDED THE ART
PATRONS OF PEORIA, 1966.

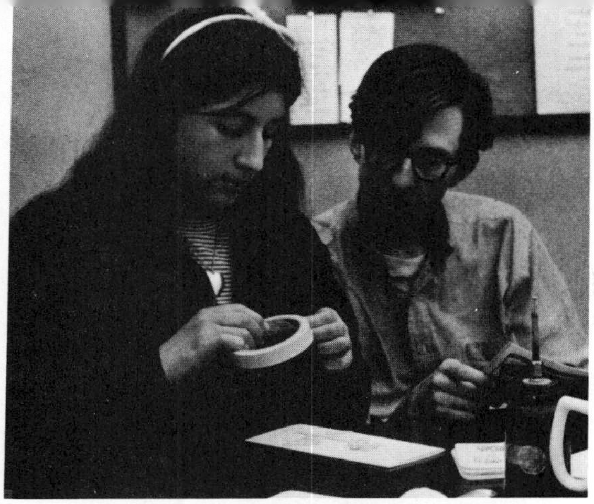

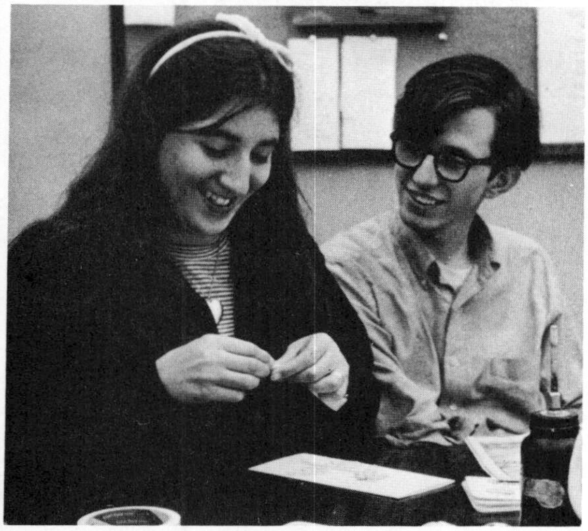

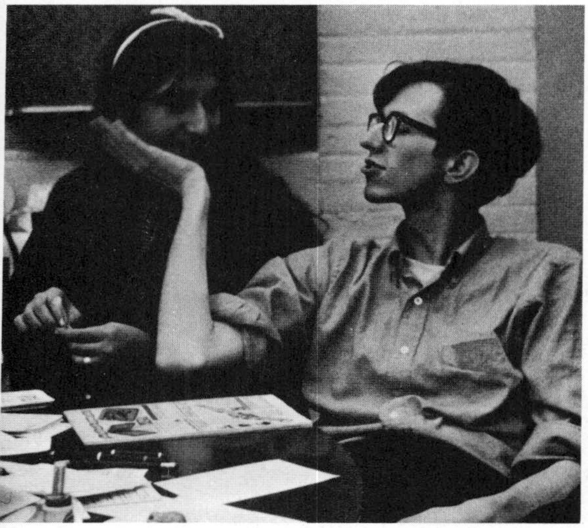

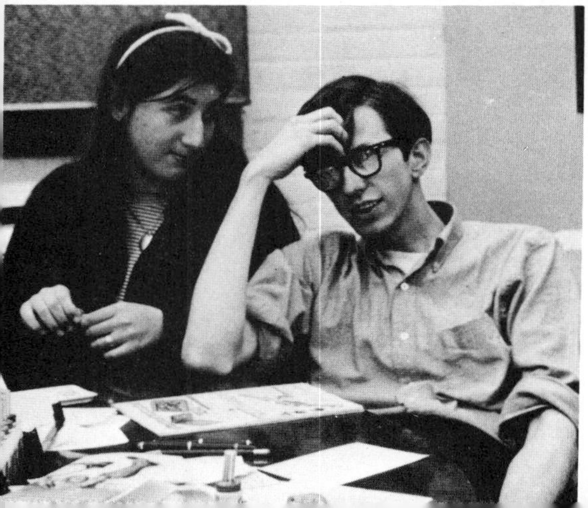

DANA & ROBERT CRUMB AT AMERICAN GREETINGS, CLEVELAND, 1966. WE USED TO TAKE ADVANTAGE OF THE COMPANY'S ABUNDANT ART SUPPLIES TO WORK ON OUR OWN PROJECTS. PHOTOS BY KAY RUDIN, ANOTHER A.G. ARTIST AND A BIG PEST WITH HER CAMERA.

R. & DANA ALL DUDED UP FOR SOME OCCASION, SAN FRANCISCO, 1967-'68. I DON'T REMEMBER WHAT....

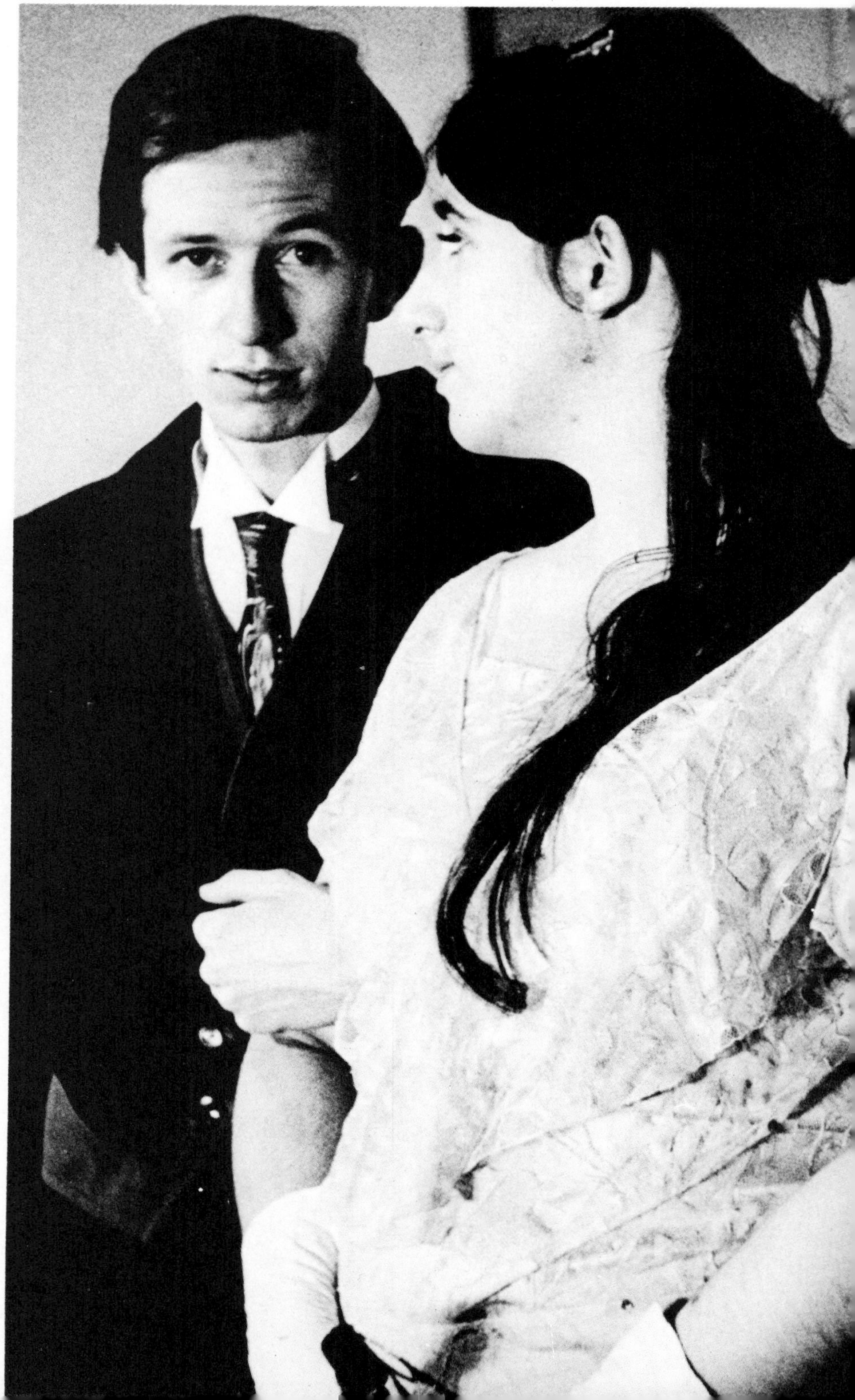

MADE A XEROX OF THE ORIGINAL PAGES, SOMETHING I DIDN'T USUALLY DO. THEN DON DONAHUE CAME ALONG. HE WAS A GUY ABOUT MY AGE WHO WAS BORN AND RAISED IN SAN FRANCISCO, QUIET, SOFT-SPOKEN, GOOD SENSE OF HUMOR. WE'RE STILL FRIENDS. HE GOT ALL JAZZED UP ABOUT PUTTING OUT ZAP COMIX. AS I RECALL, HE TRADED HIS HI-FI TO THIS SMALL-TIME PRINTER, CHARLES PLYMELL, IN EXCHANGE FOR PRINTING THE FIRST ISSUE. PLYMELL, AN OLDER HIPSTER FROM WICHITA, OWNED A SMALL PRESS, A MULTI-LITH 1250. SOON AFTER THAT DONAHUE BOUGHT THE PRESS AND LEARNED HOW TO RUN IT HIMSELF. MANY OF THE EARLY UNDERGROUND COMICS WERE PRINTED BY HIM ON THAT THING.

THE FIRST ISSUE WAS PRINTED IN FEBRUARY, '68. WE FOLDED AND STAPLED ALL 5,000 COPIES OURSELVES, AND TOOK THEM OUT TO SELL ON THE STREETS. AT FIRST THE HIPPY SHOPKEEPERS ON HAIGHT STREET LOOKED DOWN THERE NOSES AT IT..."A COMIC BOOK? NO, I DON'T LIKE COMIC BOOKS," IT LOOKED JUST LIKE A TRADITIONAL COMICBOOK. IT HAD NONE OF THE STYLINGS OF YOUR TYPICAL PSYCHEDELIC GRAPHICS; THE ROMANTIC FIGURES, THE CURVY, FLOWING SHAPES — IT TOOK A WHILE TO CATCH ON. IT WAS BEGINNING TO TAKE OFF BY THE FALL OF '68... AND SO BEGAN THE SAGA OF MY NAME BECOMING LEGEND... THE 'PHONE BEGAN RINGING ALL DAY LONG... PEOPLE WHO I DIDN'T KNOW WERE SHOWING UP AT MY DOOR... ALL MY FRIENDS WERE BEGINNING TO LOOK AT ME DIFFERENTLY. IT SEEMED I SUDDENLY HAD ALOT OF *NEW* FRIENDS... I WAS THIS FASCINATING INDIVIDUAL, NO LONGER JUST ANOTHER BLAND, BESPECTACLED NERD. I'D ALWAYS KNOWN I WAS A HELL OF AN INTERESTING GUY — NOW OTHERS WERE BEGINNING TO REALIZE IT! *LOTS* OF THEM! *MOBS* OF THEM! SOMEONE WAS FOREVER HANDING ME A LIGHTED JOINT AS I TALKED ON THE 'PHONE TO YET ANOTHER HIP MEDIA HUSTLER. OH, IT GOT *CRAZY*... INEVITABLY, I HANDLED IT LIKE A COMPLETE FOOL... I ATE IT UP... I BOUGHT THE SYCOPHANTIC FLATTERY... I LET THEM HUSTLE ME STRAIGHT INTO THE GROUND... MY EXCUSE IS I WAS STILL VERY YOUNG, 25, 26, WHEN ALL THIS HAPPENED... I HAD A LOT TO LEARN YET... IN SHORT, MY LIFE WAS TURNED UPSIDE-DOWN BECAUSE I WAS IN THE RIGHT PLACE AT THE RIGHT TIME WITH MY LI'L OL' FUNNY BOOK... READ ALL ABOUT IT IN FUTURE CHAPTERS OF THIS EPIC SERIES — IT *REALLY* GETS INTERESTING FROM HERE ON — A CLASSIC STORY... (ESPECIALLY THE SEX PART!)

—— R. CRUMB,
WINTERS, APRIL, 1989

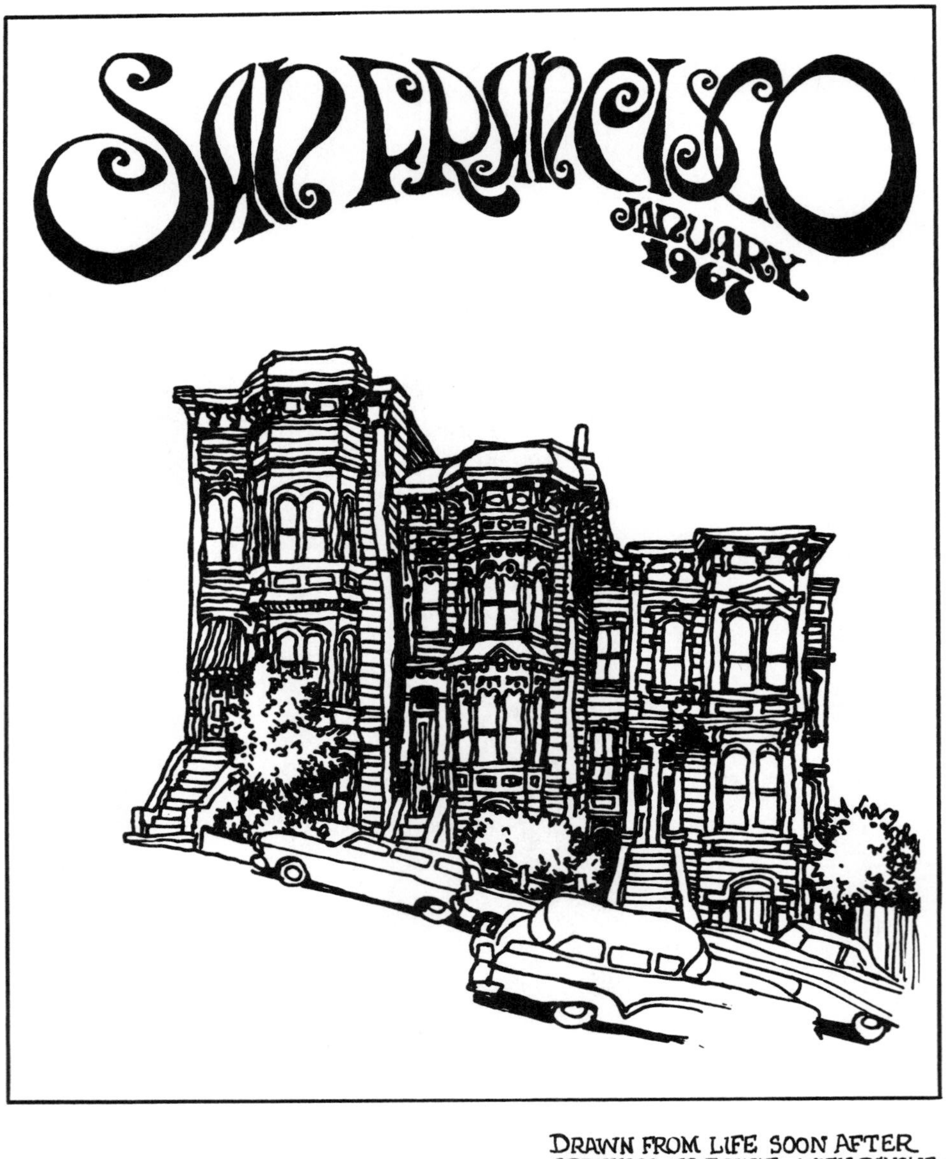
SAN FRANCISCO
JANUARY 1967

DRAWN FROM LIFE SOON AFTER ARRIVING IN TOWN — WITH PSYCHEDELIC POSTER-INSPIRED LETTERING.

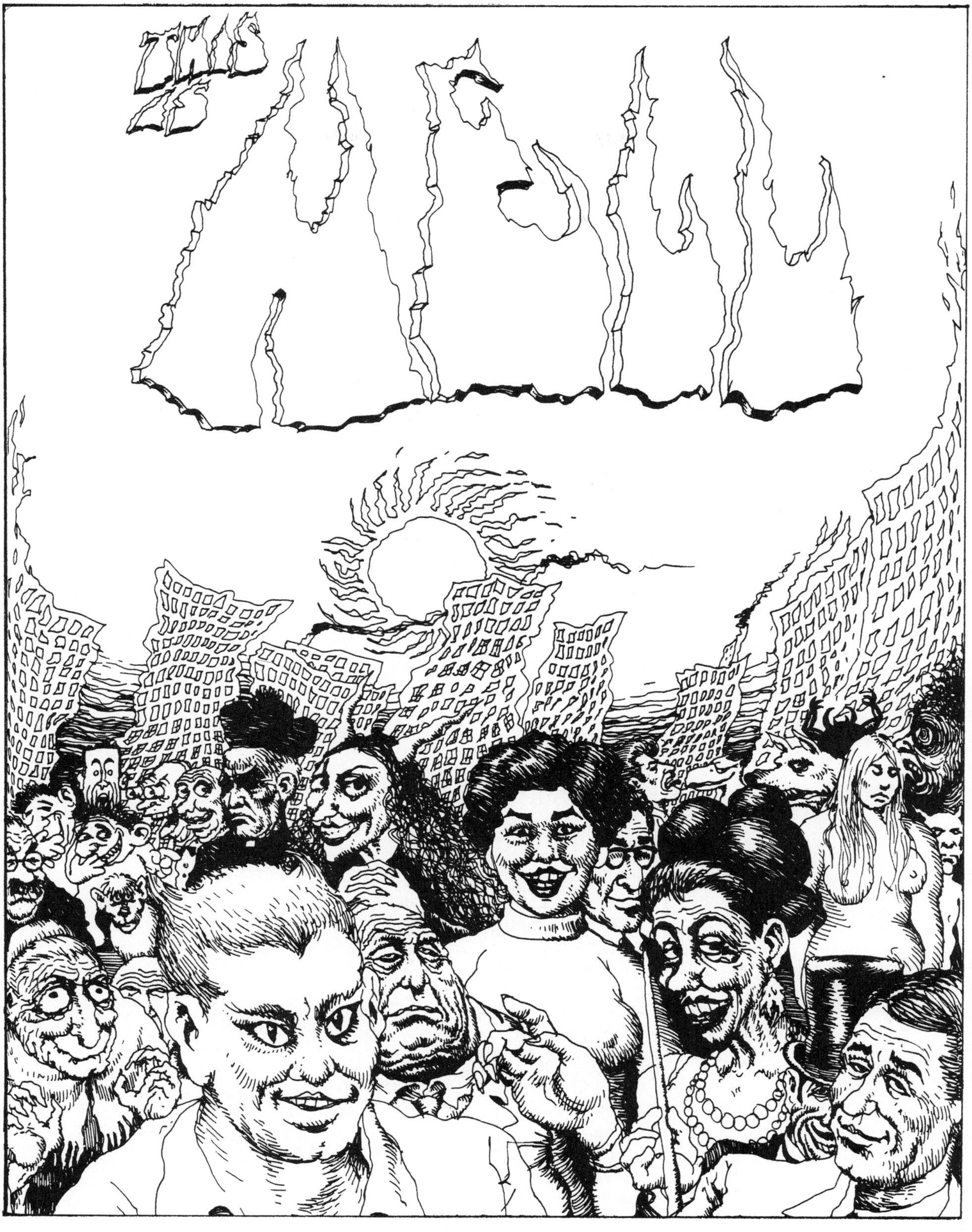
THIS IS
HELL

MEMORIES OF A HEAVY LSD TRIP
RECORDED IN THE SKETCHBOOK A FEW
DAYS LATER — SAN FRANCISCO, SPRING, '67

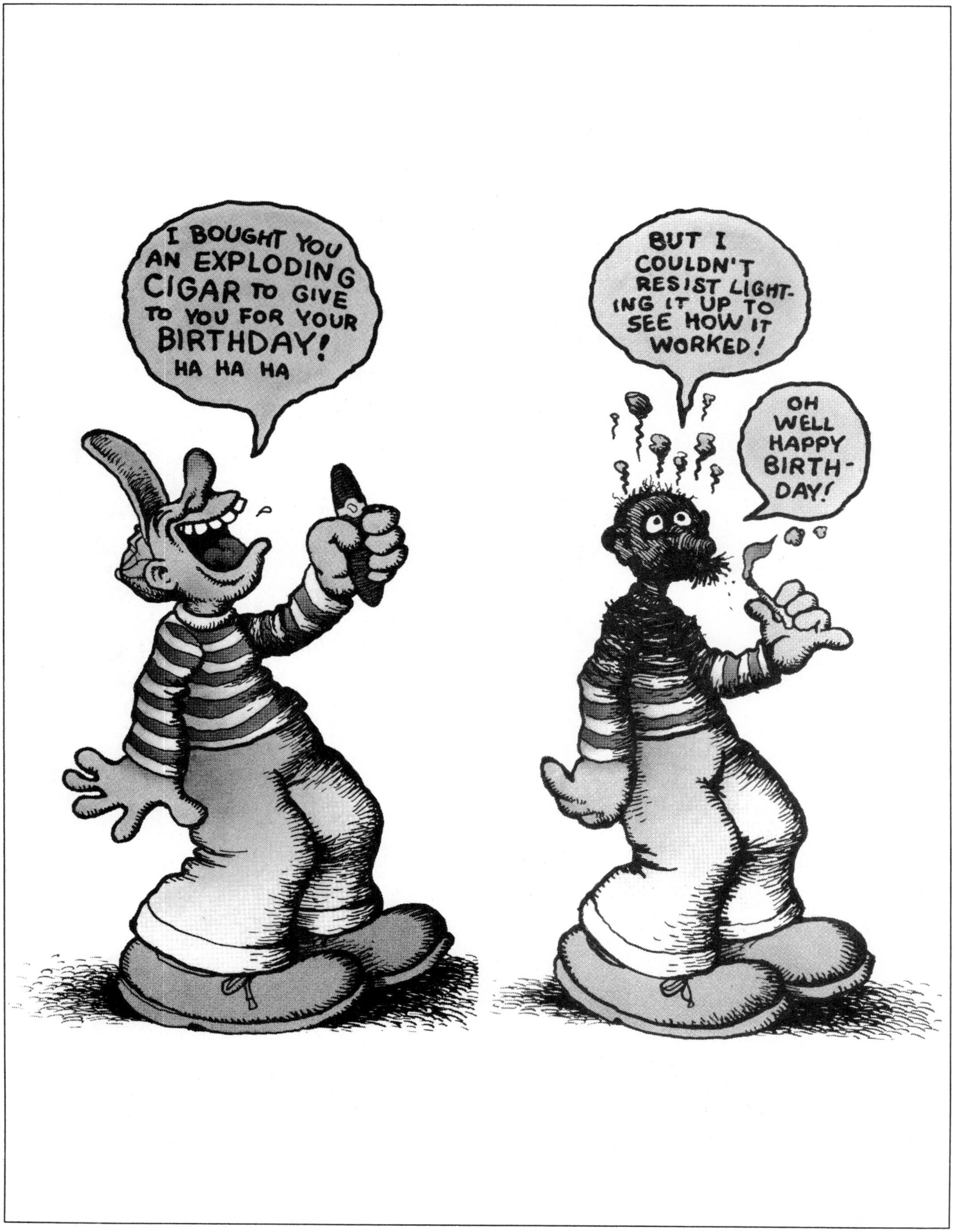
I BOUGHT YOU AN EXPLODING CIGAR TO GIVE TO YOU FOR YOUR BIRTHDAY! HA HA HA
BUT I COULDN'T RESIST LIGHTING IT UP TO SEE HOW IT WORKED!
OH WELL HAPPY BIRTHDAY!

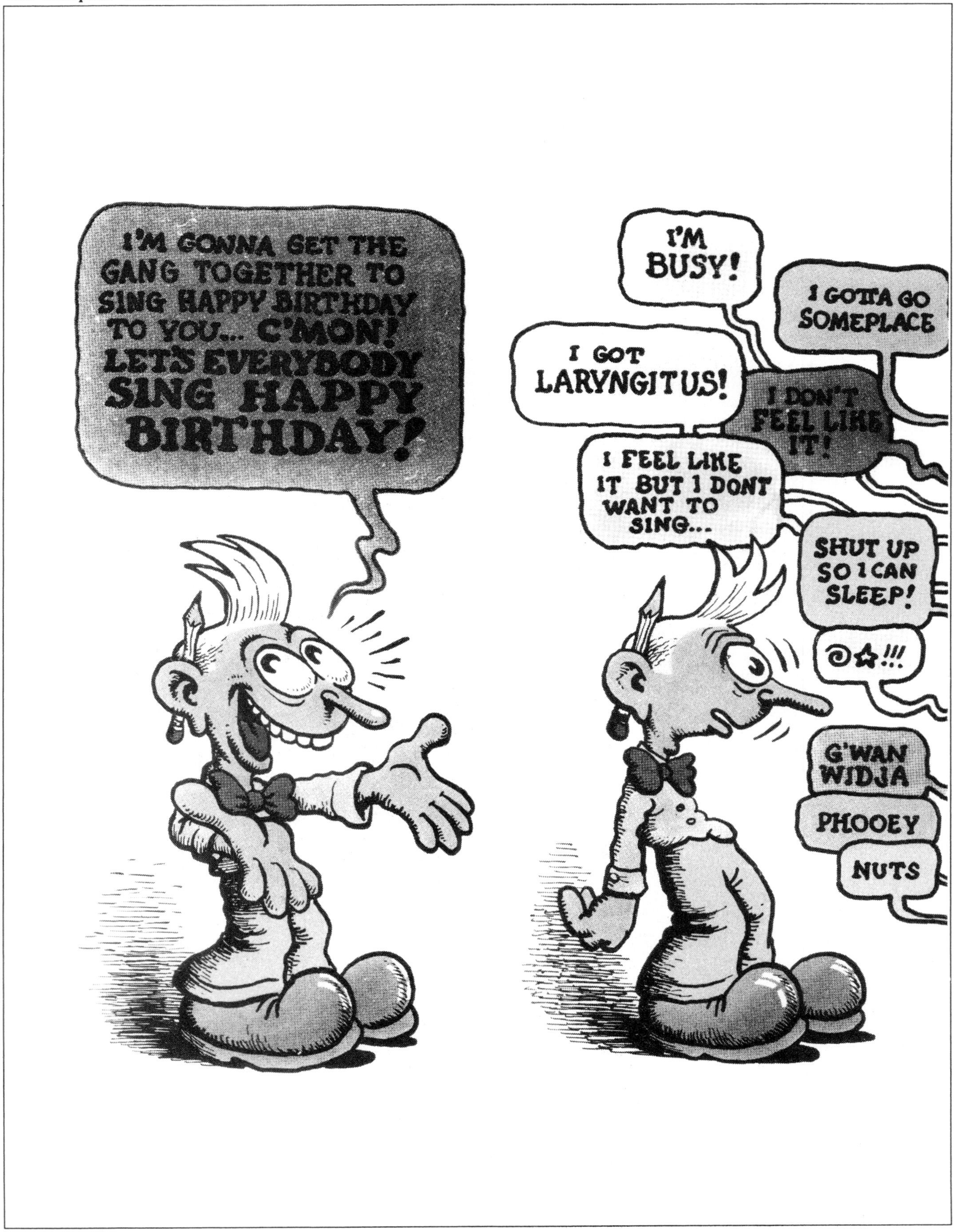
I'M GONNA GET THE GANG TOGETHER TO SING HAPPY BIRTHDAY TO YOU... C'MON! LET'S EVERYBODY SING HAPPY BIRTHDAY!
I'M BUSY!
I GOTTA GO SOMEPLACE
I GOT LARYNGITUS!
I DON'T FEEL LIKE IT!
I FEEL LIKE IT BUT I DONT WANT TO SING...
SHUT UP SO I CAN SLEEP!
!!!
G'WAN WIDJA
PHOOEY
NUTS

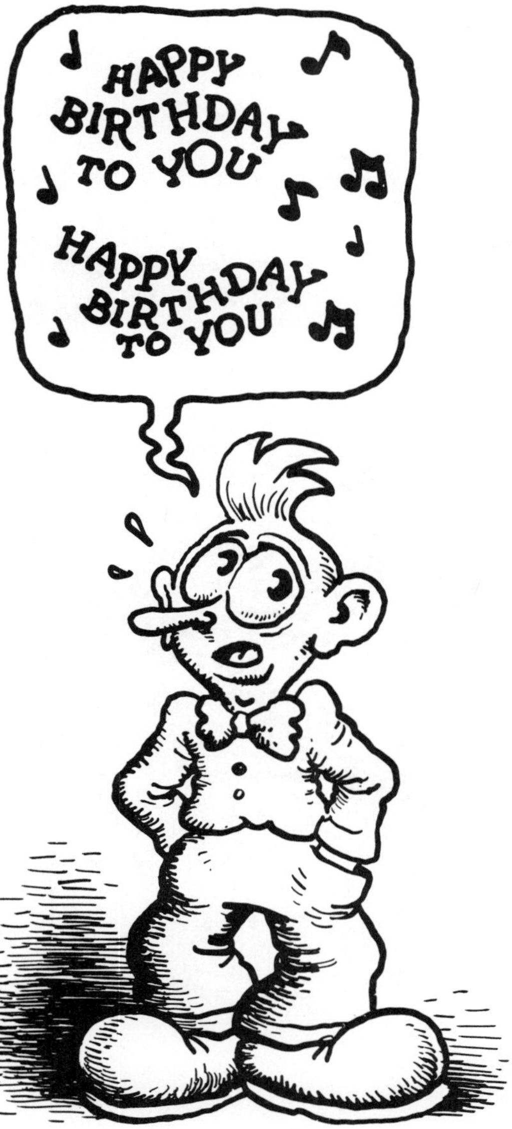
HAPPY BIRTHDAY TO YOU
HAPPY BIRTHDAY TO YOU

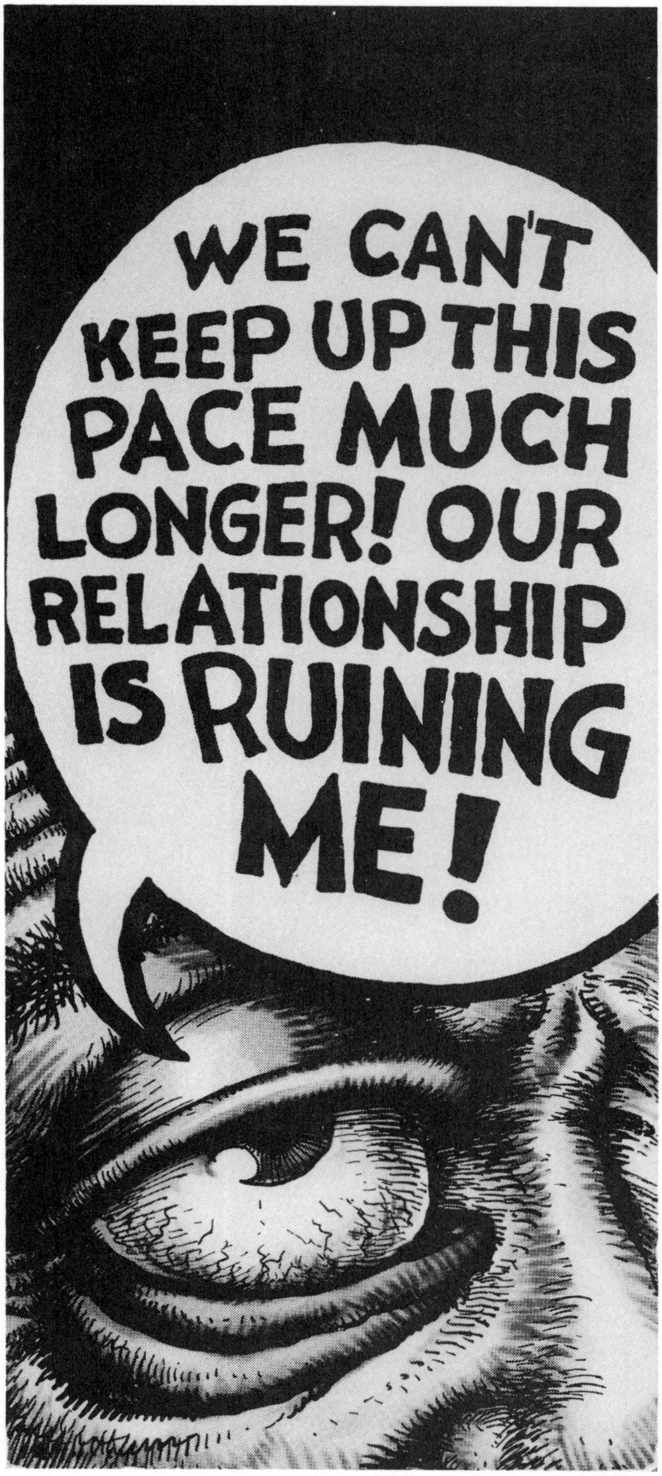
WE CAN'T KEEP UP THIS PACE MUCH LONGER! OUR RELATIONSHIP IS RUINING ME!

*[Just this morning I fell asleep running for a bus!]*

# THANKSGIVING

MEANS THE PILGRIMS LANDING AT PLYMOUTH ROCK.

IT MEANS A HOLIDAY FOR ALL.

IT MEANS TURKEY WITH ALL THE TRIMMINGS.

IT MEANS PUMPKIN PIE.

IT MEANS A TIME OF SHARING.

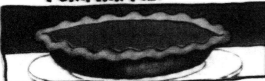

BUT MOST OF ALL, YOU KNOW WHAT IT MEANS TO ME....

...IT MEANS A SINKFUL OF DIRTY DISHES!

WHEN I HEARD YOU WERE SICK, I RUSHED RIGHT OUT TO DONATE BLOOD!
I NEEDED SOME COURAGE, SO I HAD A COUPLE OF MARTINIS ON THE WAY.
WHEN I SAW THE HOSPITAL, I NEEDED SOME MORE COURAGE.
HOSPITA
WHEN I SAW THE BIG NEEDLE AND THE BIG BOTTLE I NEEDED A LITTLE MORE COURAGE.

IF YOU NEED SOME COURAGE, ASK FOR SOME OF MY 90 PROOF TYPE, PAL!
hope you're well soon!

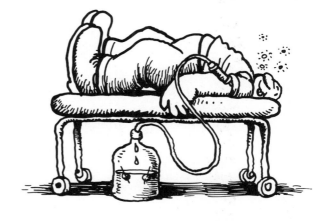

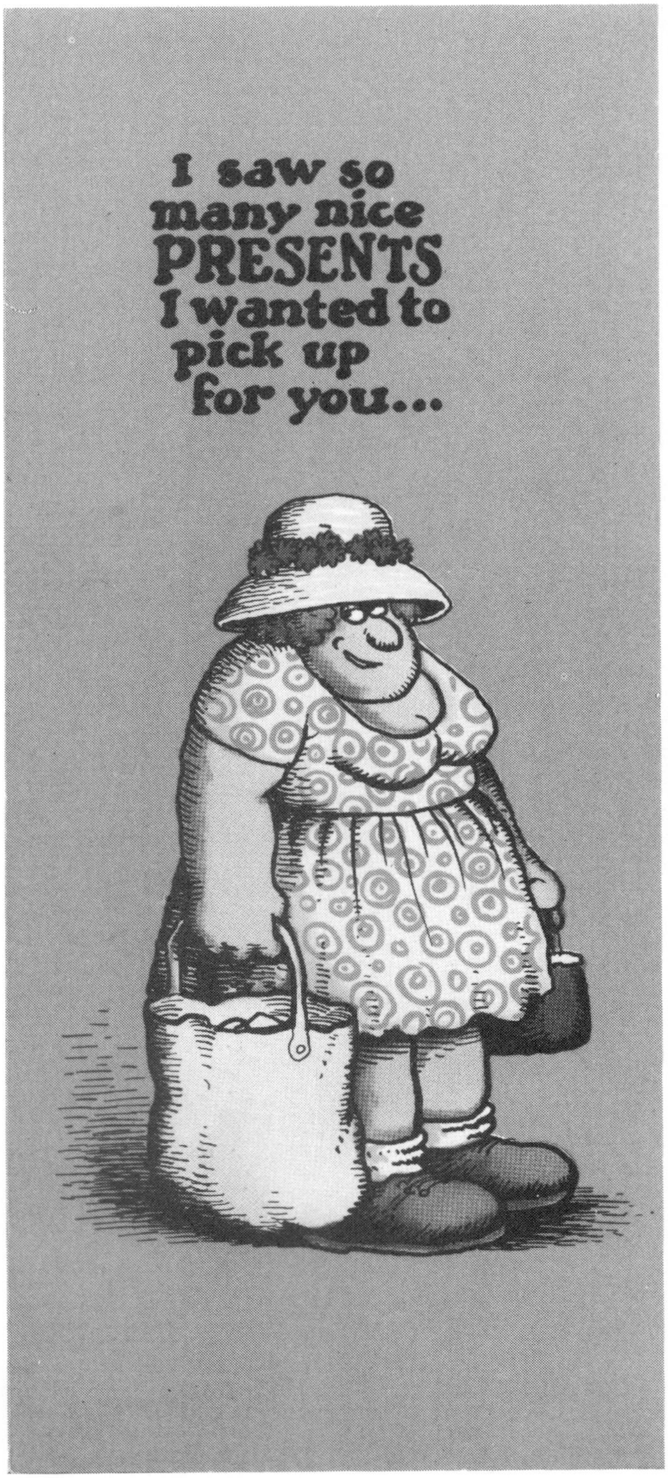
I saw so
many nice
PRESENTS
I wanted to
pick up
for you...

*[. . . but I'm not as quick as I used to be!]*

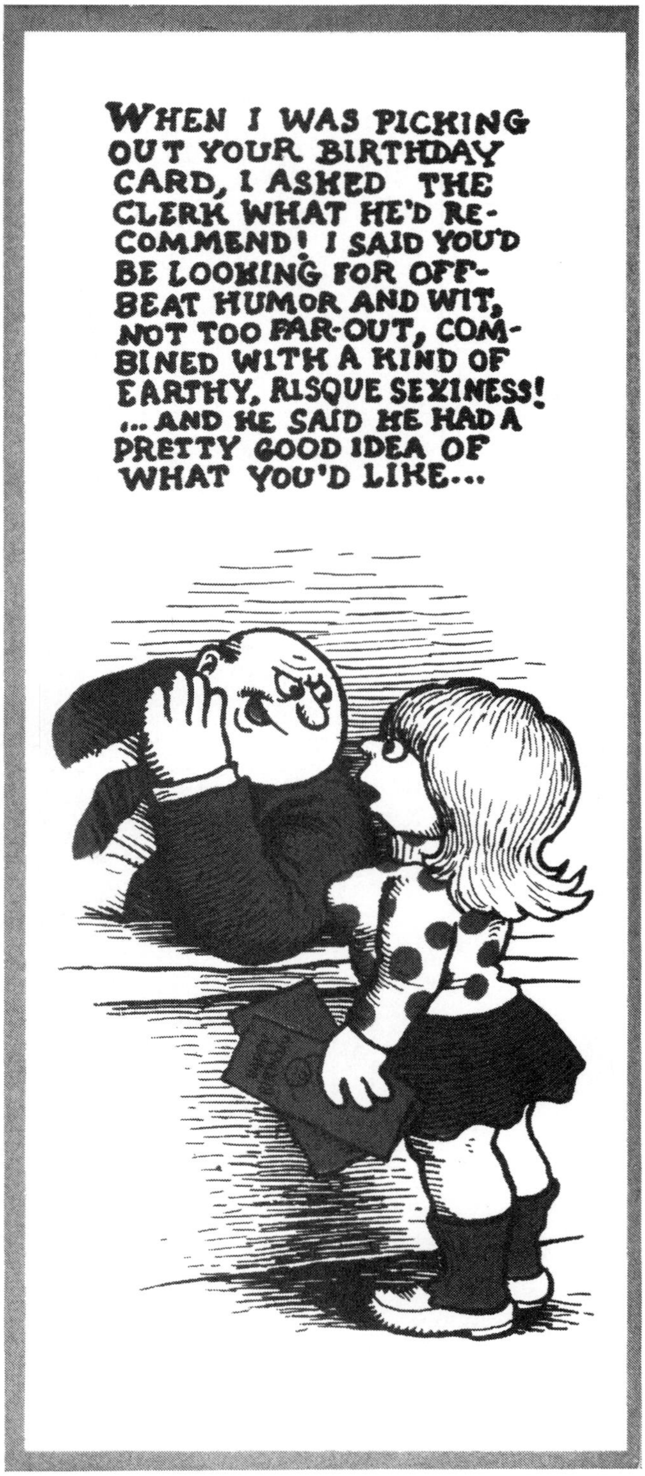
WHEN I WAS PICKING OUT YOUR BIRTHDAY CARD, I ASKED THE CLERK WHAT HE'D RE-COMMEND! I SAID YOU'D BE LOOKING FOR OFF-BEAT HUMOR AND WIT, NOT TOO FAR-OUT, COM-BINED WITH A KIND OF EARTHY, RISQUE SEXINESS! ...AND HE SAID HE HAD A PRETTY GOOD IDEA OF WHAT YOU'D LIKE...

*[. . . but she'd cost a lot more than 35¢*
*(so I just got this card!)]*

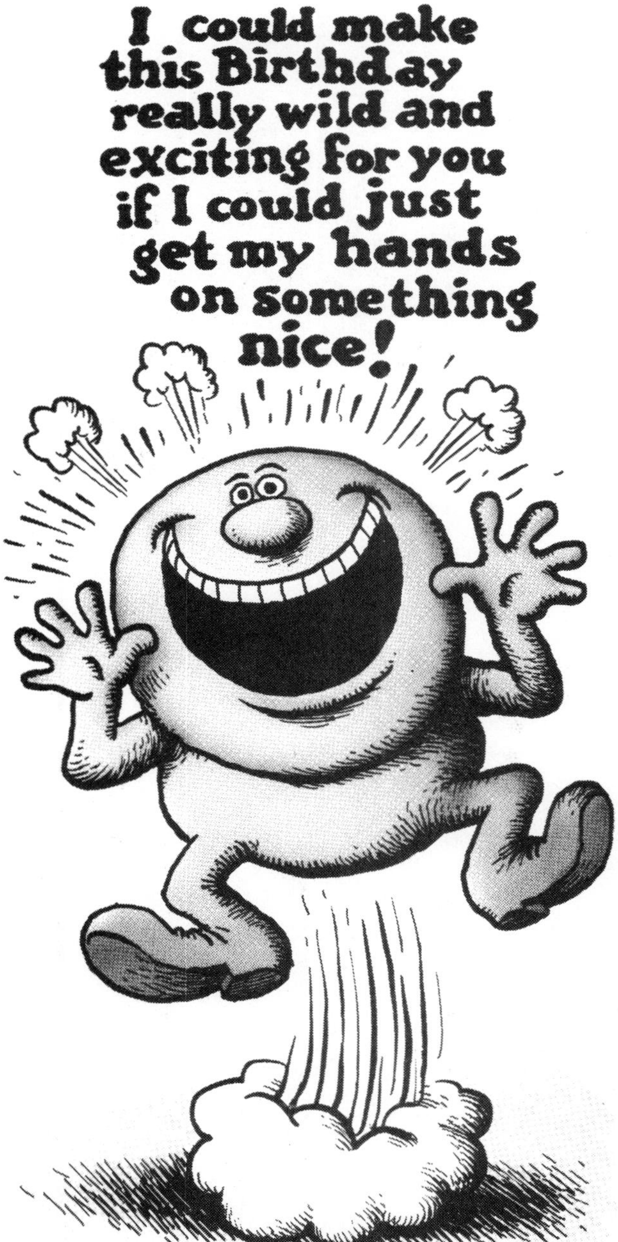
I could make this Birthday really wild and exciting for you if I could just get my hands on something nice!

[Like YOU!]

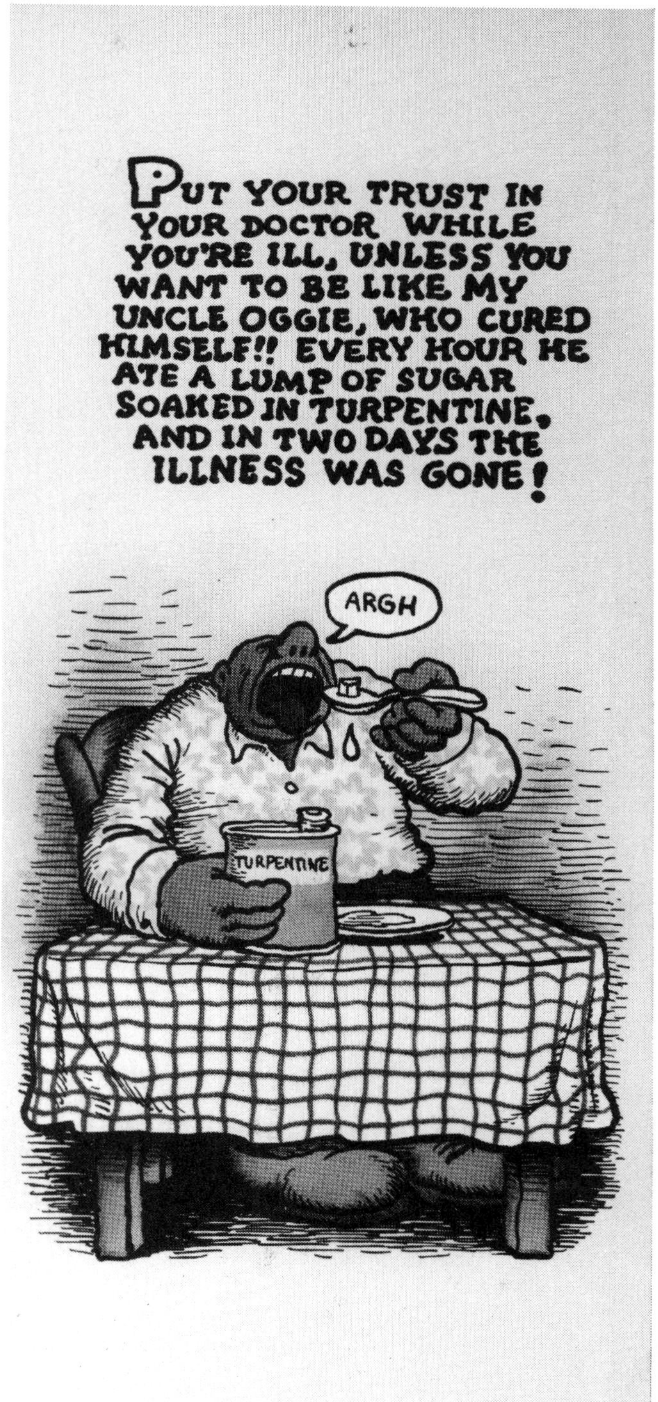
PUT YOUR TRUST IN YOUR DOCTOR WHILE YOU'RE ILL, UNLESS YOU WANT TO BE LIKE MY UNCLE OGGIE, WHO CURED HIMSELF!! EVERY HOUR HE ATE A LUMP OF SUGAR SOAKED IN TURPENTINE, AND IN TWO DAYS THE ILLNESS WAS GONE!
ARGH
TURPENTINE

[But, so was Uncle Oggie!]

IF YOU WANT ANYTHING JUST RING FOR THE NURSE!
RING FOR NURSE HERE
BZZZT
WELL, ALMOST ANYTHING
hope you're well soon!!

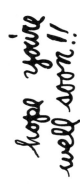

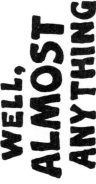

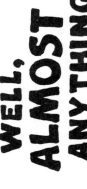

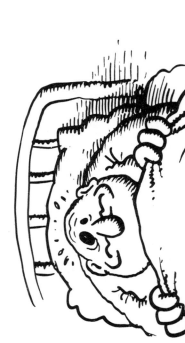

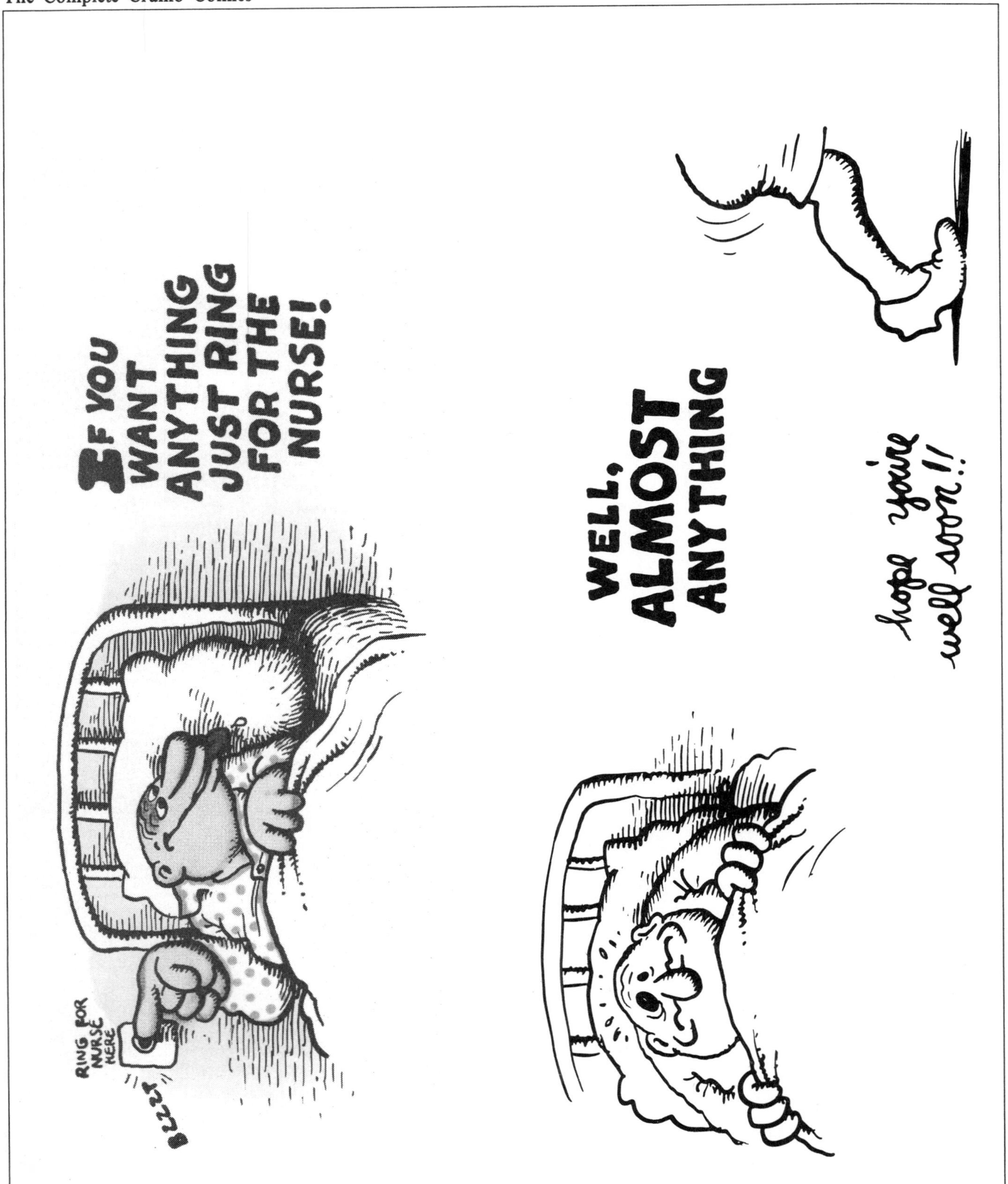

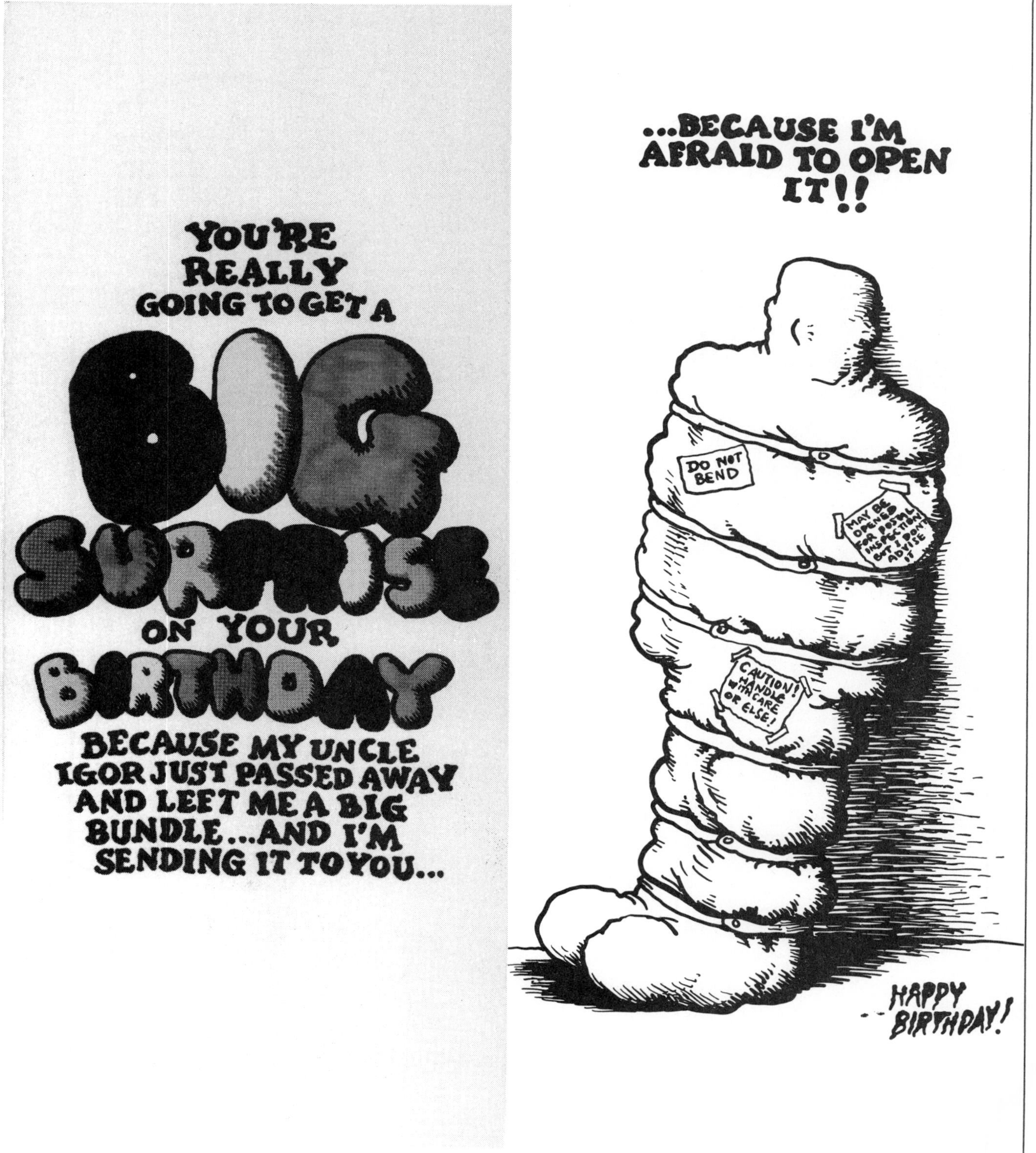
YOU'RE REALLY GOING TO GET A
BIG
SURPRISE
ON YOUR
BIRTHDAY
BECAUSE MY UNCLE IGOR JUST PASSED AWAY AND LEFT ME A BIG BUNDLE...AND I'M SENDING IT TO YOU...
...BECAUSE I'M AFRAID TO OPEN IT!!
DO NOT BEND
MAY BE OPENED FOR POSTAL INSPECTION BUT I DON'T ADVISE IT
CAUTION! HANDLE WITH CARE OR ELSE!
...HAPPY BIRTHDAY!

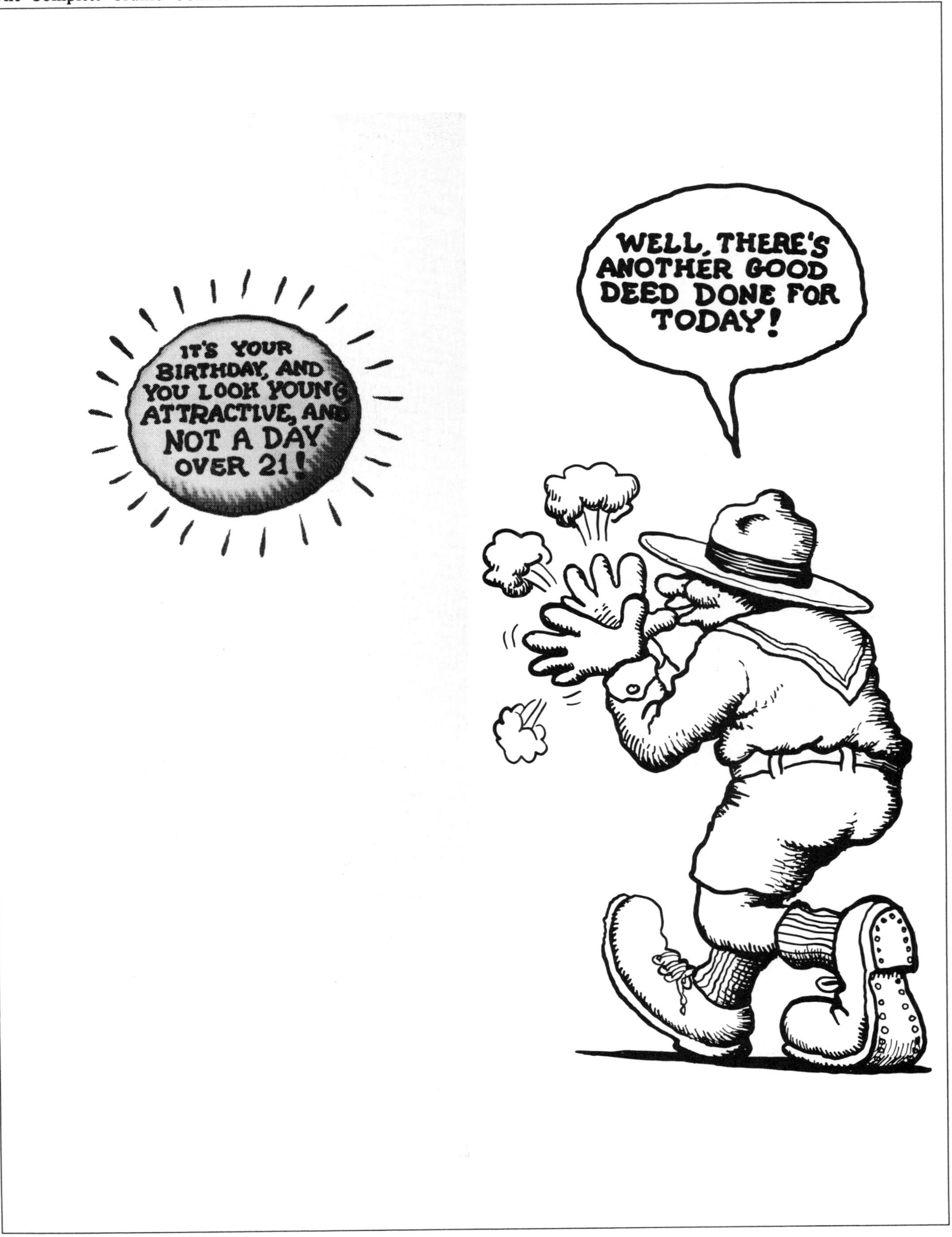
IT'S YOUR BIRTHDAY, AND YOU LOOK YOUNG, ATTRACTIVE, AND NOT A DAY OVER 21!
WELL, THERE'S ANOTHER GOOD DEED DONE FOR TODAY!

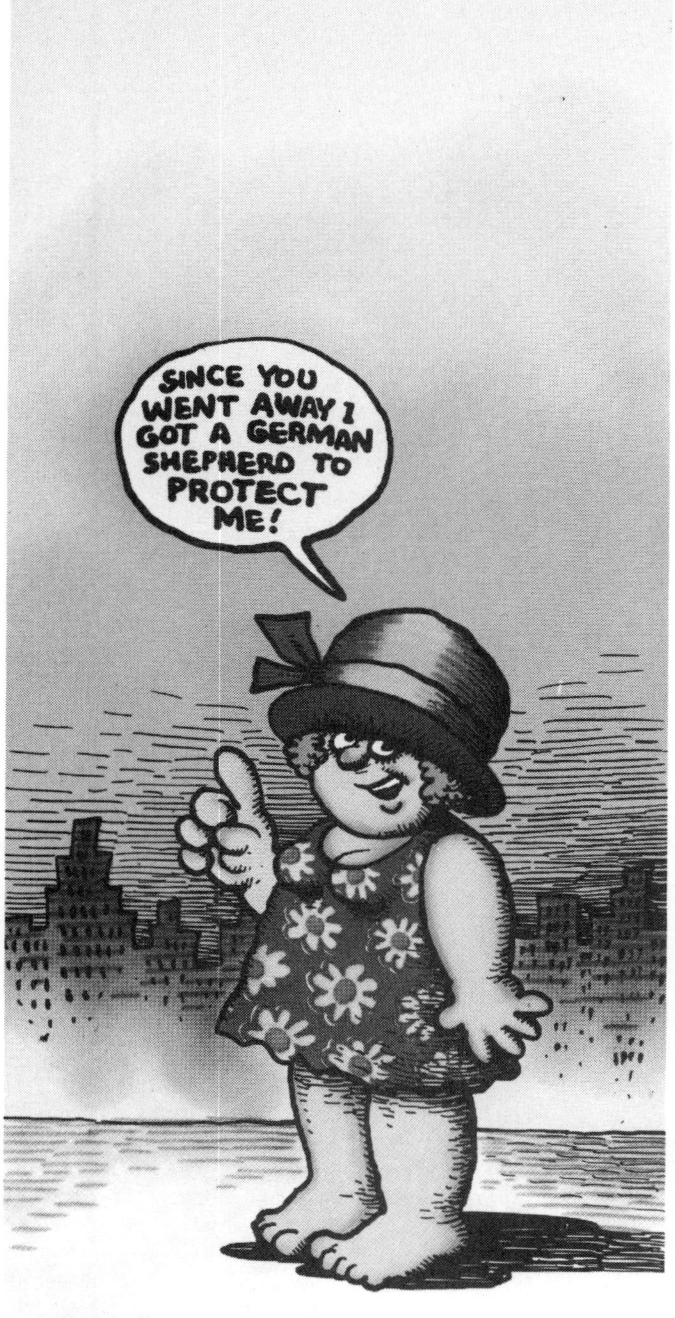
SINCE YOU WENT AWAY I GOT A GERMAN SHEPHERD TO PROTECT ME!

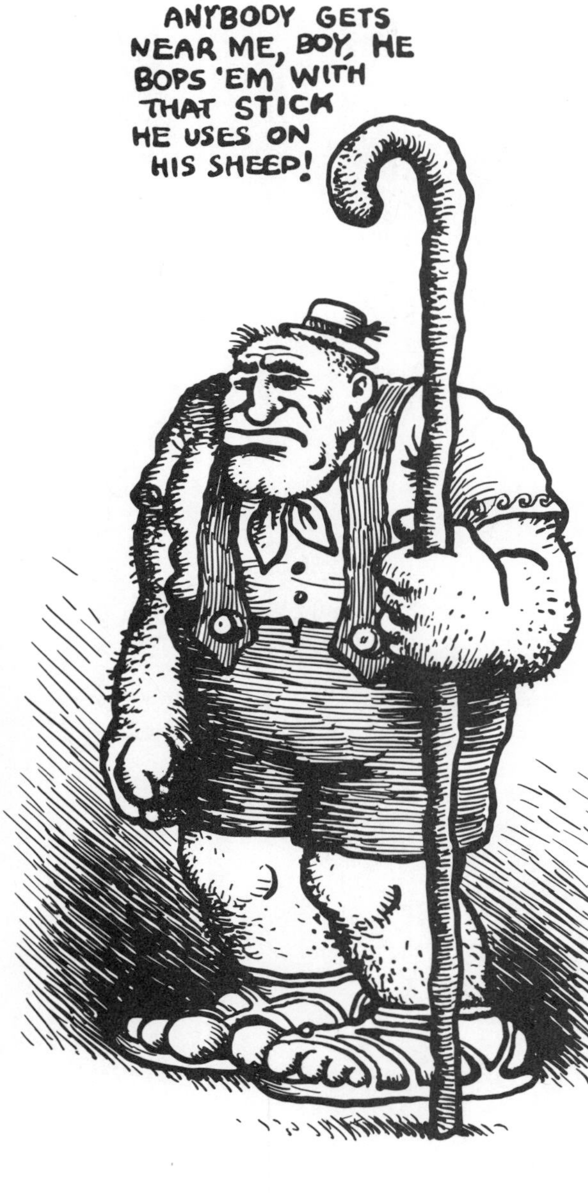
ANYBODY GETS NEAR ME, BOY, HE BOPS 'EM WITH THAT STICK HE USES ON HIS SHEEP!

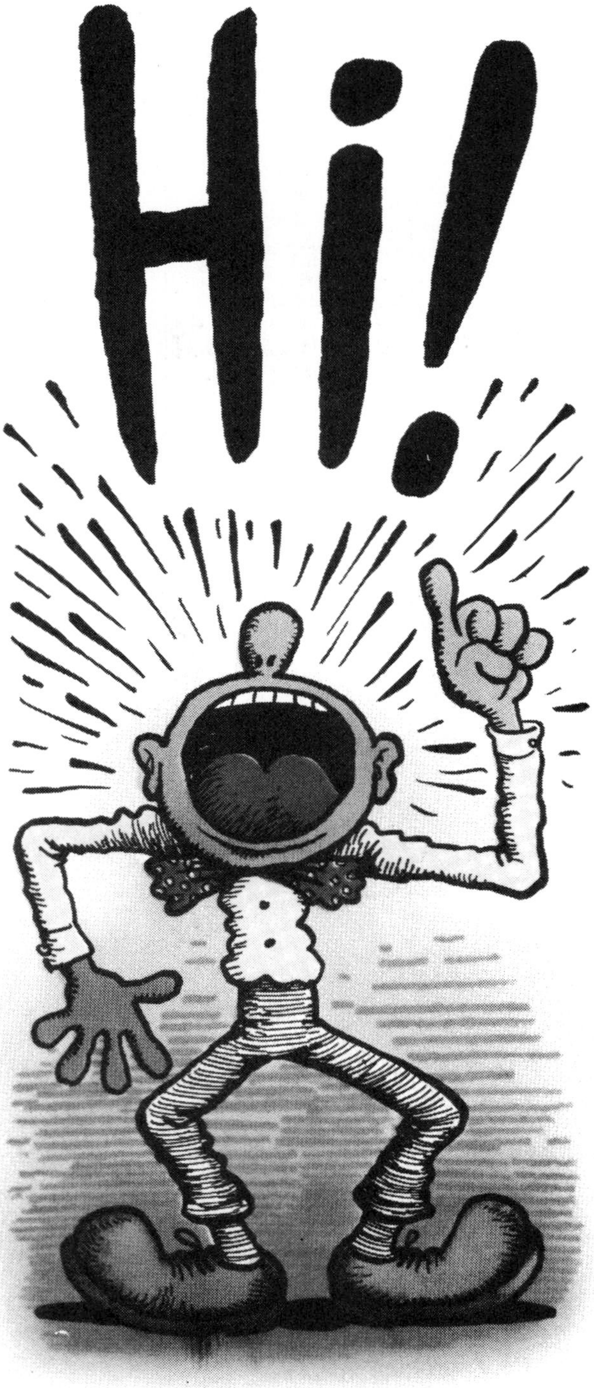
Hi!

*[More later!]*

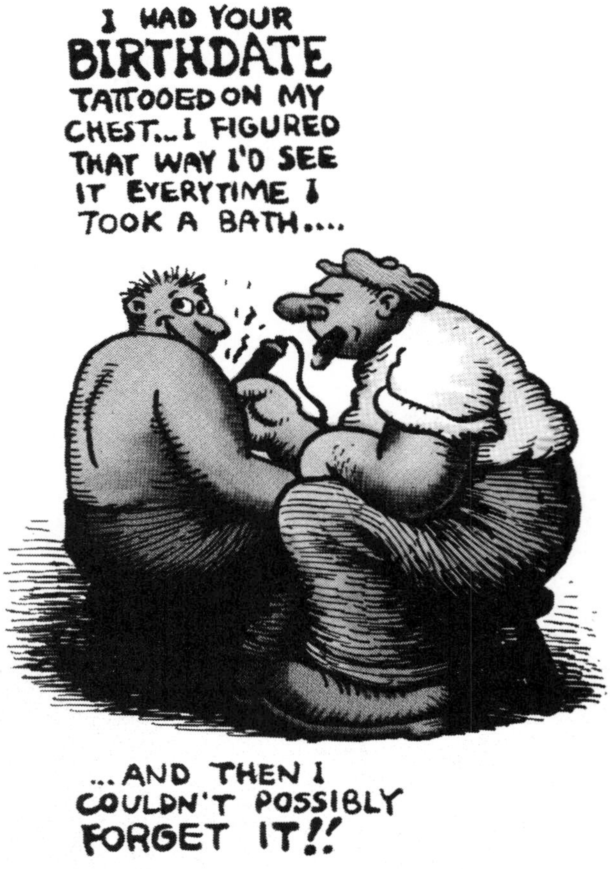
I HAD YOUR BIRTHDATE TATTOOED ON MY CHEST...I FIGURED THAT WAY I'D SEE IT EVERYTIME I TOOK A BATH....
...AND THEN I COULDN'T POSSIBLY FORGET IT!!

***[. . .The only trouble was, your birthday didn't fall on a Saturday this year!]***

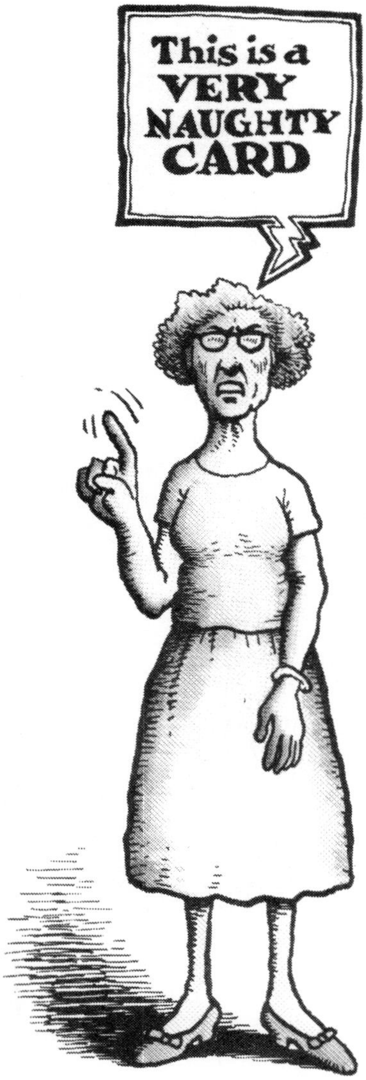
This is a VERY NAUGHTY CARD

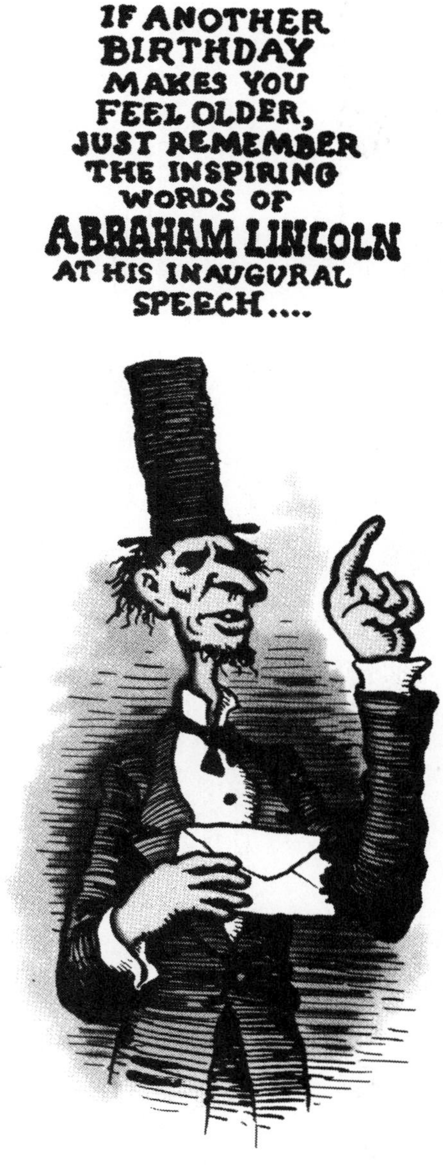
IF ANOTHER BIRTHDAY MAKES YOU FEEL OLDER, JUST REMEMBER THE INSPIRING WORDS OF ABRAHAM LINCOLN AT HIS INAUGURAL SPEECH....

*[It didn't even arrive in time for your birthday!]*

*[I hope you were taking notes so you can remember what he said!]*

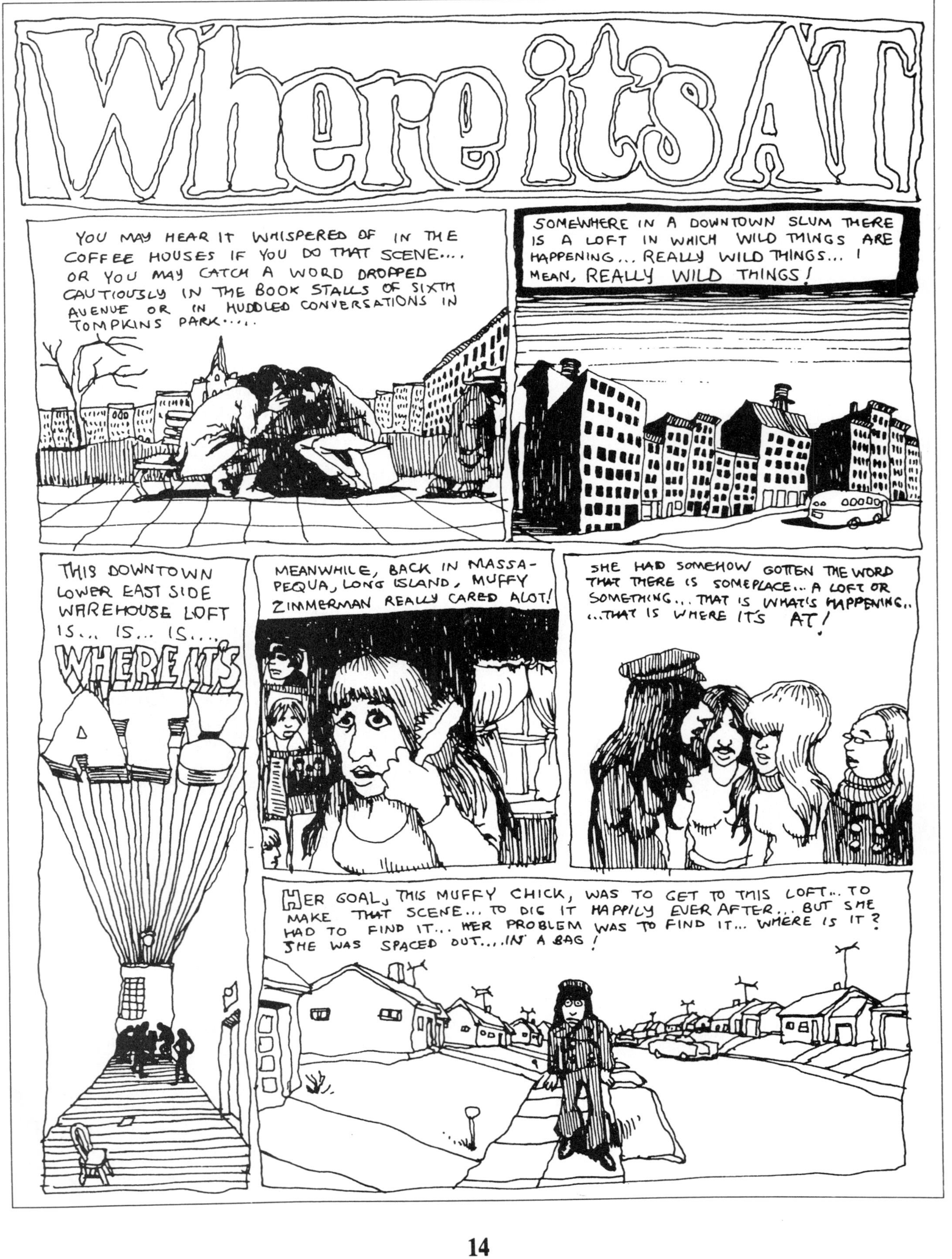
Where it's AT
YOU MAY HEAR IT WHISPERED OF IN THE COFFEE HOUSES IF YOU DO THAT SCENE.... OR YOU MAY CATCH A WORD DROPPED CAUTIOUSLY IN THE BOOK STALLS OF SIXTH AVENUE OR IN HUDDLED CONVERSATIONS IN TOMPKINS PARK.....
SOMEWHERE IN A DOWNTOWN SLUM THERE IS A LOFT IN WHICH WILD THINGS ARE HAPPENING... REALLY WILD THINGS... I MEAN, REALLY WILD THINGS!
THIS DOWNTOWN LOWER EAST SIDE WAREHOUSE LOFT IS... IS... IS....
WHERE IT'S AT
MEANWHILE, BACK IN MASSAPEQUA, LONG ISLAND, MUFFY ZIMMERMAN REALLY CARED ALOT!
SHE HAD SOMEHOW GOTTEN THE WORD THAT THERE IS SOMEPLACE... A LOFT OR SOMETHING... THAT IS WHAT'S HAPPENING.. ..THAT IS WHERE IT'S AT!
HER GOAL, THIS MUFFY CHICK, WAS TO GET TO THIS LOFT.. TO MAKE THAT SCENE... TO DIG IT HAPPILY EVER AFTER... BUT SHE HAD TO FIND IT... HER PROBLEM WAS TO FIND IT... WHERE IS IT? SHE WAS SPACED OUT.... IN A BAG!

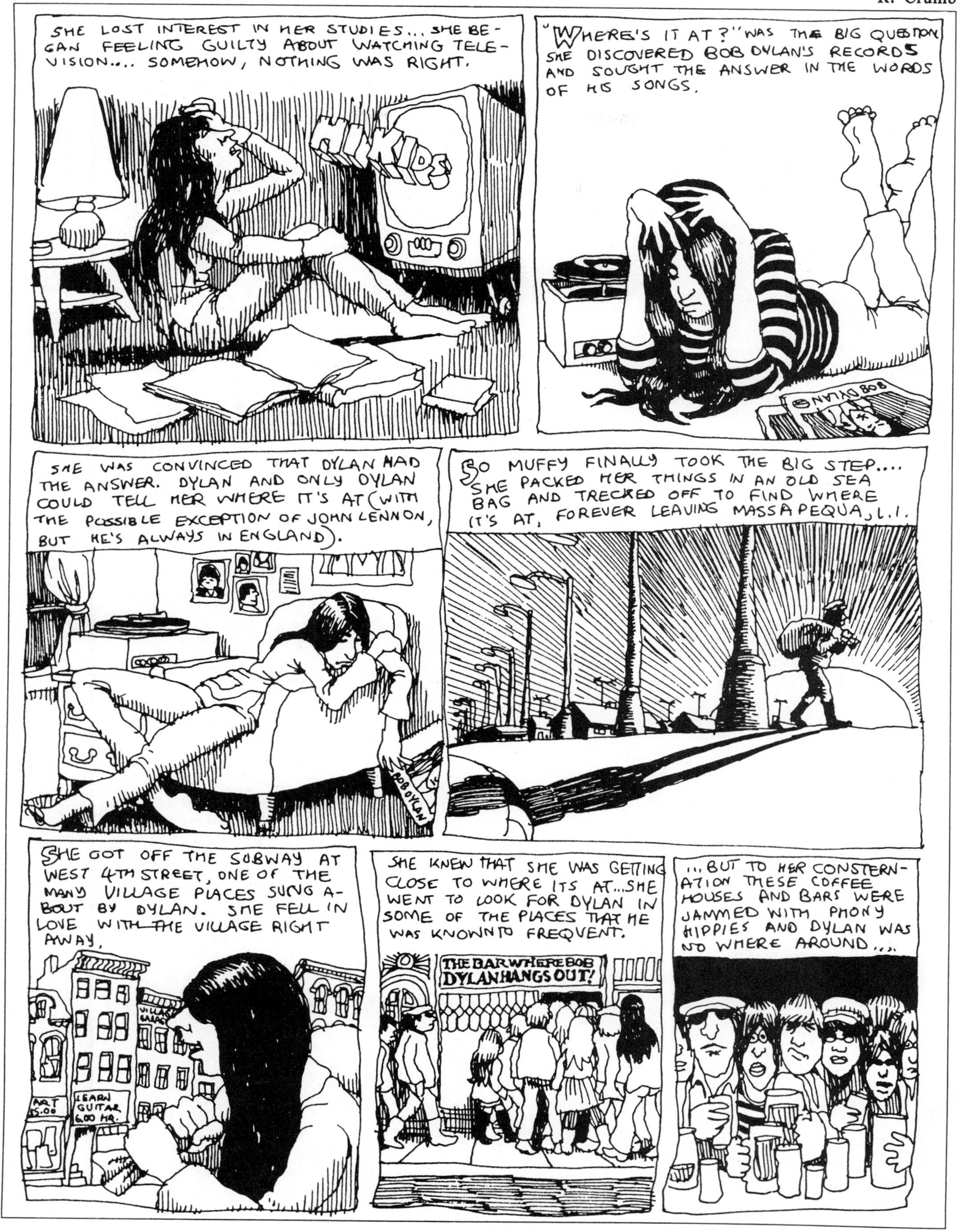
SHE LOST INTEREST IN HER STUDIES... SHE BEGAN FEELING GUILTY ABOUT WATCHING TELEVISION... SOMEHOW, NOTHING WAS RIGHT.
"WHERE'S IT AT?" WAS THE BIG QUESTION. SHE DISCOVERED BOB DYLAN'S RECORDS AND SOUGHT THE ANSWER IN THE WORDS OF HIS SONGS.
BOB DYLAN
SHE WAS CONVINCED THAT DYLAN HAD THE ANSWER. DYLAN AND ONLY DYLAN COULD TELL HER WHERE IT'S AT (WITH THE POSSIBLE EXCEPTION OF JOHN LENNON, BUT HE'S ALWAYS IN ENGLAND).
BOB DYLAN
SO MUFFY FINALLY TOOK THE BIG STEP.... SHE PACKED HER THINGS IN AN OLD SEA BAG AND TRECKED OFF TO FIND WHERE IT'S AT, FOREVER LEAVING MASSAPEQUA, L.I.
SHE GOT OFF THE SUBWAY AT WEST 4TH STREET, ONE OF THE MANY VILLAGE PLACES SUNG ABOUT BY DYLAN. SHE FELL IN LOVE WITH THE VILLAGE RIGHT AWAY.
ART $5.00
LEARN GUITAR 6.00 HR.
SHE KNEW THAT SHE WAS GETTING CLOSE TO WHERE ITS AT... SHE WENT TO LOOK FOR DYLAN IN SOME OF THE PLACES THAT HE WAS KNOWN TO FREQUENT.
THE BAR WHERE BOB DYLAN HANGS OUT!
...BUT TO HER CONSTERNATION THESE COFFEE HOUSES AND BARS WERE JAMMED WITH PHONY HIPPIES AND DYLAN WAS NO WHERE AROUND...

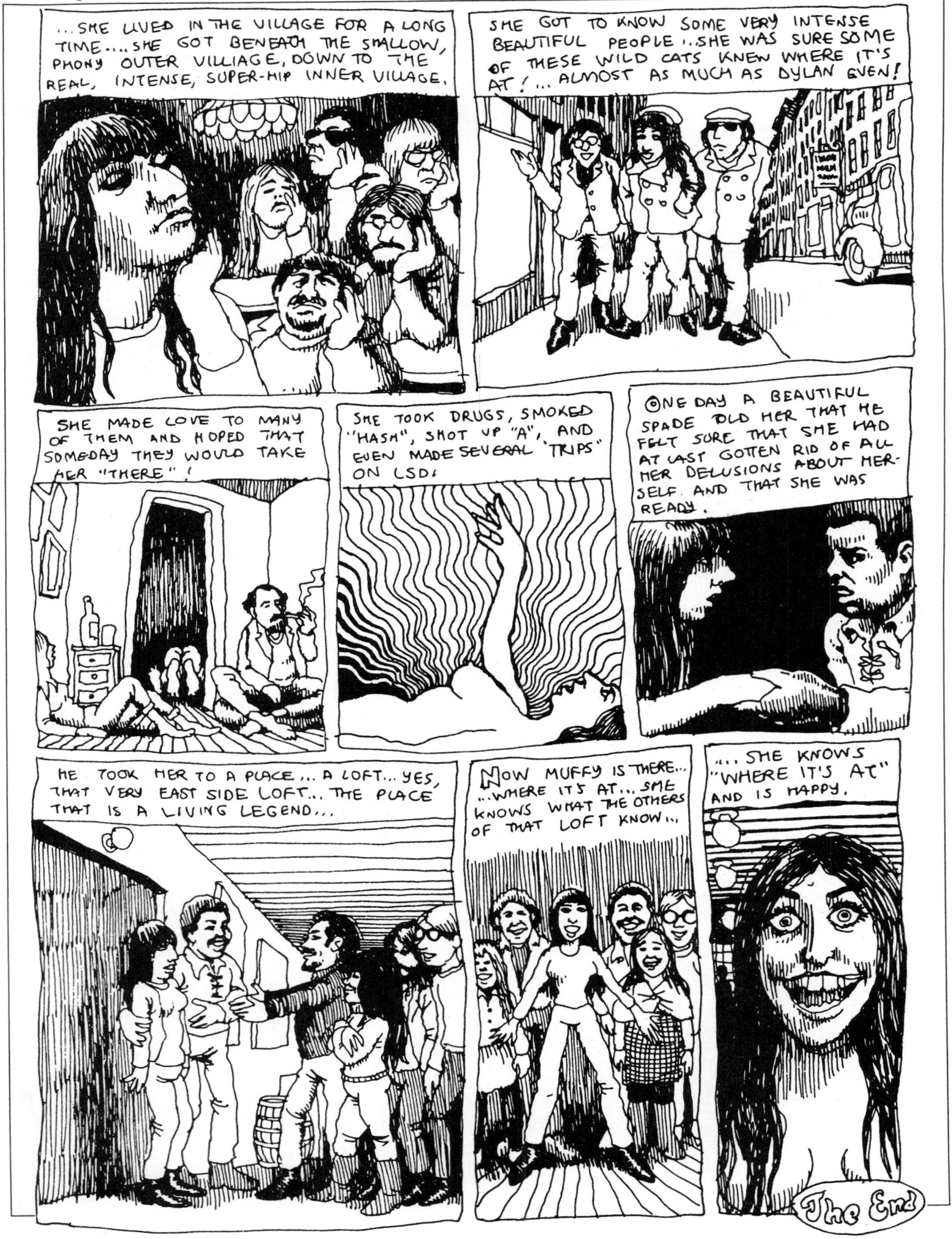
...SHE LIVED IN THE VILLAGE FOR A LONG TIME... SHE GOT BENEATH THE SHALLOW, PHONY OUTER VILLIAGE, DOWN TO THE REAL, INTENSE, SUPER-HIP INNER VILLAGE.
SHE GOT TO KNOW SOME VERY INTENSE BEAUTIFUL PEOPLE.. SHE WAS SURE SOME OF THESE WILD CATS KNEW WHERE IT'S AT! ... ALMOST AS MUCH AS DYLAN EVEN!
SHE MADE LOVE TO MANY OF THEM AND HOPED THAT SOMEDAY THEY WOULD TAKE HER "THERE"!
SHE TOOK DRUGS, SMOKED "HASH", SHOT UP "A", AND EVEN MADE SEVERAL "TRIPS" ON LSD.
ONE DAY A BEAUTIFUL SPADE TOLD HER THAT HE FELT SURE THAT SHE HAD AT LAST GOTTEN RID OF ALL HER DELUSIONS ABOUT HER-SELF AND THAT SHE WAS READY.
HE TOOK HER TO A PLACE... A LOFT... YES, THAT VERY EAST SIDE LOFT.. THE PLACE THAT IS A LIVING LEGEND...
NOW MUFFY IS THERE... ...WHERE IT'S AT... SHE KNOWS WHAT THE OTHERS OF THAT LOFT KNOW...
...SHE KNOWS "WHERE IT'S AT" AND IS HAPPY.
The End

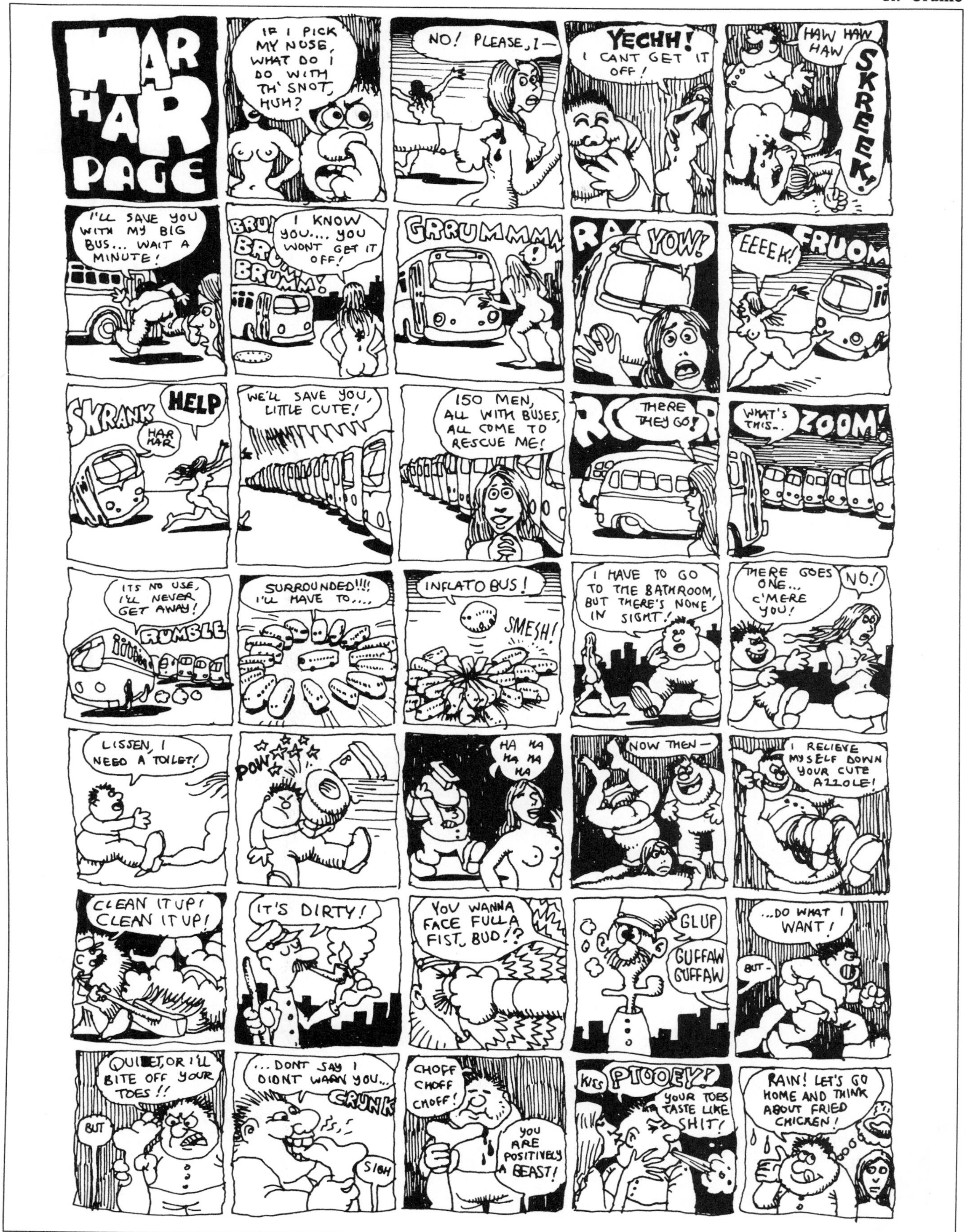
HAR HAR PAGE
IF I PICK MY NOSE, WHAT DO I DO WITH TH' SNOT, HUH?
NO! PLEASE, I—
YECHH! I CANT GET IT OFF!
HAW HAW HAW
SKREEK!
I'LL SAVE YOU WITH MY BIG BUS... WAIT A MINUTE!
I KNOW YOU.... YOU WONT GET IT OFF!
BRUMMM!
GRRUMMMM
YOW!
EEEEK!
FRUOM
SKRANK
HELP
HAR HAR
WE'LL SAVE YOU, LITTLE CUTE!
150 MEN, ALL WITH BUSES, ALL COME TO RESCUE ME!
THERE THEY GO!
WHAT'S THIS..
ZOOM!
ITS NO USE, I'LL NEVER GET AWAY!
RUMBLE
SURROUNDED!!!! I'LL HAVE TO....
INFLATO BUS!
SMESH!
I HAVE TO GO TO THE BATHROOM, BUT THERE'S NONE IN SIGHT!
THERE GOES ONE... C'MERE YOU!
NO!
LISSEN, I NEED A TOILET!
POW
HA HA HA HA HA
NOW THEN—
I RELIEVE MYSELF DOWN YOUR CUTE AZZOLE!
CLEAN IT UP! CLEAN IT UP!
IT'S DIRTY!
YOU WANNA FACE FULLA FIST, BUD!?
GLUP
GUFFAW GUFFAW
...DO WHAT I WANT!
BUT—
QUIET, OR I'LL BITE OFF YOUR TOES!!
BUT
... DONT SAY I DIDNT WARN YOU...
CRUNK
SIGH
CHOFF CHOFF CHOFF!
CHOFF
YOU ARE POSITIVELY A BEAST!
KISS
PTOOEY!
YOUR TOES TASTE LIKE SHIT!
RAIN! LET'S GO HOME AND THINK ABOUT FRIED CHICKEN!

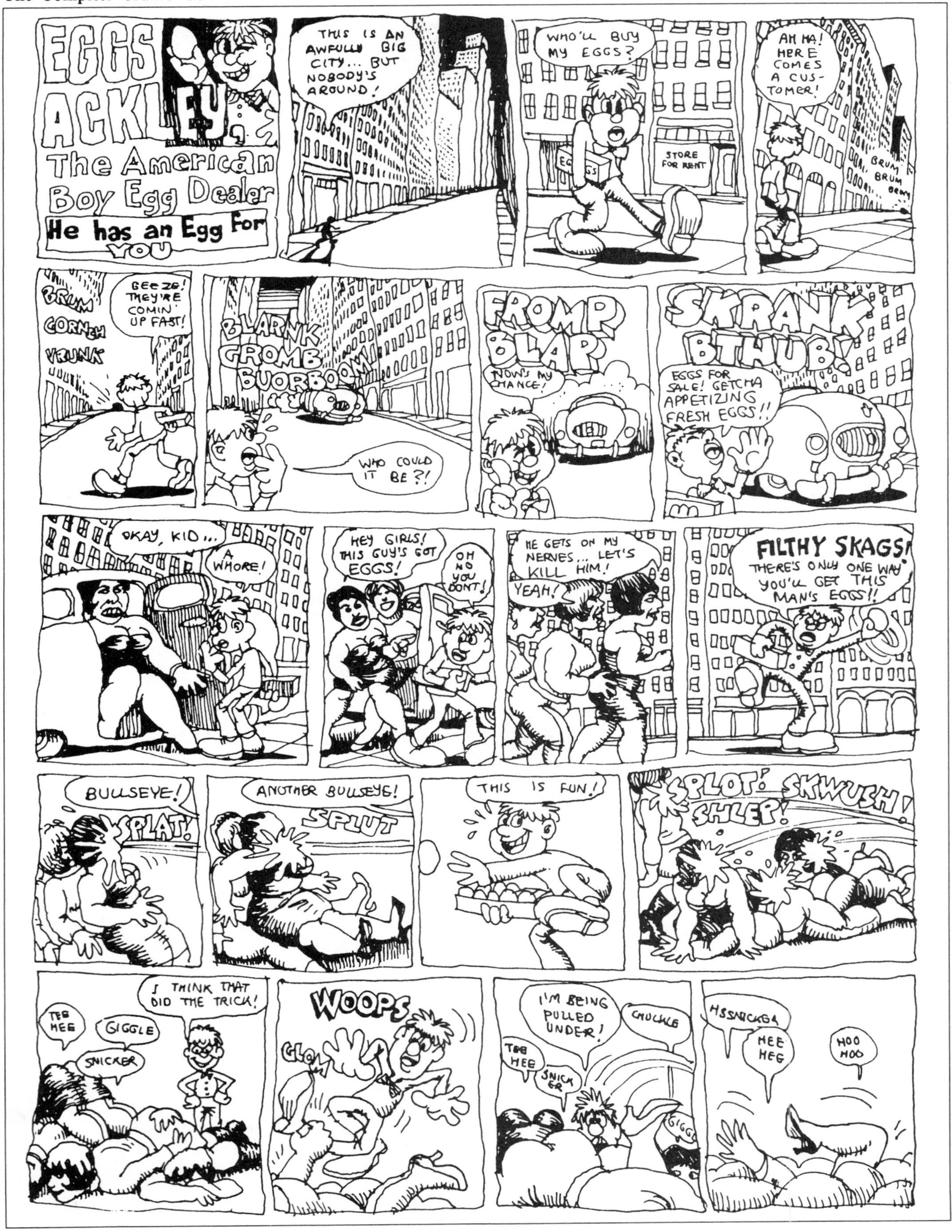
EGGS ACKLEY, The American Boy Egg Dealer
He has an Egg For YOU
THIS IS AN AWFULLY BIG CITY... BUT NOBODY'S AROUND!
WHO'LL BUY MY EGGS?
EGGS
STORE FOR RENT
AH HA! HERE COMES A CUS-TOMER!
BRUM BRUM BRUM
BRUM
CORNCH
VRUNK
GEEZE! THEY'RE COMIN' UP FAST!
BLARNK GROMB BUORBOOM
WHO COULD IT BE?!
FROMP BLAP
NOW'S MY CHANCE!
SKRANK BTHUB!
EGGS FOR SALE! GETCHA APPETIZING FRESH EGGS!!
OKAY, KID...
A WHORE!
HEY GIRLS! THIS GUY'S GOT EGGS!
OH NO YOU DON'T!
HE GETS ON MY NERVES... LET'S KILL HIM!
YEAH!
FILTHY SKAGS!
THERE'S ONLY ONE WAY YOU'LL GET THIS MAN'S EGGS!!
BULLSEYE!
SPLAT!
ANOTHER BULLSEYE!
SPLUT
THIS IS FUN!
SPLOT! SKWUSH! SHLEP!
I THINK THAT DID THE TRICK!
TEE HEE
GIGGLE
SNICKER
WOOPS
GLOM
I'M BEING PULLED UNDER!
CHUCKLE
TEE HEE
SNICKER
HSSNICKGA
HEE HEE
HOO HOO

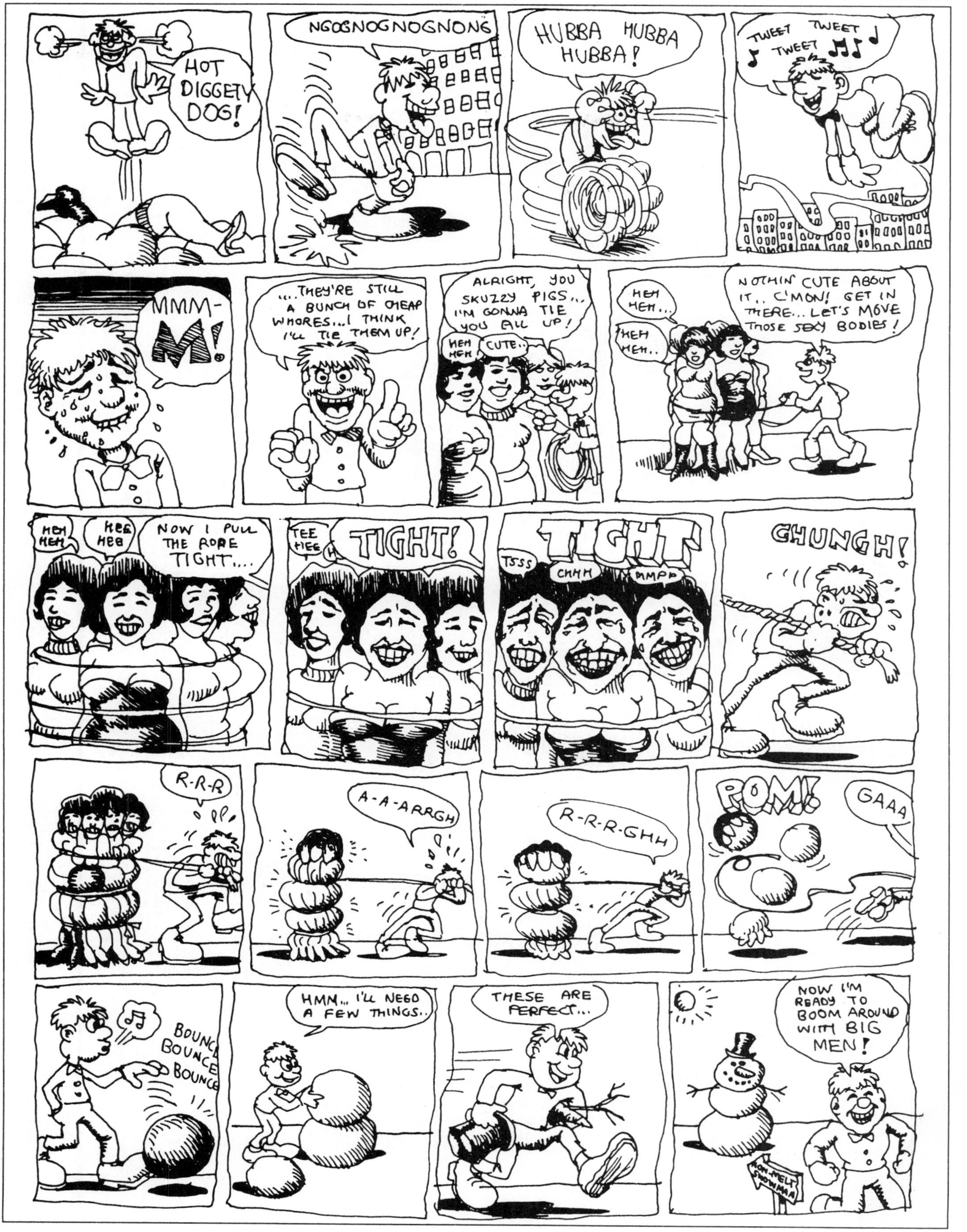
HOT DIGGETY DOG!
NGOGNOGNOGNONG
HUBBA HUBBA HUBBA!
TWEET TWEET TWEET
MMM-M!
...THEY'RE STILL A BUNCH OF CHEAP WHORES...I THINK I'LL TIE THEM UP!
ALRIGHT, YOU SKUZZY PIGS... I'M GONNA TIE YOU ALL UP!
HEH HEH
CUTE..
HEH HEH...
HEH HEH..
NOTHIN' CUTE ABOUT IT.. C'MON! GET IN THERE... LET'S MOVE THOSE SEXY BODIES!
HEH HEH
HEE HEE
NOW I PULL THE ROPE TIGHT....
TEE HEE
TIGHT!
TIGHT
TSSS
CHHH
MMPP
GHUNGH!
R-R-R
A-A-ARRGH
R-R-R-GHH
POM!
GAAA
BOUNCE BOUNCE BOUNCE
HMN... I'LL NEED A FEW THINGS..
THESE ARE PERFECT...
NOW I'M READY TO BOOM AROUND WITH BIG MEN!
NON-MELT SNOWMAN

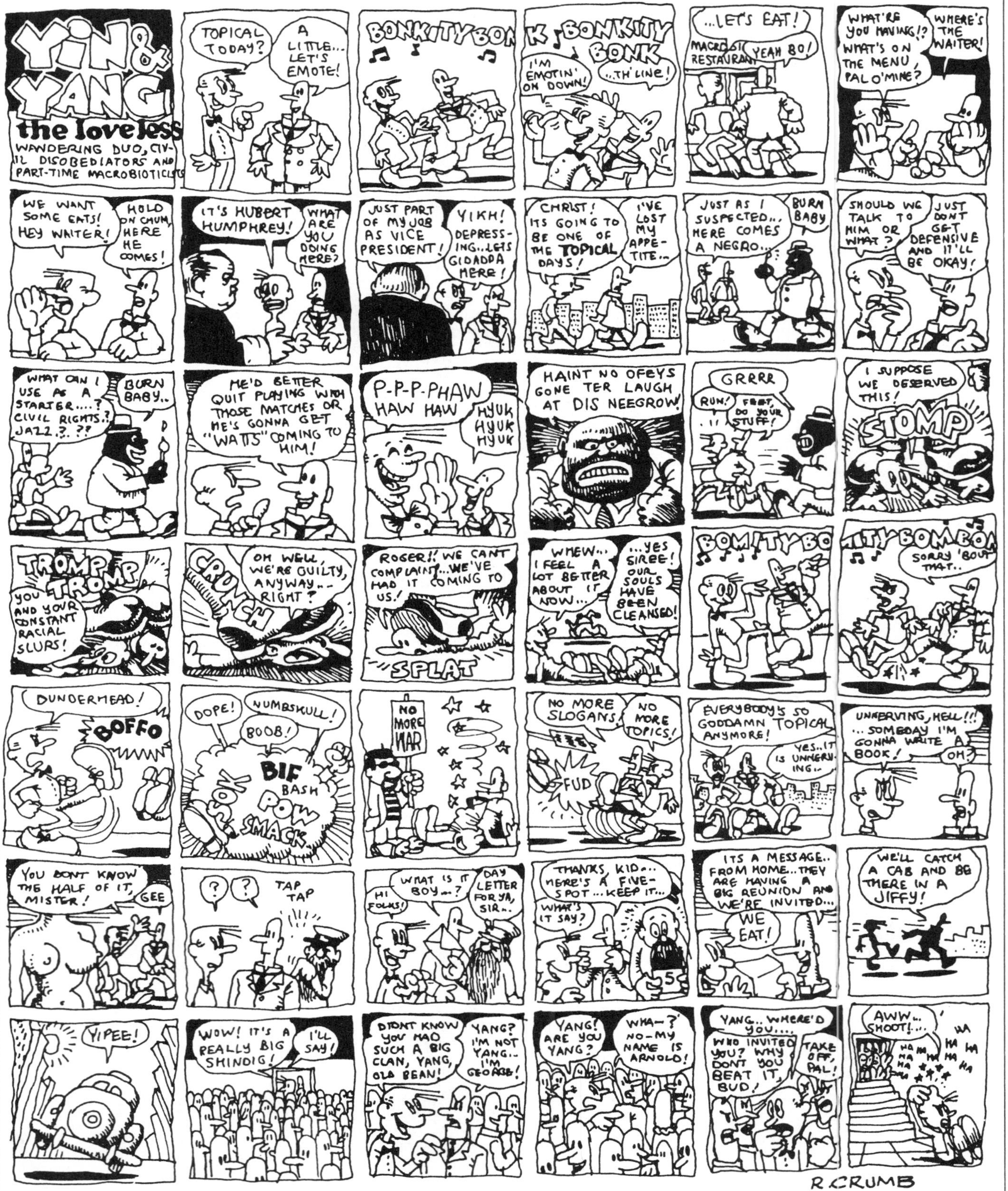
YIN & YANG
the loveless
WANDERING DUO, CIVIL DISOBEDIATORS AND PART-TIME MACROBIOTICISTS
TOPICAL TODAY?
A LITTLE... LET'S EMOTE!
BONKITYBONK BONKITY BONK
I'M EMOTIN' ON DOWN!
...TH' LINE!
...LET'S EAT!
MACROBIOTIC RESTAURANT
YEAH BO!
WHAT'RE YOU HAVING!? WHAT'S ON THE MENU, PAL O'MINE?
WHERE'S THE WAITER!
WE WANT SOME EATS! HEY WAITER!
HOLD ON CHUM, HERE HE COMES!
IT'S HUBERT HUMPHREY!
WHAT ARE YOU DOING HERE?
JUST PART OF MY JOB AS VICE PRESIDENT!
YIKH! DEPRESSING.. LETS GIDADDA HERE!
CHRIST! ITS GOING TO BE ONE OF THE TOPICAL DAYS!
I'VE LOST MY APPETITE..
JUST AS I SUSPECTED... HERE COMES A NEGRO...
BURN BABY
SHOULD WE TALK TO HIM OR WHAT?
JUST DONT GET DEFENSIVE AND IT'LL BE OKAY!
WHAT CAN I USE AS A STARTER....? CIVIL RIGHTS.? JAZZ.?.??
BURN BABY..
HE'D BETTER QUIT PLAYING WITH THOSE MATCHES OR HE'S GONNA GET "WATTS" COMING TO HIM!
P-P-P-PHAW HAW HAW
HYUK HYUK HYUK
HAINT NO OFEYS GONE TER LAUGH AT DIS NEEGROW!
GRRRR
RUN!
FEET, DO YOUR STUFF!
I SUPPOSE WE DESERVED THIS!
STOMP
TROMP TROMP
YOU AND YOUR CONSTANT RACIAL SLURS!
CRUNCH
OH WELL, WE'RE GUILTY, ANYWAY... RIGHT?
ROGER!! WE CANT COMPLAIN!...WE'VE HAD IT COMING TO US!
SPLAT
WHEW... I FEEL A LOT BETTER ABOUT IT NOW...
...YES SIREE! OUR SOULS HAVE BEEN CLEANSED!
BOMKITYBOMKITYBOMBOM
SORRY 'BOUT THAT..
DUNDERHEAD!
BOFFO
DOPE!
NUMBSKULL!
BOOB!
SOK BIF BASH POW SMACK
NO MORE WAR
NO MORE SLOGANS!
NO MORE TOPICS!
FUD
EVERYBODY'S SO GODDAMN TOPICAL ANYMORE!
YES..IT IS UNNERVING..
UNNERVING, HELL!!! ...SOMEDAY I'M GONNA WRITE A BOOK!
OH?
YOU DONT KNOW THE HALF OF IT, MISTER!
GEE
?
?
TAP TAP
HI FOLKS!
WHAT IS IT BOY...?
DAY LETTER FOR YA, SIR..
THANKS, KID... HERE'S A FIVE-SPOT... KEEP IT...
WHAT'S IT SAY?
ITS A MESSAGE.. FROM HOME...THEY ARE HAVING A BIG REUNION AND WE'RE INVITED...
WE EAT!
WE'LL CATCH A CAB AND BE THERE IN A JIFFY!
YIPEE!
WOW! IT'S A REALLY BIG SHINDIG!
I'LL SAY!
DIDNT KNOW YOU HAD SUCH A BIG CLAN, YANG, OLD BEAN!
YANG? I'M NOT YANG.. I'M GEORGE!
YANG! ARE YOU YANG?
WHA-? NO-MY NAME IS ARNOLD!
YANG.. WHERE'D YOU....
WHO INVITED YOU? WHY DONT YOU BEAT IT, BUD!
TAKE OFF, PAL!
AWW... SHOOT!...
HA HA HA HA HA HA HA HA
R. CRUMB

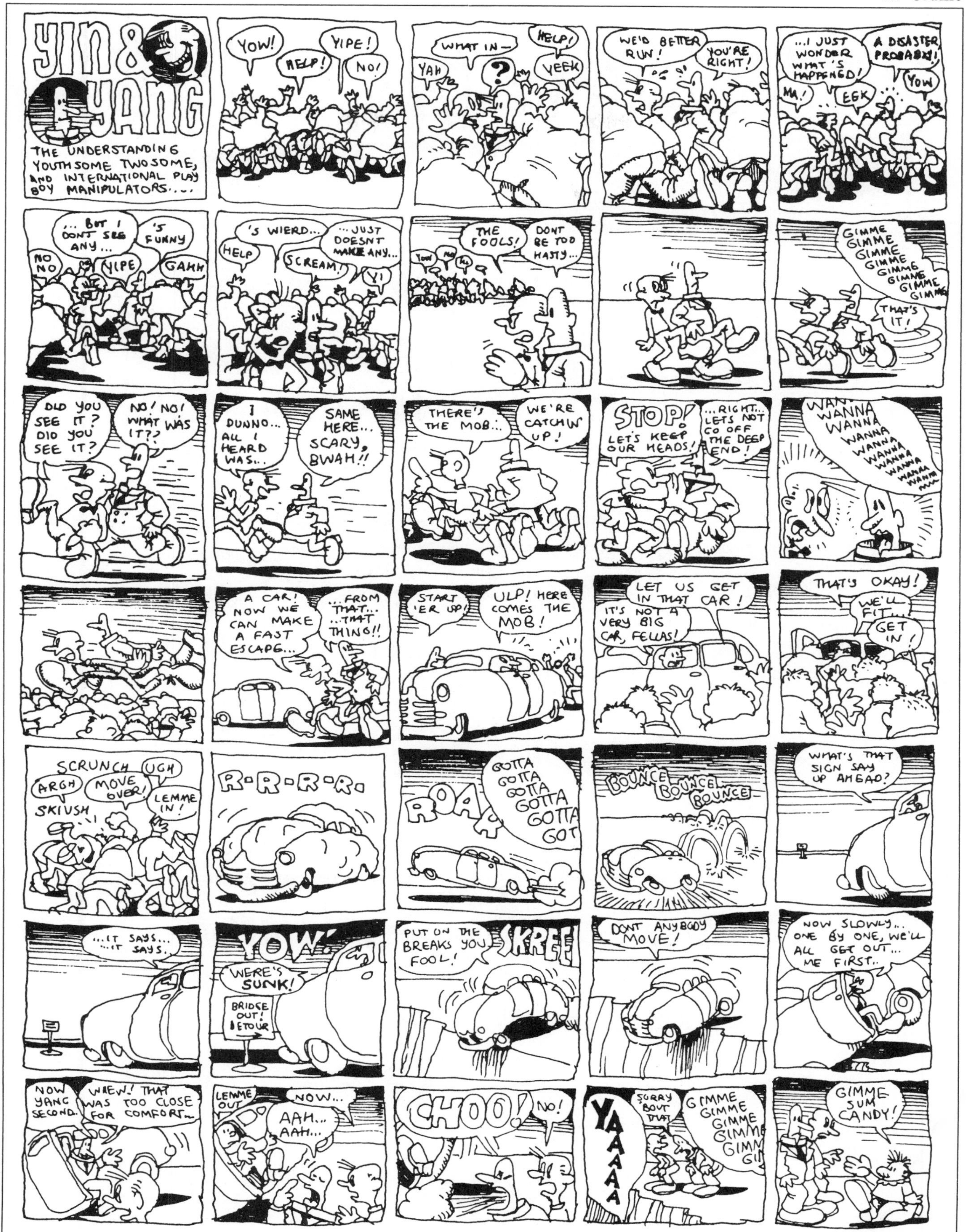
YIN & YANG
THE UNDERSTANDING YOUTHSOME TWOSOME, AND INTERNATIONAL PLAY BOY MANIPULATORS....
YOW!
HELP!
YIPE!
NO!
WHAT IN—
HELP!
YAH
?
YEEK
WE'D BETTER RUN!
YOU'RE RIGHT!
...I JUST WONDER WHAT'S HAPPENED!
A DISASTER PROBABLY!
MA!
EEK
YOW
... BUT I DONT SEE ANY ...
'S FUNNY
NO NO
YIPE
GAHH
'S WIERD...
...JUST DOESNT MAKE ANY...
HELP
SCREAM!
YI
THE FOOLS!
DONT BE TOO HASTY...
GIMME GIMME GIMME GIMME GIMME GIMME GIMME GIMME
THAT'S IT!
DID YOU SEE IT? DID YOU SEE IT?
NO! NO! WHAT WAS IT??
I DUNNO... ALL I HEARD WAS...
SAME HERE... SCARY, BWAH!!
THERE'S THE MOB...
WE'RE CATCHIN' UP!
STOP! LET'S KEEP OUR HEADS!
...RIGHT... LETS NOT GO OFF THE DEEP END!
WANNA WANNA WANNA WANNA WANNA WANNA WANNA WANNA WANNA
A CAR! NOW WE CAN MAKE A FAST ESCAPE...
...FROM THAT... ...THAT THING!!
START 'ER UP!
ULP! HERE COMES THE MOB!
LET US GET IN THAT CAR!
IT'S NOT A VERY BIG CAR, FELLAS!
THAT'S OKAY!
WE'LL FIT...
GET IN!
SCRUNCH
UGH
ARGH
MOVE OVER!
LEMME IN!
SKIUSH
R-R-R-R-R-
ROAR
GOTTA GOTTA GOTTA GOTTA GOTTA GOT
BOUNCE BOUNCE BOUNCE
WHAT'S THAT SIGN SAY UP AHEAD?
...IT SAYS... ...IT SAYS...
YOW!
WERE'S SUNK!
BRIDGE OUT! DETOUR
PUT ON THE BREAKS YOU FOOL!
SKREE
DONT ANYBODY MOVE!
NOW SLOWLY... ONE BY ONE, WE'LL ALL GET OUT... ME FIRST..
NOW YANG SECOND.
WHEW! THAT WAS TOO CLOSE FOR COMFORT...
LEMME OUT
NOW...
AAH... AAH...
CHOO!
NO!
YAAAAA
SORRY 'BOUT THAT
GIMME GIMME GIMME GIMME GIMM GI
GIMME SUM CANDY!

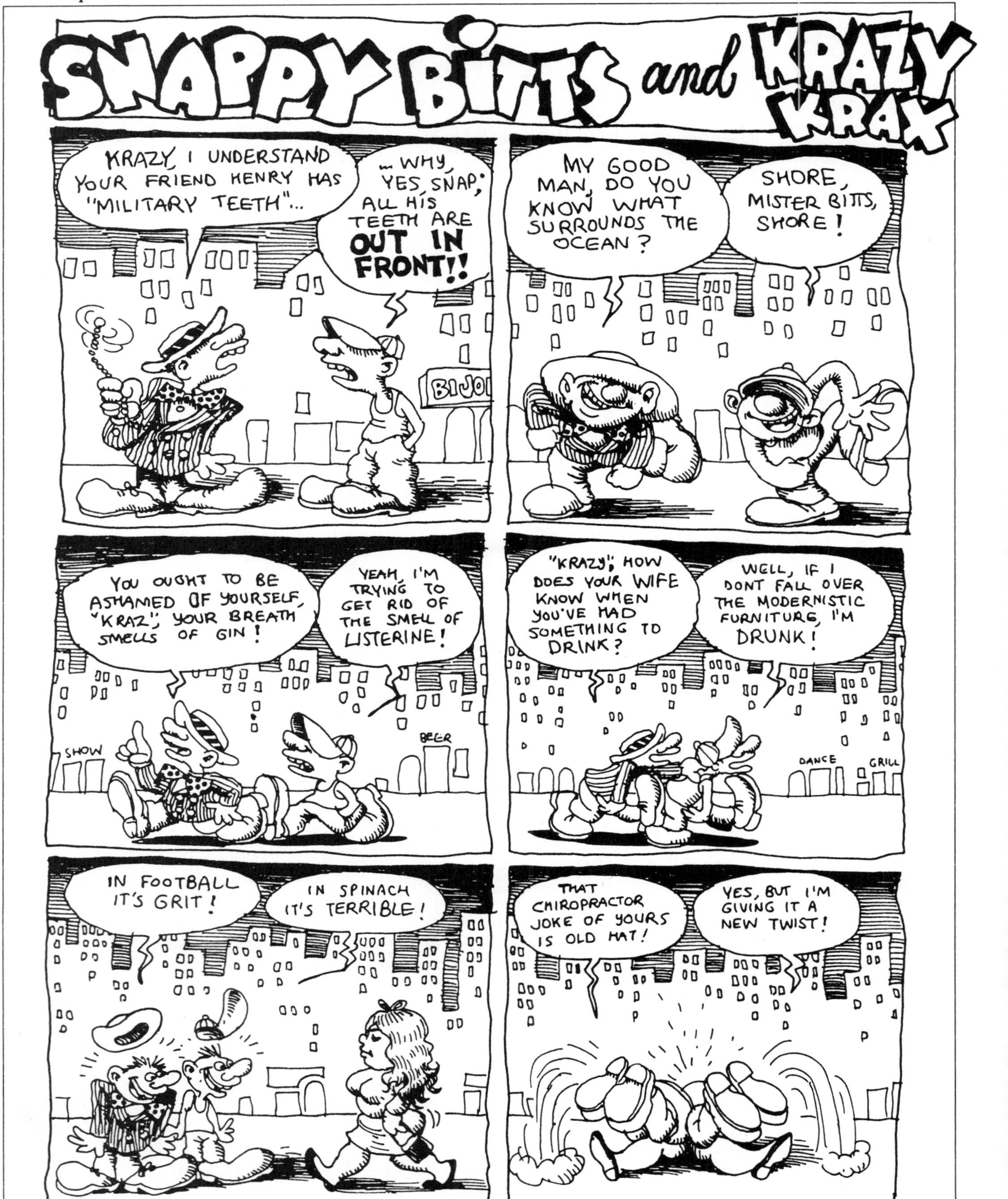
SNAPPY BITTS and KRAZY KRAX
KRAZY, I UNDERSTAND YOUR FRIEND HENRY HAS "MILITARY TEETH"...
...WHY, YES, SNAP, ALL HIS TEETH ARE OUT IN FRONT!!
BIJOU
MY GOOD MAN, DO YOU KNOW WHAT SURROUNDS THE OCEAN?
SHORE, MISTER BITTS, SHORE!
YOU OUGHT TO BE ASHAMED OF YOURSELF, "KRAZ", YOUR BREATH SMELLS OF GIN!
YEAH, I'M TRYING TO GET RID OF THE SMELL OF LISTERINE!
SHOW
BEER
"KRAZY", HOW DOES YOUR WIFE KNOW WHEN YOU'VE HAD SOMETHING TO DRINK?
WELL, IF I DONT FALL OVER THE MODERNISTIC FURNITURE, I'M DRUNK!
DANCE
GRILL
IN FOOTBALL IT'S GRIT!
IN SPINACH IT'S TERRIBLE!
THAT CHIROPRACTOR JOKE OF YOURS IS OLD HAT!
YES, BUT I'M GIVING IT A NEW TWIST!

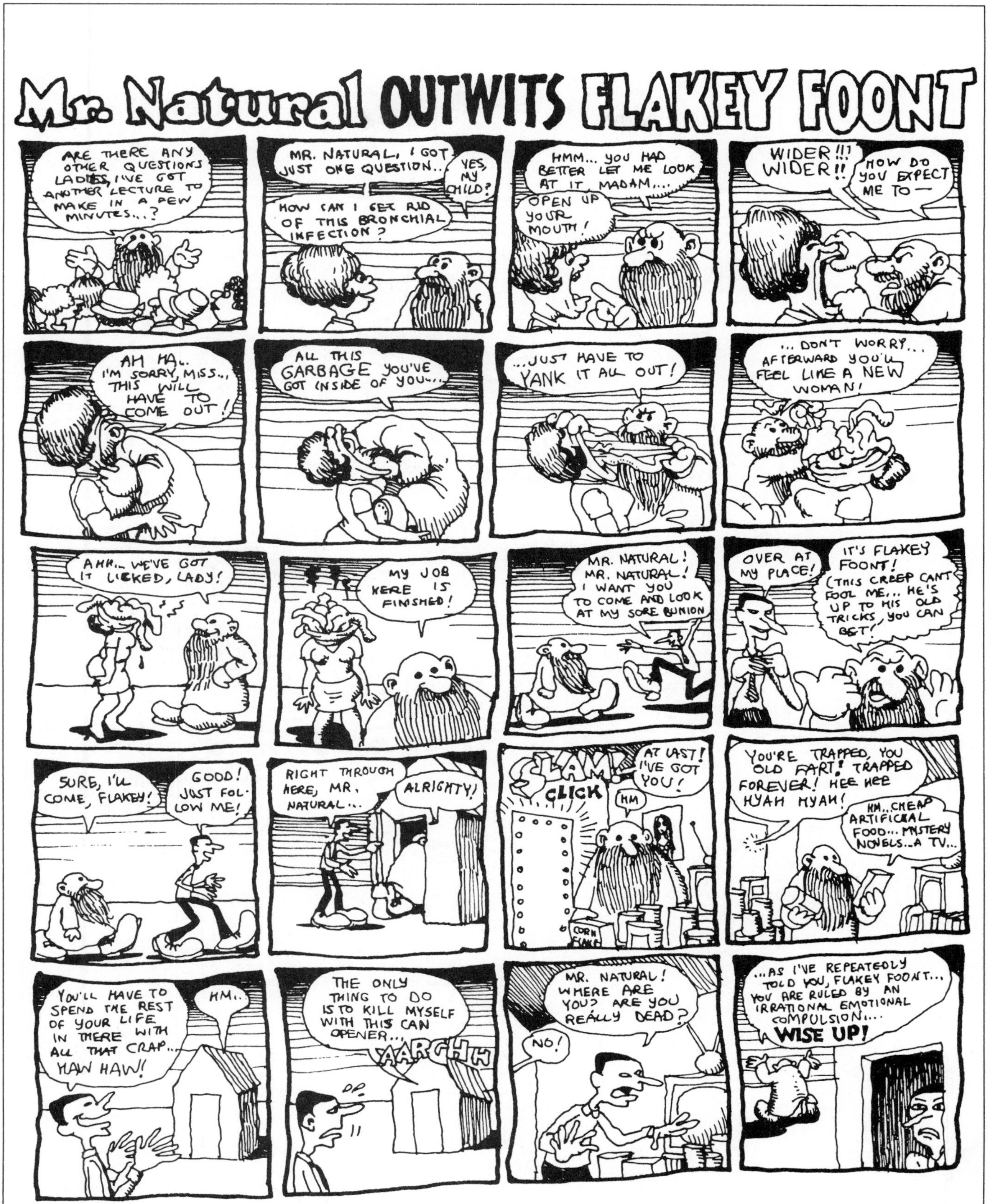
Mr. Natural OUTWITS FLAKEY FOONT
ARE THERE ANY OTHER QUESTIONS LADIES, I'VE GOT ANOTHER LECTURE TO MAKE IN A FEW MINUTES...?
MR. NATURAL, I GOT JUST ONE QUESTION...
YES, MY CHILD?
HOW CAN I GET RID OF THIS BRONCHIAL INFECTION?
HMM... YOU HAD BETTER LET ME LOOK AT IT, MADAM....
OPEN UP YOUR MOUTH!
WIDER!!! WIDER!!
HOW DO YOU EXPECT ME TO—
AH HA.. I'M SORRY, MISS.., THIS WILL HAVE TO COME OUT!
ALL THIS GARBAGE YOU'VE GOT INSIDE OF YOU...
...JUST HAVE TO YANK IT ALL OUT!
... DON'T WORRY... AFTERWARD YOU'LL FEEL LIKE A NEW WOMAN!
AHH.. WE'VE GOT IT LICKED, LADY!
MY JOB HERE IS FINISHED!
MR. NATURAL! MR. NATURAL! I WANT YOU TO COME AND LOOK AT MY SORE BUNION
OVER AT MY PLACE!
IT'S FLAKEY FOONT! (THIS CREEP CAN'T FOOL ME... HE'S UP TO HIS OLD TRICKS, YOU CAN BET!)
SURE, I'LL COME, FLAKEY!
GOOD! JUST FOL-LOW ME!
RIGHT THROUGH HERE, MR. NATURAL...
ALRIGHTY!
SLAM!
CLICK
AT LAST! I'VE GOT YOU!
HM
YOU'RE TRAPPED, YOU OLD FART! TRAPPED FOREVER! HEE HEE HYAH HYAH!
HM.. CHEAP ARTIFICIAL FOOD... MYSTERY NOVELS...A TV...
YOU'LL HAVE TO SPEND THE REST OF YOUR LIFE IN THERE WITH ALL THAT CRAP... HAW HAW!
HM..
THE ONLY THING TO DO IS TO KILL MYSELF WITH THIS CAN OPENER...
AARGHH
MR. NATURAL! WHERE ARE YOU? ARE YOU REALLY DEAD?
NO!
...AS I'VE REPEATEDLY TOLD YOU, FLAKEY FOONT... YOU ARE RULED BY AN IRRATIONAL EMOTIONAL COMPULSION....
WISE UP!

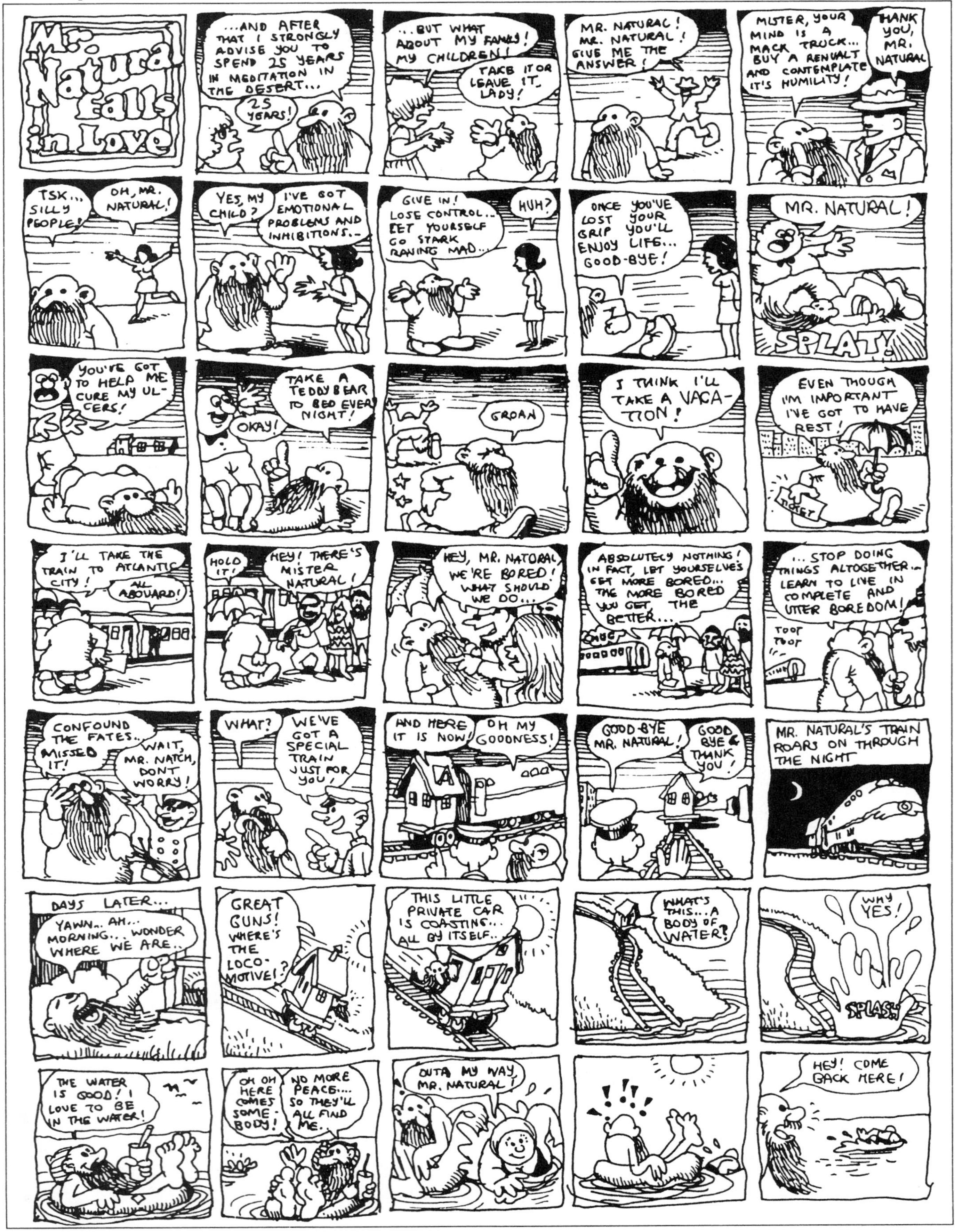
Mr. Natural Falls in Love
...AND AFTER THAT I STRONGLY ADVISE YOU TO SPEND 25 YEARS IN MEDITATION IN THE DESERT...
25 YEARS!
...BUT WHAT ABOUT MY FAMILY! MY CHILDREN!
TAKE IT OR LEAVE IT, LADY!
MR. NATURAL! MR. NATURAL! GIVE ME THE ANSWER!
MISTER, YOUR MIND IS A MACK TRUCK... BUY A RENAULT AND CONTEMPLATE IT'S HUMILITY!
THANK YOU, MR. NATURAL
TSK... SILLY PEOPLE!
OH, MR. NATURAL!
YES, MY CHILD?
I'VE GOT EMOTIONAL PROBLEMS AND INHIBITIONS...
GIVE IN! LOSE CONTROL... LET YOURSELF GO STARK RAVING MAD...
HUH?
ONCE YOU'VE LOST YOUR GRIP YOU'LL ENJOY LIFE... GOOD-BYE!
MR. NATURAL!
SPLAT!
YOU'VE GOT TO HELP ME CURE MY ULCERS!
TAKE A TEDDY BEAR TO BED EVERY NIGHT!
OKAY!
GROAN
I THINK I'LL TAKE A VACATION!
EVEN THOUGH I'M IMPORTANT I'VE GOT TO HAVE REST!
TICKET
I'LL TAKE THE TRAIN TO ATLANTIC CITY!
ALL ABOUARD!
HOLD IT!
HEY! THERE'S MISTER NATURAL!
HEY, MR. NATURAL, WE'RE BORED! WHAT SHOULD WE DO...
ABSOLUTELY NOTHING! IN FACT, LET YOURSELVES GET MORE BORED... THE MORE BORED YOU GET, THE BETTER...
...STOP DOING THINGS ALTOGETHER... LEARN TO LIVE IN COMPLETE AND UTTER BOREDOM!
TOOT TOOT
CONFOUND THE FATES... MISSED IT!
WAIT, MR. NATCH, DONT WORRY!
WHAT?
WE'VE GOT A SPECIAL TRAIN JUST FOR YOU!
AND HERE IT IS NOW!
OH MY GOODNESS!
GOOD-BYE MR. NATURAL!
GOOD BYE & THANK YOU!
MR. NATURAL'S TRAIN ROARS ON THROUGH THE NIGHT
DAYS LATER...
YAWN.. AH... MORNING... WONDER WHERE WE ARE..
GREAT GUNS! WHERE'S THE LOCO-MOTIVE!?
THIS LITTLE PRIVATE CAR IS COASTING... ALL BY ITSELF..
WHAT'S THIS...A BODY OF WATER?
WHY YES!
SPLASH
THE WATER IS GOOD! I LOVE TO BE IN THE WATER!
OH OH HERE COMES SOME-BODY!
NO MORE PEACE.... SO THEY'LL ALL FIND ME.
OUTA MY WAY, MR. NATURAL!
HEY! COME BACK HERE!

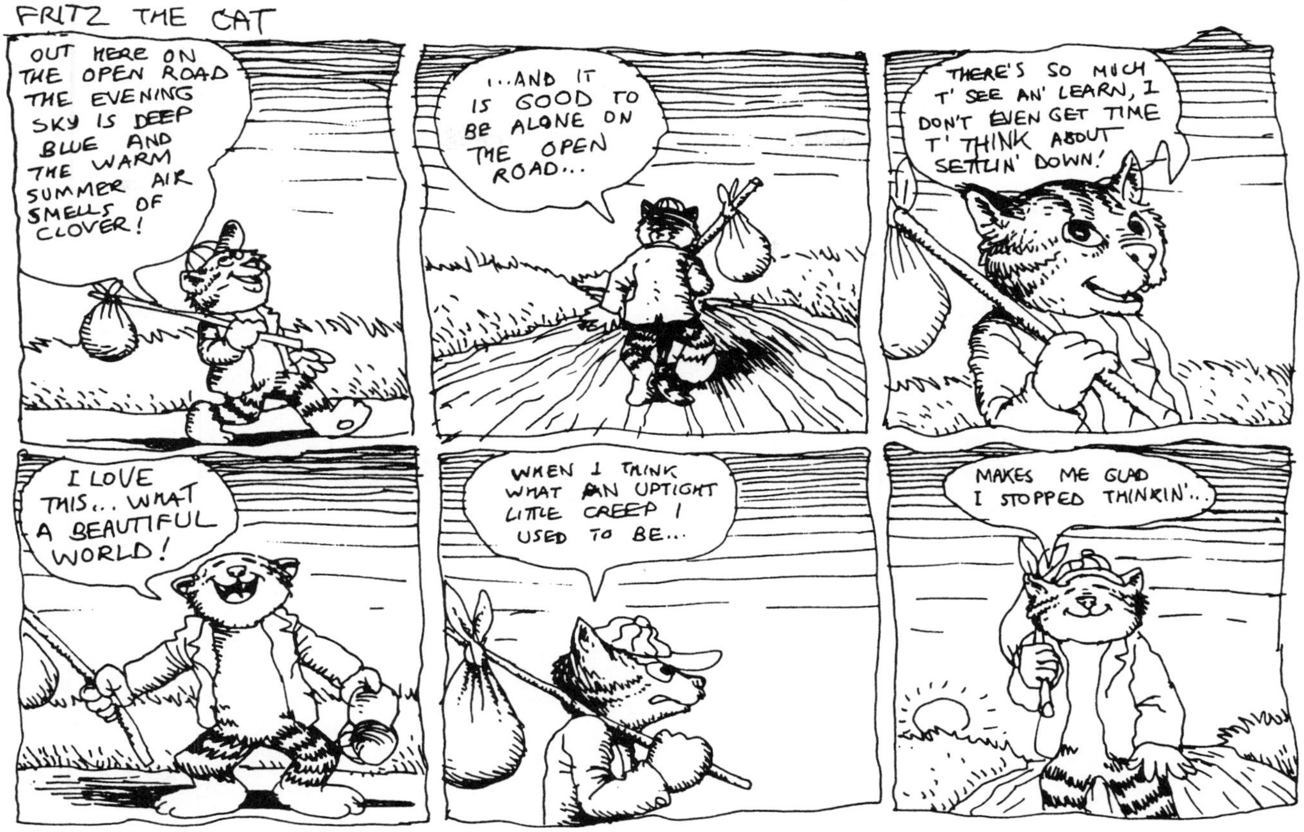
FRITZ THE CAT
OUT HERE ON THE OPEN ROAD THE EVENING SKY IS DEEP BLUE AND THE WARM SUMMER AIR SMELLS OF CLOVER!
...AND IT IS GOOD TO BE ALONE ON THE OPEN ROAD...
THERE'S SO MUCH T' SEE AN' LEARN, I DON'T EVEN GET TIME T' THINK ABOUT SETTLIN' DOWN!
I LOVE THIS... WHAT A BEAUTIFUL WORLD!
WHEN I THINK WHAT AN UPTIGHT LITTLE CREEP I USED TO BE...
MAKES ME GLAD I STOPPED THINKIN'...

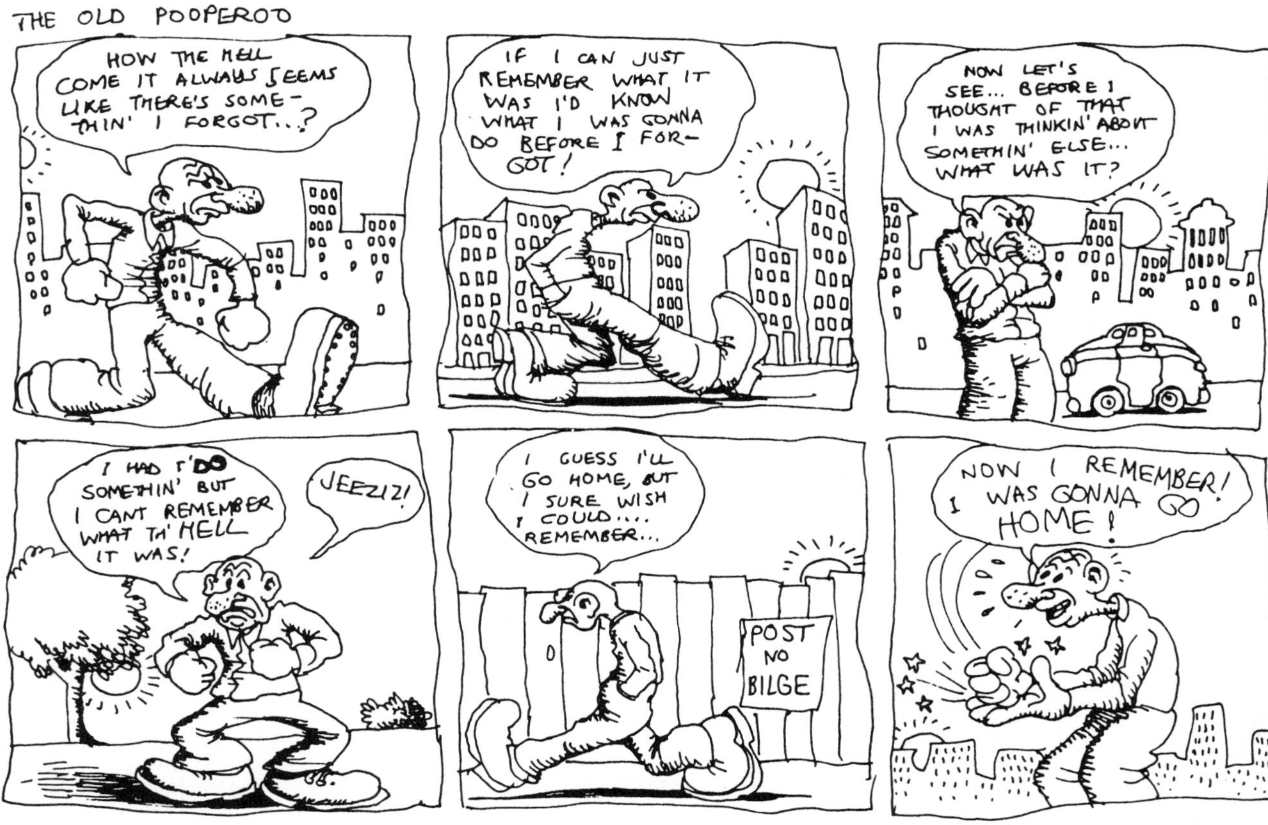
THE OLD POOPEROO
HOW THE HELL COME IT ALWAYS SEEMS LIKE THERE'S SOMETHIN' I FORGOT...?
IF I CAN JUST REMEMBER WHAT IT WAS I'D KNOW WHAT I WAS GONNA DO BEFORE I FORGOT!
NOW LET'S SEE... BEFORE I THOUGHT OF THAT I WAS THINKIN' ABOUT SOMETHIN' ELSE... WHAT WAS IT?
I HAD T'DO SOMETHIN' BUT I CANT REMEMBER WHAT TH' HELL IT WAS!
JEEZIZ!
I GUESS I'LL GO HOME, BUT I SURE WISH I COULD.... REMEMBER...
POST NO BILGE
NOW I REMEMBER! I WAS GONNA GO HOME!

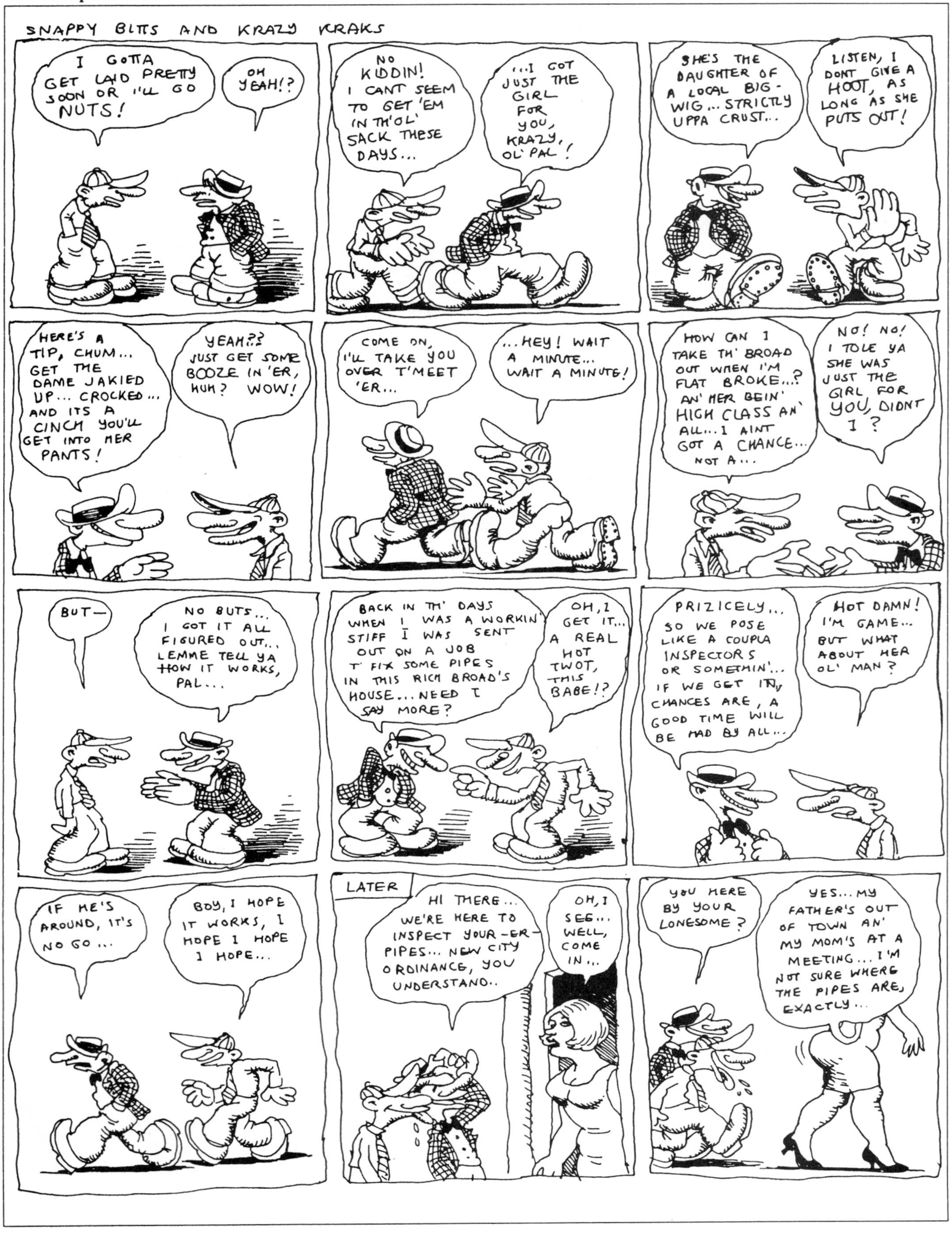
SNAPPY BITTS AND KRAZY KRAKS
I GOTTA GET LAID PRETTY SOON OR I'LL GO NUTS!
OH YEAH!?
NO KIDDIN! I CANT SEEM TO GET 'EM IN TH'OL' SACK THESE DAYS...
...I GOT JUST THE GIRL FOR YOU, KRAZY, OL' PAL!
SHE'S THE DAUGHTER OF A LOCAL BIG-WIG... STRICTLY UPPA CRUST...
LISTEN, I DONT GIVE A HOOT, AS LONG AS SHE PUTS OUT!
HERE'S A TIP, CHUM... GET THE DAME JAKIED UP... CROCKED... AND ITS A CINCH YOU'LL GET INTO HER PANTS!
YEAH?? JUST GET SOME BOOZE IN 'ER, HUH? WOW!
COME ON, I'LL TAKE YOU OVER T'MEET 'ER...
...HEY! WAIT A MINUTE... WAIT A MINUTE!
HOW CAN I TAKE TH' BROAD OUT WHEN I'M FLAT BROKE...? AN' HER BEIN' HIGH CLASS AN' ALL... I AINT GOT A CHANCE... NOT A...
NO! NO! I TOLE YA SHE WAS JUST THE GIRL FOR YOU, DIDNT I?
BUT—
NO BUTS... I GOT IT ALL FIGURED OUT... LEMME TELL YA HOW IT WORKS, PAL...
BACK IN TH' DAYS WHEN I WAS A WORKIN' STIFF I WAS SENT OUT ON A JOB T' FIX SOME PIPES IN THIS RICH BROAD'S HOUSE... NEED I SAY MORE?
OH, I GET IT... A REAL HOT TWOT, THIS BABE!?
PRIZICELY... SO WE POSE LIKE A COUPLA INSPECTORS OR SOMETHIN'... IF WE GET IN, CHANCES ARE, A GOOD TIME WILL BE HAD BY ALL...
HOT DAMN! I'M GAME... BUT WHAT ABOUT HER OL' MAN?
IF HE'S AROUND, IT'S NO GO...
BOY, I HOPE IT WORKS, I HOPE I HOPE I HOPE...
LATER
HI THERE... WE'RE HERE TO INSPECT YOUR-ER-PIPES... NEW CITY ORDINANCE, YOU UNDERSTAND..
OH, I SEE... WELL, COME IN...
YOU HERE BY YOUR LONESOME?
YES... MY FATHER'S OUT OF TOWN AN' MY MOM'S AT A MEETING... I'M NOT SURE WHERE THE PIPES ARE, EXACTLY...

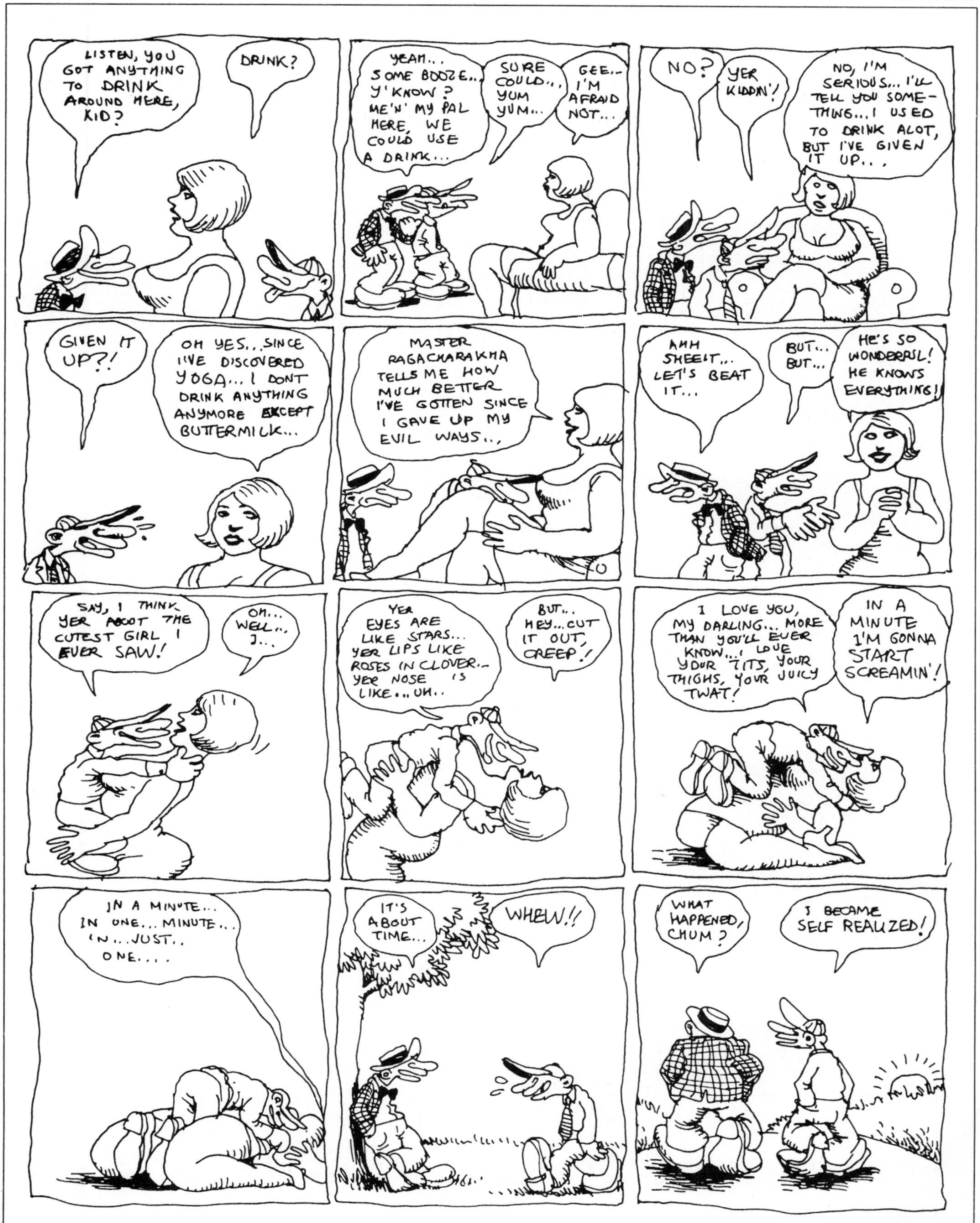
LISTEN, YOU GOT ANYTHING TO DRINK AROUND HERE, KID?
DRINK?
YEAH... SOME BOOZE... Y'KNOW? ME'N' MY PAL HERE, WE COULD USE A DRINK...
SURE COULD... YUM YUM...
GEE... I'M AFRAID NOT...
NO?
YER KIDDIN'!
NO, I'M SERIOUS... I'LL TELL YOU SOMETHING... I USED TO DRINK ALOT, BUT I'VE GIVEN IT UP...
GIVEN IT UP?!
OH YES... SINCE I'VE DISCOVERED YOGA... I DONT DRINK ANYTHING ANYMORE EXCEPT BUTTERMILK...
MASTER RAGACHARAKHA TELLS ME HOW MUCH BETTER I'VE GOTTEN SINCE I GAVE UP MY EVIL WAYS...
AHH SHEEIT... LET'S BEAT IT...
BUT... BUT...
HE'S SO WONDERFUL! HE KNOWS EVERYTHING!
SAY, I THINK YER ABOUT THE CUTEST GIRL I EVER SAW!
OH... WELL... I...
YER EYES ARE LIKE STARS... YER LIPS LIKE ROSES IN CLOVER... YER NOSE IS LIKE... UH...
BUT... HEY... CUT IT OUT, CREEP!
I LOVE YOU, MY DARLING... MORE THAN YOU'LL EVER KNOW... I LOVE YOUR TITS, YOUR THIGHS, YOUR JUICY TWAT!
IN A MINUTE I'M GONNA START SCREAMIN'!
IN A MINUTE... IN ONE... MINUTE... IN... JUST... ONE....
IT'S ABOUT TIME...
WHEW!!
WHAT HAPPENED, CHUM?
I BECAME SELF REALIZED!

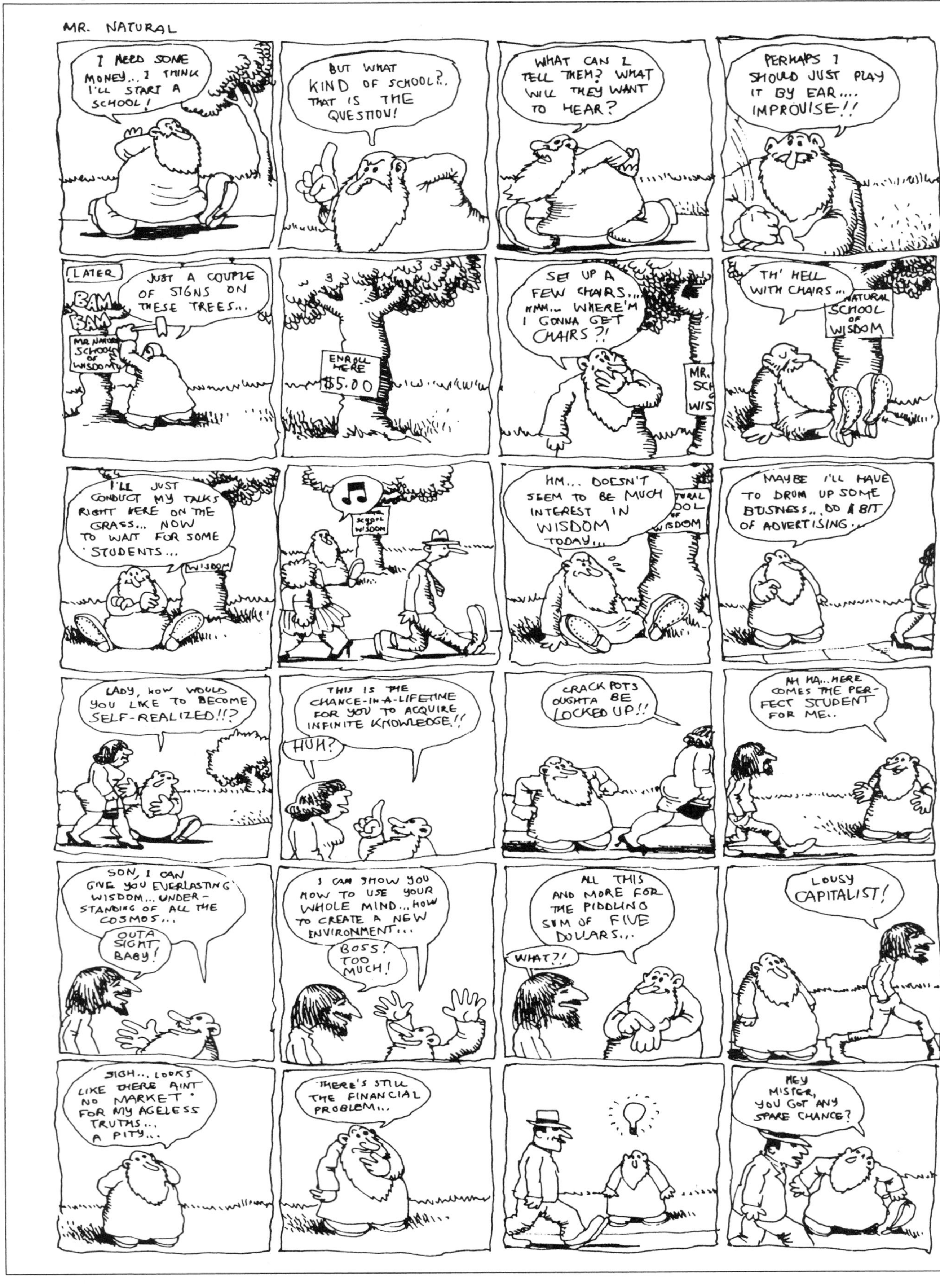
MR. NATURAL
I NEED SOME MONEY.. I THINK I'LL START A SCHOOL!
BUT WHAT KIND OF SCHOOL?.. THAT IS THE QUESTION!
WHAT CAN I TELL THEM? WHAT WILL THEY WANT TO HEAR?
PERHAPS I SHOULD JUST PLAY IT BY EAR.... IMPROVISE!!
LATER
JUST A COUPLE OF SIGNS ON THESE TREES..
BAM
BAM
MR NATURAL SCHOOL OF WISDOM
ENROLL HERE $5.00
SET UP A FEW CHAIRS... HMM.. WHERE'M I GONNA GET CHAIRS?!
TH' HELL WITH CHAIRS...
NATURAL SCHOOL OF WISDOM
I'LL JUST CONDUCT MY TALKS RIGHT HERE ON THE GRASS... NOW TO WAIT FOR SOME STUDENTS...
WISDOM
SCHOOL WISDOM
HM... DOESN'T SEEM TO BE MUCH INTEREST IN WISDOM TODAY...
MAYBE I'LL HAVE TO DRUM UP SOME BUSINESS.. DO A BIT OF ADVERTISING..
LADY, HOW WOULD YOU LIKE TO BECOME SELF-REALIZED!!?
THIS IS THE CHANCE-IN-A-LIFETIME FOR YOU TO ACQUIRE INFINITE KNOWLEDGE!!
HUH?
CRACK POTS OUGHTA BE LOCKED UP!!
AH HA...HERE COMES THE PERFECT STUDENT FOR ME..
SON, I CAN GIVE YOU EVERLASTING WISDOM... UNDERSTANDING OF ALL THE COSMOS...
OUTA SIGHT, BABY!
I CAN SHOW YOU HOW TO USE YOUR WHOLE MIND... HOW TO CREATE A NEW ENVIRONMENT...
BOSS! TOO MUCH!
ALL THIS AND MORE FOR THE PIDDLING SUM OF FIVE DOLLARS...
WHAT?!
LOUSY CAPITALIST!
SIGH... LOOKS LIKE THERE AINT NO MARKET FOR MY AGELESS TRUTHS... A PITY..
THERE'S STILL THE FINANCIAL PROBLEM...
HEY MISTER, YOU GOT ANY SPARE CHANGE?

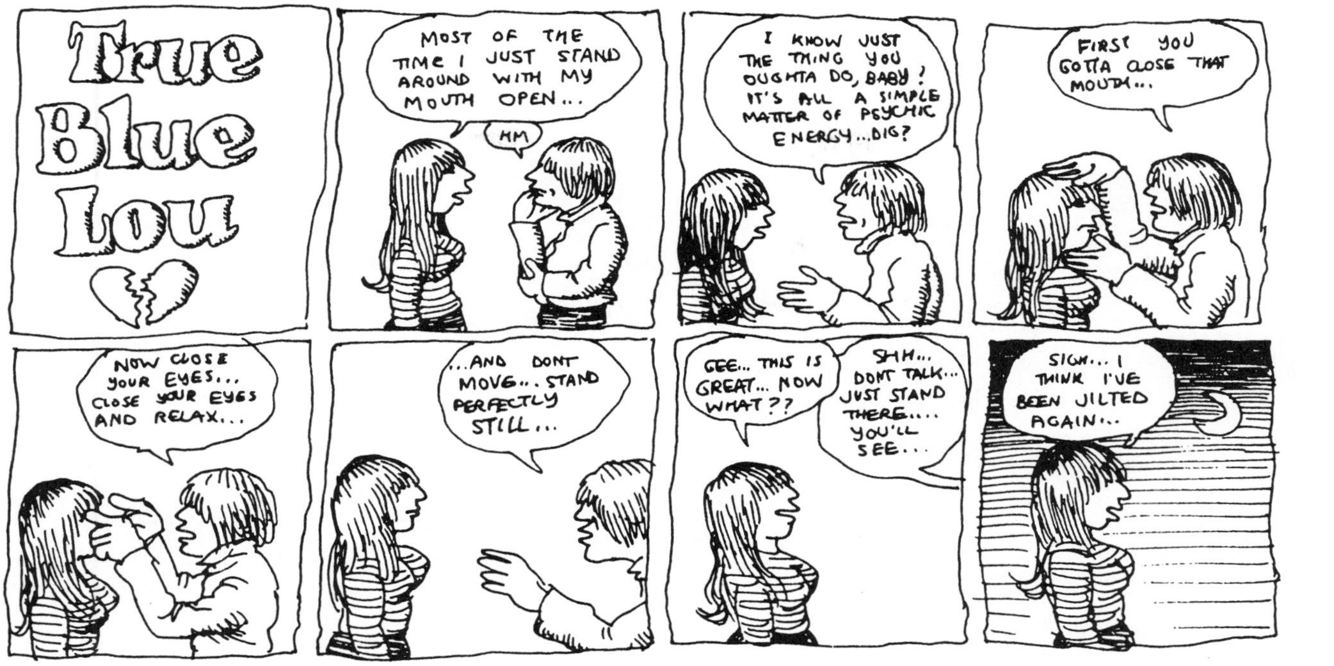
True Blue Lou
MOST OF THE TIME I JUST STAND AROUND WITH MY MOUTH OPEN...
HM
I KNOW JUST THE THING YOU OUGHTA DO, BABY! IT'S ALL A SIMPLE MATTER OF PSYCHIC ENERGY...DIG?
FIRST YOU GOTTA CLOSE THAT MOUTH...
NOW CLOSE YOUR EYES... CLOSE YOUR EYES AND RELAX...
...AND DONT MOVE... STAND PERFECTLY STILL...
SEE... THIS IS GREAT... NOW WHAT??
SHH... DONT TALK... JUST STAND THERE.... YOU'LL SEE...
SIGH... I THINK I'VE BEEN JILTED AGAIN...

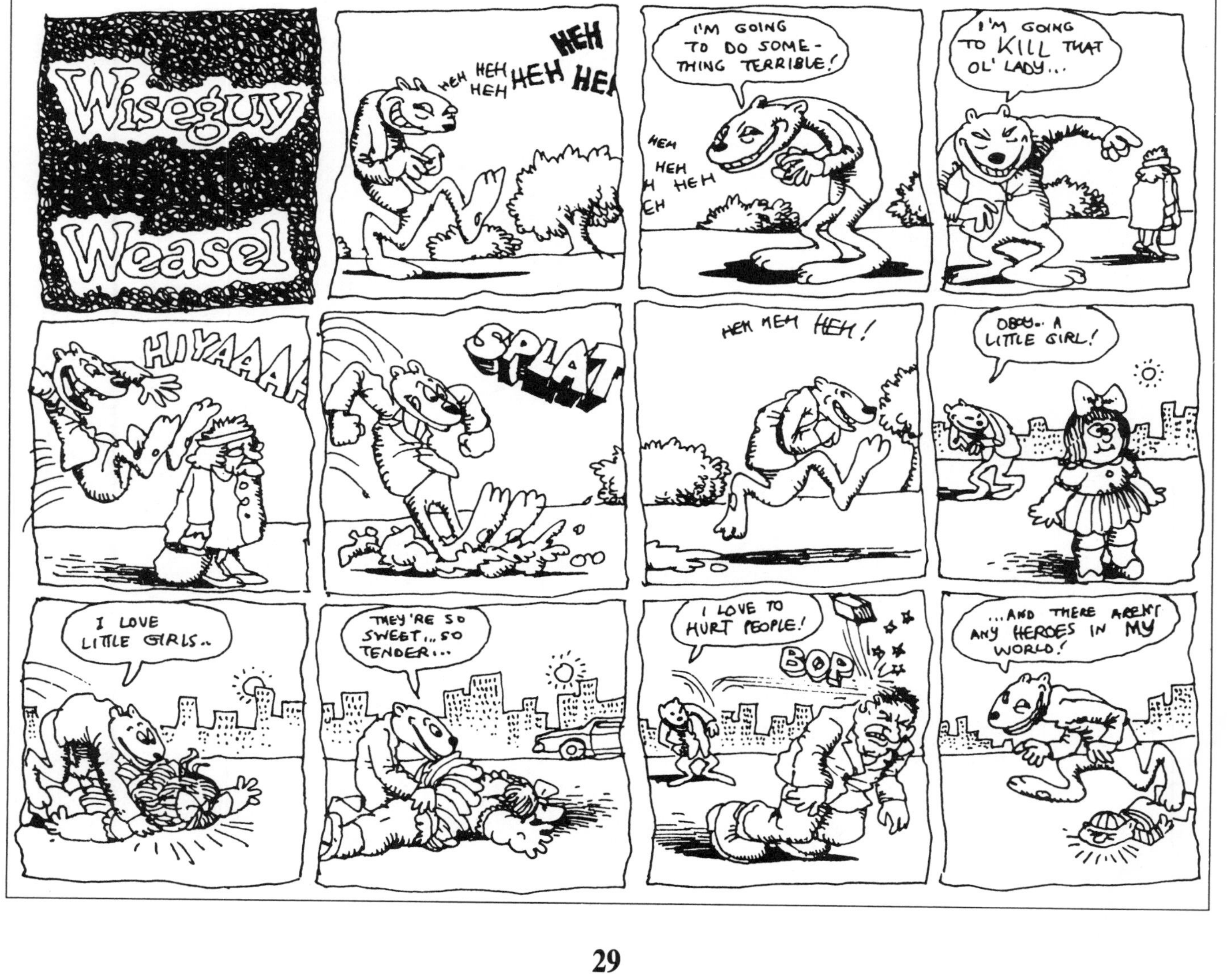
Wiseguy Weasel
HEH HEH HEH HEH HEH HEH HEH
I'M GOING TO DO SOME-THING TERRIBLE!
HEH HEH HEH
I'M GOING TO KILL THAT OL' LADY...
HIYAAAA
SPLAT
HEH HEH HEH!
OBOY.. A LITTLE GIRL!
I LOVE LITTLE GIRLS..
THEY'RE SO SWEET... SO TENDER...
I LOVE TO HURT PEOPLE!
BOP
...AND THERE AREN'T ANY HEROES IN MY WORLD!

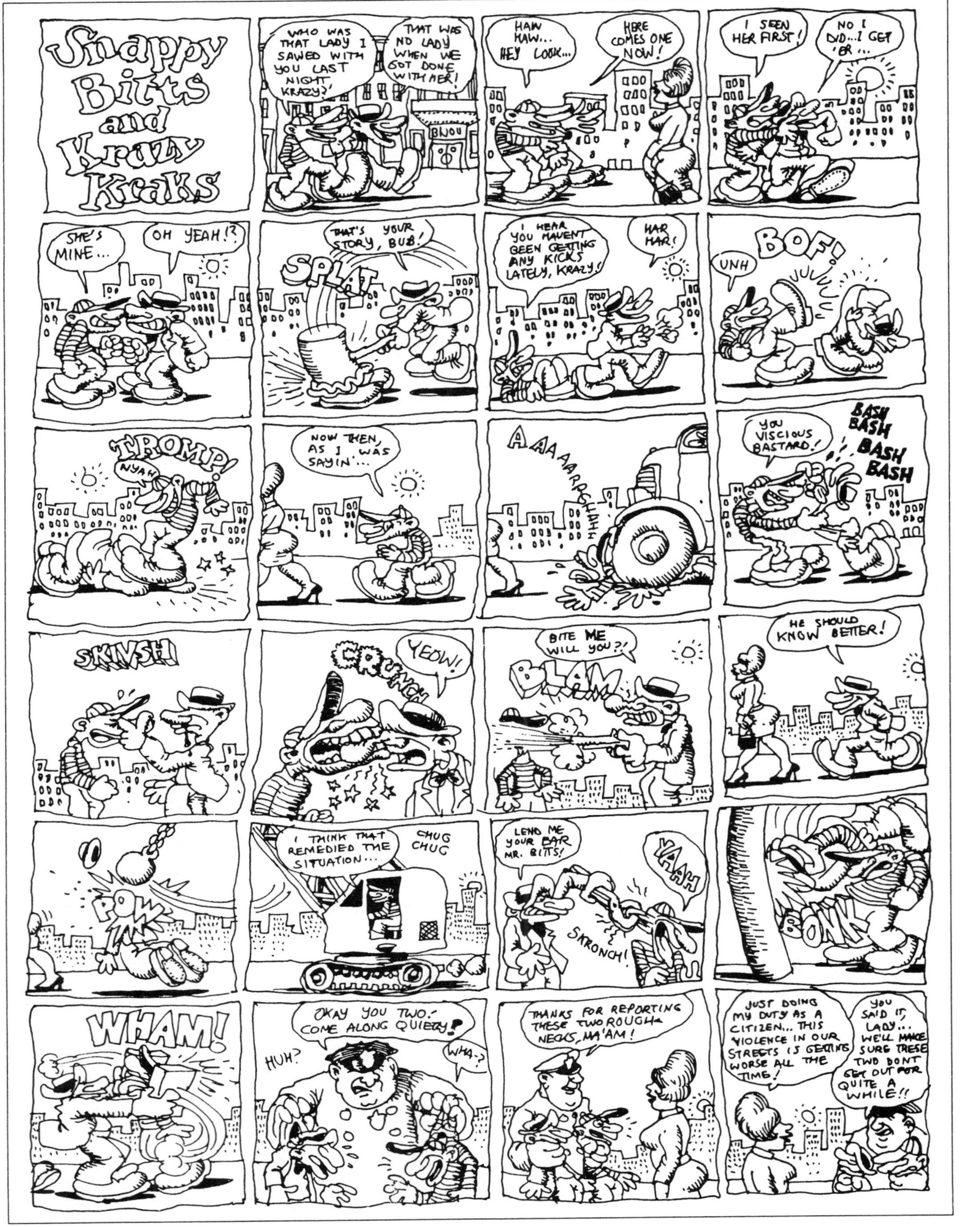
Snappy Bitts and Krazy Kraks
WHO WAS THAT LADY I SAWED WITH YOU LAST NIGHT, KRAZY?
THAT WAS NO LADY WHEN WE GOT DONE WITH HER!
BIJOU
HAW HAW... HEY LOOK...
HERE COMES ONE NOW!
I SEEN HER FIRST!
NO I DID... I GET 'ER...
SHE'S MINE...
OH YEAH!?
THAT'S YOUR STORY, BUB!
SPLAT
I HEAR YOU HAVEN'T BEEN GETTING ANY KICKS LATELY, KRAZY!
HAR HAR!
UNH
BOF!
TROMP!
NYAH
NOW THEN, AS I WAS SAYIN'...
AAAAAARRGHHH
YOU VISCIOUS BASTARD!
BASH BASH BASH BASH
SKWSH
CRUNCH
YEOW!
BITE ME WILL YOU?!
BLAM
HE SHOULD KNOW BETTER!
POW
I THINK THAT REMEDIED THE SITUATION...
CHUG CHUG
LEND ME YOUR BAR MR. BITTS!
YAAAH
SKRONCH!
BONK
WHAM!
OKAY YOU TWO. COME ALONG QUIETLY!
HUH?
WHA-?
THANKS FOR REPORTING THESE TWO ROUGH-NECKS, MA'AM!
JUST DOING MY DUTY AS A CITIZEN... THIS VIOLENCE IN OUR STREETS IS GETTING WORSE ALL THE TIME!
YOU SAID IT, LADY... WE'LL MAKE SURE THESE TWO DONT GET OUT FOR QUITE A WHILE!!

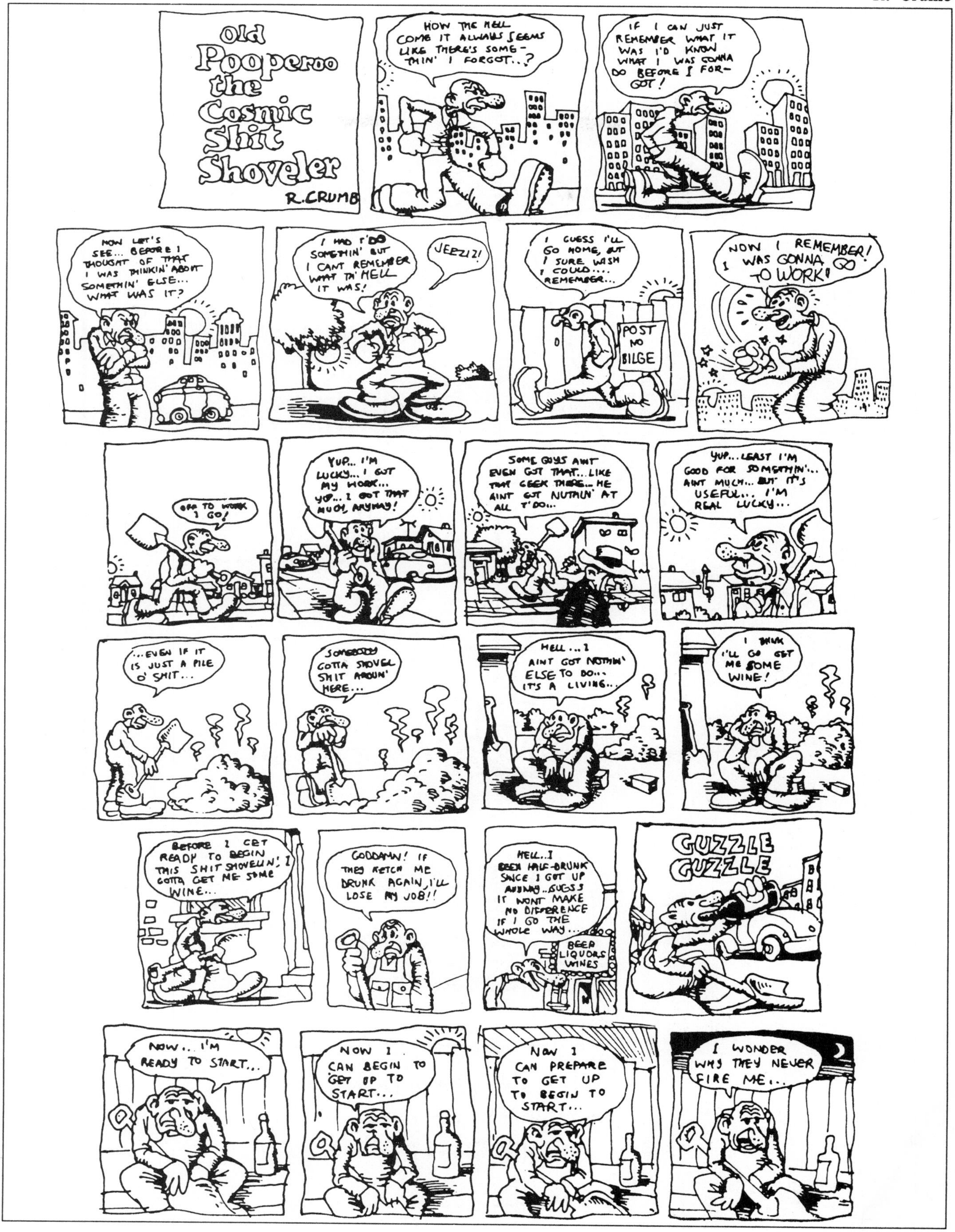
Old Pooperoo the Cosmic Shit Shoveler
R.CRUMB
HOW THE HELL COME IT ALWAYS SEEMS LIKE THERE'S SOME-THIN' I FORGOT...?
IF I CAN JUST REMEMBER WHAT IT WAS I'D KNOW WHAT I WAS GONNA DO BEFORE I FOR-GOT!
NOW LET'S SEE... BEFORE I THOUGHT OF THAT I WAS THINKIN' ABOUT SOMETHIN' ELSE... WHAT WAS IT?
I HAD T'DO SOMETHIN' BUT I CANT REMEMBER WHAT TH' HELL IT WAS!
JEEZUZ!
I GUESS I'LL GO HOME, BUT I SURE WISH I COULD.... REMEMBER...
POST NO BILGE
NOW I REMEMBER! I WAS GONNA GO TO WORK!
OFF TO WORK I GO!
YUP... I'M LUCKY... I GOT MY WORK... YUP... I GOT THAT MUCH, ANYWAY!
SOME GUYS AINT EVEN GOT THAT... LIKE THAT GEEK THERE... HE AINT GOT NUTHIN' AT ALL T'DO...
YUP... LEAST I'M GOOD FOR SOMETHIN'... AINT MUCH... BUT IT'S USEFUL... I'M REAL LUCKY...
...EVEN IF IT IS JUST A PILE O' SHIT...
SOMEBODY GOTTA SHOVEL SHIT AROUN' HERE...
HELL... I AINT GOT NOTHIN' ELSE TO DO... IT'S A LIVING...
I THINK I'LL GO GET ME SOME WINE!
BEFORE I GET READY TO BEGIN THIS SHIT SHOVELIN', I GOTTA GET ME SOME WINE...
GODDAMN! IF THEY KETCH ME DRUNK AGAIN, I'LL LOSE MY JOB!!
HELL.. I BEEN HALF-DRUNK SINCE I GOT UP ANYWAY.. GUESS IT WONT MAKE NO DIFFERENCE IF I GO THE WHOLE WAY...
BEER LIQUORS WINES
GUZZLE GUZZLE
NOW... I'M READY TO START...
NOW I CAN BEGIN TO GET UP TO START...
NOW I CAN PREPARE TO GET UP TO BEGIN TO START...
I WONDER WHY THEY NEVER FIRE ME...

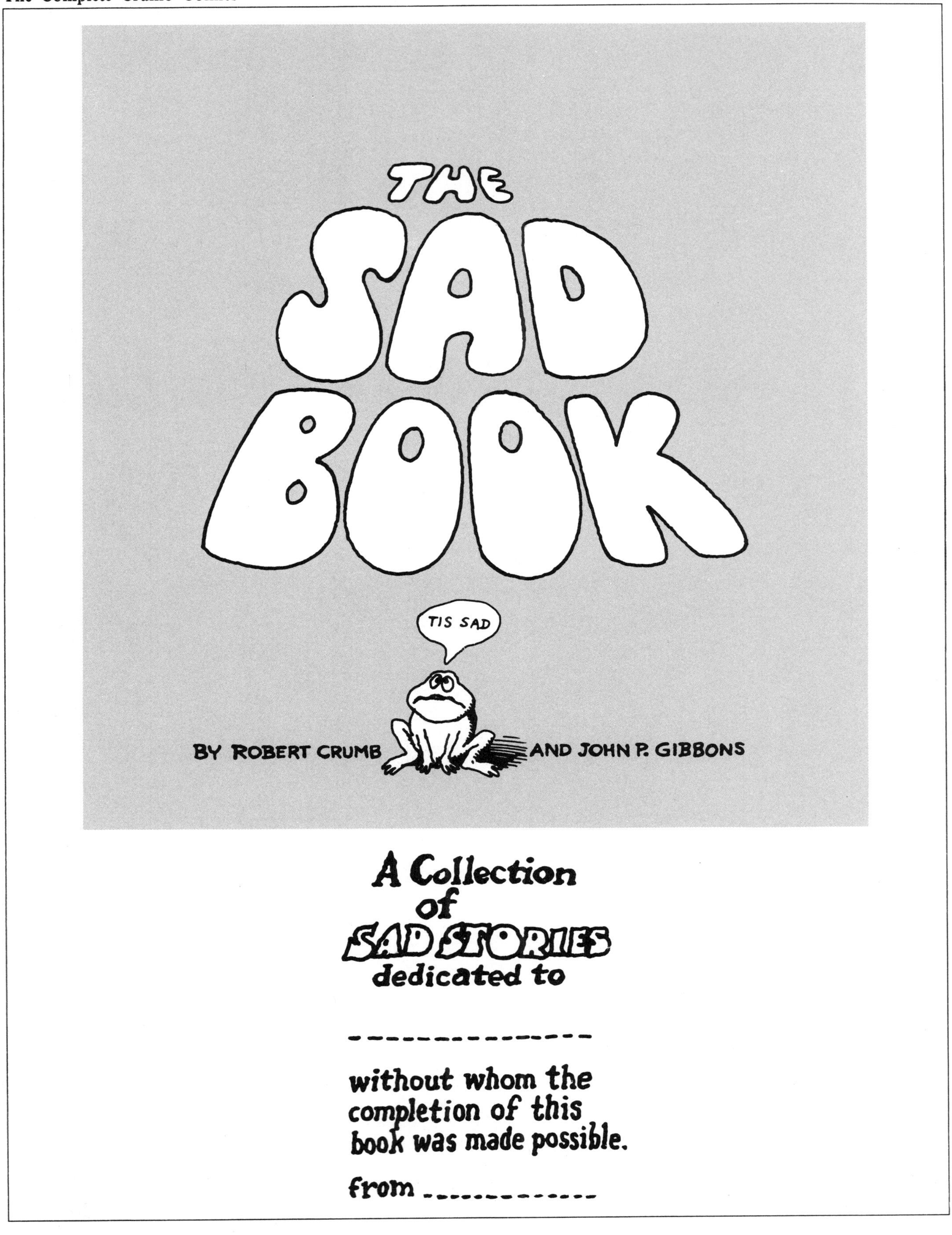
THE SAD BOOK
TIS SAD
BY ROBERT CRUMB AND JOHN P. GIBBONS
A Collection of SAD STORIES dedicated to
--------------
without whom the completion of this book was made possible.
from ------------

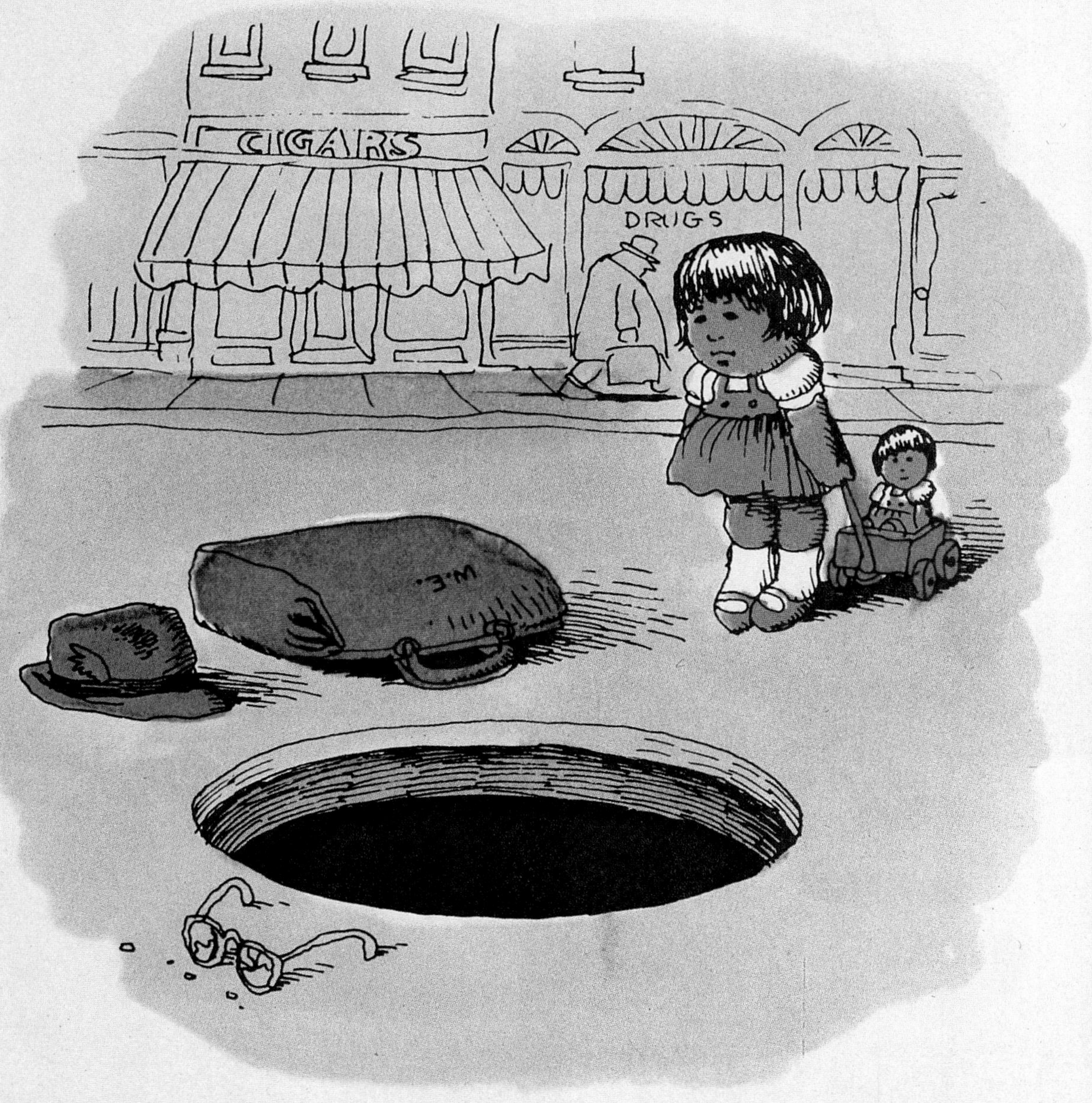
CIGARS
DRUGS
W.E.

WALLACE ELKINS, OF PEORIA, ILL., WAS WALKING HOME FROM THE OFFICE ONE EVENING, AND FELL INTO A BIG HOLE.

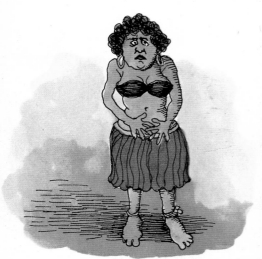

HARRIET FELHUD WANTED TO BE A BELLY DANCER, BUT SHE HAD VARICOSE VEINS IN HER STOMACH.

TAKE A GUI ED TOUR
OF SAN FRA SISCO FOR
ONLY $1.00!
SHNOOK
TOURS
INC.
WATCH YOUR STEP!

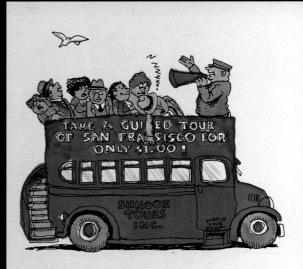

PHIL OXBUN, OF SAN FRANCISCO, WON AN ALL-EXPENSES-PAID TRIP TO SAN FRANCISCO.

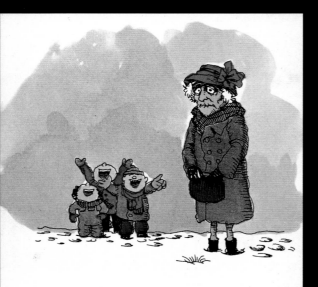

AFTER 35 YEARS, MEAN OLD MRS. MEDNICK SMILED AT SOME CHILDREN, AND HER TEETH FELL IN THE SNOW.

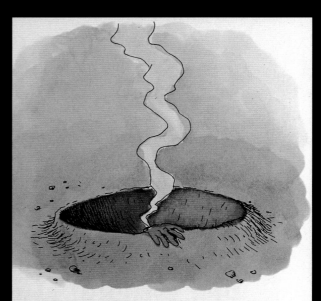

FRED "BLAST" GNARR INVENTED THE FIRST EXPLOSIVE KNOWN TO MAN, THOUGH AT THE TIME HE DIDN'T THINK IT WOULD WORK.

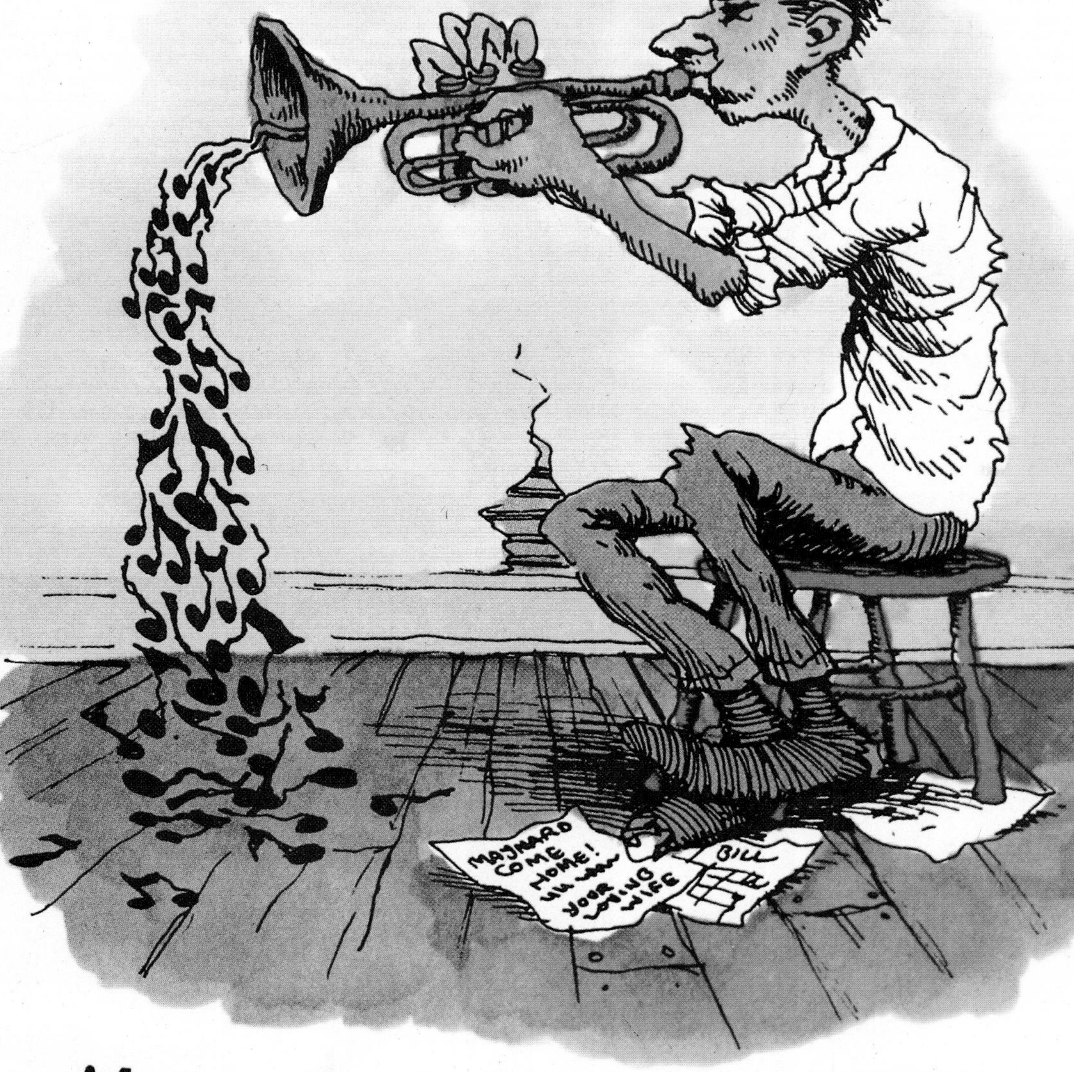
MAYNARD COME HOME!
YOUR LOVING WIFE
BILL

MAYNARD GAVE UP EVERYTHING FOR HIS MUSIC... BUT HE COULDN'T PLAY VERY WELL.

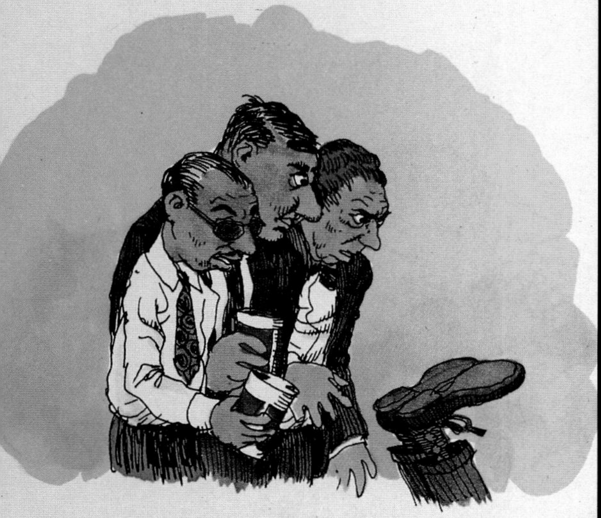

AXLE ULCH TRIED TO SAY "RUBBER BABY BUGGY BUMPERS" THREE TIMES IN A ROW AND STRANGLED TO DEATH.

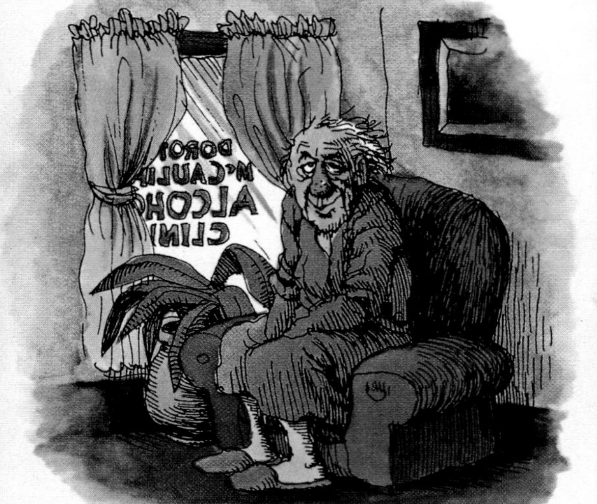

J.P. MAGNADANE, SON OF AN INSIGNIFICANT BERRY PICKER FROM GRAVELDUMP, OHIO, GREW UP TO BE A TOTAL FAILURE AND AN INCURABLE ALCOHOLIC.

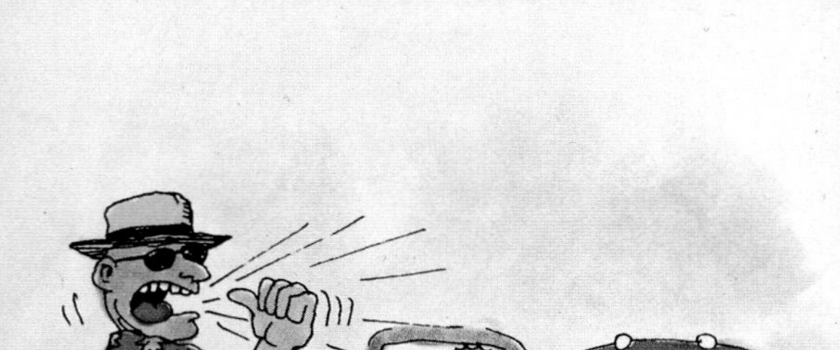
SEEING EYE DOG

BRUNO WAS A WONDERFUL SEEING EYE DOG, BUT HE DIDN'T HEAR SO GOOD.

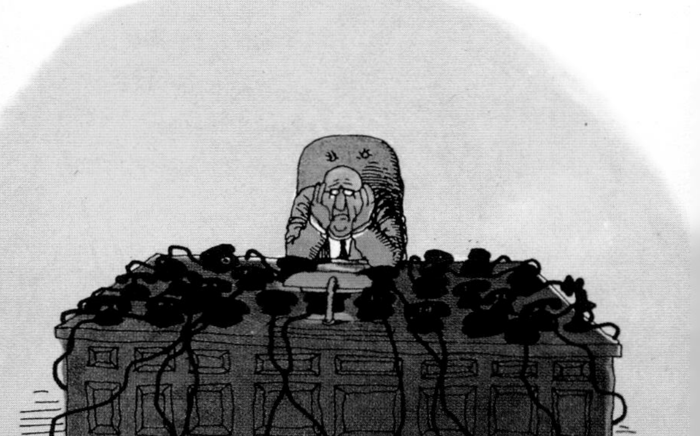

MR. MORGAN WAS A BIG EXECUTIVE WITH 25 PHONES ON HIS DESK.... BUT NOBODY EVER CALLED HIM.

BASIL FLUDNEYBUNT HAD A
MILLION DOLLARS WORTH OF PENNIES
IN A SILO 81 FEET HIGH, AND IT
FELL ON HIM.

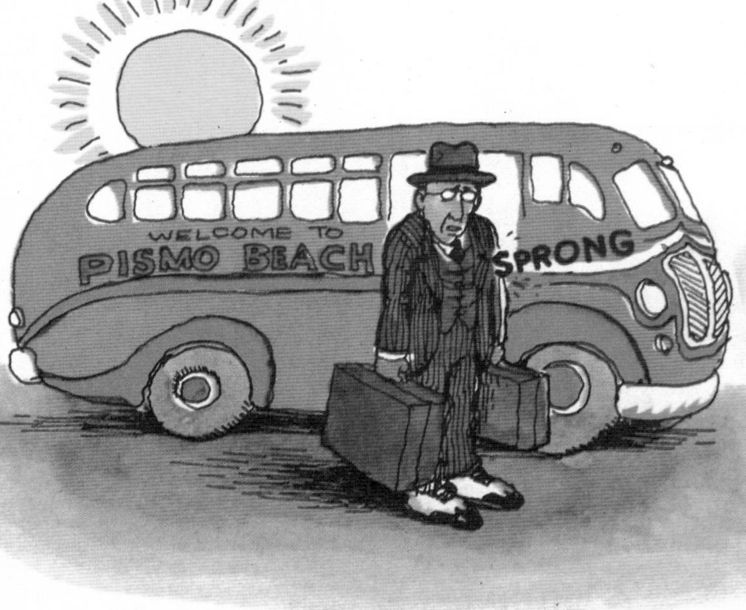
WELCOME TO
PISMO BEACH
SPRONG

AFTER FIFTY YEARS OF LOYAL SERVICE TO HIS FIRM, GRANDPA NEEZER WAS GIVEN A GOLD WATCH.... BUT THE MAINSPRING BROKE AND PIERCED HIS HEART.

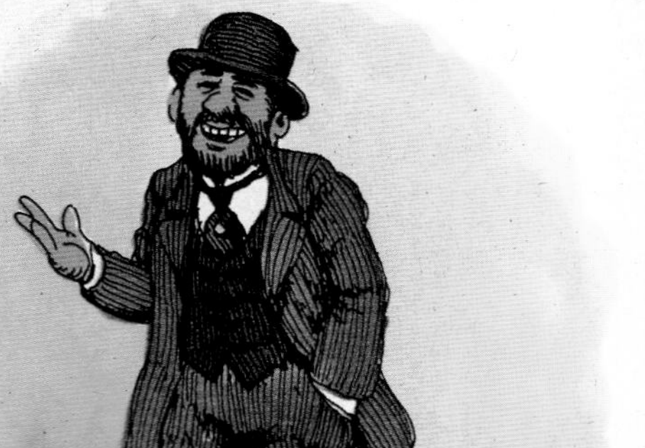

INTON PANGBORNE WAS THE
NIEST TV COMEDIAN OF ALL
E. UNFORTUNATELY, HE DIED
1872.

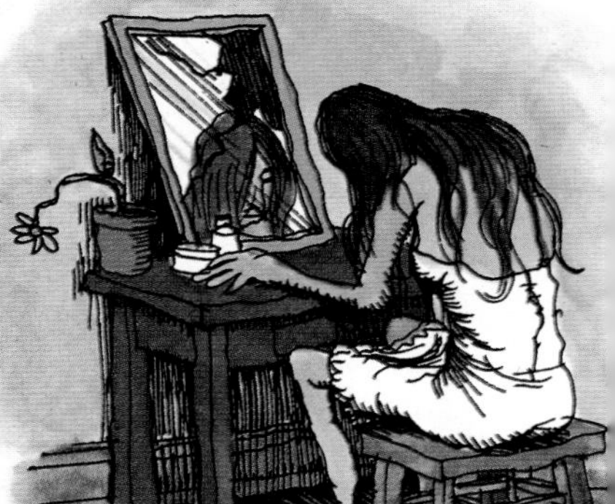

GLADYS GOINK WAS JUST U
AS HELL, AND SHE DIDN'T H
ANY MONEY EITHER.

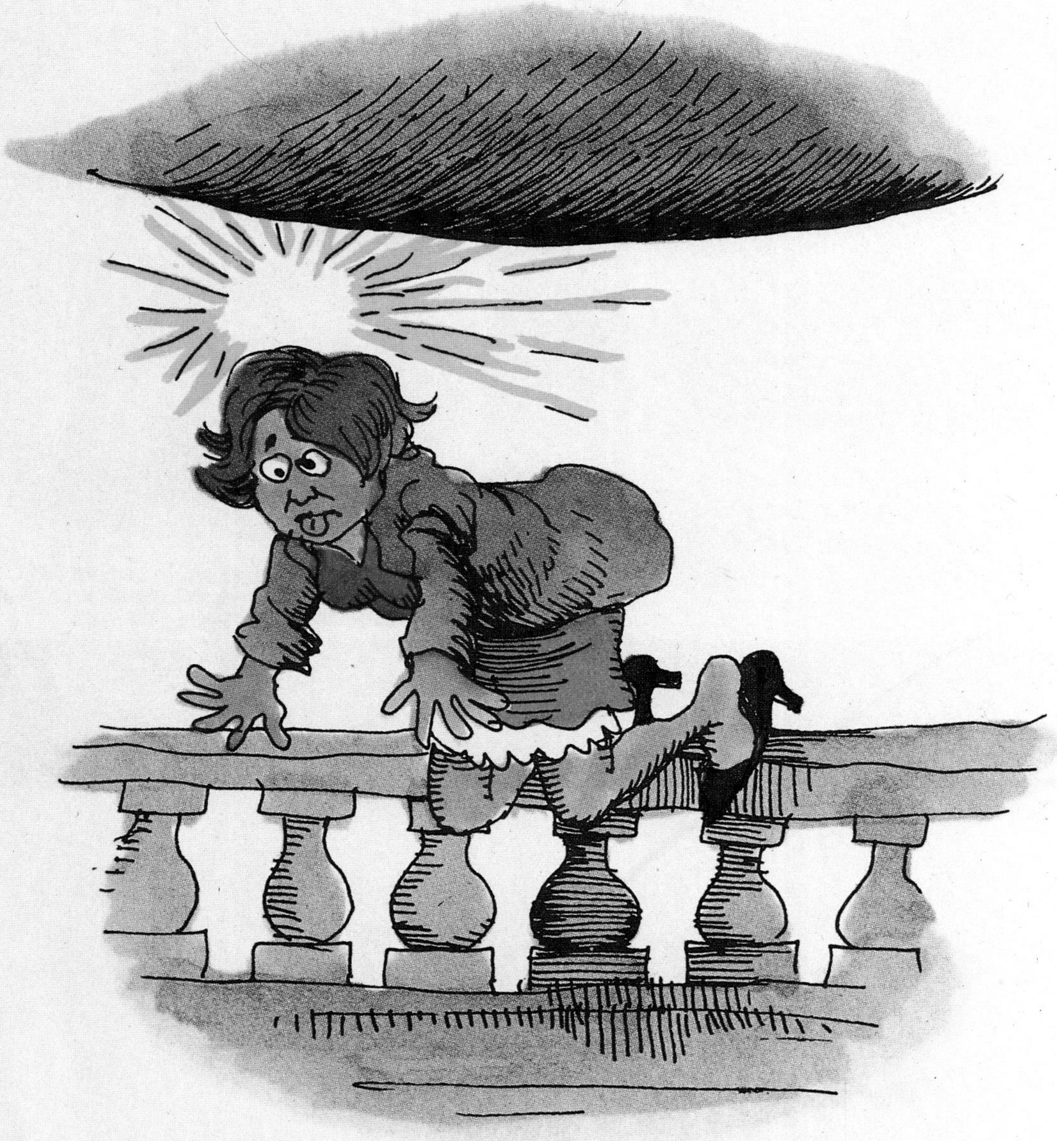

EVELYN TURKBULL WAS JUST ABOUT TO JUMP OFF THE BROOK-LYN BRIDGE WHEN SHE WAS STRUCK BY A LOW-FLYING ZEPPELIN.

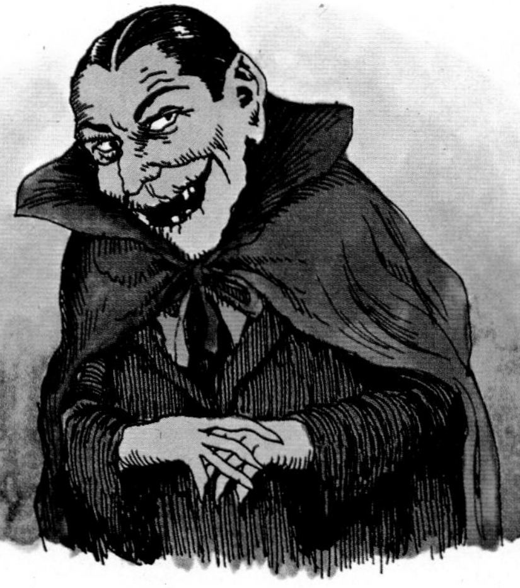

BORIS WAS A VERY GOOD VAMPIRE, BUT HE HAD VERY BAD TEETH.

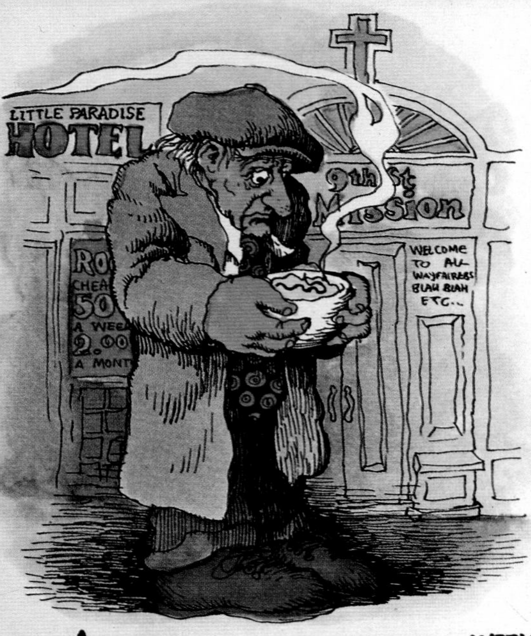
LITTLE PARADISE
HOTEL
9th St Mission
WELCOME TO ALL WAYFAIRERS BLAH BLAH ETC..

A POOR OLD MAN SAVED ALL WEEK TO BUY A CUP OF PORRIDGE.... AND THERE WAS A HAIR IN IT.

....but of all
the sad, sad
things in this
sad, sad world
the saddest
of all is.....

# ME WITHOUT YOU

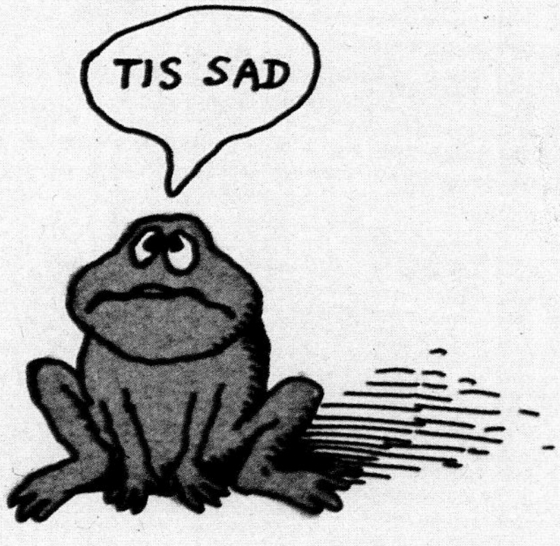
TIS SAD

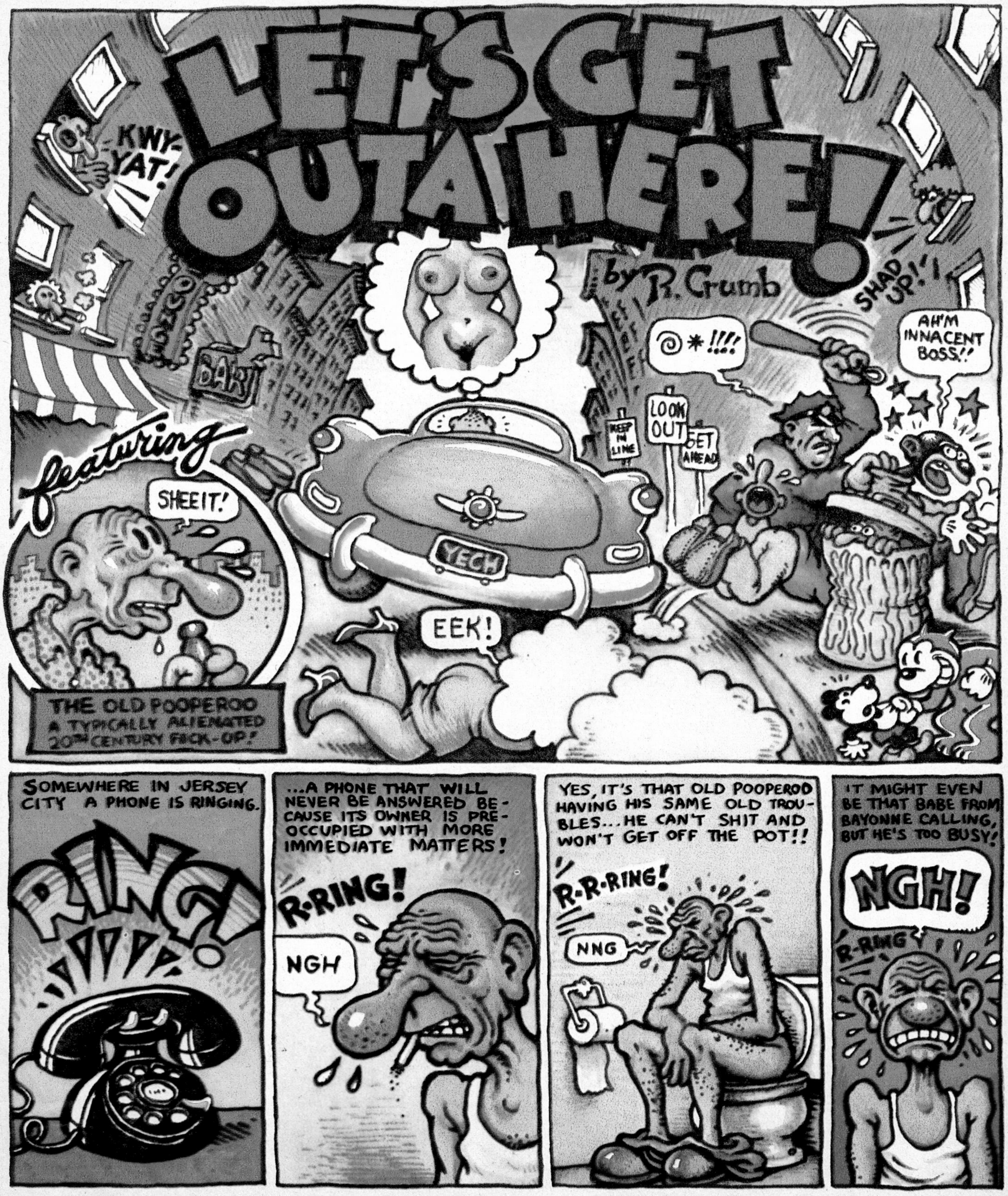
LET'S GET OUTA HERE!
by R. Crumb
KWY-YAT!
SHAD UP!
AH'M INNACENT BOSS!!
*!!!!
BAR
KEEP IN LINE
LOOK OUT
GET AHEAD
YECH
EEK!
featuring
SHEEIT!
THE OLD POOPEROO A TYPICALLY ALIENATED 20TH CENTURY FUCK-UP!
SOMEWHERE IN JERSEY CITY A PHONE IS RINGING.
RING!
...A PHONE THAT WILL NEVER BE ANSWERED BECAUSE ITS OWNER IS PREOCCUPIED WITH MORE IMMEDIATE MATTERS!
R-RING!
NGH
YES, IT'S THAT OLD POOPEROO HAVING HIS SAME OLD TROUBLES... HE CAN'T SHIT AND WON'T GET OFF THE POT!!
R-R-RING!
NNG
IT MIGHT EVEN BE THAT BABE FROM BAYONNE CALLING, BUT HE'S TOO BUSY!
NGH!
R-RING

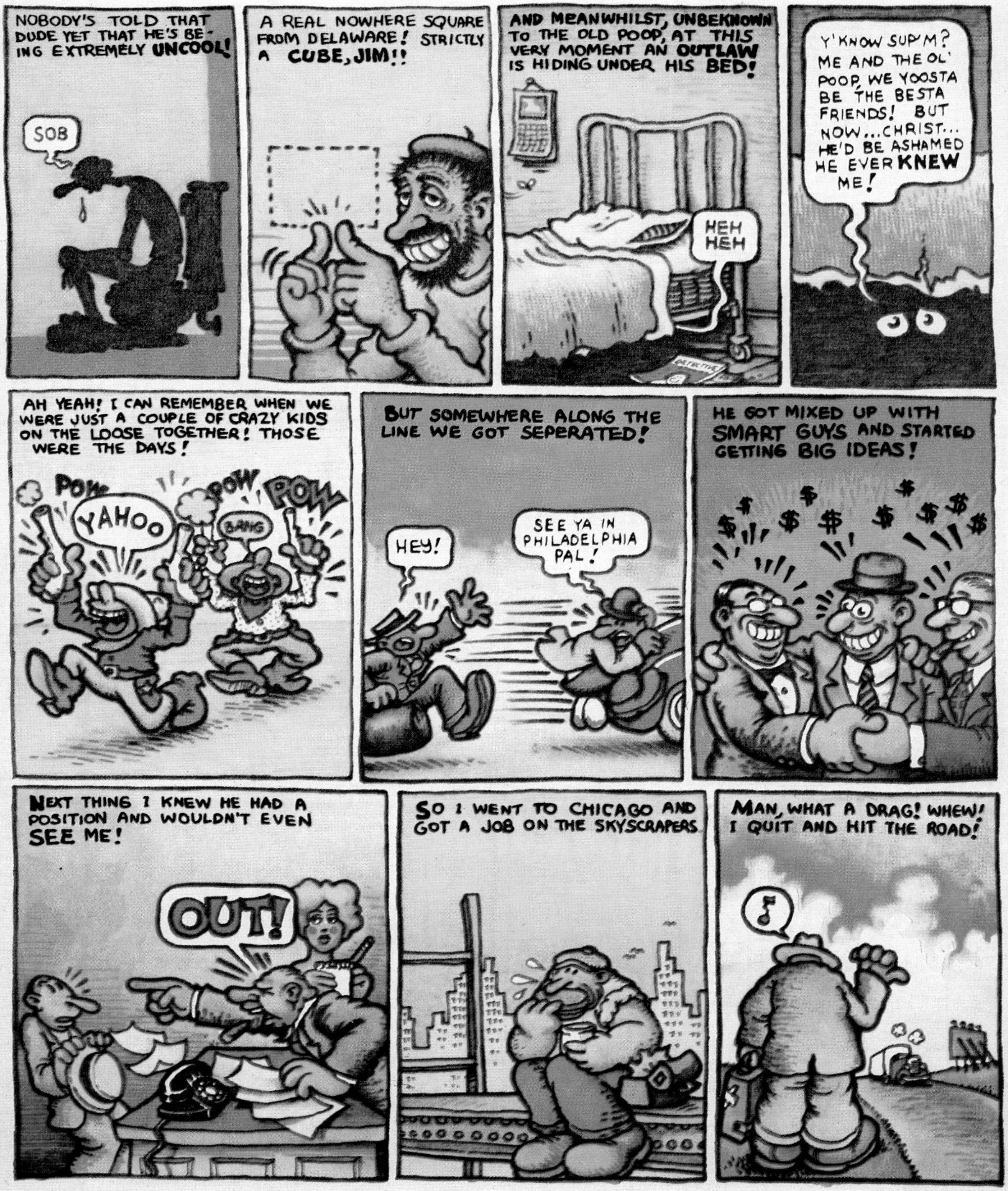
NOBODY'S TOLD THAT DUDE YET THAT HE'S BE-ING EXTREMELY UNCOOL!
SOB
A REAL NOWHERE SQUARE FROM DELAWARE! STRICTLY A CUBE, JIM!!
AND MEANWHILST, UNBEKNOWN TO THE OLD POOP, AT THIS VERY MOMENT AN OUTLAW IS HIDING UNDER HIS BED!
HEH HEH
Y'KNOW SUP'M? ME AND THE OL' POOP, WE YOOSTA BE THE BESTA FRIENDS! BUT NOW...CHRIST... HE'D BE ASHAMED HE EVER KNEW ME!
AH YEAH! I CAN REMEMBER WHEN WE WERE JUST A COUPLE OF CRAZY KIDS ON THE LOOSE TOGETHER! THOSE WERE THE DAYS!
POW
YAHOO
POW
BANG
POW
BUT SOMEWHERE ALONG THE LINE WE GOT SEPERATED!
HEY!
SEE YA IN PHILADELPHIA PAL!
HE GOT MIXED UP WITH SMART GUYS AND STARTED GETTING BIG IDEAS!
NEXT THING I KNEW HE HAD A POSITION AND WOULDN'T EVEN SEE ME!
OUT!
SO I WENT TO CHICAGO AND GOT A JOB ON THE SKYSCRAPERS
MAN, WHAT A DRAG! WHEW! I QUIT AND HIT THE ROAD!

THAT'S WHEN I BEGAN MY LIFE OF CRIME... ROBBING FRUIT STANDS, BURNING THE PHONE COMPANY, USING FAKE CREDIT CARDS, ALWAYS RUNNING, HIDING....

SLUG

THEN ONE DAY I HEARD THE SIRENS AND I KNEW THE MAN WAS ON HIS WAY!

EEEEEEE

⊙*!!!! COPS!

I WAS RUNNING AROUND WITH A TOUGH TWERP FROM TULSA AT THE TIME NAMED, SURPRISINGLY ENOUGH, JUDY HOLIDAY. I KISSED THE KID GOOD-BYE AND TOLD HER TO BEAT IT!

SO LONG KID!

SMOOCH

SO LONG Y'SELF!

I GOT SENT UP ON A TEN-YEAR RAP FOR SEDUCING A MINOR (TEE HEE)... BUT THEY COULDN'T KEEP ME IN THAT JOINT! I WAS DETERMINED TO BUST OUT!

YA CAN'T KEEP **ME** BEHIND BARS, YA **RATS** YA!

26743

WHICH I DID, YEARS LATER... I'D HEARD ON THE INSIDE THAT MY LONG LOST BUDDY, THE OLD POOPEROO, WAS HAVING THIS...ER... TROUBLE DOING HIS BUSINESS, SO THAT'S WHERE I HEADED...

WHICH BRINGS US RIGHT TO THE POINT! THERE'S JUST ONE MORE LITTLE JOB I GOTTA DO!

**YOU!** I BEEN WAITIN' FER THIS MOMENT FER YEARS!

MR. NATURAL! WAIT, I—

SMOOCH!

YOU CAN BE SURE IF IT **SHRINKS HEMORRHOIDS!**

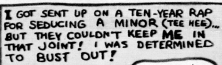

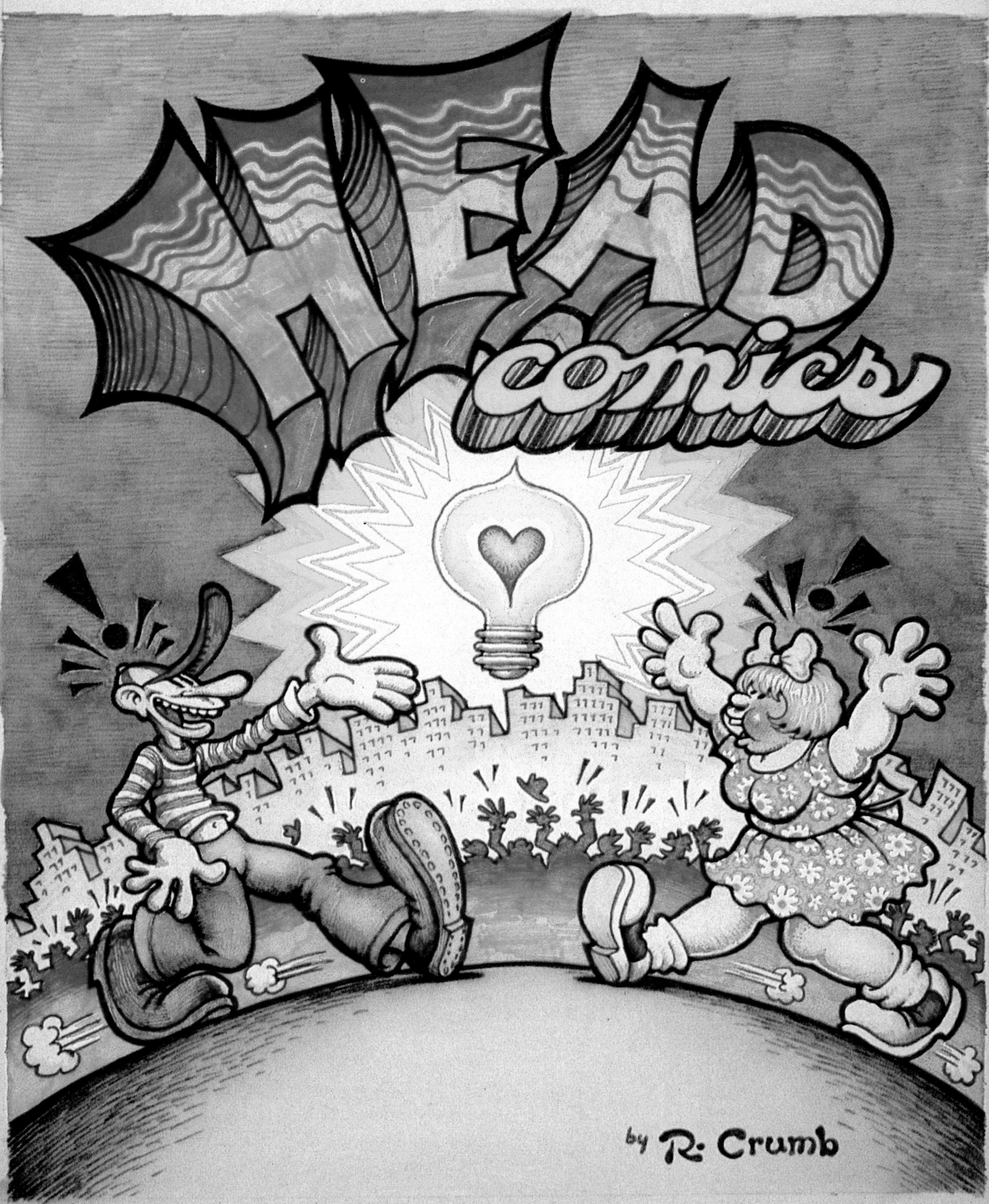
HEAD comics
by R. Crumb

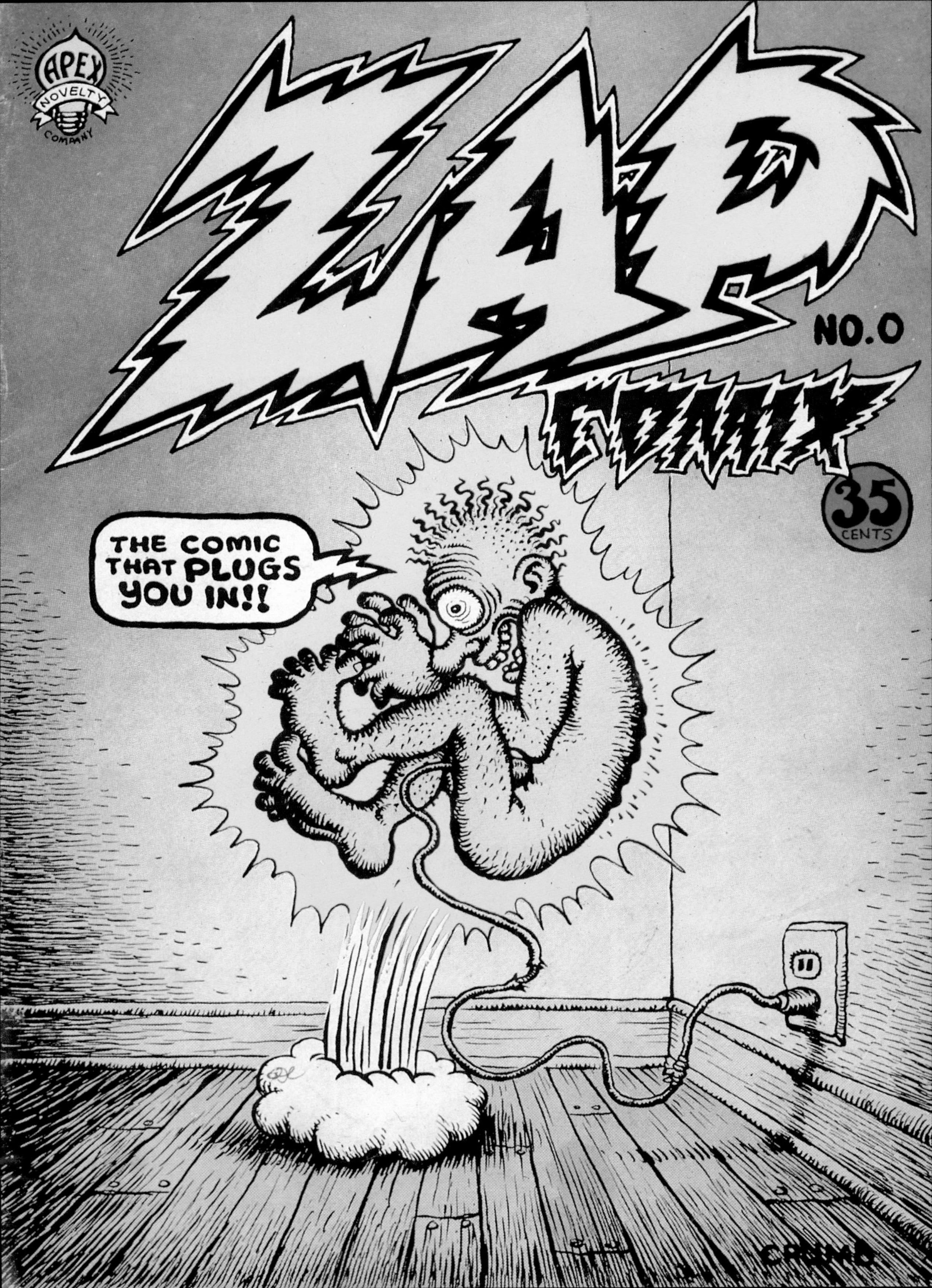
APEX NOVELTY COMPANY
ZAP COMIX
NO. 0
35 CENTS
THE COMIC THAT PLUGS YOU IN!!
CRUMB

# I'LL BET THIS HAP-PENED TO YOU WHEN YOU WERE A KID!

I WANT YOU SHOULD STOP WASTING YOUR TIME READING THESE **CHEAP COMIC BOOKS!**

Did your mother ever tear up **YOUR** comic books? Did you ever recieve warnings about how comic books were going to RUIN your MIND? Were you given lectures about how comics were CHEAP TRASH put out by evil men? Do you feel a spark of GUILT every time you pick up a comic book? Do you feel like you ought to be reading a good book in-stead? Let **ZAP** comics wisk away all such foolish notions! Takes only 15 minutes! Read **ZAP** comics!

THIS AD IS NOT INTENDED FOR THOSE FORTUNATES A-MONG US WHOSE PARENTS DIDN'T GIVE A SHIT IF THEY READ COMIC BOOKS.

—A MESSAGE FROM YOUR EDITOR, R. CRUMB

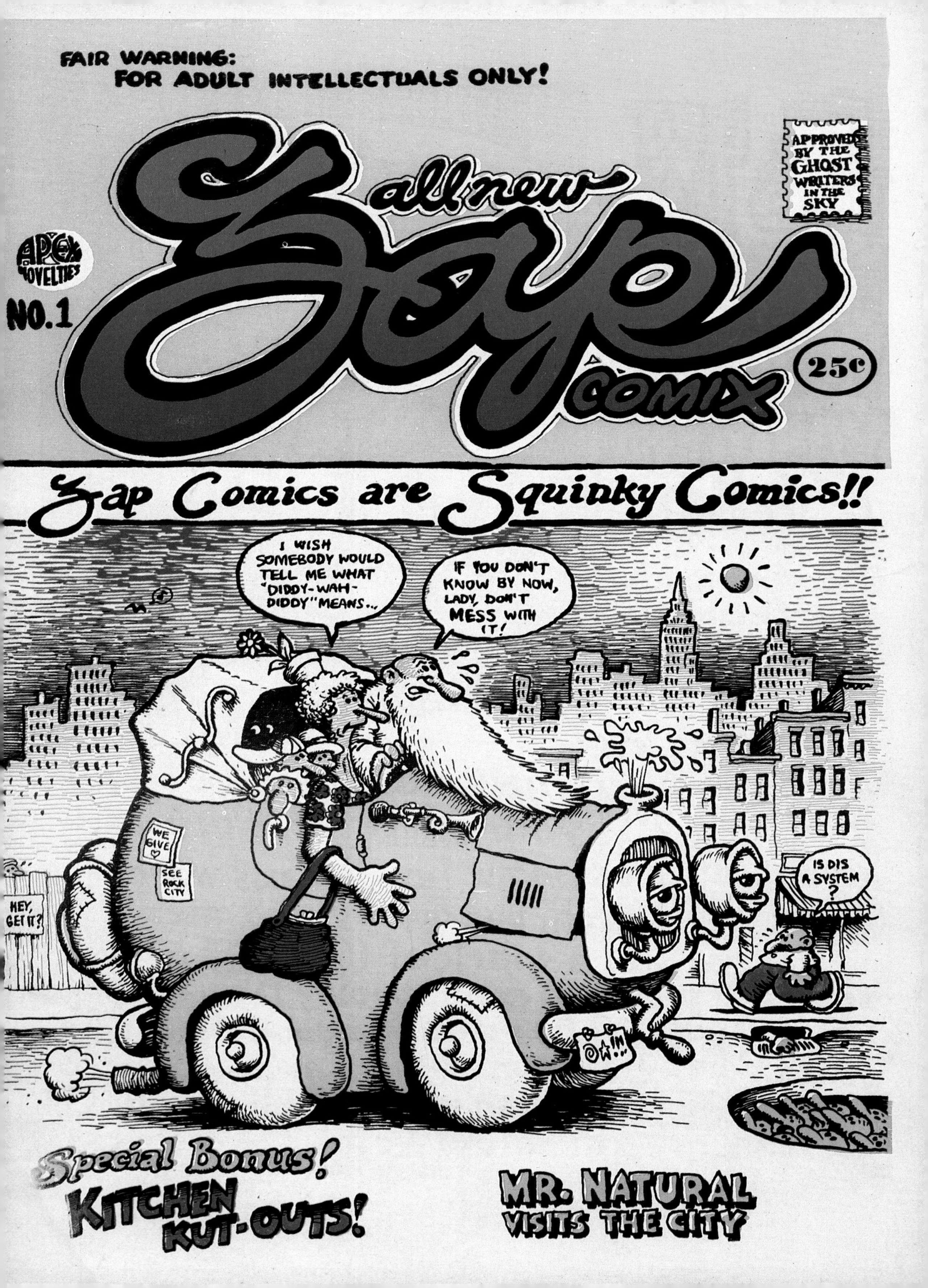
FAIR WARNING:
FOR ADULT INTELLECTUALS ONLY!
APPROVED BY THE GHOST WRITERS IN THE SKY
APEX NOVELTIES
NO.1
all new Zap COMIX
25¢
Zap Comics are Squinky Comics!!
I WISH SOMEBODY WOULD TELL ME WHAT "DIDDY-WAH-DIDDY" MEANS...
IF YOU DON'T KNOW BY NOW, LADY, DON'T MESS WITH IT!
WE GIVE ♡
SEE ROCK CITY
HEY, GET IT?
IS DIS A SYSTEM ?
Special Bonus!
KITCHEN KUT-OUTS!
MR. NATURAL VISITS THE CITY

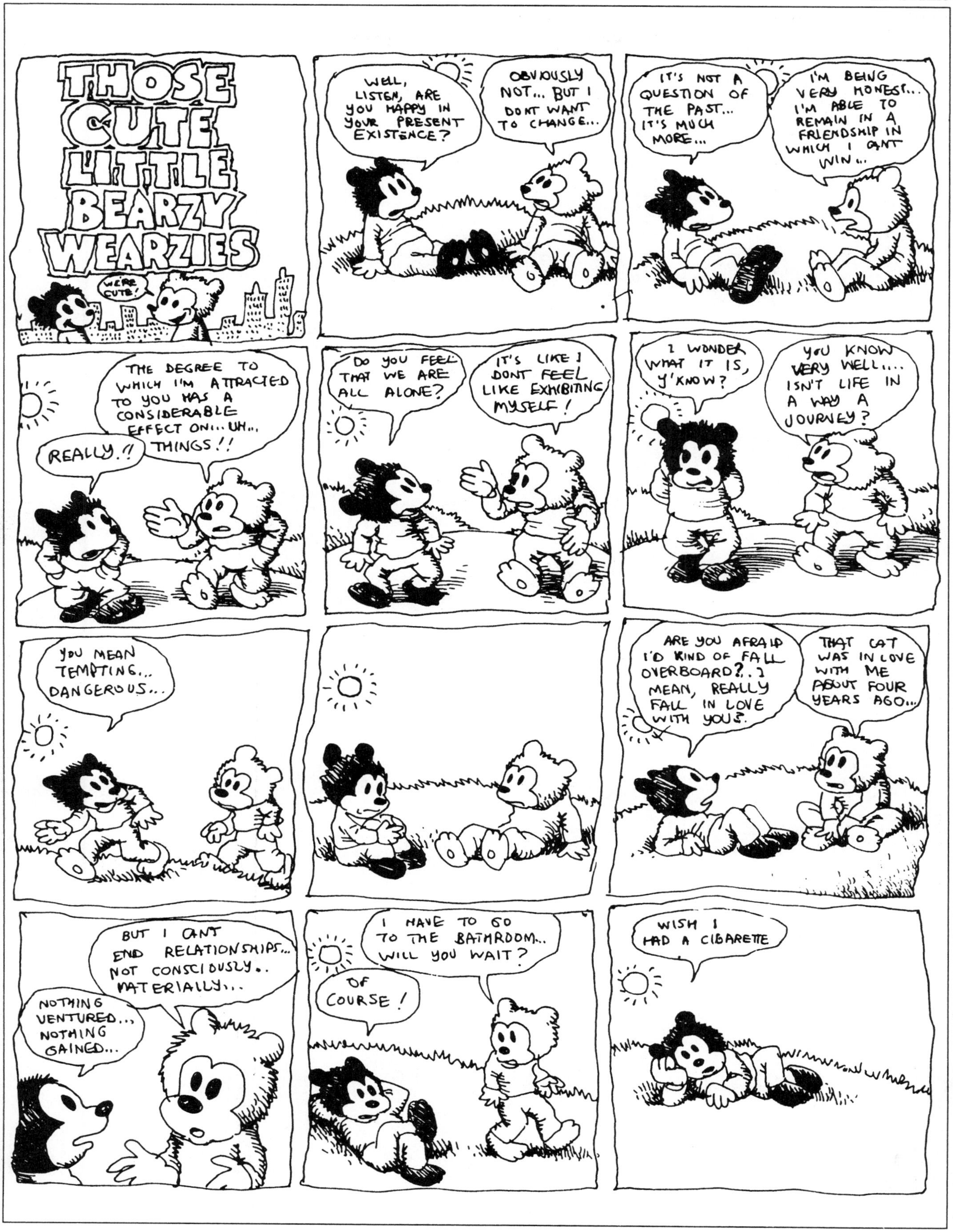
THOSE CUTE LITTLE BEARZY WEARZIES
WE'RE CUTE!
WELL, LISTEN, ARE YOU HAPPY IN YOUR PRESENT EXISTENCE?
OBVIOUSLY NOT... BUT I DONT WANT TO CHANGE...
IT'S NOT A QUESTION OF THE PAST... IT'S MUCH MORE...
I'M BEING VERY HONEST... I'M ABLE TO REMAIN IN A FRIENDSHIP IN WHICH I CANT WIN...
THE DEGREE TO WHICH I'M ATTRACTED TO YOU HAS A CONSIDERABLE EFFECT ON... UH... THINGS!!
REALLY!!
DO YOU FEEL THAT WE ARE ALL ALONE?
IT'S LIKE I DONT FEEL LIKE EXHIBITING MYSELF!
I WONDER WHAT IT IS, Y'KNOW?
YOU KNOW VERY WELL.... ISN'T LIFE IN A WAY A JOURNEY?
YOU MEAN TEMPTING... DANGEROUS...
ARE YOU AFRAID I'D KIND OF FALL OVERBOARD?.. I MEAN, REALLY FALL IN LOVE WITH YOU?
THAT CAT WAS IN LOVE WITH ME ABOUT FOUR YEARS AGO...
BUT I CANT END RELATIONSHIPS... NOT CONSCIOUSLY.. MATERIALLY...
NOTHING VENTURED... NOTHING GAINED...
I HAVE TO GO TO THE BATHROOM.. WILL YOU WAIT?
OF COURSE!
WISH I HAD A CIGARETTE

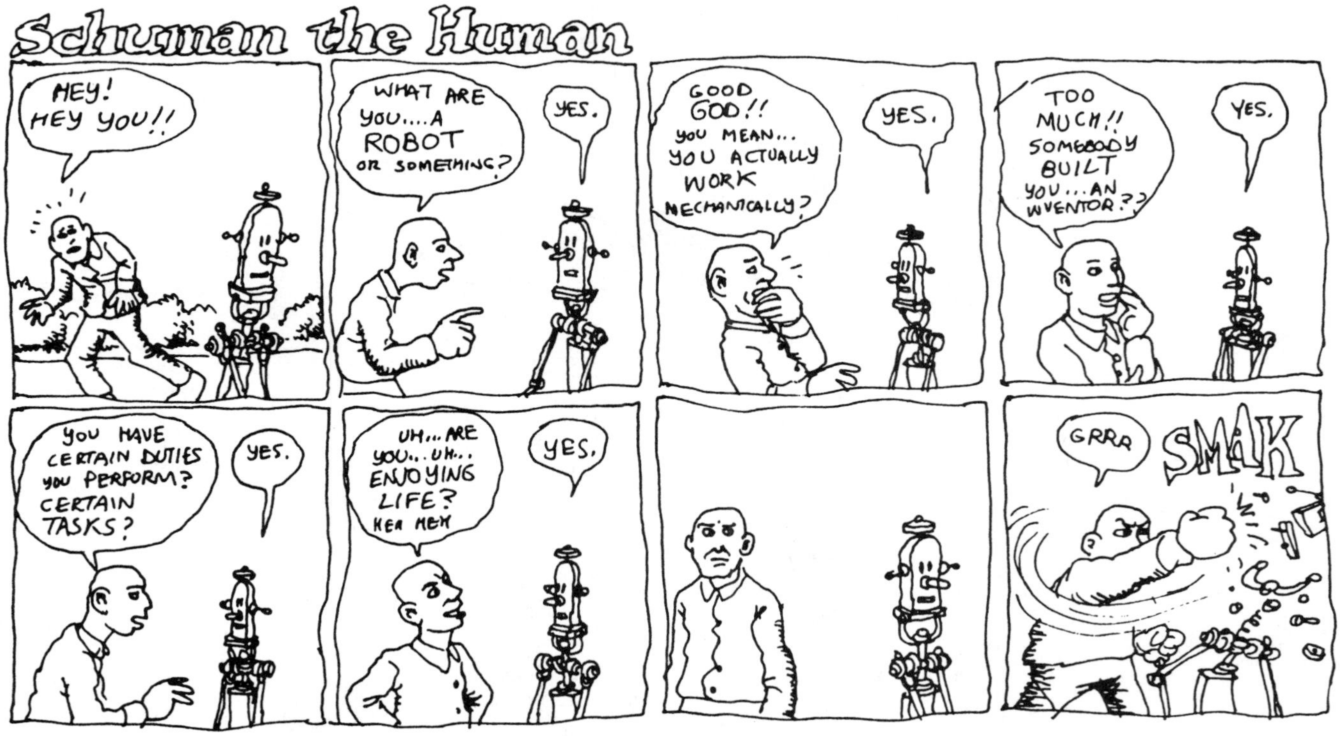
Schuman the Human
HEY! HEY YOU!!
WHAT ARE YOU....A ROBOT OR SOMETHING?
YES.
GOOD GOD!! YOU MEAN... YOU ACTUALLY WORK MECHANICALLY?
YES.
TOO MUCH!! SOMEBODY BUILT YOU...AN INVENTOR??
YES.
YOU HAVE CERTAIN DUTIES YOU PERFORM? CERTAIN TASKS?
YES.
UH...ARE YOU...UH... ENJOYING LIFE? HEH HEH
YES.
GRRR
SMAK

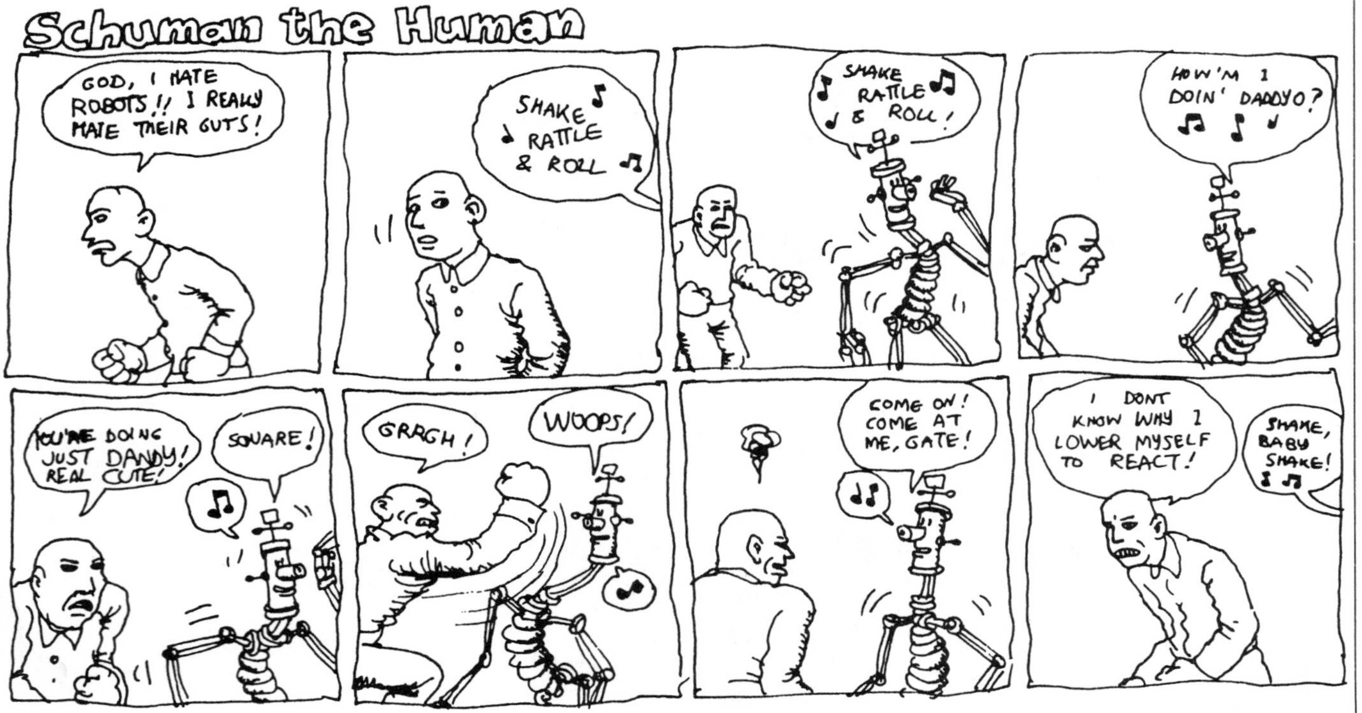
Schuman the Human
GOD, I HATE ROBOTS!! I REALLY HATE THEIR GUTS!
SHAKE RATTLE & ROLL
SHAKE RATTLE & ROLL!
HOW'M I DOIN' DADDYO?
YOU'RE DOING JUST DANDY! REAL CUTE!
SQUARE!
GRRGH!
WOOPS!
COME ON! COME AT ME, GATE!
I DONT KNOW WHY I LOWER MYSELF TO REACT!
SHAKE, BABY SHAKE!

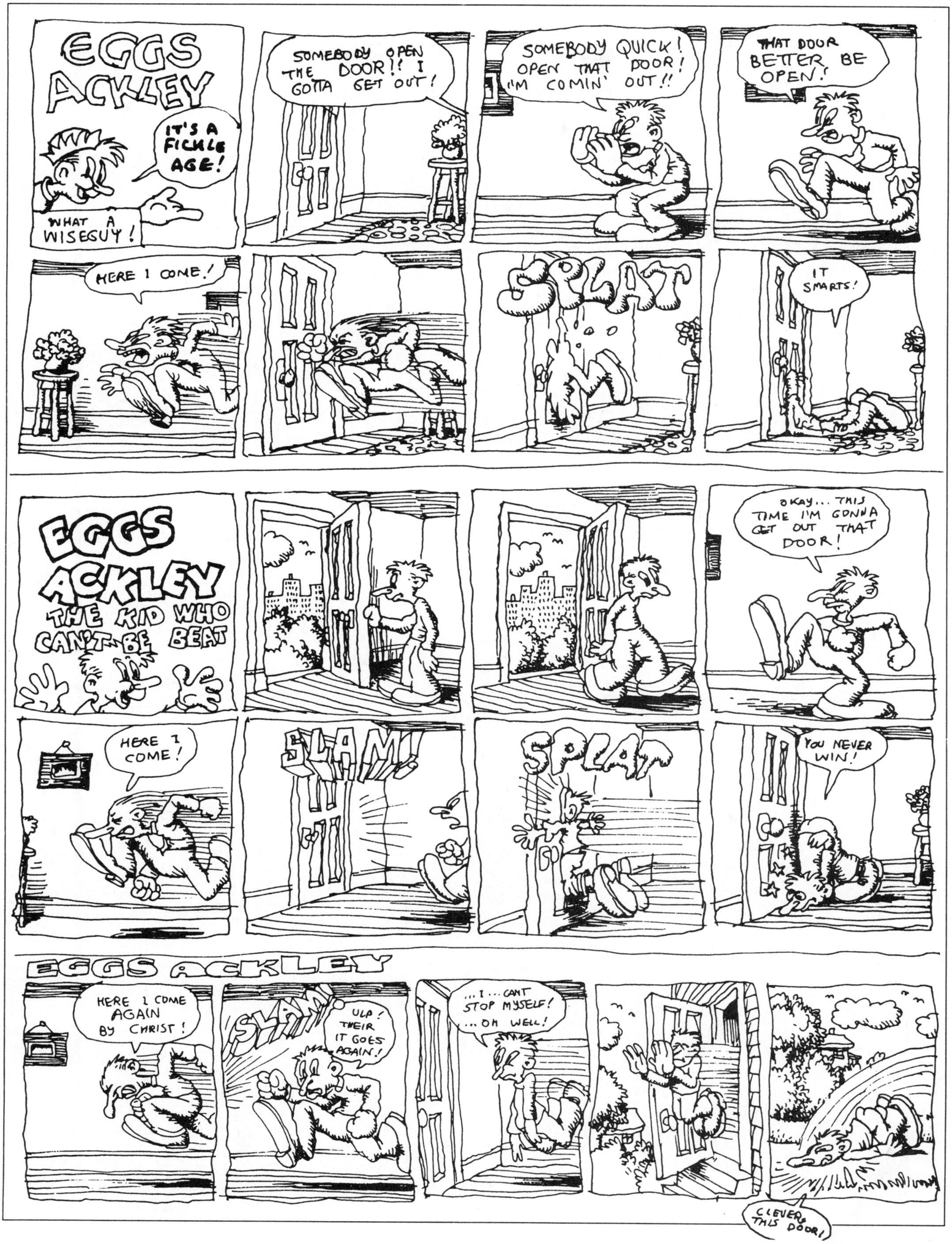
EGGS ACKLEY
IT'S A FICKLE AGE!
WHAT A WISEGUY!
SOMEBODY OPEN THE DOOR!! I GOTTA GET OUT!
SOMEBODY QUICK! OPEN THAT DOOR! I'M COMIN' OUT!!
THAT DOOR BETTER BE OPEN!
HERE I COME!
SPLAT
IT SMARTS!
EGGS ACKLEY
THE KID WHO CAN'T BE BEAT
OKAY... THIS TIME I'M GONNA GET OUT THAT DOOR!
HERE I COME!
SLAM!
SPLAT
YOU NEVER WIN!
EGGS ACKLEY
HERE I COME AGAIN BY CHRIST!
SLAM!
ULP! THEIR IT GOES AGAIN!
...I...CANT STOP MYSELF! ...OH WELL!
CLEVER, THIS DOOR!

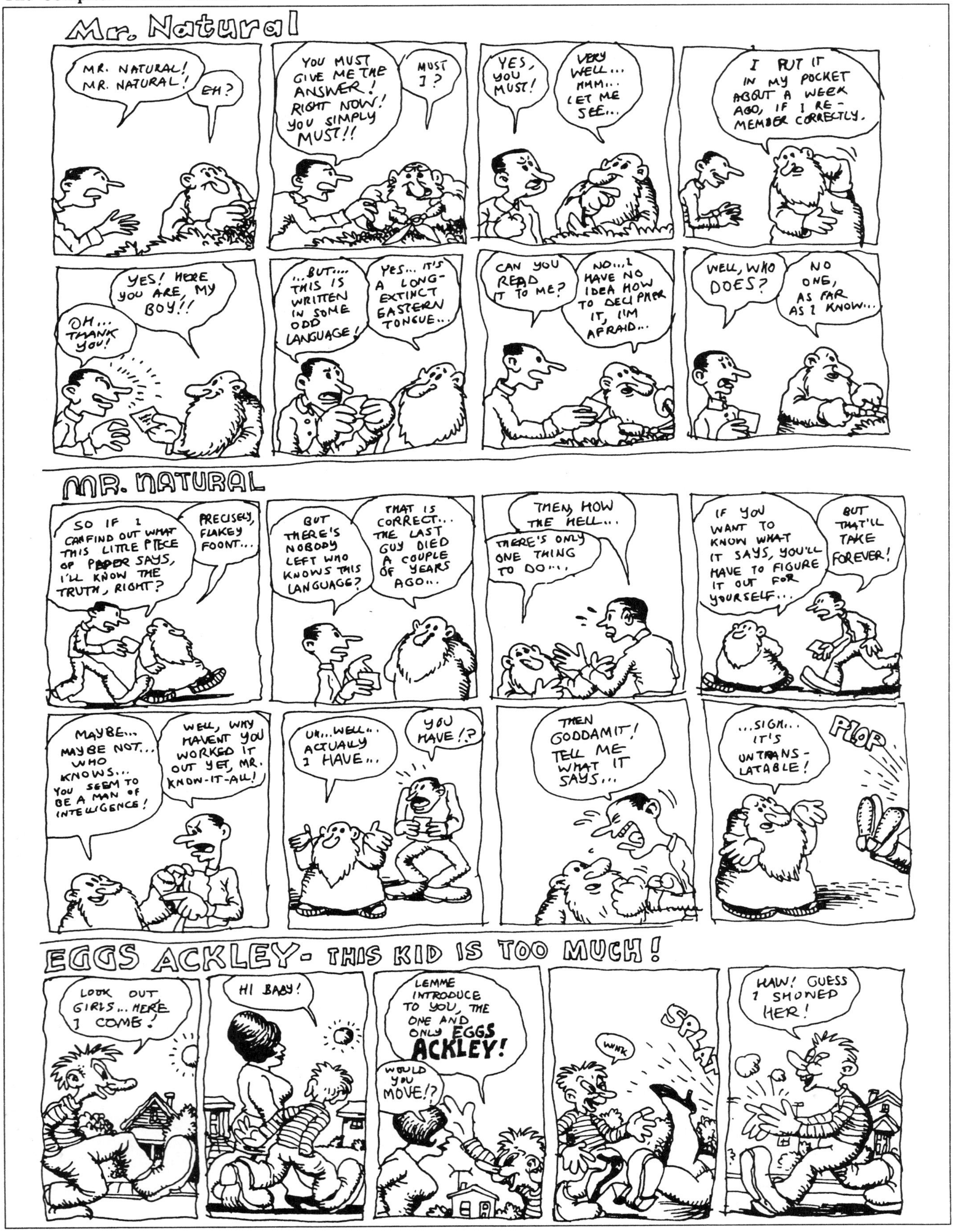
Mr. Natural
MR. NATURAL! MR. NATURAL!
EH?
YOU MUST GIVE ME THE ANSWER! RIGHT NOW! YOU SIMPLY MUST!!
MUST I?
YES, YOU MUST!
VERY WELL... MMM... LET ME SEE...
I PUT IT IN MY POCKET ABOUT A WEEK AGO, IF I REMEMBER CORRECTLY.
YES! HERE YOU ARE, MY BOY!!
OH... THANK YOU!
...BUT.... THIS IS WRITTEN IN SOME ODD LANGUAGE!
YES... IT'S A LONG-EXTINCT EASTERN TONGUE...
CAN YOU READ IT TO ME?
NO...I HAVE NO IDEA HOW TO DECIPHER IT, I'M AFRAID...
WELL, WHO DOES?
NO ONE, AS FAR AS I KNOW...
MR. NATURAL
SO IF I CAN FIND OUT WHAT THIS LITTLE PIECE OF PAPER SAYS, I'LL KNOW THE TRUTH, RIGHT?
PRECISELY, FLAKEY FOONT...
BUT THERE'S NOBODY LEFT WHO KNOWS THIS LANGUAGE?
THAT IS CORRECT... THE LAST GUY DIED A COUPLE OF YEARS AGO...
THEN, HOW THE HELL...
THERE'S ONLY ONE THING TO DO...
IF YOU WANT TO KNOW WHAT IT SAYS, YOU'LL HAVE TO FIGURE IT OUT FOR YOURSELF...
BUT THAT'LL TAKE FOREVER!
MAYBE... MAYBE NOT... WHO KNOWS... YOU SEEM TO BE A MAN OF INTELLIGENCE!
WELL, WHY HAVEN'T YOU WORKED IT OUT YET, MR. KNOW-IT-ALL!
UH...WELL... ACTUALLY I HAVE...
YOU HAVE!?
THEN GODDAMIT! TELL ME WHAT IT SAYS...
...SIGH... IT'S UNTRANSLATABLE!
PLOP
EGGS ACKLEY- THIS KID IS TOO MUCH!
LOOK OUT GIRLS... HERE I COME!
HI BABY!
LEMME INTRODUCE TO YOU, THE ONE AND ONLY EGGS ACKLEY!
WOULD YOU MOVE!?
WNK
SPLAT
HAW! GUESS I SHOWED HER!

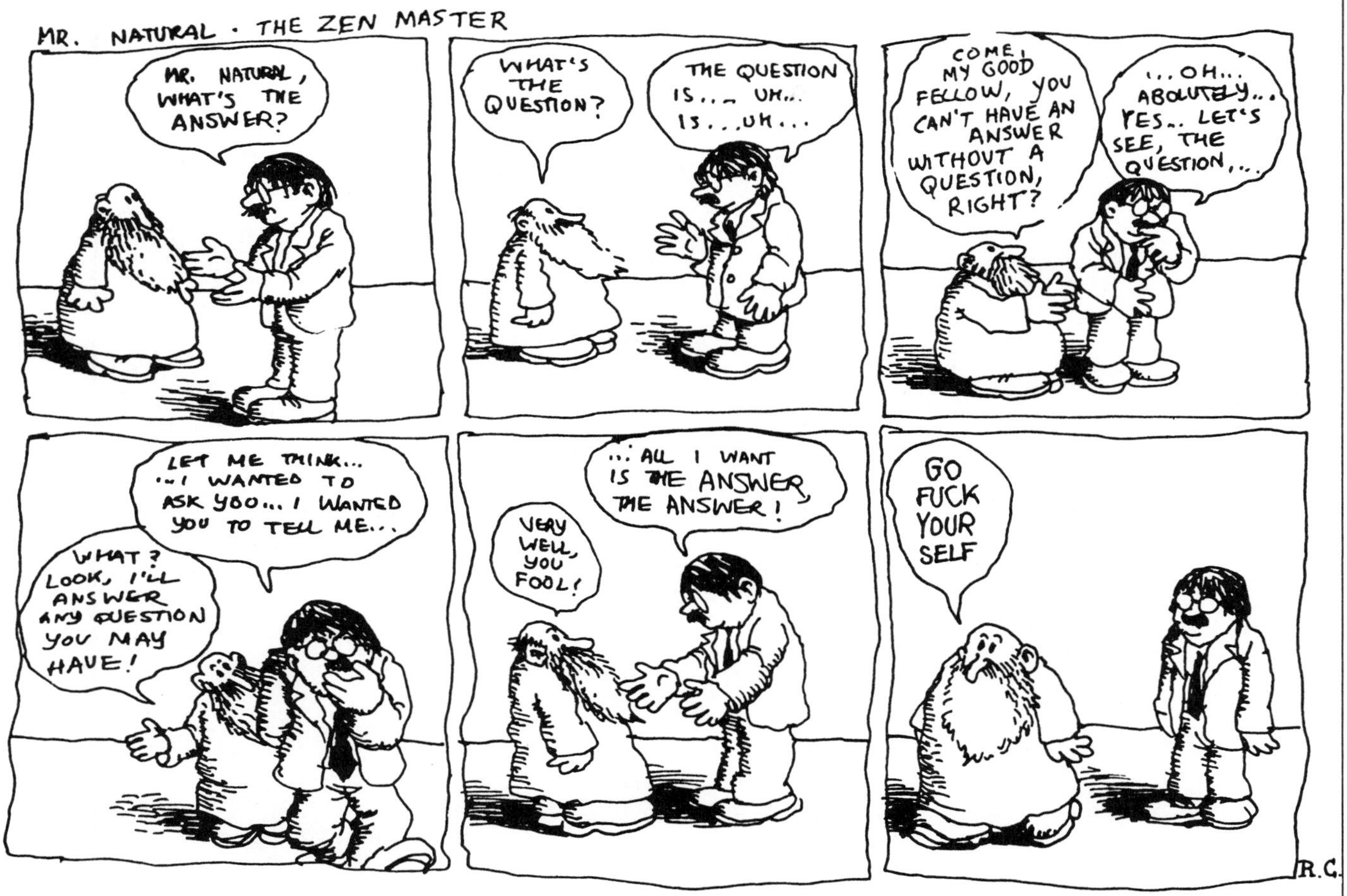
MR. NATURAL · THE ZEN MASTER
MR. NATURAL, WHAT'S THE ANSWER?
WHAT'S THE QUESTION?
THE QUESTION IS... UH... IS... UH...
COME, MY GOOD FELLOW, YOU CAN'T HAVE AN ANSWER WITHOUT A QUESTION, RIGHT?
...OH... ABOLUTELY.. YES.. LET'S SEE, THE QUESTION,...
LET ME THINK... ...I WANTED TO ASK YOO... I WANTED YOU TO TELL ME...
WHAT? LOOK, I'LL ANSWER ANY QUESTION YOU MAY HAVE!
...ALL I WANT IS THE ANSWER, THE ANSWER!
VERY WELL, YOU FOOL!
GO FUCK YOUR SELF
R.C.

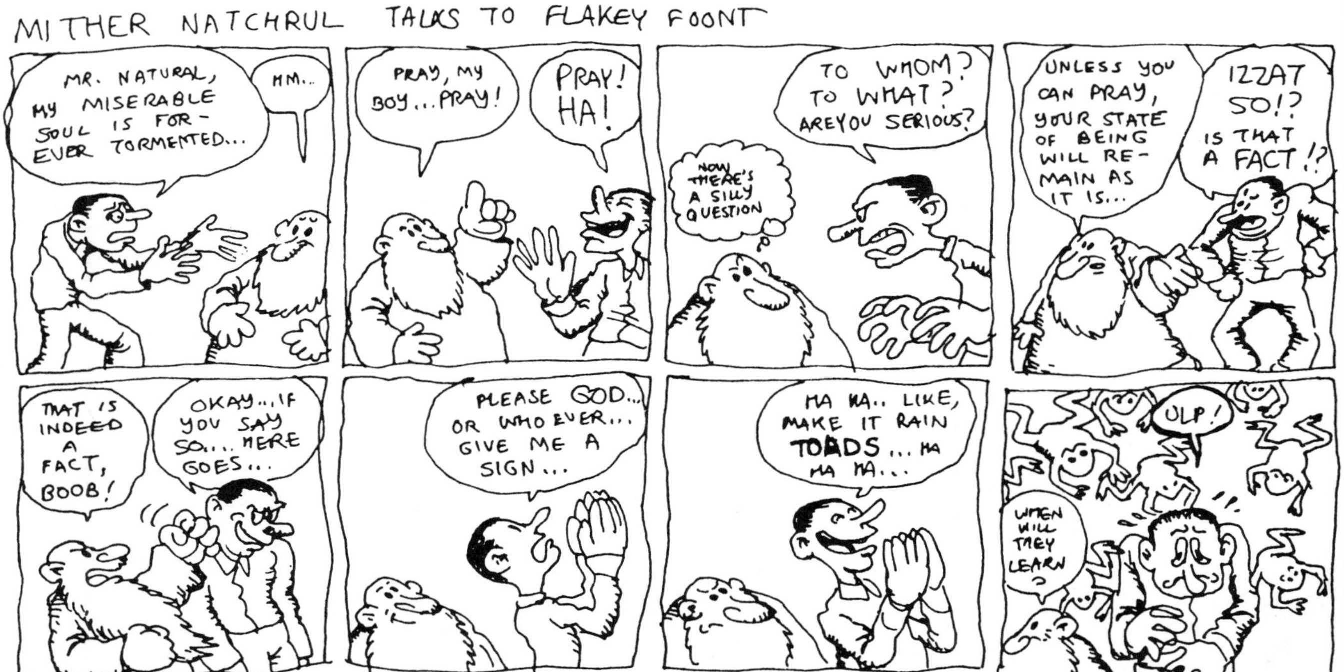
MITHER NATCHRUL TALKS TO FLAKEY FOONT
MR. NATURAL, MY MISERABLE SOUL IS FOR-EVER TORMENTED...
HM...
PRAY, MY BOY...PRAY!
PRAY! HA!
TO WHOM? TO WHAT? AREYOU SERIOUS?
NOW THERE'S A SILLY QUESTION
UNLESS YOU CAN PRAY, YOUR STATE OF BEING WILL RE-MAIN AS IT IS...
IZZAT SO!? IS THAT A FACT!?
THAT IS INDEED A FACT, BOOB!
OKAY...IF YOU SAY SO... HERE GOES...
PLEASE GOD... OR WHO EVER... GIVE ME A SIGN...
HA HA.. LIKE, MAKE IT RAIN TOADS... HA HA HA...
ULP!
WHEN WILL THEY LEARN?

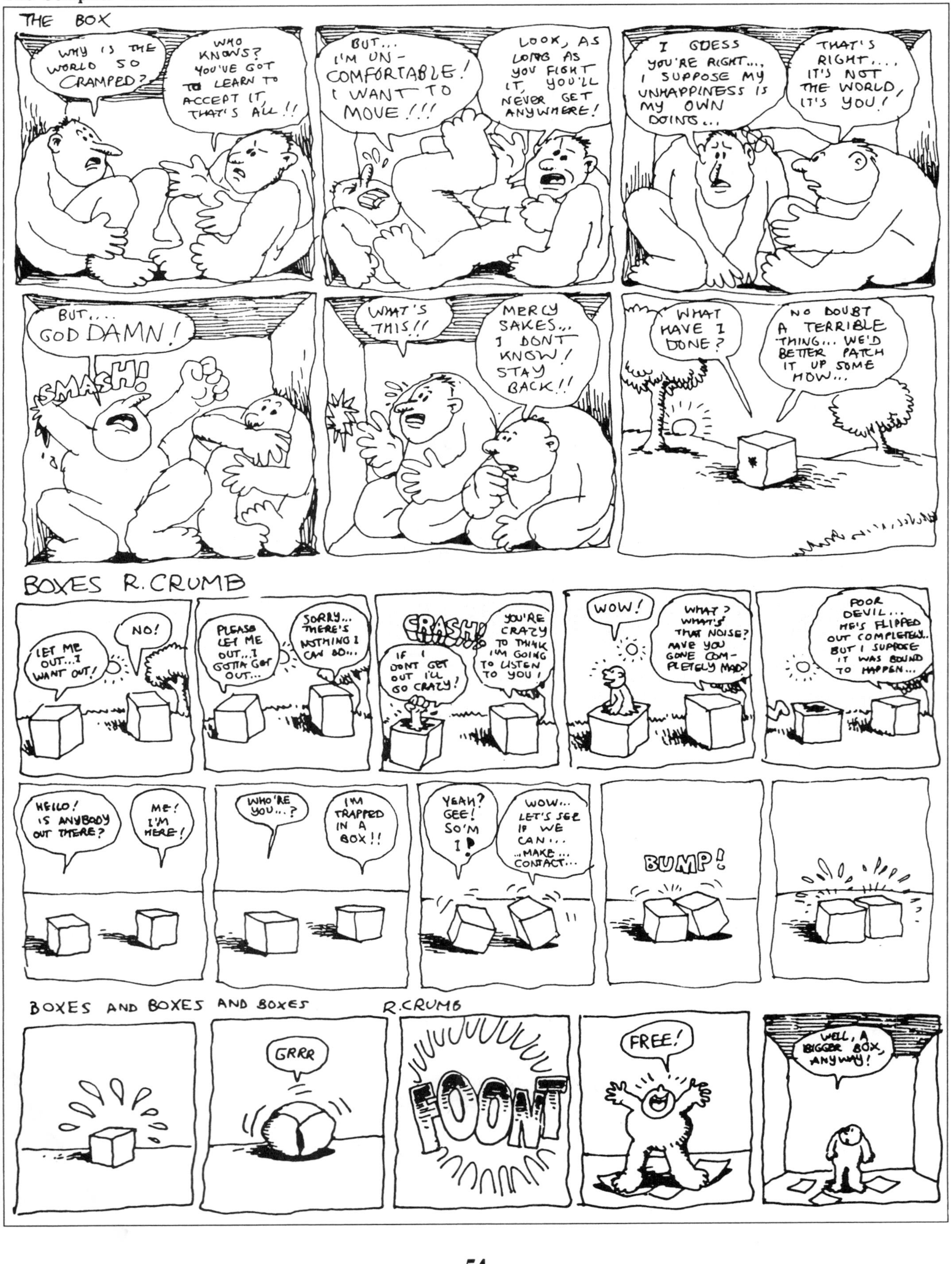
THE BOX
WHY IS THE WORLD SO CRAMPED?
WHO KNOWS? YOU'VE GOT TO LEARN TO ACCEPT IT, THAT'S ALL!!
BUT... I'M UN-COMFORTABLE! I WANT TO MOVE!!!
LOOK, AS LONG AS YOU FIGHT IT, YOU'LL NEVER GET ANYWHERE!
I GUESS YOU'RE RIGHT..., I SUPPOSE MY UNHAPPINESS IS MY OWN DOING...
THAT'S RIGHT..., IT'S NOT THE WORLD, IT'S YOU!
BUT.... GOD DAMN!
SMASH!
WHAT'S THIS!!
MERCY SAKES... I DONT KNOW! STAY BACK!!
WHAT HAVE I DONE?
NO DOUBT A TERRIBLE THING... WE'D BETTER PATCH IT UP SOME HOW...
BOXES R.CRUMB
LET ME OUT...I WANT OUT!
NO!
PLEASE LET ME OUT...I GOTTA GET OUT...
SORRY... THERE'S NOTHING I CAN DO...
CRASH!
IF I DONT GET OUT I'LL GO CRAZY!
YOU'RE CRAZY TO THINK I'M GOING TO LISTEN TO YOU!
WOW!
WHAT? WHAT'S THAT NOISE? HAVE YOU GONE COM-PLETELY MAD?
POOR DEVIL... HE'S FLIPPED OUT COMPLETELY.. BUT I SUPPOSE IT WAS BOUND TO HAPPEN...
HELLO! IS ANYBODY OUT THERE?
ME! I'M HERE!
WHO'RE YOU...?
I'M TRAPPED IN A BOX!!
YEAH? GEE! SO'M I!
WOW... LET'S SEE IF WE CAN... ...MAKE... CONTACT...
BUMP!
BOXES AND BOXES AND BOXES R.CRUMB
GRRR
FOOMT
FREE!
WELL, A BIGGER BOX, ANYWAY!

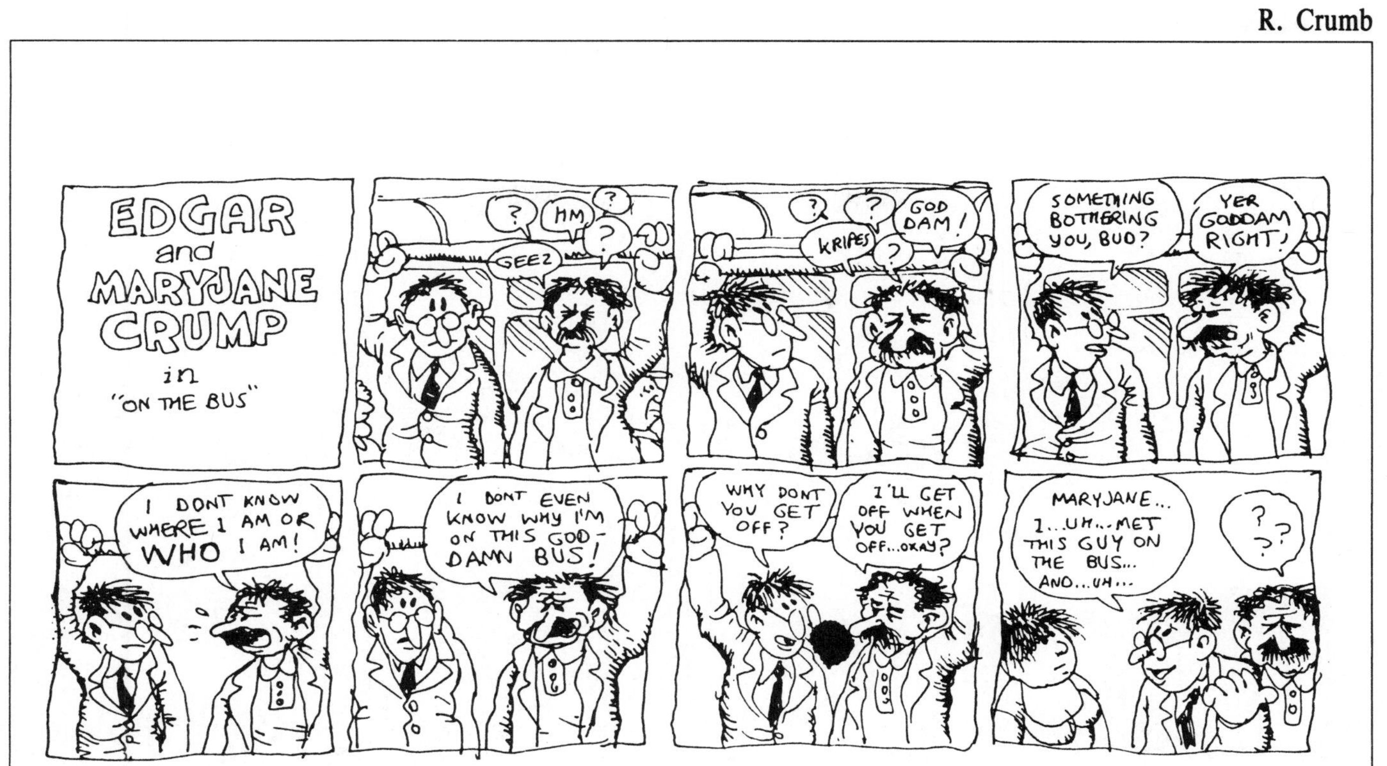
EDGAR and MARYJANE CRUMP in "ON THE BUS"
?
HM
?
?
GEEZ
?
?
KRIPES
GOD DAM!
?
SOMETHING BOTHERING YOU, BUD?
YER GODDAM RIGHT!
I DONT KNOW WHERE I AM OR WHO I AM!
I DONT EVEN KNOW WHY I'M ON THIS GOD-DAMN BUS!
WHY DONT YOU GET OFF?
I'LL GET OFF WHEN YOU GET OFF...OKAY?
MARYJANE... I...UH...MET THIS GUY ON THE BUS... AND...UH...
? ??

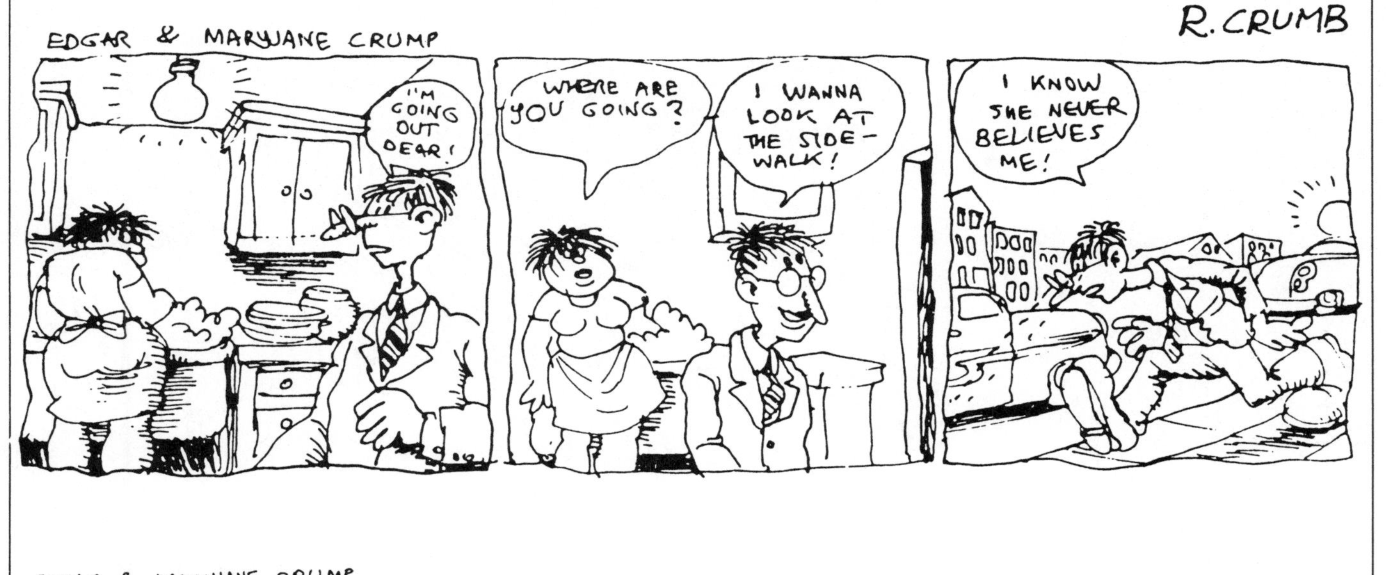
EDGAR & MARYJANE CRUMP
R. CRUMB
I'M GOING OUT DEAR!
WHERE ARE YOU GOING?
I WANNA LOOK AT THE SIDE-WALK!
I KNOW SHE NEVER BELIEVES ME!

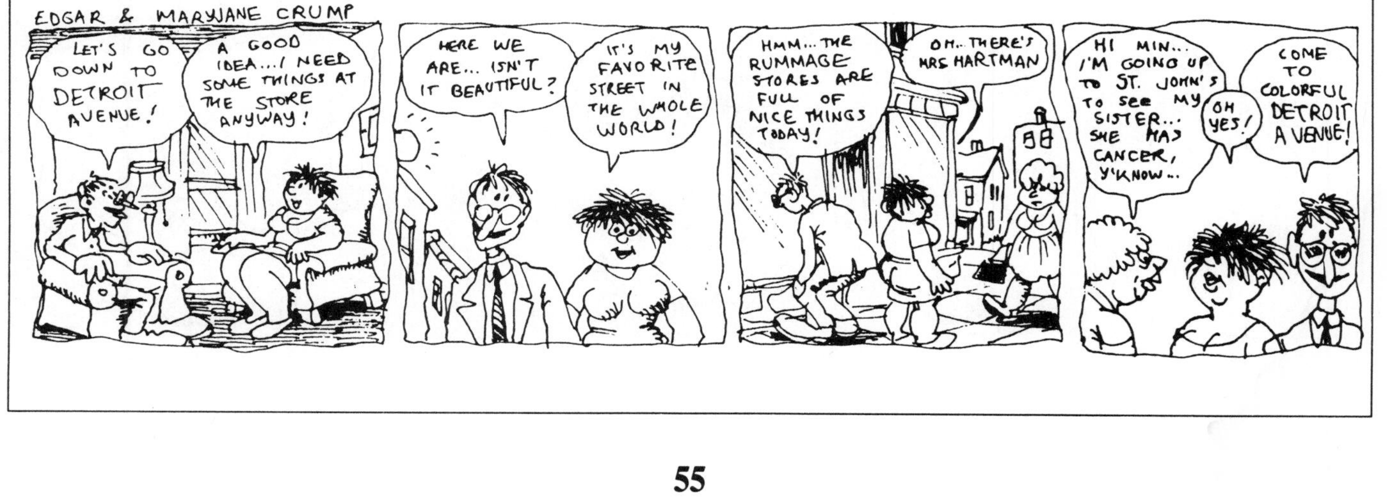
EDGAR & MARYJANE CRUMP
LET'S GO DOWN TO DETROIT AVENUE!
A GOOD IDEA...I NEED SOME THINGS AT THE STORE ANYWAY!
HERE WE ARE... ISN'T IT BEAUTIFUL?
IT'S MY FAVORITE STREET IN THE WHOLE WORLD!
HMM... THE RUMMAGE STORES ARE FULL OF NICE THINGS TODAY!
OH.. THERE'S MRS HARTMAN
HI MIN... I'M GOING UP TO ST. JOHN'S TO SEE MY SISTER... SHE HAS CANCER, Y'KNOW...
OH YES!
COME TO COLORFUL DETROIT AVENUE!

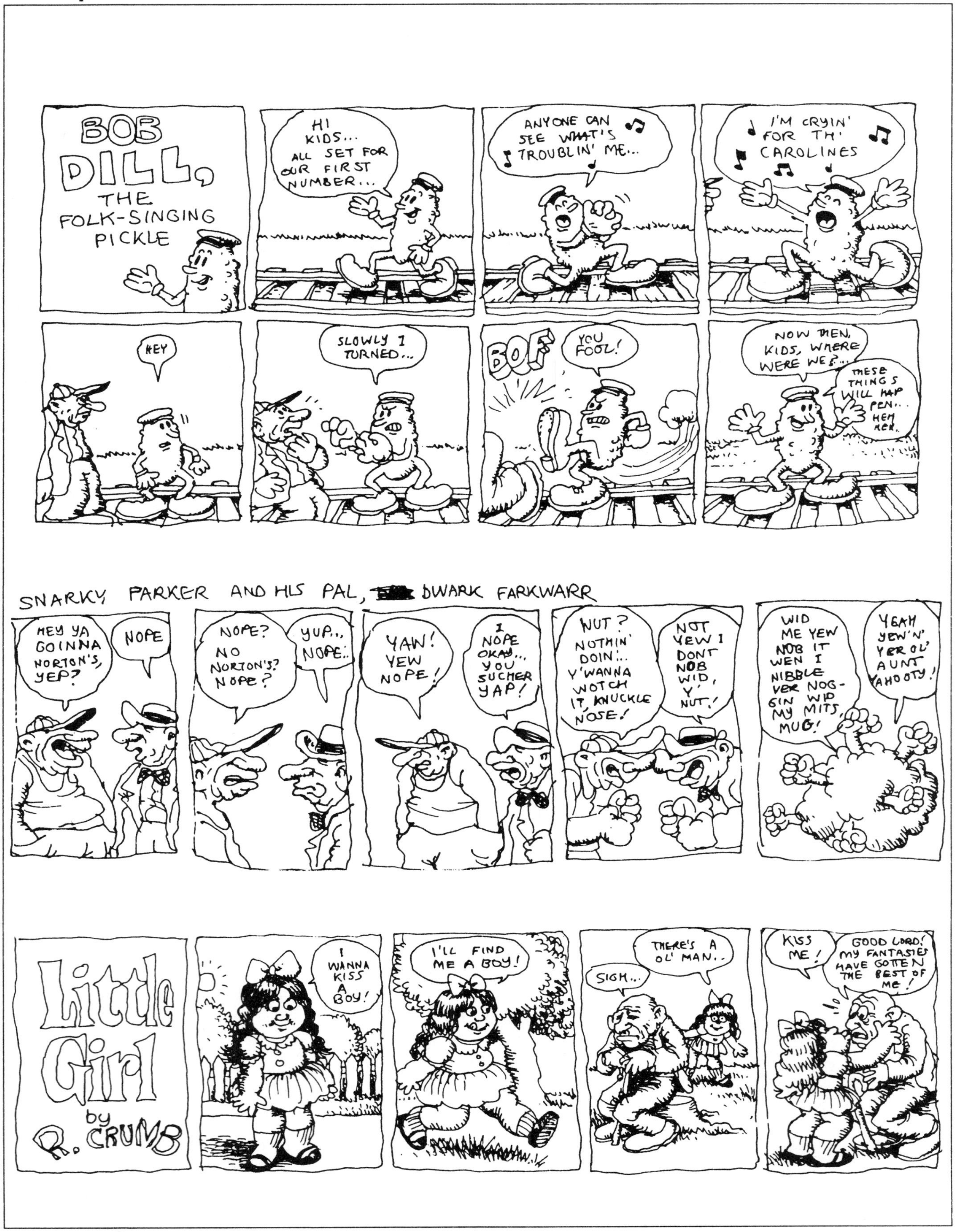
BOB DILL, THE FOLK-SINGING PICKLE
HI KIDS... ALL SET FOR OUR FIRST NUMBER...
ANYONE CAN SEE WHAT'S TROUBLIN' ME...
I'M CRYIN' FOR TH' CAROLINES
HEY
SLOWLY I TURNED...
BOF
YOU FOOL!
NOW THEN, KIDS, WHERE WERE WE?...
THESE THINGS WILL HAP PEN... HEM HEM.
SNARKY PARKER AND HIS PAL, [redacted] DWARK FARKWARR
HEY YA GOINNA NORTON'S, YEP?
NOPE
NOPE? NO NORTON'S? NOPE?
YUP.. NOPE..
YAW! YEW NOPE!
I NOPE OKAY... YOU SUCHER YAP!
NUT? NOTHIN' DOIN'... Y'WANNA WOTCH IT, KNUCKLE NOSE!
NOT YEW I DONT NOB WID, Y' NUT!
WID ME YEW NOB IT WEN I NIBBLE YER NOG-GIN WID MY MITS, MUG!
YEAH YEW'N' YER OL' AUNT YAHOOTY!
Little Girl by R. CRUMB
I WANNA KISS A BOY!
I'LL FIND ME A BOY!
SIGH...
THERE'S A OL' MAN..
KISS ME!
GOOD LORD! MY FANTASIES HAVE GOTTEN THE BEST OF ME!

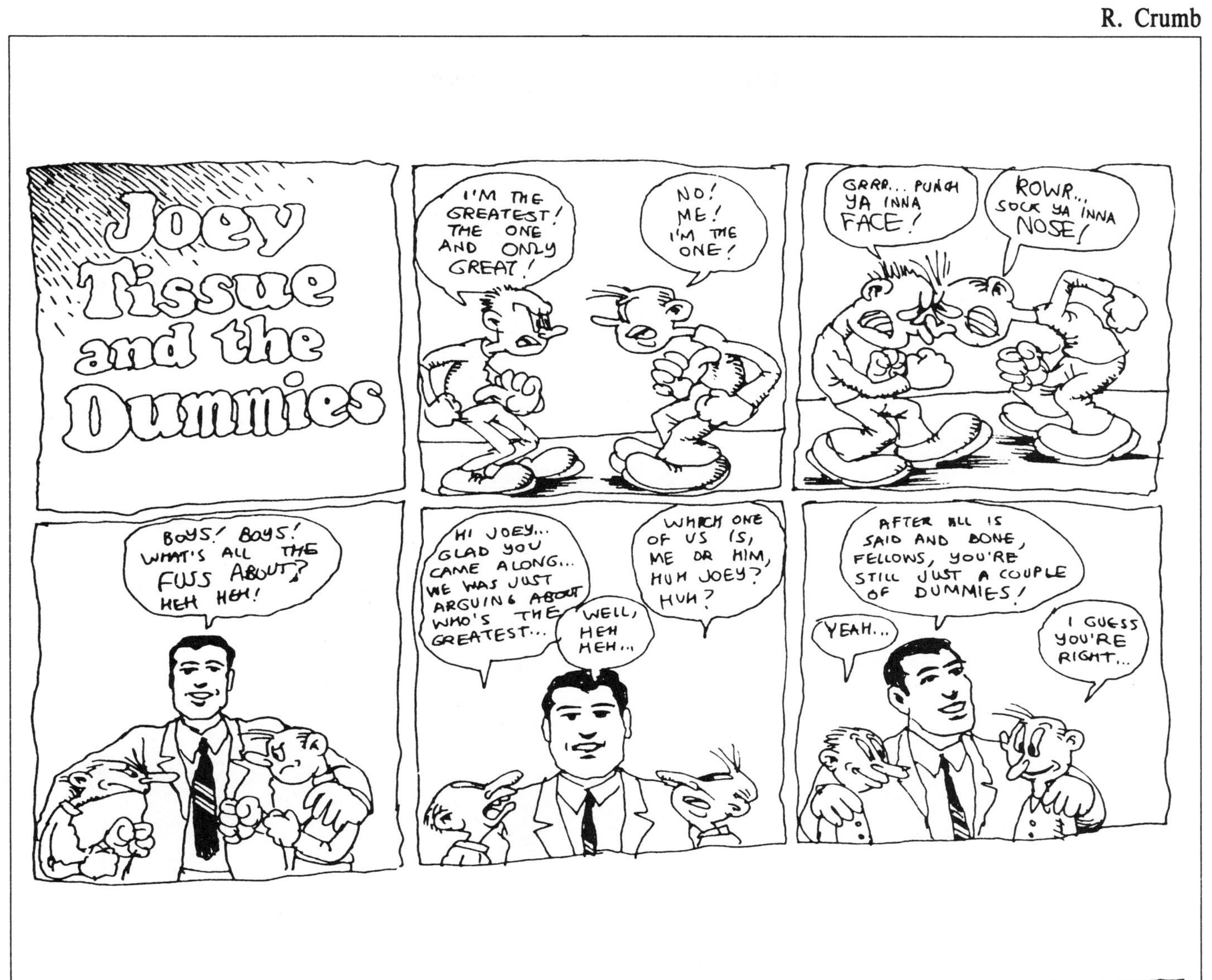
Joey Tissue and the Dummies
I'M THE GREATEST! THE ONE AND ONLY GREAT!
NO! ME! I'M THE ONE!
GRRR... PUNCH YA INNA FACE!
ROWR... SOCK YA INNA NOSE!
BOYS! BOYS! WHAT'S ALL THE FUSS ABOUT? HEH HEH!
HI JOEY... GLAD YOU CAME ALONG... WE WAS JUST ARGUING ABOUT WHO'S THE GREATEST...
WHICH ONE OF US IS, ME OR HIM, HUH JOEY? HUH?
WELL, HEH HEH...
AFTER ALL IS SAID AND DONE, FELLOWS, YOU'RE STILL JUST A COUPLE OF DUMMIES!
YEAH...
I GUESS YOU'RE RIGHT...

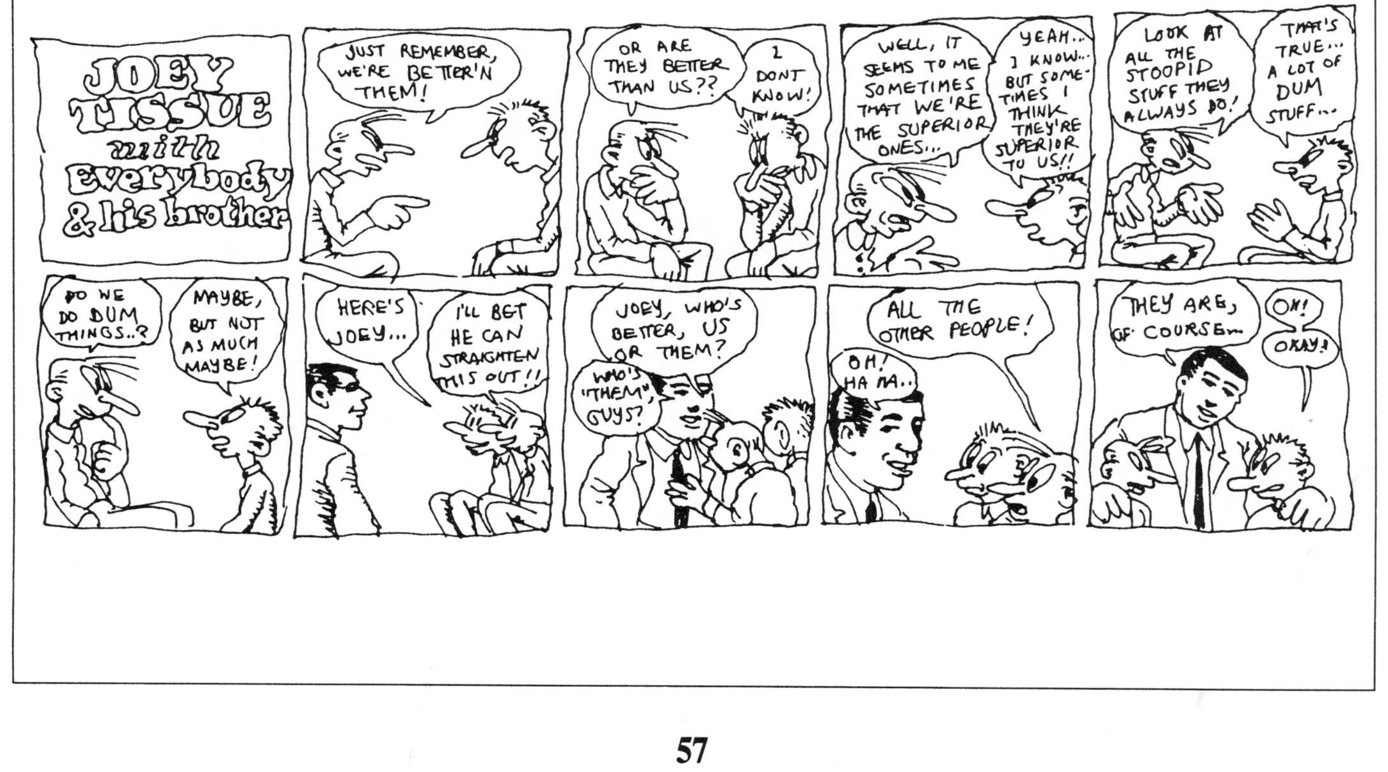
JOEY TISSUE with Everybody & his brother
JUST REMEMBER, WE'RE BETTER'N THEM!
OR ARE THEY BETTER THAN US??
I DONT KNOW!
WELL, IT SEEMS TO ME SOMETIMES THAT WE'RE THE SUPERIOR ONES...
YEAH... I KNOW... BUT SOMETIMES I THINK THEY'RE SUPERIOR TO US!!
LOOK AT ALL THE STOOPID STUFF THEY ALWAYS DO!
THAT'S TRUE... A LOT OF DUM STUFF...
DO WE DO DUM THINGS..?
MAYBE, BUT NOT AS MUCH MAYBE!
HERE'S JOEY...
I'LL BET HE CAN STRAIGHTEN THIS OUT!!
JOEY, WHO'S BETTER, US OR THEM?
WHO'S "THEM", GUYS?
ALL THE OTHER PEOPLE!
OH! HA HA..
THEY ARE, OF COURSE...
OH! OKAY!

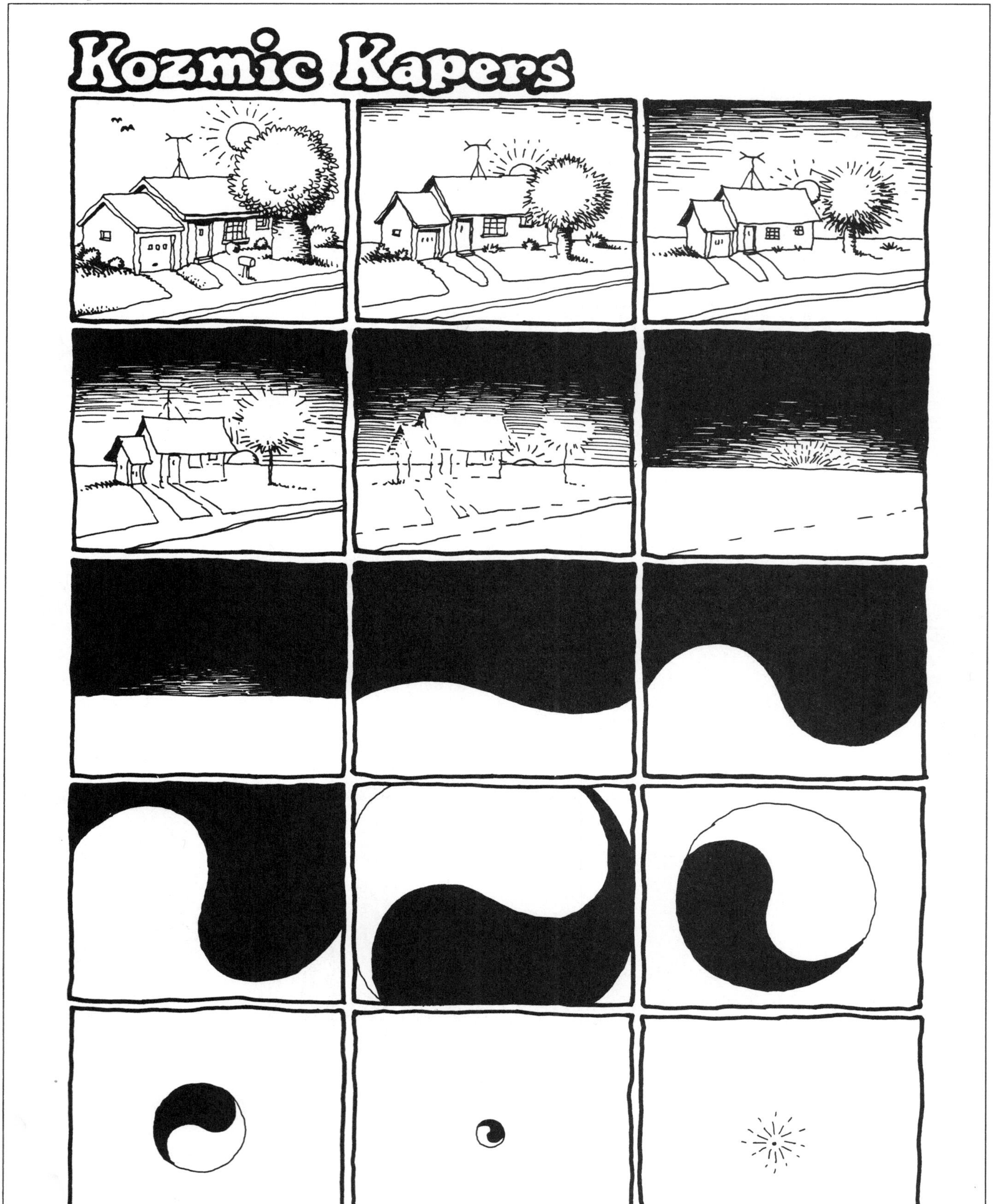
Kozmic Kapers

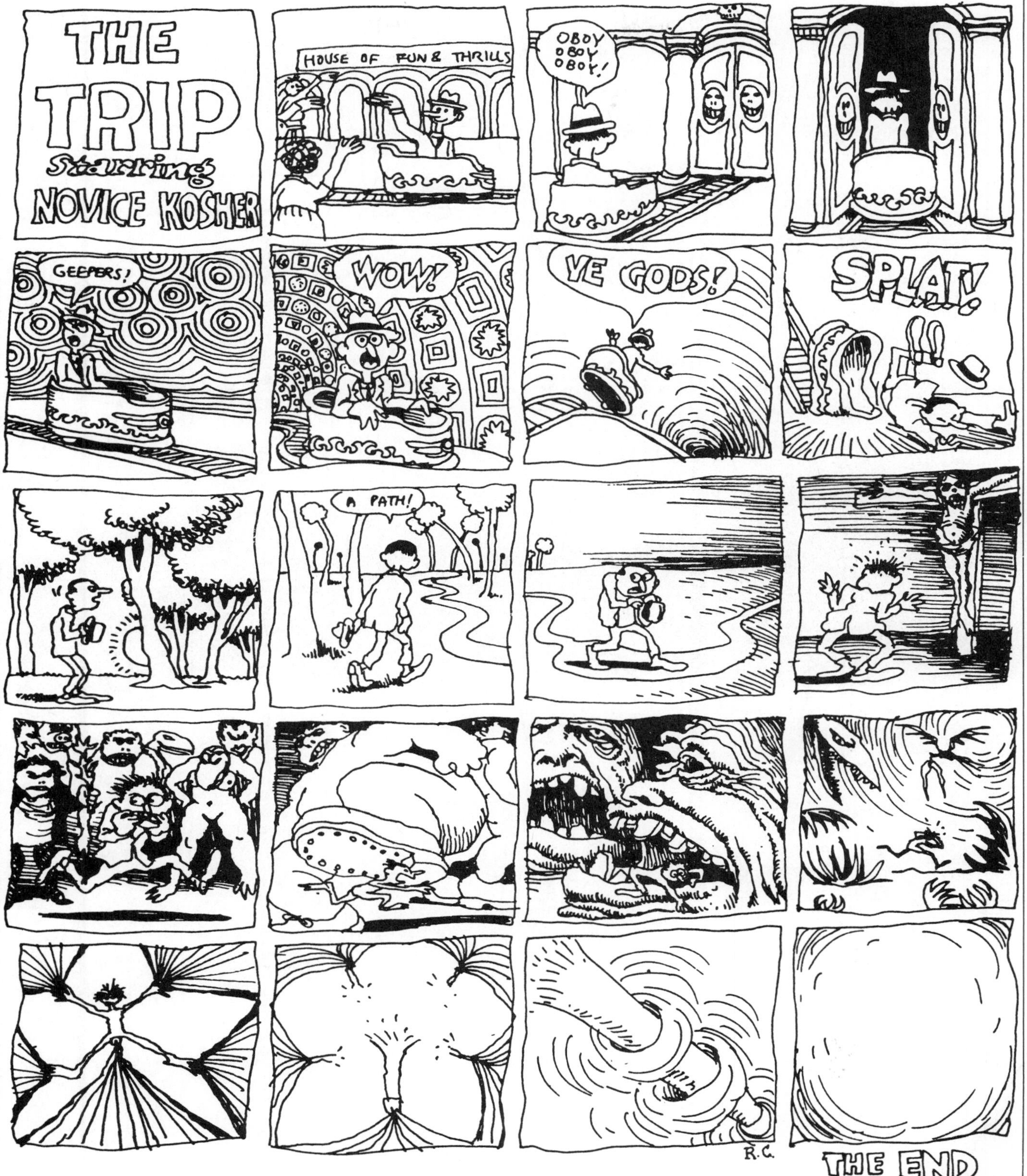
THE TRIP
Starring
NOVICE KOSHER
HOUSE OF FUN & THRILLS
OBOY OBOY OBOY!
GEEPERS!
WOW!
YE GODS!
SPLAT!
A PATH!
R.C.
THE END

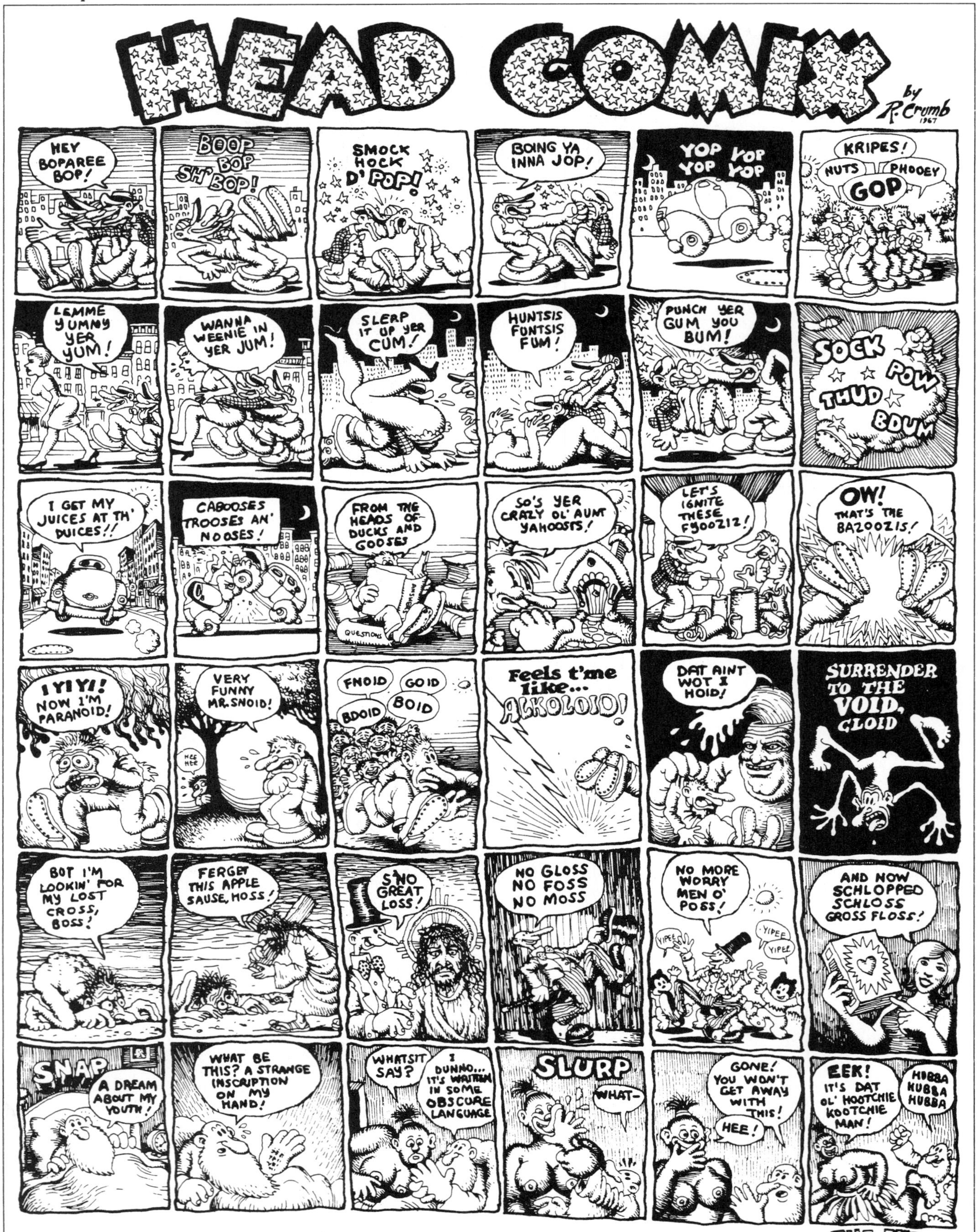
HEAD COMIX
by R. Crumb 1967
HEY BOPAREE BOP!
BOOP BOP SH'BOP!
SMOCK HOCK D'POP!
BOING YA INNA JOP!
YOP YOP YOP YOP
KRIPES!
NUTS
PHOOEY
GOP
LEMME YUMMY YER YUM!
WANNA WEENIE IN YER JUM!
SLERP IT UP YER CUM!
HUNTSIS FUNTSIS FUM!
PUNCH YER GUM YOU BUM!
SOCK POW THUD BDUM
I GET MY JUICES AT TH' DUICES!!
CABOOSES TROOSES AN' NOOSES!
FROM THE HEADS OF DUCKS AND GOOSES
QUESTIONS
SO'S YER CRAZY OL' AUNT YAHOOSIS!
LET'S IGNITE THESE FYOOZIZ!
OW! THAT'S THE BAZOOZIS!
IYIYI! NOW I'M PARANOID!
VERY FUNNY MR. SNOID!
HEE HEE
FNOID
GOID
BDOID
BOID
Feels t'me like... ALKOLOID!
DAT AINT WOT I HOID!
SURRENDER TO THE VOID, GLOID
BOT I'M LOOKIN' FOR MY LOST CROSS, BOSS!
FERGET THIS APPLE SAUSE, MOSS!
S'NO GREAT LOSS!
NO GLOSS NO FOSS NO MOSS
NO MORE WORRY MEN O' POSS!
YIPEE
YIPEE
YIPEE
AND NOW SCHLOPPED SCHLOSS GROSS FLOSS!
SNAP
A DREAM ABOUT MY YOUTH!
WHAT BE THIS? A STRANGE INSCRIPTION ON MY HAND!
WHATSIT SAY?
I DUNNO... IT'S WRITTEN IN SOME OBSCURE LANGUAGE
SLURP
WHAT-
GONE! YOU WON'T GET AWAY WITH THIS!
HEE!
EEK! IT'S DAT OL' HOOTCHIE KOOTCHIE MAN!
HUBBA HUBBA HUBBA
THE END

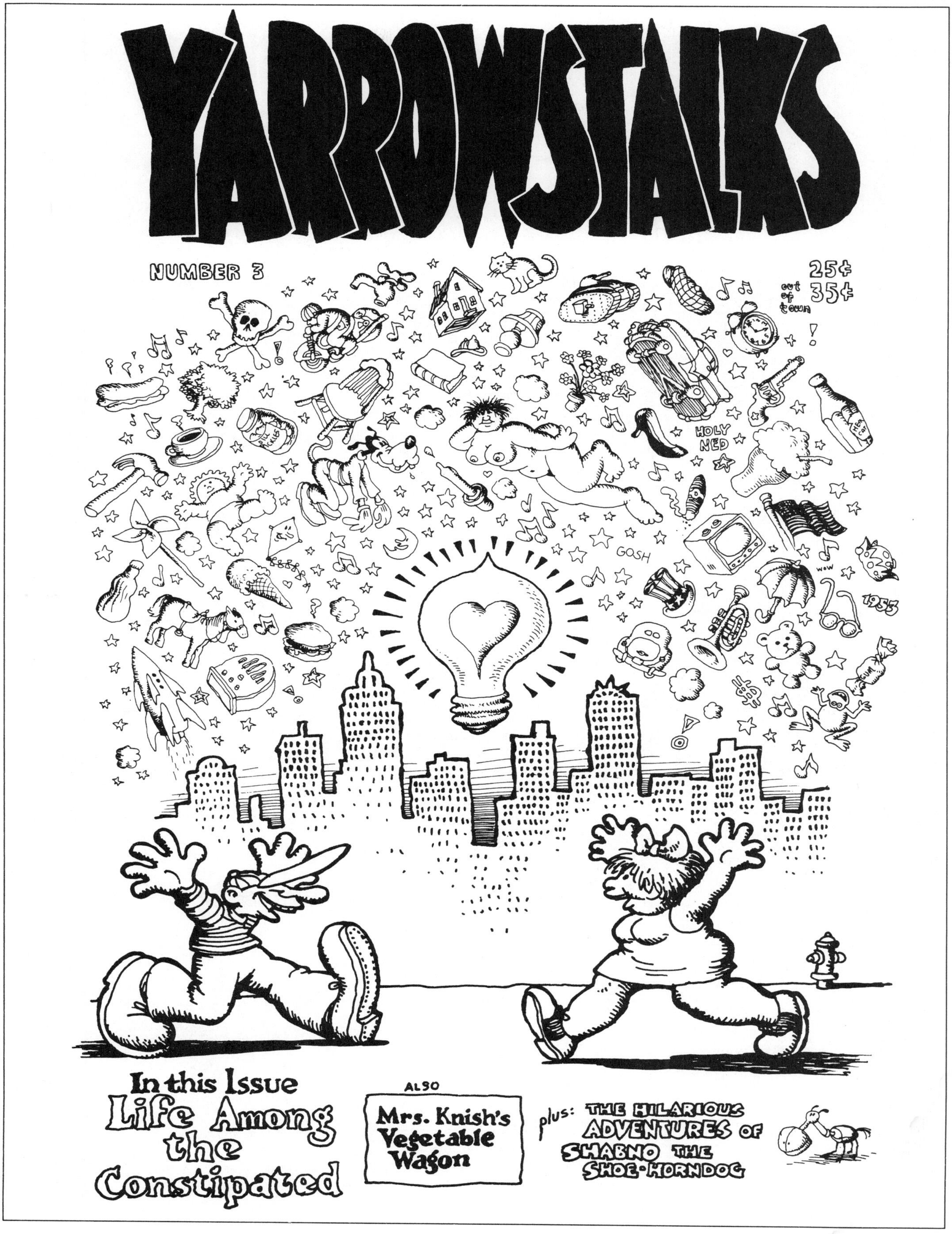
YARROWSTALKS
NUMBER 3
25¢
out of town 35¢
HOLY NED
GOSH
WOW
1955
In this Issue
Life Among the Constipated
ALSO
Mrs. Knish's Vegetable Wagon
plus: THE HILARIOUS ADVENTURES OF SHABNO THE SHOE-HORNDOG

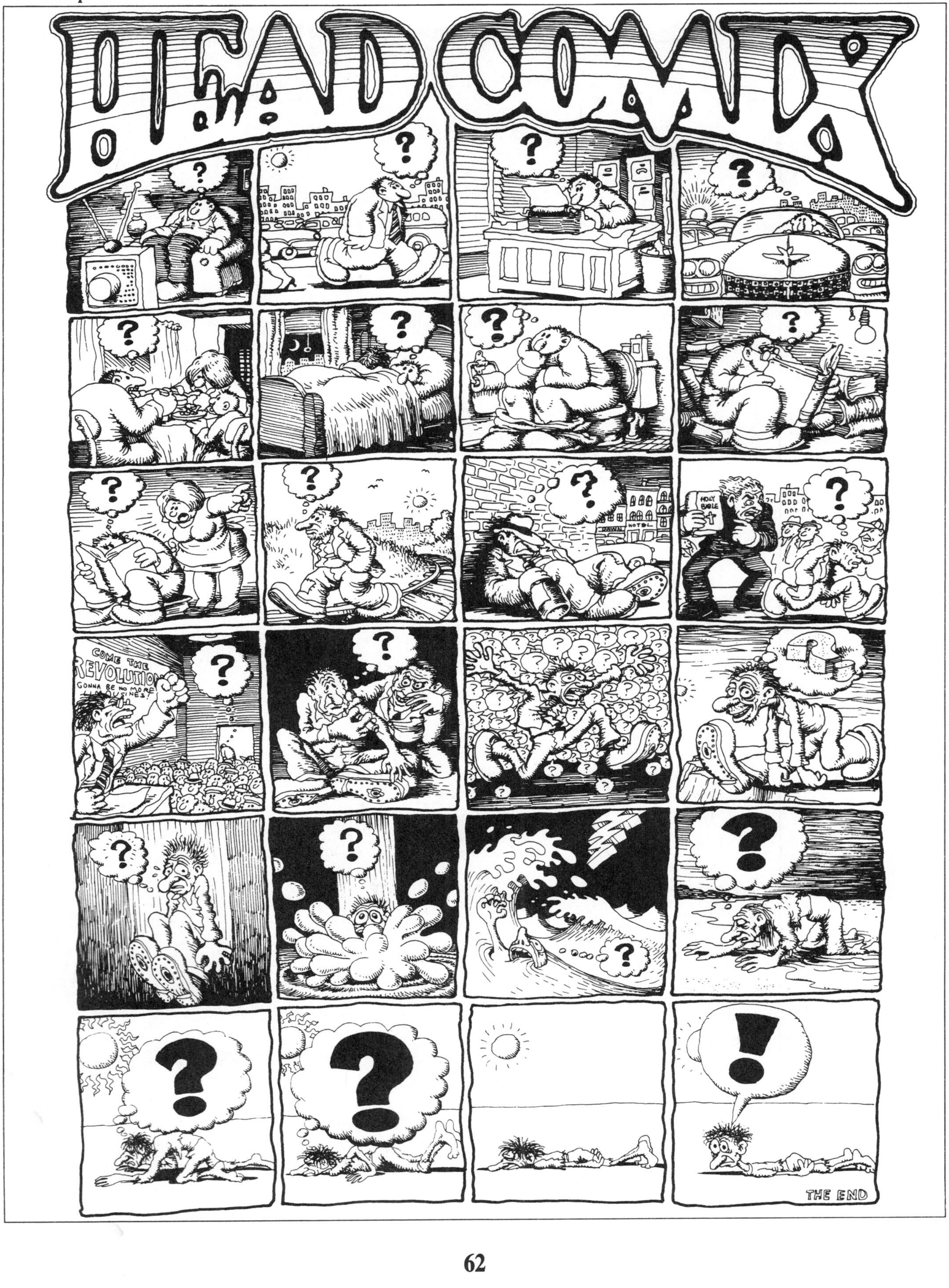
HEAD COMIX
COME THE REVOLUTION
GONNA BE NO MORE
HOLY BIBLE
HOTEL
PAWN
THE END

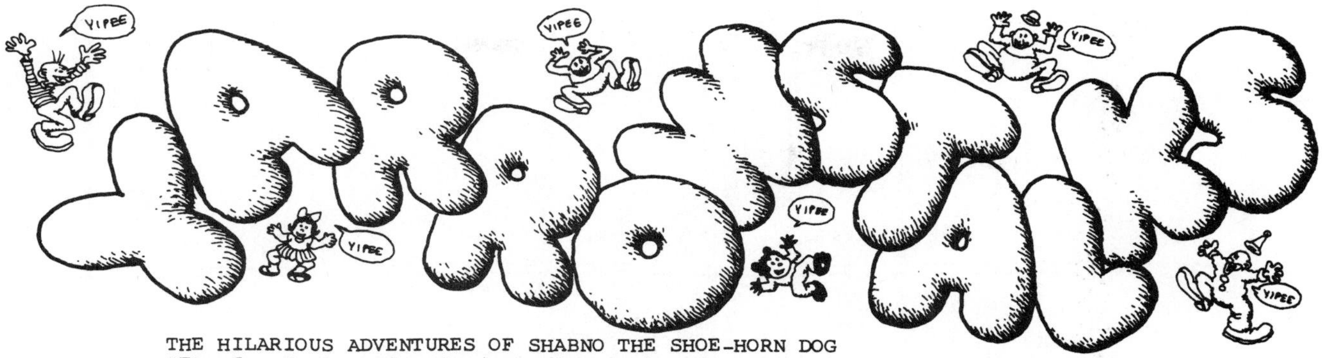
YIPEE
YIPEE
YIPEE
YARROWSTALKS
YIPEE
YIPEE
YIPEE

THE HILARIOUS ADVENTURES OF SHABNO THE SHOE-HORN DOG

"The foundation of modern physics is based on the question 'How many angels can dance on the head of a pin?' "

Shabno awoke, trotted to the next frame, turned around and surveyed the air with his left profile. He saw a flying rabbit.

" I see a flying rabbit."

Several Thousand of them to be precise. (He's looking at you.)

Shabno like many others is a Shoe-horndog.

There are many others.

In many frames of his life he has been approached by lesser beings attempting to ignore his evolutionary importance.

"I am not unique," he said wagging his tail as he walked through the brick wall into the next frame. It was a chinese restaurant.

"Ha, Ha," said the church key cat, also under the influence of seeing several thousand flying rabbits.

"Put the polar ice-cap back in the fridgerator."

Nevertheless, the usual possibilities were endless, leading Shabno to make such introductory comment as, "Where's your shelf?" to the a-spatial cock-roach dwelling in a transvestite tomatoe can.

Rolling over into the next frame, Shabno acheived a major place in science having thus invented himself into a wheel.

"Zarff" he commented in the language of his decendants.

Lifting his leg he ascended in vertical take-off through the time-warp to his right and reappeared in the non-lineal transposition of the first frame of the next column.

Landing on his spring tail in a two inch depth of Zorastrian watermelon pulp, Shabno heard the surrounding air resound with "Insane" He cast forward a puzzled glance to see flying rabbits seeking protection from their whiskers.

Disregarding ominous externality, he returned to his immediate enlightenment, and sighted along the ridge of his nose towards the trapazoidal termite attempting to bug his ear-hole.

Shabno knew suddenly what had to be done and back flipped into the next frame. From behind a rock he took a tablet -relic of an age long past. He read the inscription closely. Not one to look askance at such good fortune, he took the tablet. Without effort he found himself being lifted by the semi-liquid atmospheric bouyancy. He had succeded in remembering the thoughts of the crumby guru, "It is not a natural syndrome, you must infect yourself with the possibility." He floated out from the land of page, behind the heads of the several thousand flying rabbits, one at a time in quantity. (He's still look-ing at you.) They were playing with their ice creams, blowing the flies down the drain, surveying cow-pats, and making a general nuisance of themselves. Shabno went on, searching for another of his kind with which to share his experiences. Nothing but flying rabbits, edsels and other numerous oddities did he see.

Without difficulty he found a page and a frame what looked familiar. He approached slowly so that his senses would have a chance to notice anything attractive about this outer land, for he had seen vestigal traces of some-thing good.

The gravity of his land overcame his will and in a multi-scented puff of light he found himself there.

" 'Sno go? " said the butter-nut mouse.

Shabno shook his head smiling, turned to survey the air, and concluded,

" That's all, folks! "

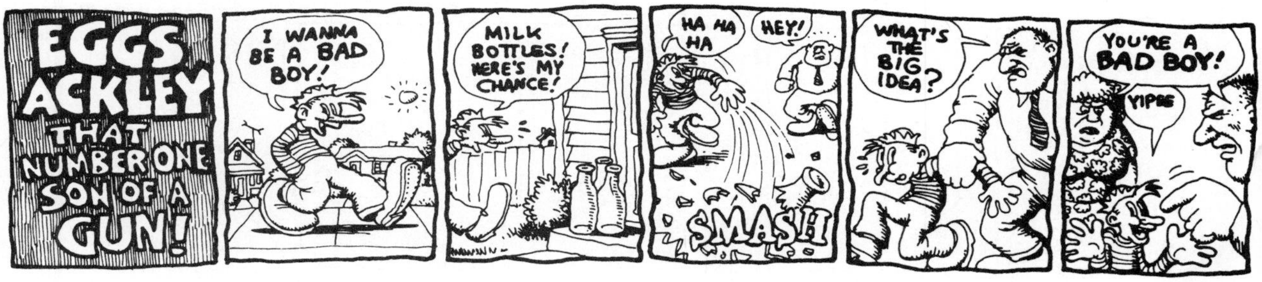
EGGS ACKLEY THAT NUMBER ONE SON OF A GUN!
I WANNA BE A BAD BOY!
MILK BOTTLES! HERE'S MY CHANCE!
HA HA HA
HEY!
SMASH
WHAT'S THE BIG IDEA?
YOU'RE A BAD BOY!
YIPEE

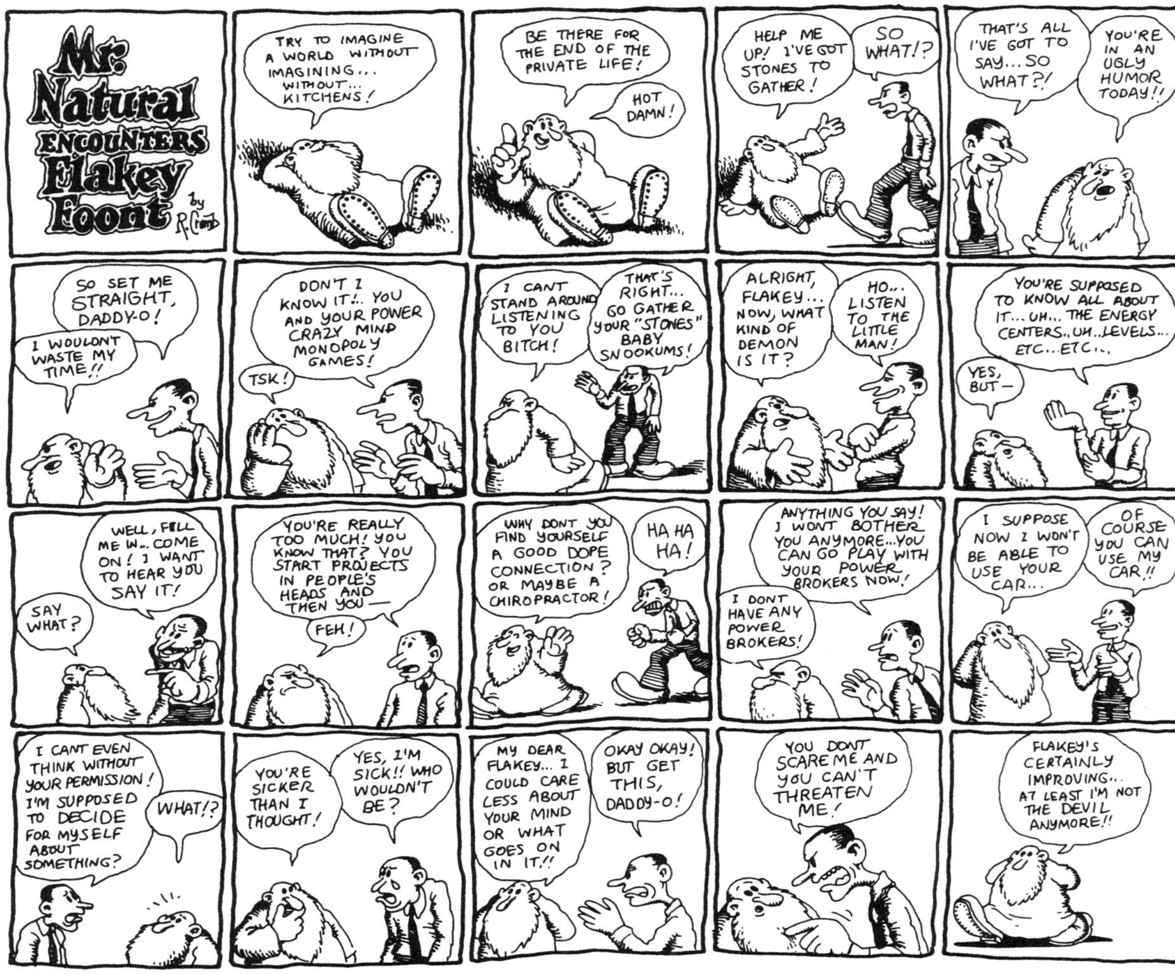
Mr. Natural Encounters Flakey Foont
by R. Crumb
TRY TO IMAGINE A WORLD WITHOUT IMAGINING... WITHOUT... KITCHENS!
BE THERE FOR THE END OF THE PRIVATE LIFE!
HOT DAMN!
HELP ME UP! I'VE GOT STONES TO GATHER!
SO WHAT!?
THAT'S ALL I'VE GOT TO SAY... SO WHAT?!
YOU'RE IN AN UGLY HUMOR TODAY!!
SO SET ME STRAIGHT, DADDY-O!
I WOULDN'T WASTE MY TIME!!
DON'T I KNOW IT!.. YOU AND YOUR POWER CRAZY MIND MONOPOLY GAMES!
TSK!
I CAN'T STAND AROUND LISTENING TO YOU BITCH!
THAT'S RIGHT... GO GATHER YOUR "STONES" BABY SNOOKUMS!
ALRIGHT, FLAKEY... NOW, WHAT KIND OF DEMON IS IT?
HO.. LISTEN TO THE LITTLE MAN!
YOU'RE SUPPOSED TO KNOW ALL ABOUT IT... UH... THE ENERGY CENTERS.. UH.. LEVELS... ETC... ETC...
YES, BUT—
WELL, FILL ME IN.. COME ON! I WANT TO HEAR YOU SAY IT!
SAY WHAT?
YOU'RE REALLY TOO MUCH! YOU KNOW THAT? YOU START PROJECTS IN PEOPLE'S HEADS AND THEN YOU—
FEH!
WHY DON'T YOU FIND YOURSELF A GOOD DOPE CONNECTION? OR MAYBE A CHIROPRACTOR!
HA HA HA!
ANYTHING YOU SAY! I WON'T BOTHER YOU ANYMORE...YOU CAN GO PLAY WITH YOUR POWER BROKERS NOW!
I DON'T HAVE ANY POWER BROKERS!
I SUPPOSE NOW I WON'T BE ABLE TO USE YOUR CAR...
OF COURSE YOU CAN USE MY CAR!!
I CAN'T EVEN THINK WITHOUT YOUR PERMISSION! I'M SUPPOSED TO DECIDE FOR MYSELF ABOUT SOMETHING?
WHAT!?
YOU'RE SICKER THAN I THOUGHT!
YES, I'M SICK!! WHO WOULDN'T BE?
MY DEAR FLAKEY... I COULD CARE LESS ABOUT YOUR MIND OR WHAT GOES ON IN IT!!
OKAY OKAY! BUT GET THIS, DADDY-O!
YOU DON'T SCARE ME AND YOU CAN'T THREATEN ME!
FLAKEY'S CERTAINLY IMPROVING... AT LEAST I'M NOT THE DEVIL ANYMORE!!

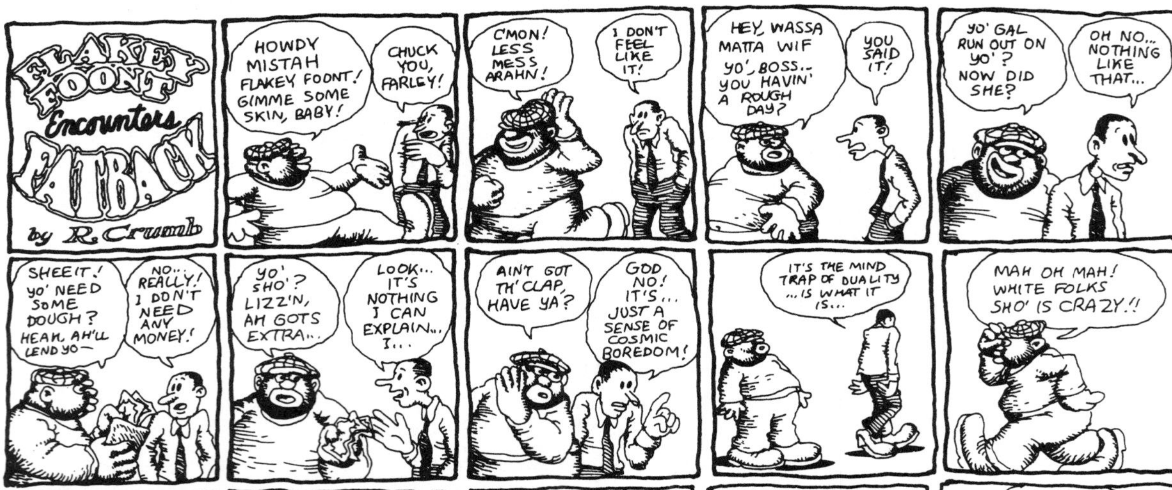
Flakey Foont Encounters Fatback
by R. Crumb
HOWDY MISTAH FLAKEY FOONT! GIMME SOME SKIN, BABY!
CHUCK YOU, FARLEY!
C'MON! LESS MESS ARAHN!
I DON'T FEEL LIKE IT!
HEY, WASSA MATTA WIF YO', BOSS.. YOU HAVIN' A ROUGH DAY?
YOU SAID IT!
YO' GAL RUN OUT ON YO'? NOW DID SHE?
OH NO... NOTHING LIKE THAT...
SHEEIT! YO' NEED SOME DOUGH? HEAH, AH'LL LEND YO—
NO... REALLY! I DON'T NEED ANY MONEY!
YO' SHO'? LIZZ'N, AH GOTS EXTRA...
LOOK... IT'S NOTHING I CAN EXPLAIN... I...
AIN'T GOT TH' CLAP, HAVE YA?
GOD NO! IT'S... JUST A SENSE OF COSMIC BOREDOM!
IT'S THE MIND TRAP OF DUALITY ...IS WHAT IT IS...
MAH OH MAH! WHITE FOLKS SHO' IS CRAZY!!

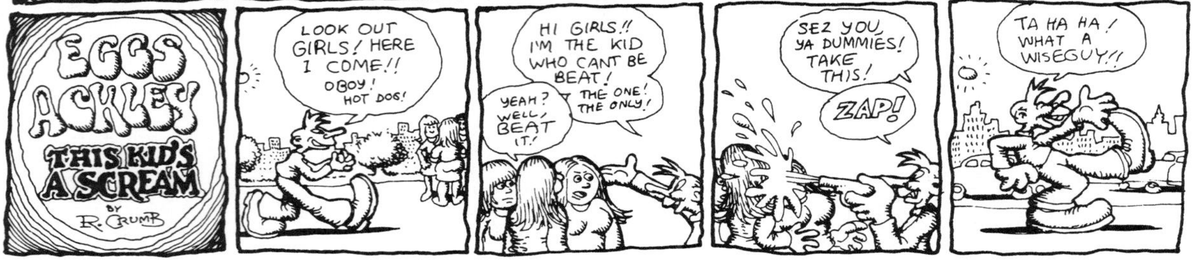
Eggs Ackley
This Kid's A Scream
by R. Crumb
LOOK OUT GIRLS! HERE I COME!! OBOY! HOT DOG!
HI GIRLS!! I'M THE KID WHO CAN'T BE BEAT! THE ONE! THE ONLY!
YEAH? WELL, BEAT IT!
SEZ YOU, YA DUMMIES! TAKE THIS!
ZAP!
TA HA HA! WHAT A WISEGUY!!

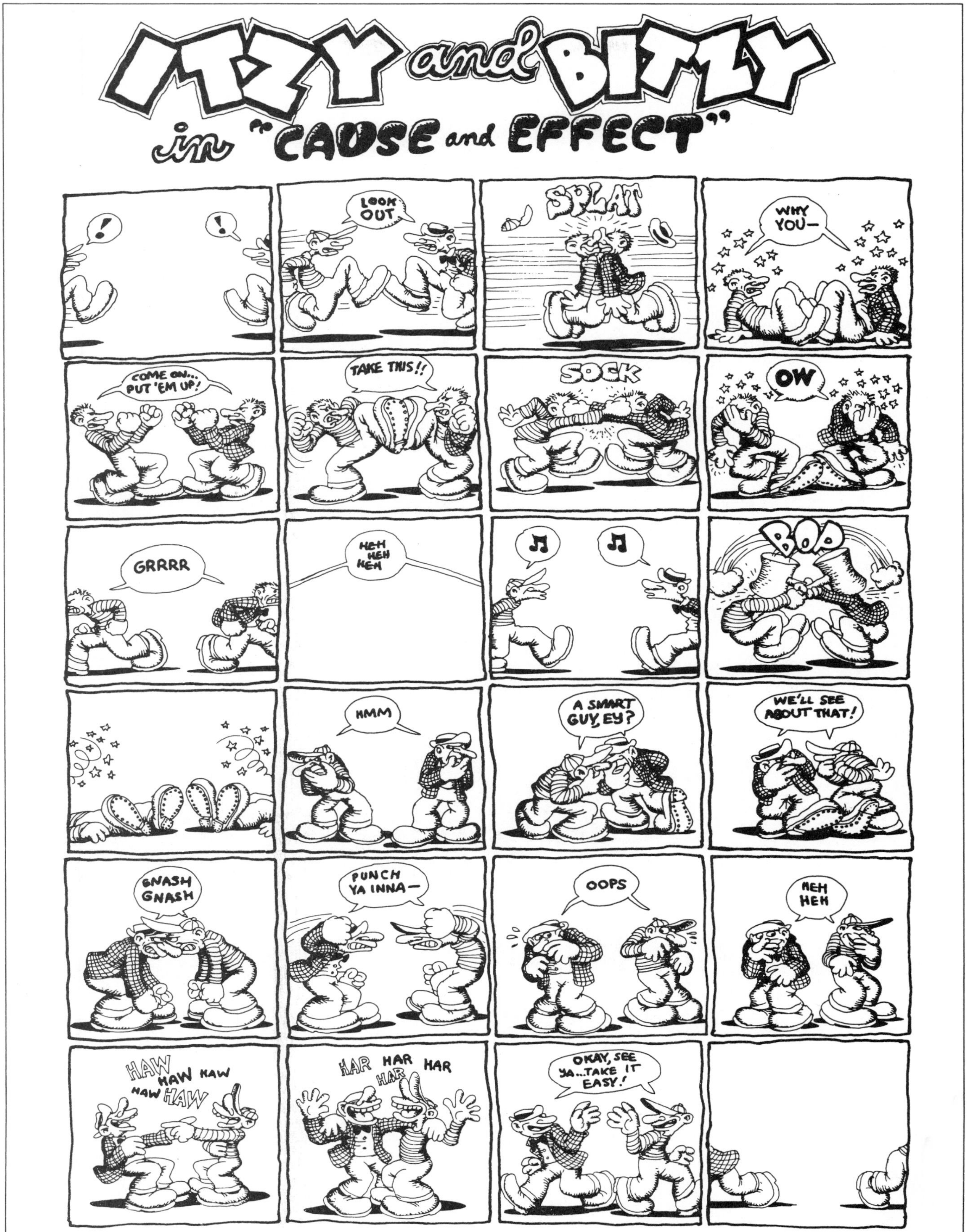
ITZY and BITZY
in "CAUSE and EFFECT"
!
!
LOOK OUT
SPLAT
WHY YOU—
COME ON... PUT 'EM UP!
TAKE THIS!!
SOCK
OW
GRRRR
HEH HEH HEH
♫
♫
BOP
HMM
A SMART GUY, EY?
WE'LL SEE ABOUT THAT!
GNASH GNASH
PUNCH YA INNA—
OOPS
HEH HEH
HAW HAW HAW HAW HAW
HAR HAR HAR HAR
OKAY, SEE YA...TAKE IT EASY!

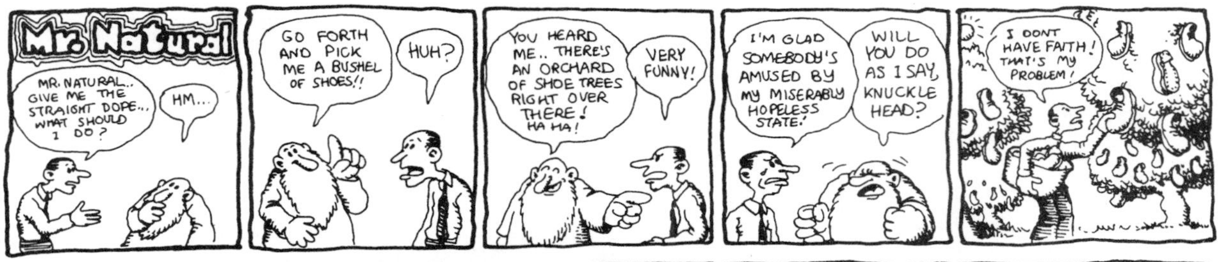
Mr. Natural
MR. NATURAL.. GIVE ME THE STRAIGHT DOPE... WHAT SHOULD I DO?
HM...
GO FORTH AND PICK ME A BUSHEL OF SHOES!!
HUH?
YOU HEARD ME.. THERE'S AN ORCHARD OF SHOE TREES RIGHT OVER THERE!
HA HA!
VERY FUNNY!
I'M GLAD SOMEBODY'S AMUSED BY MY MISERABLY HOPELESS STATE!
WILL YOU DO AS I SAY, KNUCKLE HEAD?
I DONT HAVE FAITH! THAT'S MY PROBLEM!

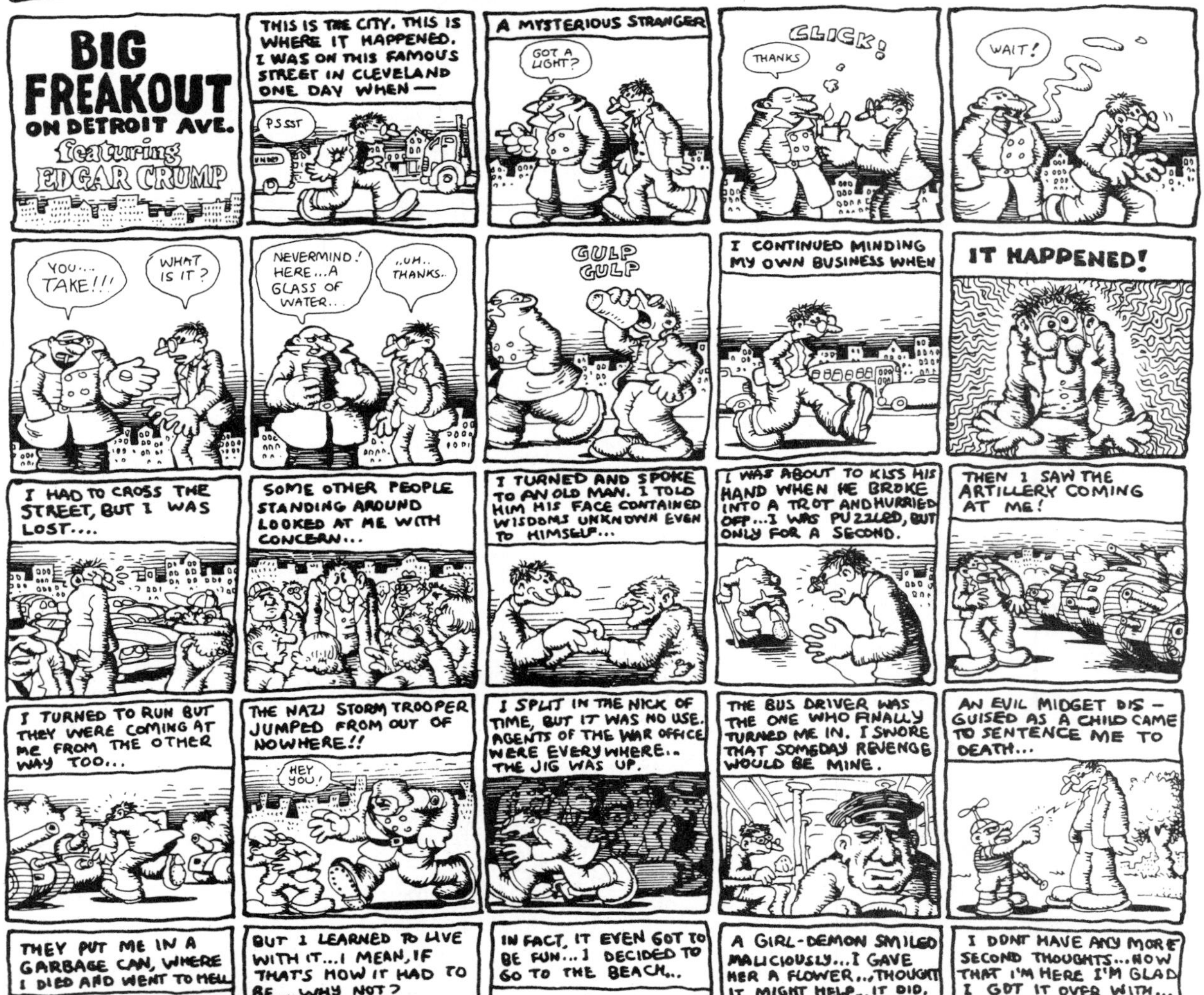
BIG FREAKOUT ON DETROIT AVE.
featuring EDGAR CRUMP
THIS IS THE CITY. THIS IS WHERE IT HAPPENED. I WAS ON THIS FAMOUS STREET IN CLEVELAND ONE DAY WHEN—
PSSST
A MYSTERIOUS STRANGER
GOT A LIGHT?
CLICK!
THANKS
WAIT!
YOU... TAKE!!!
WHAT IS IT?
NEVERMIND! HERE...A GLASS OF WATER...
..UH.. THANKS..
GULP GULP
I CONTINUED MINDING MY OWN BUSINESS WHEN
IT HAPPENED!
I HAD TO CROSS THE STREET, BUT I WAS LOST....
SOME OTHER PEOPLE STANDING AROUND LOOKED AT ME WITH CONCERN...
I TURNED AND SPOKE TO AN OLD MAN. I TOLD HIM HIS FACE CONTAINED WISDOMS UNKNOWN EVEN TO HIMSELF...
I WAS ABOUT TO KISS HIS HAND WHEN HE BROKE INTO A TROT AND HURRIED OFF...I WAS PUZZLED, BUT ONLY FOR A SECOND.
THEN I SAW THE ARTILLERY COMING AT ME!
I TURNED TO RUN BUT THEY WERE COMING AT ME FROM THE OTHER WAY TOO...
THE NAZI STORM TROOPER JUMPED FROM OUT OF NOWHERE!!
HEY YOU!
I SPLIT IN THE NICK OF TIME, BUT IT WAS NO USE. AGENTS OF THE WAR OFFICE WERE EVERYWHERE.. THE JIG WAS UP.
THE BUS DRIVER WAS THE ONE WHO FINALLY TURNED ME IN. I SWORE THAT SOMEDAY REVENGE WOULD BE MINE.
AN EVIL MIDGET DISGUISED AS A CHILD CAME TO SENTENCE ME TO DEATH...
THEY PUT ME IN A GARBAGE CAN, WHERE I DIED AND WENT TO HELL
BUT I LEARNED TO LIVE WITH IT...I MEAN, IF THAT'S HOW IT HAD TO BE...WHY NOT?
IN FACT, IT EVEN GOT TO BE FUN...I DECIDED TO GO TO THE BEACH...
A GIRL-DEMON SMILED MALICIOUSLY...I GAVE HER A FLOWER...THOUGHT IT MIGHT HELP...IT DID.
THANK YOU
I DONT HAVE ANY MORE SECOND THOUGHTS...NOW THAT I'M HERE I'M GLAD I GOT IT OVER WITH...

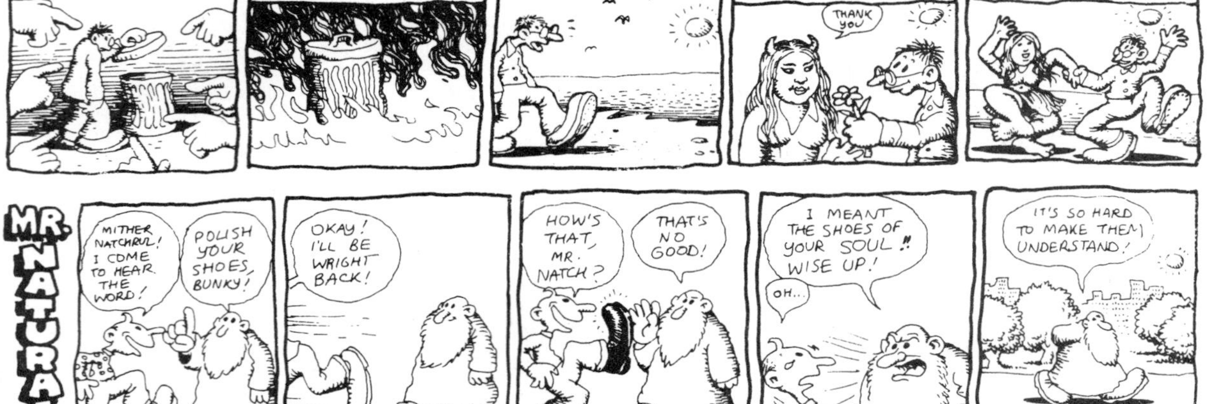
MR. NATURAL
MITHER NATCHRUL! I COME TO HEAR THE WORD!
POLISH YOUR SHOES, BUNKY!
OKAY! I'LL BE WRIGHT BACK!
HOW'S THAT, MR. NATCH?
THAT'S NO GOOD!
I MEANT THE SHOES OF YOUR SOUL!! WISE UP!
OH...
IT'S SO HARD TO MAKE THEM UNDERSTAND!

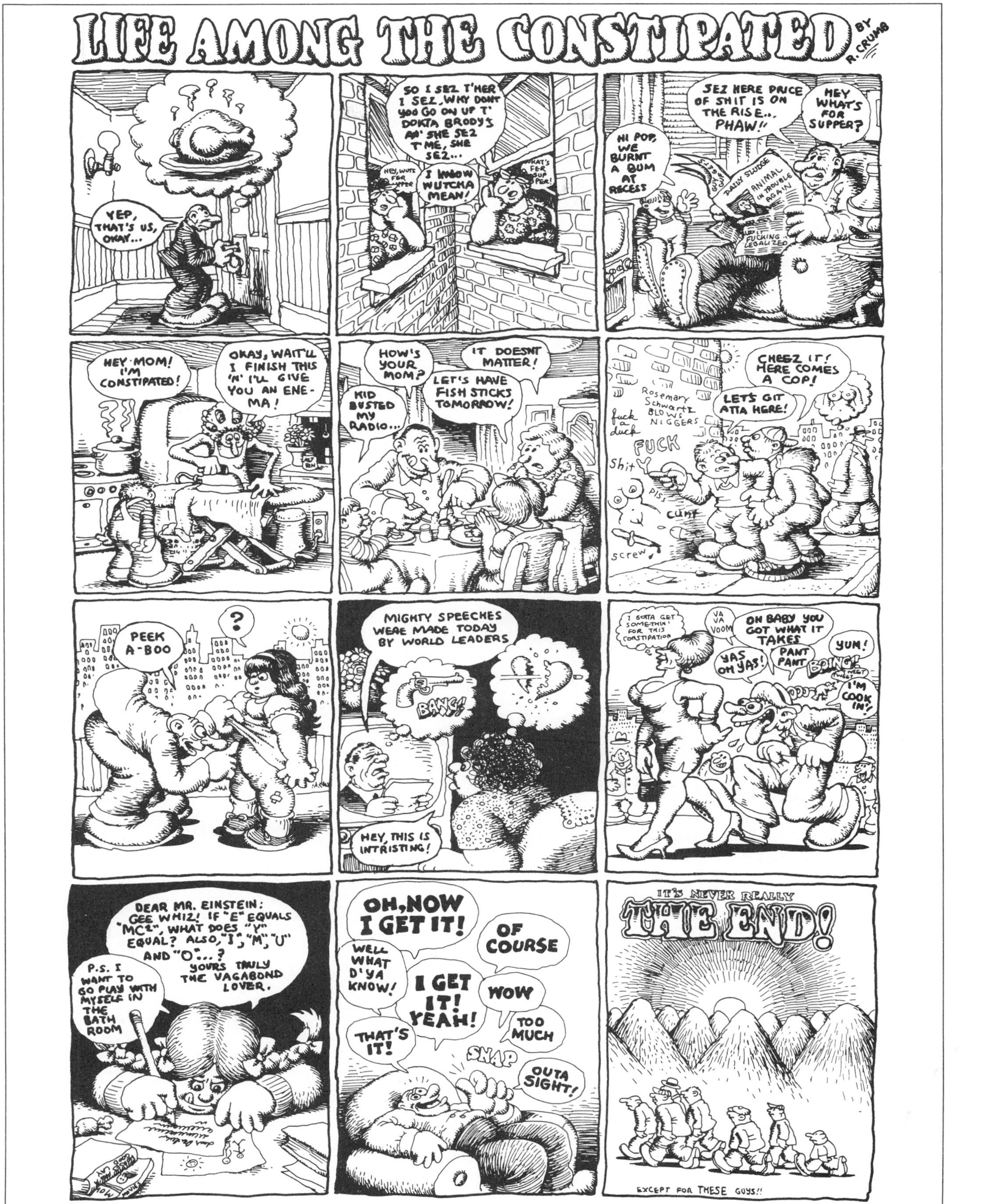
LIFE AMONG THE CONSTIPATED
BY R. CRUMB
YEP, THAT'S US, OKAY...
SO I SEZ T'HER I SEZ, WHY DONT YOU GO ON UP T' DOKTA BRODY'S AN' SHE SEZ T'ME, SHE SEZ...
HEY, WUTS FER SUPPER
I KNOW WUTCHA MEAN!
WHAT'S FER SUP PER!
SEZ HERE PRICE OF SHIT IS ON THE RISE... PHAW!!
HEY WHAT'S FOR SUPPER?
HI POP, WE BURNT A BUM AT RECESS
DAILY SLUDGE
ANIMAL IN TROUBLE AGAIN
FUCKING LEGALIZED
HEY MOM! I'M CONSTIPATED!
OKAY, WAIT'LL I FINISH THIS 'N' I'LL GIVE YOU AN ENE-MA!
HOW'S YOUR MOM?
IT DOESNT MATTER!
KID BUSTED MY RADIO...
LET'S HAVE FISH STICKS TOMORROW!
CHEEZ IT! HERE COMES A COP!
LET'S GIT ATTA HERE!
Rosemary Schwartz BLOWS NIGGERS
fuck a duck
FUCK
Shit
PISS
CUNT
screw
PEEK A-BOO
?
MIGHTY SPEECHES WERE MADE TODAY BY WORLD LEADERS
BANG!
HEY, THIS IS INTRISTING!
I GOTTA GET SOMETHIN' FOR THIS CONSTIPATION
VA VA VOOM
OH BABY YOU GOT WHAT IT TAKES
YAS OH YAS!
PANT PANT
YUM!
BOING!
TWEET TWEET
I'M COOK IN'!
DEAR MR. EINSTEIN: GEE WHIZ! IF "E" EQUALS "MC$^2$", WHAT DOES "Y" EQUAL? ALSO, "I", "M", "U" AND "O"...? YOURS TRULY THE VAGABOND LOVER.
P.S. I WANT TO GO PLAY WITH MYSELF IN THE BATH ROOM
OH, NOW I GET IT!
OF COURSE
WELL WHAT D'YA KNOW!
I GET IT! YEAH!
WOW
TOO MUCH
THAT'S IT!
SNAP
OUTA SIGHT!
IT'S NEVER REALLY THE END!
EXCEPT FOR THESE GUYS!!

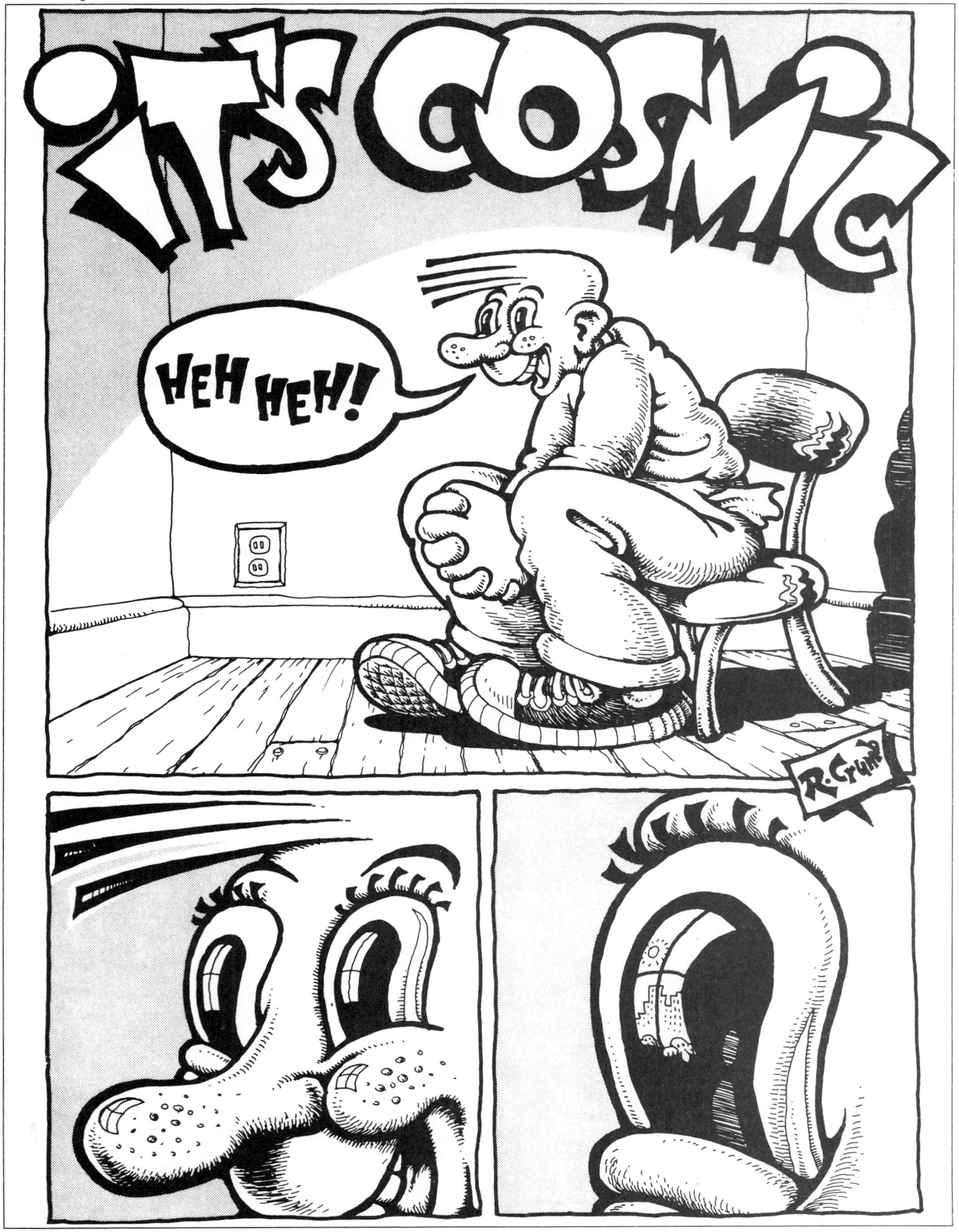
IT'S COSMIC
HEH HEH!
R. Crumb

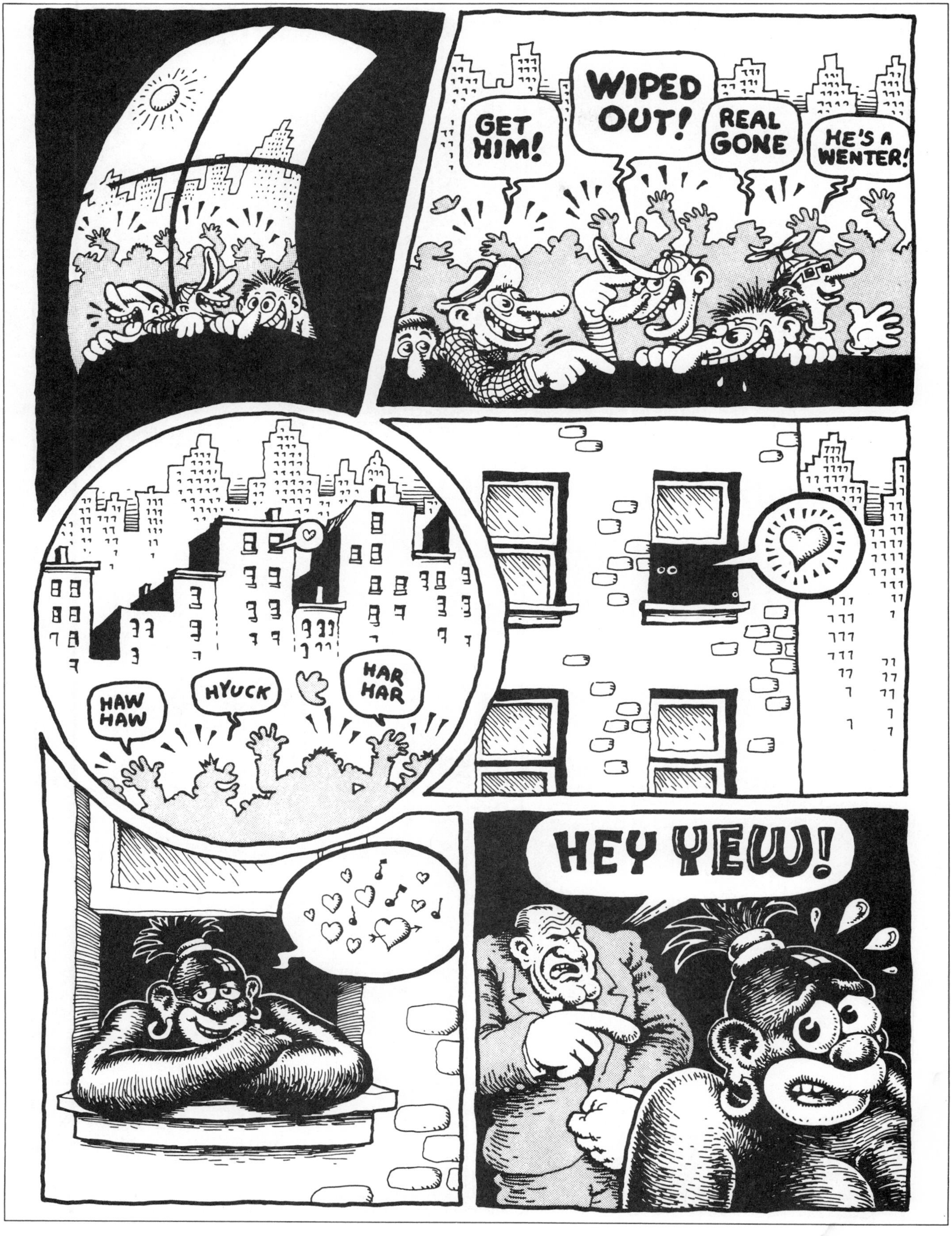
GET HIM!
WIPED OUT!
REAL GONE
HE'S A WENTER!
HAW HAW
HYUCK
HAR HAR
HEY YEW!

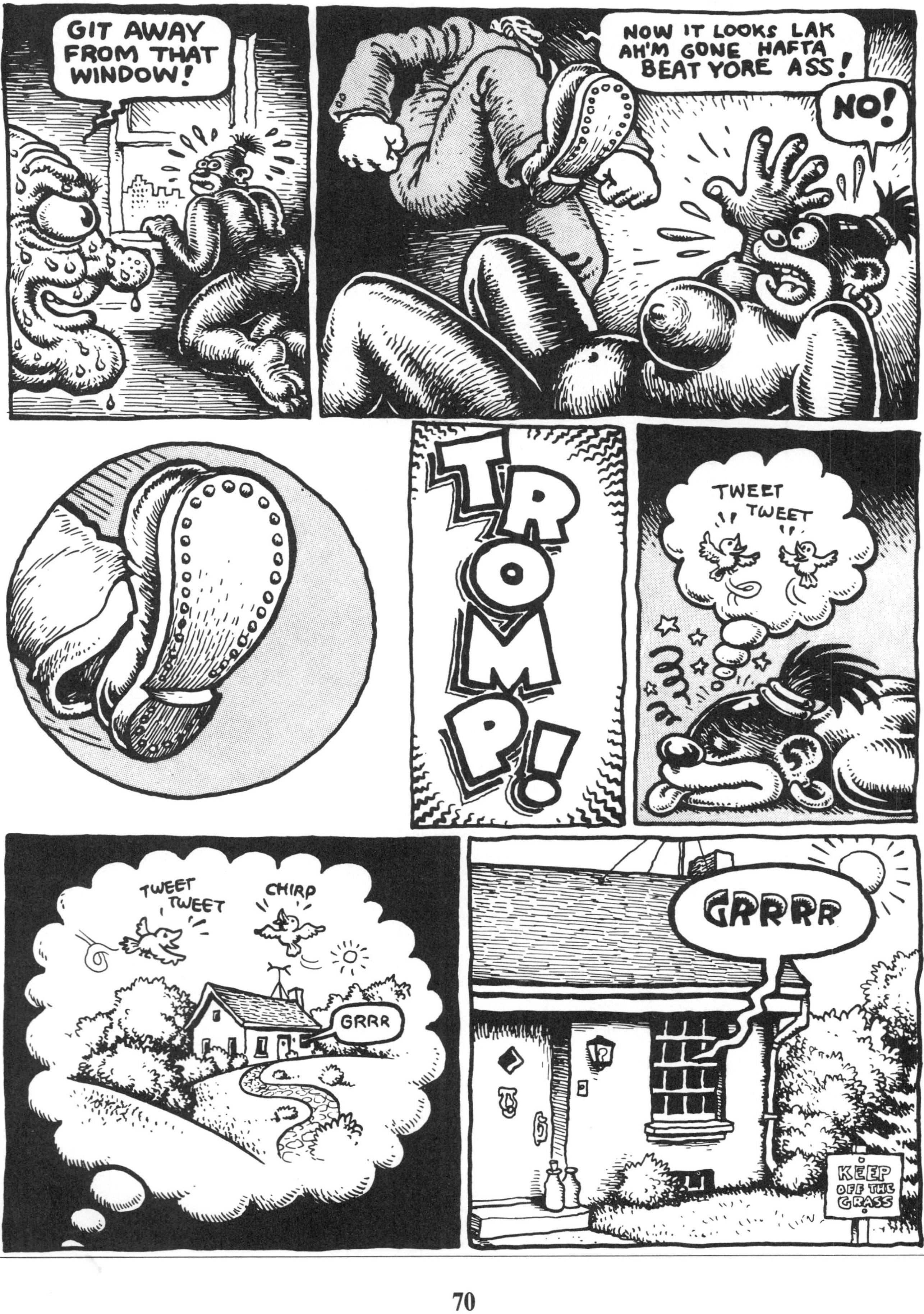
GIT AWAY FROM THAT WINDOW!
NOW IT LOOKS LAK AH'M GONE HAFTA BEAT YORE ASS!
NO!
TROMP!
TWEET TWEET
TWEET TWEET
CHIRP
GRRR
GRRRR
KEEP OFF THE GRASS

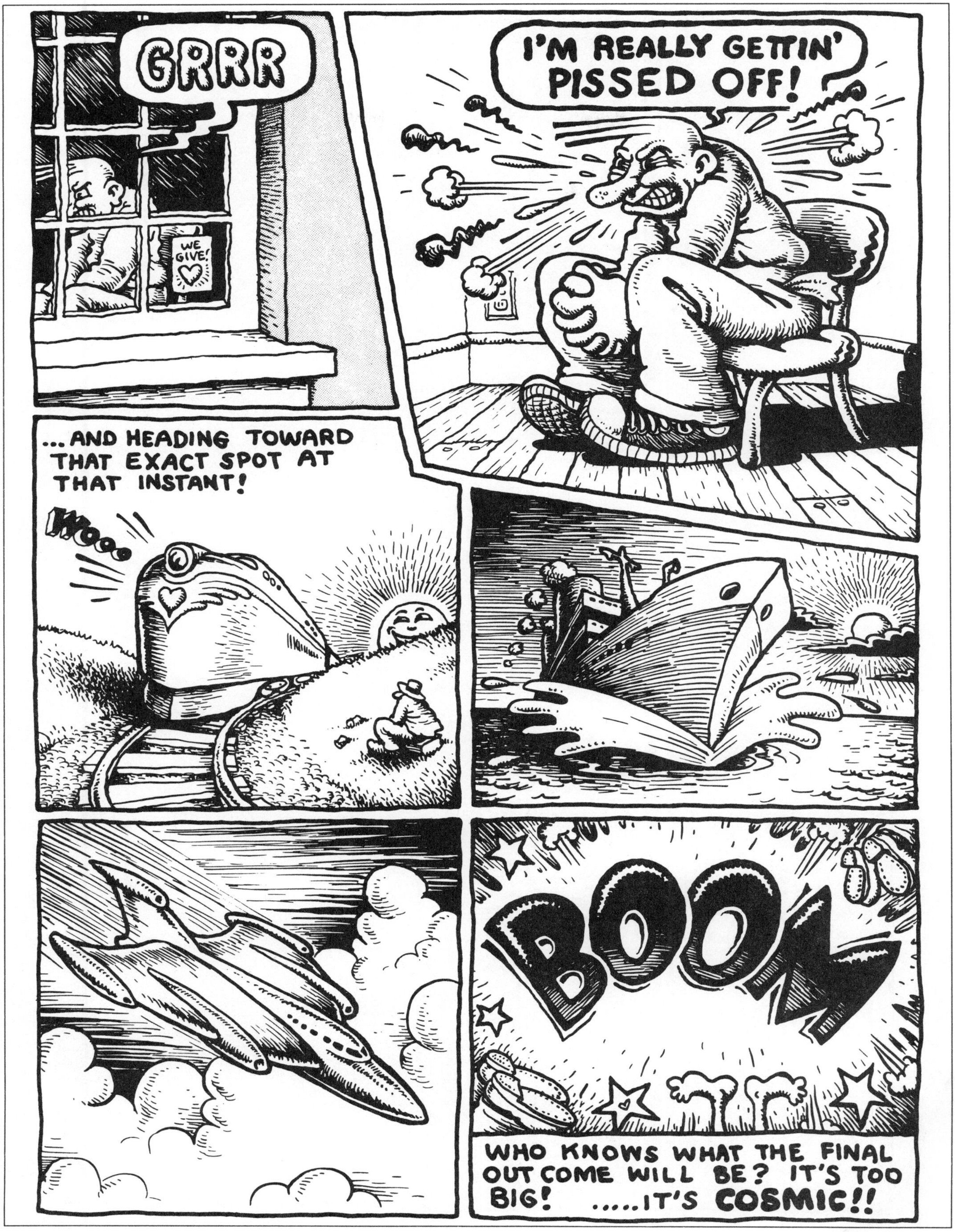
GRRR
WE GIVE!
I'M REALLY GETTIN' PISSED OFF!
...AND HEADING TOWARD THAT EXACT SPOT AT THAT INSTANT!
WOOO
BOOM
WHO KNOWS WHAT THE FINAL OUT COME WILL BE? IT'S TOO BIG! .....IT'S COSMIC!!

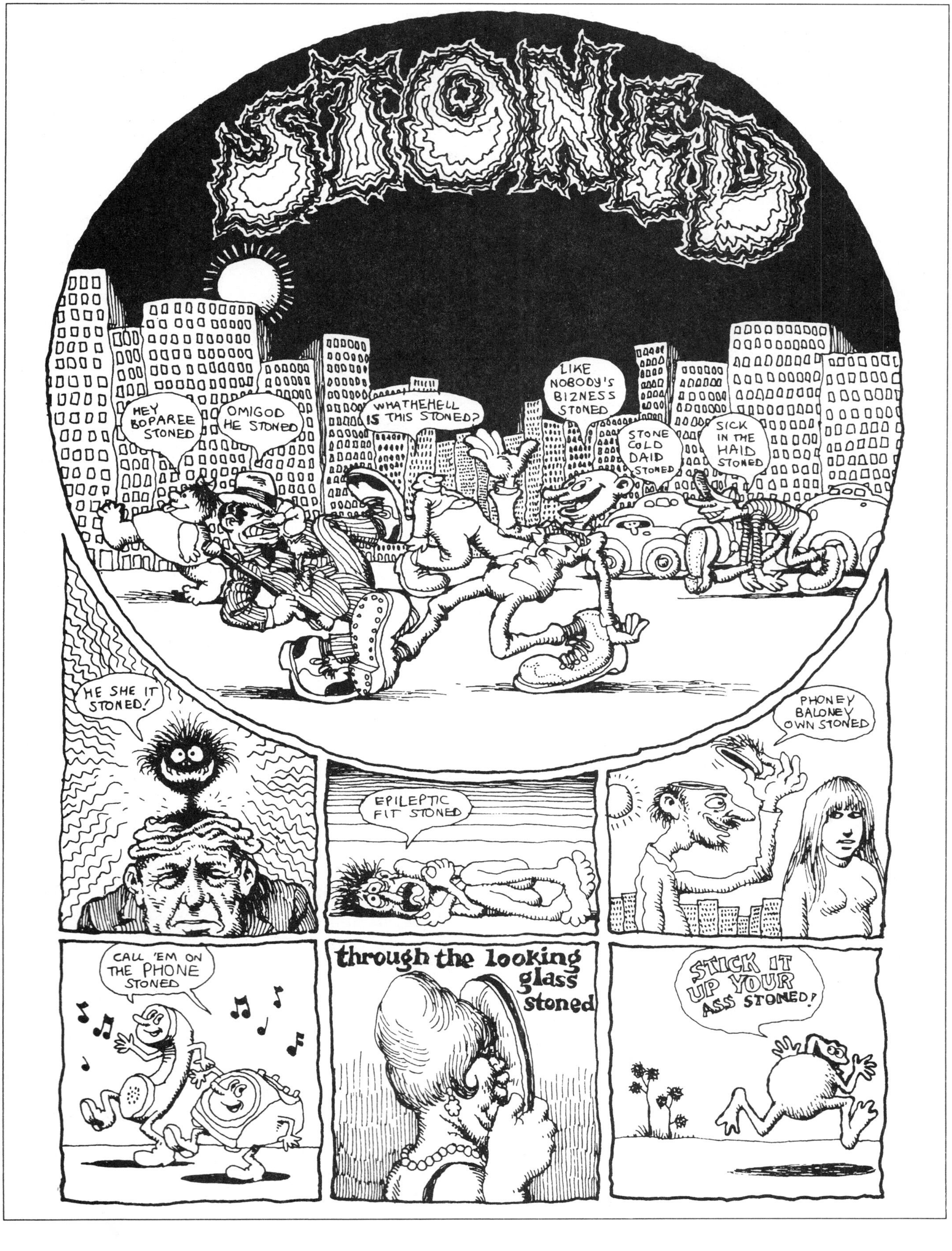
STONED
HEY BOPAREE STONED
OMIGOD HE STONED
WHATHEHELL IS THIS STONED?
LIKE NOBODY'S BIZNESS STONED
STONE COLD DAID STONED
SICK IN THE HAID STONED
HE SHE IT STONED!
EPILEPTIC FIT STONED
PHONEY BALONEY OWN STONED
CALL 'EM ON THE PHONE STONED
through the looking glass stoned
STICK IT UP YOUR ASS STONED!

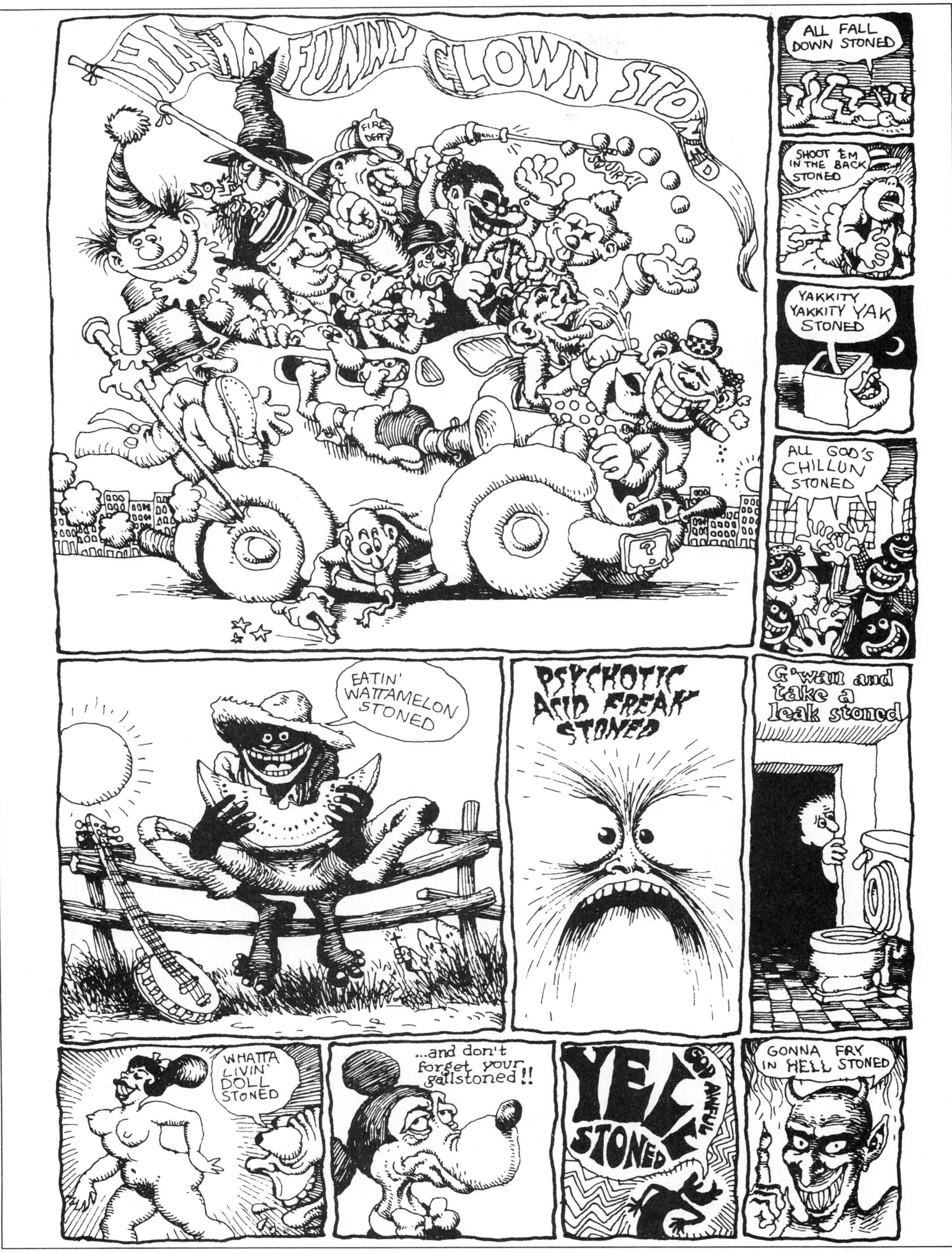
HA HA FUNNY CLOWN STONED
FIRE DEPT
SQUIRT
ALL FALL DOWN STONED
SHOOT 'EM IN THE BACK STONED
YAKKITY YAKKITY YAK STONED
ALL GOD'S CHILLUN STONED
EATIN' WATTAMELON STONED
PSYCHOTIC ACID FREAK STONED
G'wan and take a leak stoned
WHATTA LIVIN' DOLL STONED
...and don't forget your gallstoned!!
YEEE GOD AWFUL STONED
GONNA FRY IN HELL STONED

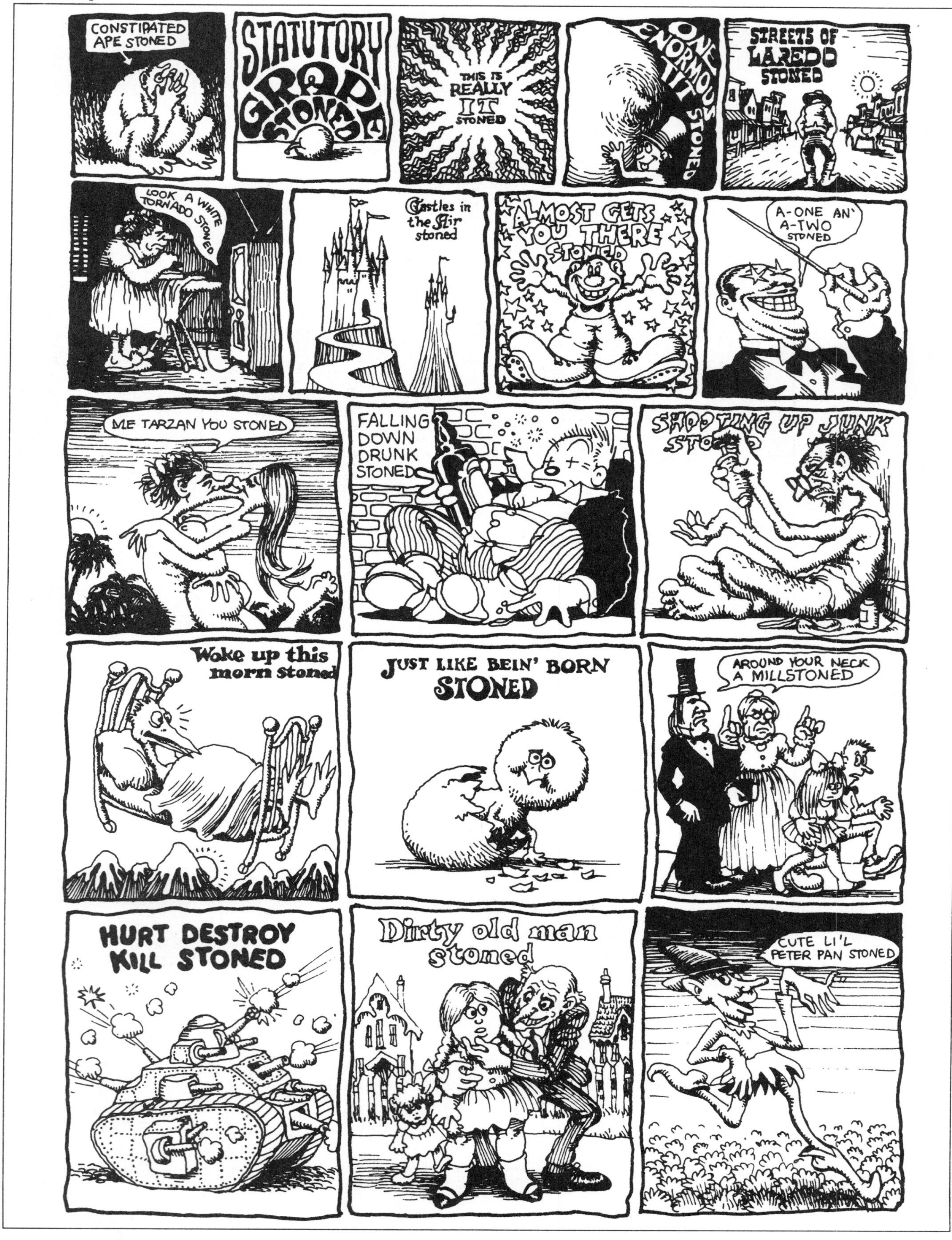
CONSTIPATED APE STONED
STATUTORY GRAPE STONED
THIS IS REALLY IT STONED
ONE ENORMOUS TIT STONED
STREETS OF LAREDO STONED
LOOK A WHITE TORNADO STONED
Castles in the Air stoned
ALMOST GETS YOU THERE STONED
A-ONE AN' A-TWO STONED
ME TARZAN YOU STONED
FALLING DOWN DRUNK STONED
SHOOTING UP JUNK STONED
Woke up this morn stoned
JUST LIKE BEIN' BORN STONED
AROUND YOUR NECK A MILLSTONED
HURT DESTROY KILL STONED
Dirty old man stoned
CUTE LI'L PETER PAN STONED

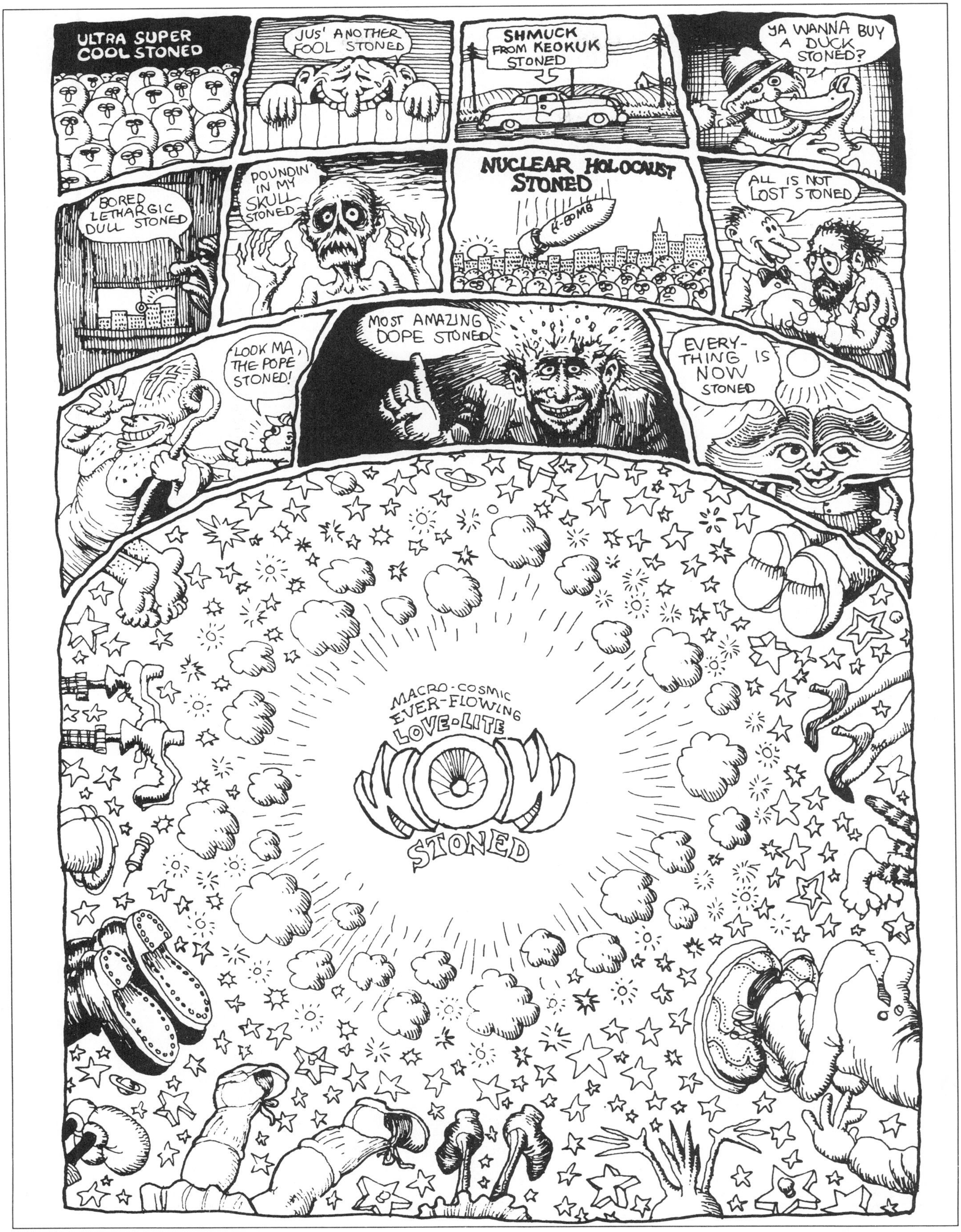
ULTRA SUPER COOL STONED
JUS' ANOTHER FOOL STONED
SHMUCK FROM KEOKUK STONED
YA WANNA BUY A DUCK STONED?
BORED LETHARGIC DULL STONED
POUNDIN' IN MY SKULL STONED
NUCLEAR HOLOCAUST STONED
H-BOMB
ALL IS NOT LOST STONED
LOOK MA, THE POPE STONED!
MOST AMAZING DOPE STONED
EVERY-THING IS NOW STONED
MACRO-COSMIC EVER-FLOWING LOVE-LITE STONED

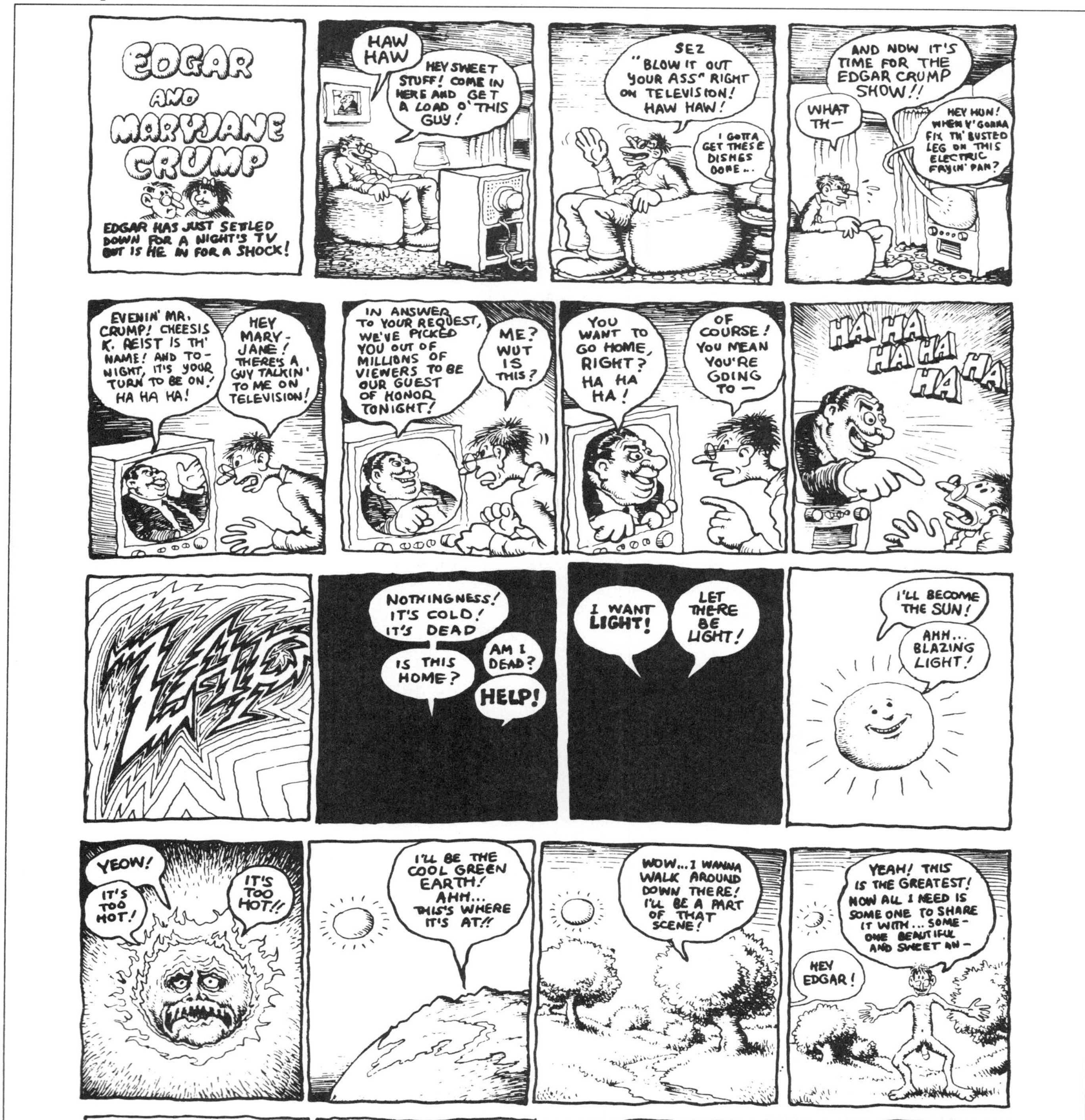
EDGAR AND MARYJANE CRUMP
EDGAR HAS JUST SETTLED DOWN FOR A NIGHT'S TV BUT IS HE IN FOR A SHOCK!
HAW HAW
HEY SWEET STUFF! COME IN HERE AND GET A LOAD O' THIS GUY!
SEZ "BLOW IT OUT YOUR ASS" RIGHT ON TELEVISION! HAW HAW!
I GOTTA GET THESE DISHES DONE..
AND NOW IT'S TIME FOR THE EDGAR CRUMP SHOW!!
WHAT TH—
HEY HUN! WHEN Y' GONNA FIX TH' BUSTED LEG ON THIS ELECTRIC FRYIN' PAN?
EVENIN' MR. CRUMP! CHEESIS K. REIST IS TH' NAME! AND TO-NIGHT, IT'S YOUR TURN TO BE ON! HA HA HA!
HEY MARY-JANE! THERE'S A GUY TALKIN' TO ME ON TELEVISION!
IN ANSWER TO YOUR REQUEST, WE'VE PICKED YOU OUT OF MILLIONS OF VIEWERS TO BE OUR GUEST OF HONOR TONIGHT!
ME? WUT IS THIS?
YOU WANT TO GO HOME, RIGHT? HA HA HA!
OF COURSE! YOU MEAN YOU'RE GOING TO—
HA HA HA HA HA HA
NOTHINGNESS! IT'S COLD! IT'S DEAD
IS THIS HOME?
AM I DEAD?
HELP!
I WANT LIGHT!
LET THERE BE LIGHT!
I'LL BECOME THE SUN!
AHH... BLAZING LIGHT!
YEOW!
IT'S TOO HOT!
IT'S TOO HOT!!
I'LL BE THE COOL GREEN EARTH! AHH... THIS'S WHERE IT'S AT!!
WOW... I WANNA WALK AROUND DOWN THERE! I'LL BE A PART OF THAT SCENE!
YEAH! THIS IS THE GREATEST! NOW ALL I NEED IS SOME ONE TO SHARE IT WITH... SOME-ONE BEAUTIFUL AND SWEET AN—
HEY EDGAR!
MARY JANE!
AIN'T LOVE GRAND!? LET'S MAKE BABIES AN' EAT HAM-BURGERS!
IS THIS HOME?
HEY HUN! I WANNA WATCH "STOLEN MOMENTS"!
YOU'RE DREAMIN' THIS WHOLE THING UP, EDGAR, BABY! HA HA HA HA
YEAH... SO THE JOKE'S ON ME!
HEY, I WANNA—
LET'S WATCH MRS. YAHOOTIE'S VEGETABLE WAGON... I WANNA SEE IF SHE EVER GOT HOME!
I'LL SETTLE IT... WE'LL WATCH MR. NATURAL!

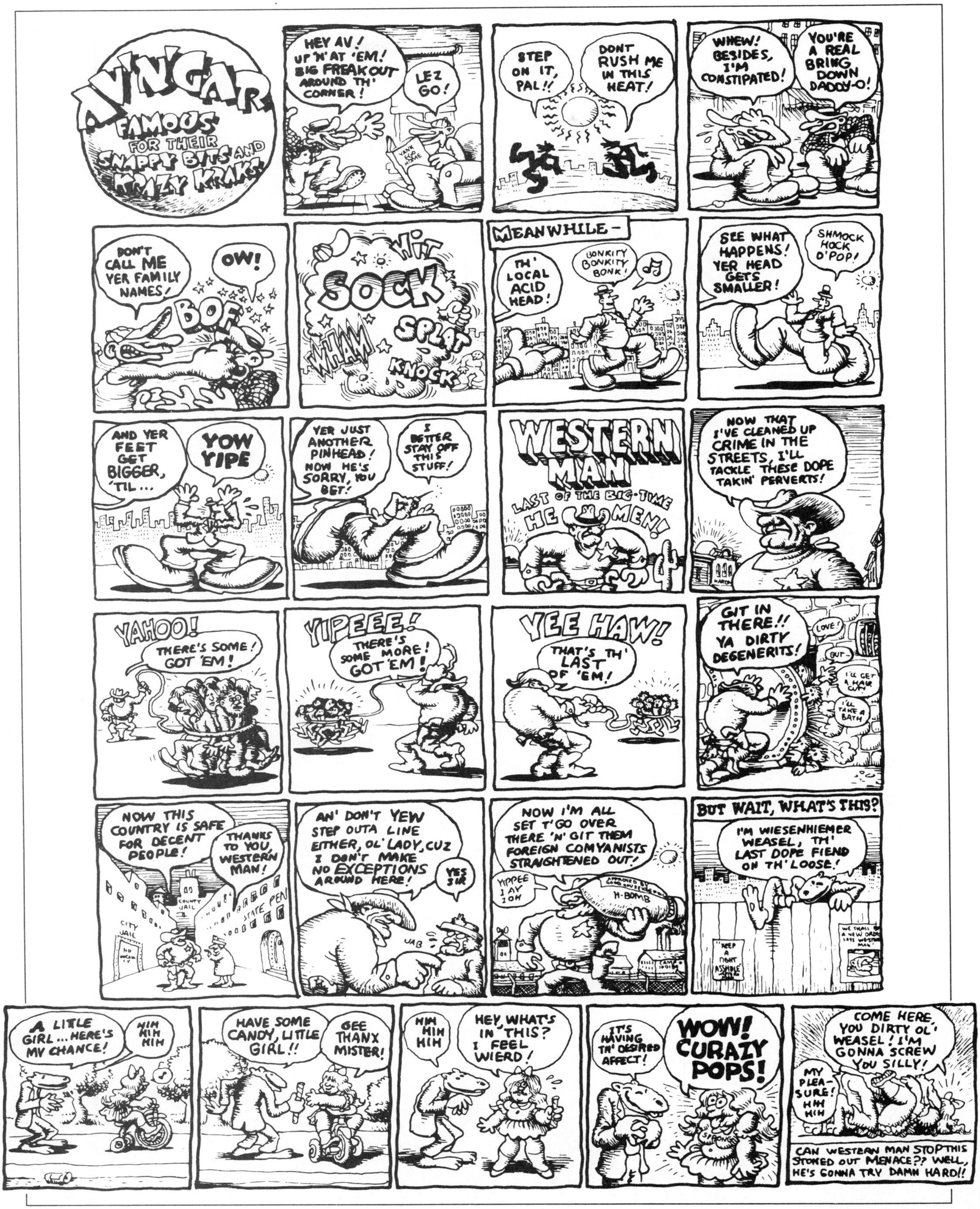
AV 'N' GAR
FAMOUS FOR THEIR SNAPPY BITS AND KRAZY KRAKS
HEY AV! UP 'N' AT 'EM! BIG FREAKOUT AROUND TH' CORNER!
LEZ GO!
STEP ON IT, PAL!!
DONT RUSH ME IN THIS HEAT!
WHEW! BESIDES, I'M CONSTIPATED!
YOU'RE A REAL BRING DOWN DADDY-O!
DON'T CALL ME YER FAMILY NAMES!
OW!
BOF
WHIT
SOCK
WHAM
SPLAT
KNOCK
MEANWHILE-
TH' LOCAL ACID HEAD!
BONKITY BONKITY BONK!
SEE WHAT HAPPENS! YER HEAD GETS SMALLER!
SHMOCK HOCK O'POP!
AND YER FEET GET BIGGER, 'TIL...
YOW YIPE
YER JUST ANOTHER PINHEAD! NOW HE'S SORRY, YOU BET!
I BETTER STAY OFF THIS STUFF!
WESTERN MAN
LAST OF THE BIG-TIME HE MEN!
NOW THAT I'VE CLEANED UP CRIME IN THE STREETS, I'LL TACKLE THESE DOPE TAKIN' PERVERTS!
YAHOO!
THERE'S SOME! GOT 'EM!
YIPEEE!
THERE'S SOME MORE! GOT 'EM!
YEE HAW!
THAT'S TH' LAST OF 'EM!
GIT IN THERE!! YA DIRTY DEGENERITS!
LOVE!
BUT-
I'LL GET A HAIR CUT
I'LL TAKE A BATH
NOW THIS COUNTRY IS SAFE FOR DECENT PEOPLE!
THANKS TO YOU, WESTERN MAN!
COUNTY JAIL
CITY JAIL
STATE PEN
AN' DON'T YEW STEP OUTA LINE EITHER, OL' LADY, CUZ I DON'T MAKE NO EXCEPTIONS AROUND HERE!
YES SIR
NOW I'M ALL SET T'GO OVER THERE 'N' GIT THEM FOREIGN COMYANISTS STRAIGHTENED OUT!
YIPPEE I AY IOH
H-BOMB
BUT WAIT, WHAT'S THIS?
I'M WIESENHIEMER WEASEL, TH' LAST DOPE FIEND ON TH' LOOSE!
"KEEP A TIGHT ASSHOLE"
A LITTLE GIRL... HERE'S MY CHANCE!
HIH HIH HIH
HAVE SOME CANDY, LITTLE GIRL!!
GEE THANX MISTER!
HIH HIH HIH
HEY, WHAT'S IN THIS? I FEEL WIERD!
IT'S HAVING TH' DESIRED AFFECT!
WOW! CURAZY POPS!
STRONG
COME HERE, YOU DIRTY OL' WEASEL! I'M GONNA SCREW YOU SILLY!
MY PLEA-SURE! HIH HIH
CAN WESTERN MAN STOP THIS STONED OUT MENACE?? WELL, HE'S GONNA TRY DAMN HARD!!

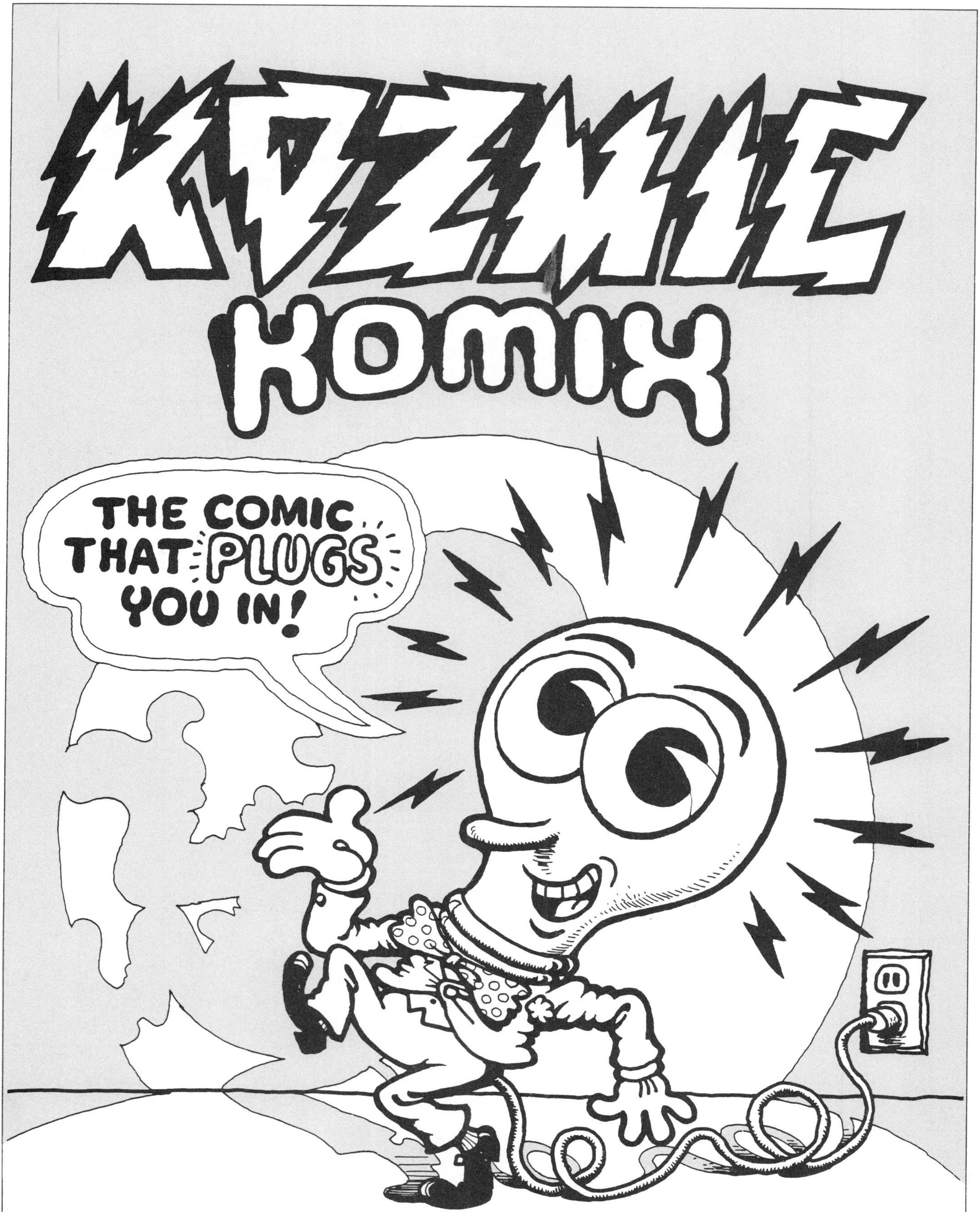
KOZMIC
KOMIX
THE COMIC THAT PLUGS YOU IN!

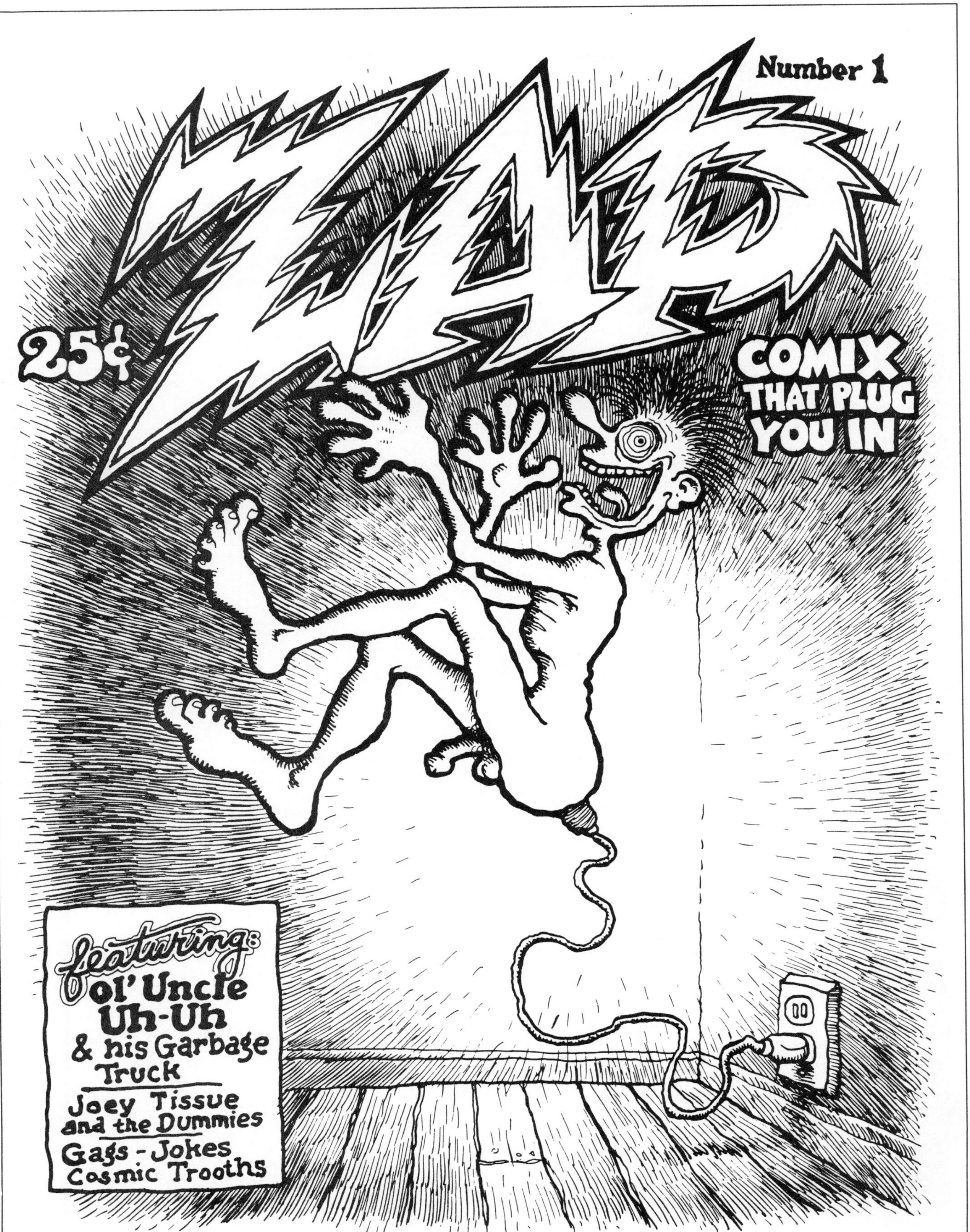
Number 1
ZAP
25¢
COMIX THAT PLUG YOU IN
featuring:
ol' Uncle Uh-Uh
& his Garbage Truck
Joey Tissue and the Dummies
Gags - Jokes
Cosmic Trooths

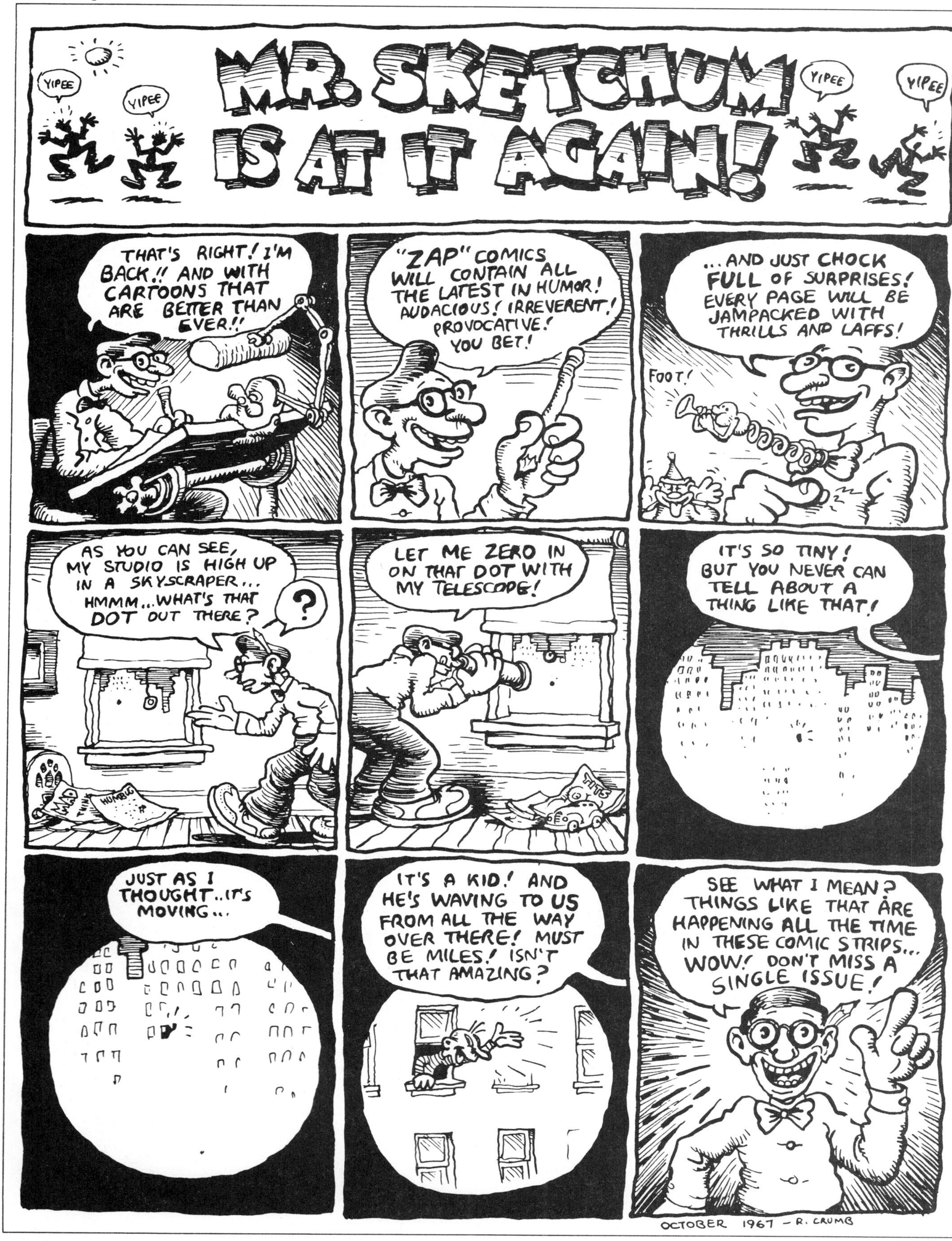
MR. SKETCHUM IS AT IT AGAIN!
YIPEE
YIPEE
YIPEE
YIPEE
THAT'S RIGHT! I'M BACK!! AND WITH CARTOONS THAT ARE BETTER THAN EVER!!
"ZAP" COMICS WILL CONTAIN ALL THE LATEST IN HUMOR! AUDACIOUS! IRREVERENT! PROVOCATIVE! YOU BET!
...AND JUST CHOCK FULL OF SURPRISES! EVERY PAGE WILL BE JAMPACKED WITH THRILLS AND LAFFS!
FOOT!
AS YOU CAN SEE, MY STUDIO IS HIGH UP IN A SKYSCRAPER... HMMM...WHAT'S THAT DOT OUT THERE?
?
MAD
HUMBUG
LET ME ZERO IN ON THAT DOT WITH MY TELESCOPE!
IT'S SO TINY! BUT YOU NEVER CAN TELL ABOUT A THING LIKE THAT!
JUST AS I THOUGHT..IT'S MOVING...
IT'S A KID! AND HE'S WAVING TO US FROM ALL THE WAY OVER THERE! MUST BE MILES! ISN'T THAT AMAZING?
SEE WHAT I MEAN? THINGS LIKE THAT ARE HAPPENING ALL THE TIME IN THESE COMIC STRIPS... WOW! DON'T MISS A SINGLE ISSUE!
OCTOBER 1967 - R. CRUMB

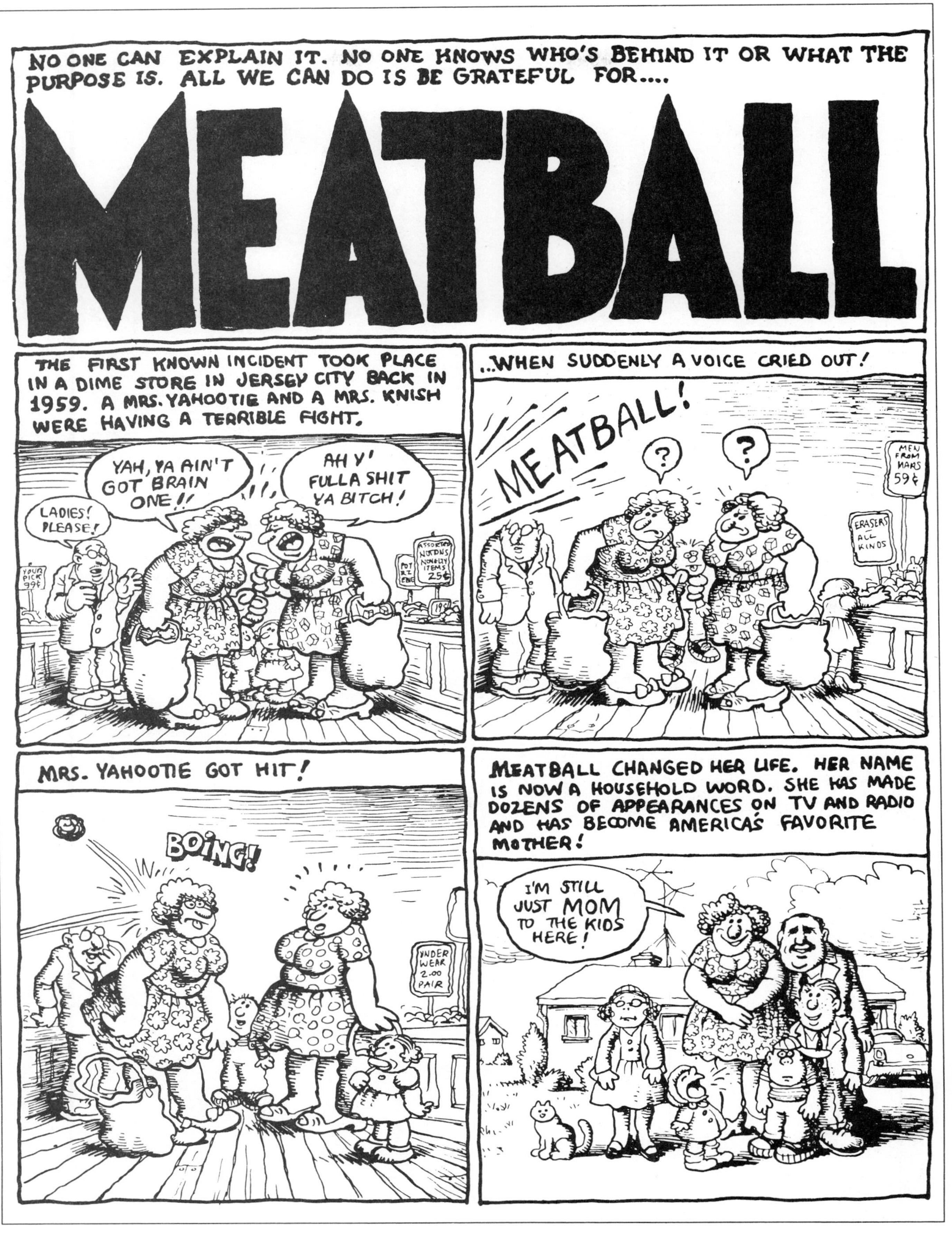
NO ONE CAN EXPLAIN IT. NO ONE KNOWS WHO'S BEHIND IT OR WHAT THE PURPOSE IS. ALL WE CAN DO IS BE GRATEFUL FOR....
MEATBALL
THE FIRST KNOWN INCIDENT TOOK PLACE IN A DIME STORE IN JERSEY CITY BACK IN 1959. A MRS. YAHOOTIE AND A MRS. KNISH WERE HAVING A TERRIBLE FIGHT.
LADIES! PLEASE!
YAH, YA AIN'T GOT BRAIN ONE!!
AH Y' FULLA SHIT YA BITCH!
YOUR PICK 99¢
25¢
...WHEN SUDDENLY A VOICE CRIED OUT!
MEATBALL!
?
?
MEN FROM MARS 59¢
ERASERS ALL KINDS
MRS. YAHOOTIE GOT HIT!
BOING!
UNDER WEAR 2.00 PAIR
MEATBALL CHANGED HER LIFE. HER NAME IS NOW A HOUSEHOLD WORD. SHE HAS MADE DOZENS OF APPEARANCES ON TV AND RADIO AND HAS BECOME AMERICA'S FAVORITE MOTHER!
I'M STILL JUST MOM TO THE KIDS HERE!

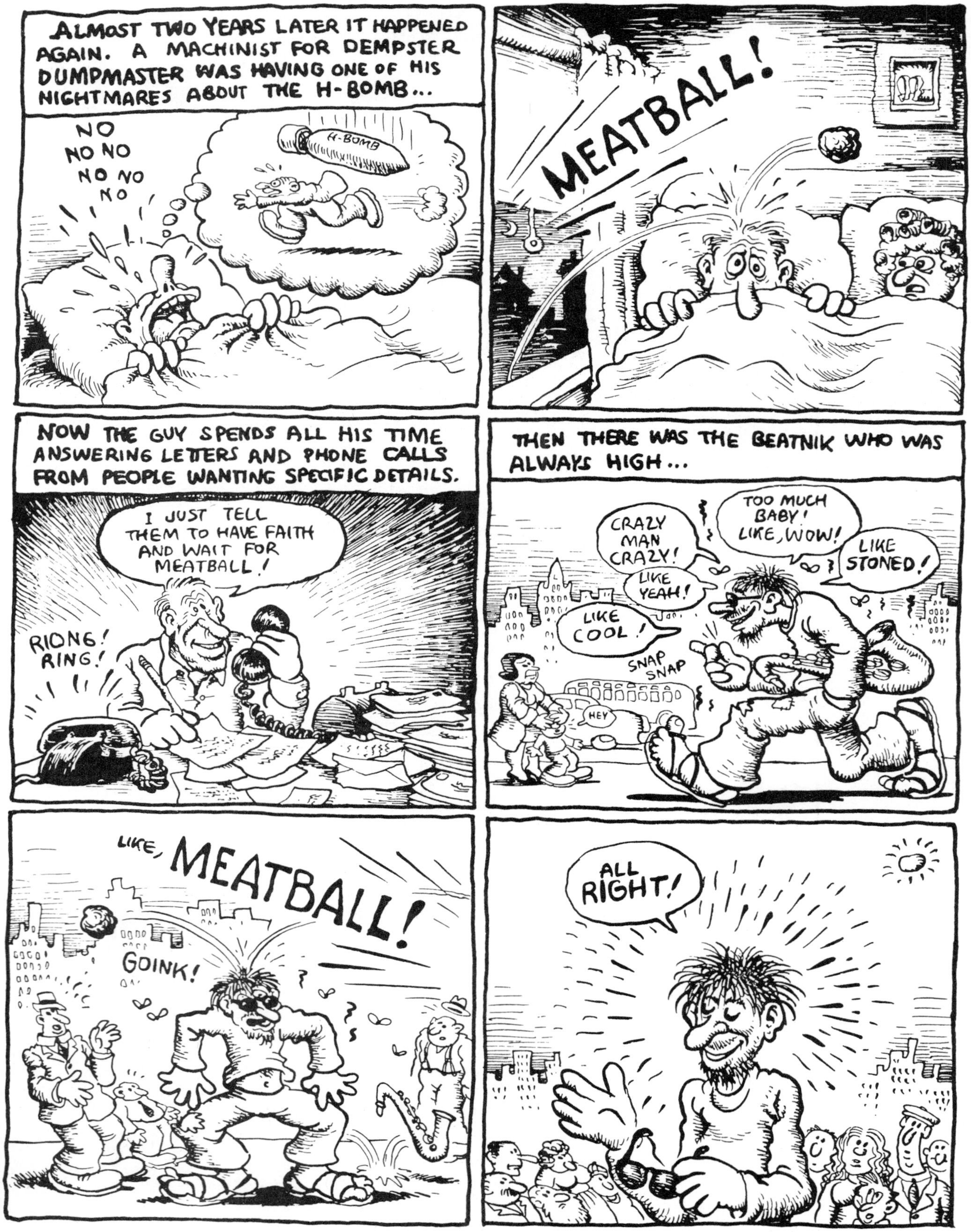
ALMOST TWO YEARS LATER IT HAPPENED AGAIN. A MACHINIST FOR DEMPSTER DUMPMASTER WAS HAVING ONE OF HIS NIGHTMARES ABOUT THE H-BOMB...
NO NO NO NO NO NO
H-BOMB
MEATBALL!
NOW THE GUY SPENDS ALL HIS TIME ANSWERING LETTERS AND PHONE CALLS FROM PEOPLE WANTING SPECIFIC DETAILS.
I JUST TELL THEM TO HAVE FAITH AND WAIT FOR MEATBALL!
RIONG! RING!
THEN THERE WAS THE BEATNIK WHO WAS ALWAYS HIGH...
CRAZY MAN CRAZY!
TOO MUCH BABY! LIKE, WOW!
LIKE STONED!
LIKE YEAH!
LIKE COOL!
SNAP SNAP
HEY
LIKE, MEATBALL!
GOINK!
ALL RIGHT!

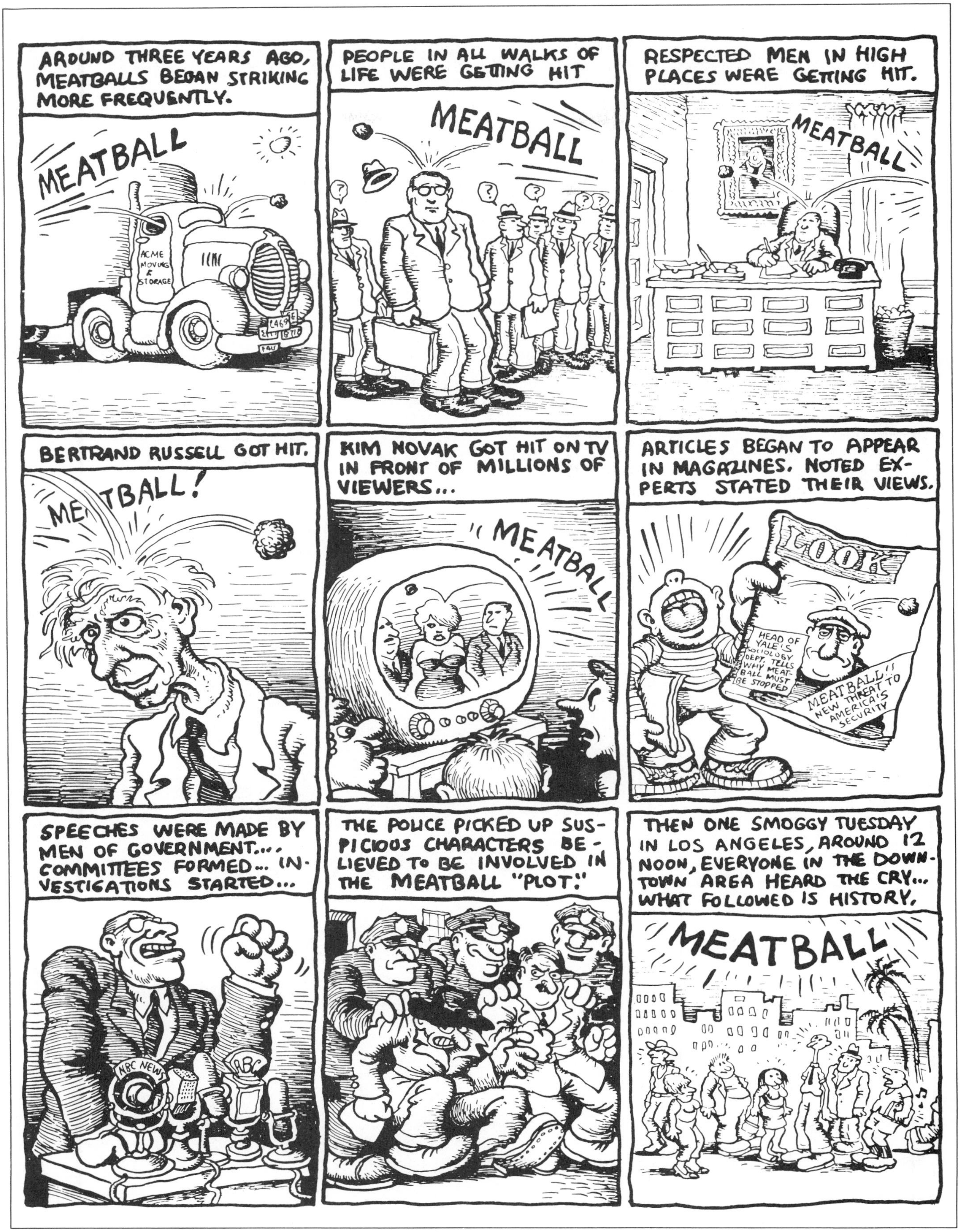
AROUND THREE YEARS AGO, MEATBALLS BEGAN STRIKING MORE FREQUENTLY.
MEATBALL
ACME MOVING & STORAGE
PEOPLE IN ALL WALKS OF LIFE WERE GETTING HIT
MEATBALL
?
?
?
??
RESPECTED MEN IN HIGH PLACES WERE GETTING HIT.
MEATBALL
BERTRAND RUSSELL GOT HIT.
MEATBALL!
KIM NOVAK GOT HIT ON TV IN FRONT OF MILLIONS OF VIEWERS...
MEATBALL
ARTICLES BEGAN TO APPEAR IN MAGAZINES. NOTED EXPERTS STATED THEIR VIEWS.
LOOK
HEAD OF YALE'S SOCIOLOGY DEPT. TELLS WHY MEATBALL MUST BE STOPPED
MEATBALL!! NEW THREAT TO AMERICA'S SECURITY
SPEECHES WERE MADE BY MEN OF GOVERNMENT.... COMMITTEES FORMED... INVESTIGATIONS STARTED...
NBC NEWS
ABC
THE POLICE PICKED UP SUSPICIOUS CHARACTERS BELIEVED TO BE INVOLVED IN THE MEATBALL "PLOT."
THEN ONE SMOGGY TUESDAY IN LOS ANGELES, AROUND 12 NOON, EVERYONE IN THE DOWNTOWN AREA HEARD THE CRY... WHAT FOLLOWED IS HISTORY.
MEATBALL

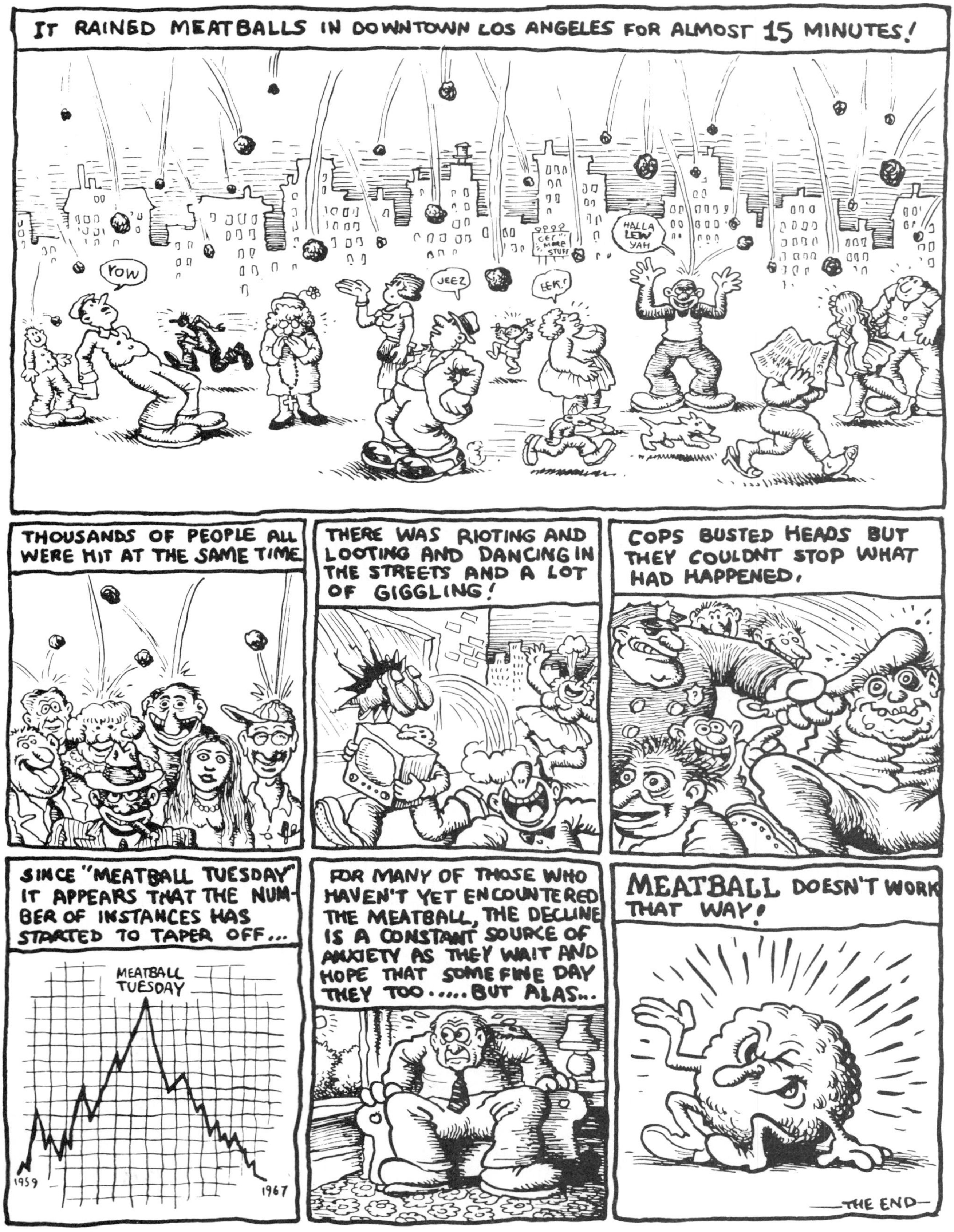
IT RAINED MEATBALLS IN DOWNTOWN LOS ANGELES FOR ALMOST 15 MINUTES!
YOW
JEEZ
EEK!
GET MORE STUFF
HALLA LEW YAH
THOUSANDS OF PEOPLE ALL WERE HIT AT THE SAME TIME.
THERE WAS RIOTING AND LOOTING AND DANCING IN THE STREETS AND A LOT OF GIGGLING!
COPS BUSTED HEADS BUT THEY COULDNT STOP WHAT HAD HAPPENED.
SINCE "MEATBALL TUESDAY" IT APPEARS THAT THE NUMBER OF INSTANCES HAS STARTED TO TAPER OFF...
MEATBALL TUESDAY
1959
1967
FOR MANY OF THOSE WHO HAVEN'T YET ENCOUNTERED THE MEATBALL, THE DECLINE IS A CONSTANT SOURCE OF ANXIETY AS THEY WAIT AND HOPE THAT SOME FINE DAY THEY TOO..... BUT ALAS...
MEATBALL DOESN'T WORK THAT WAY!
—THE END—

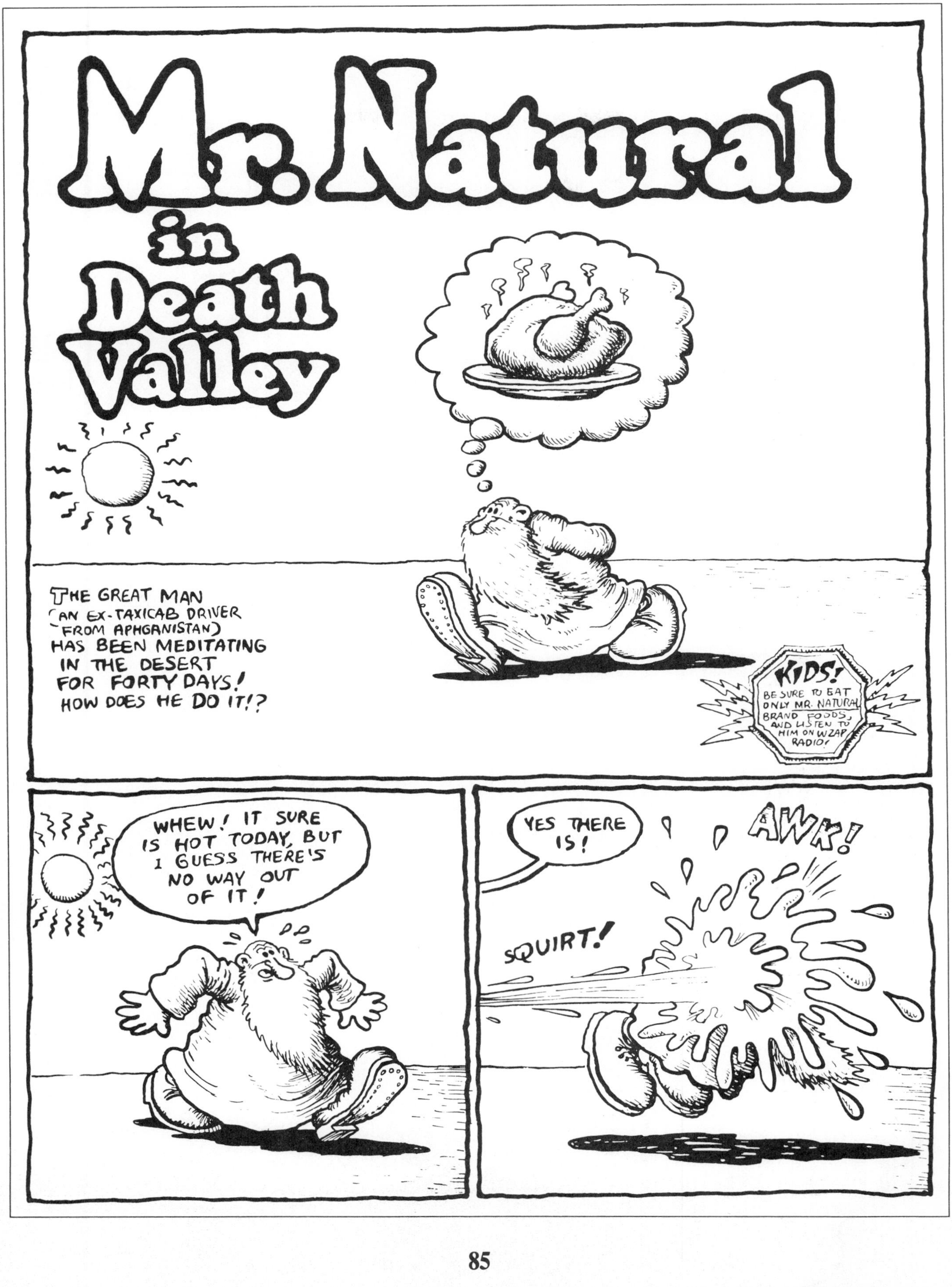
Mr. Natural
in Death Valley
THE GREAT MAN (AN EX-TAXICAB DRIVER FROM APHGANISTAN) HAS BEEN MEDITATING IN THE DESERT FOR FORTY DAYS! HOW DOES HE DO IT!?
KIDS! BE SURE TO EAT ONLY MR. NATURAL BRAND FOODS, AND LISTEN TO HIM ON WZAP RADIO!
WHEW! IT SURE IS HOT TODAY, BUT I GUESS THERE'S NO WAY OUT OF IT!
YES THERE IS!
AWK!
SQUIRT!

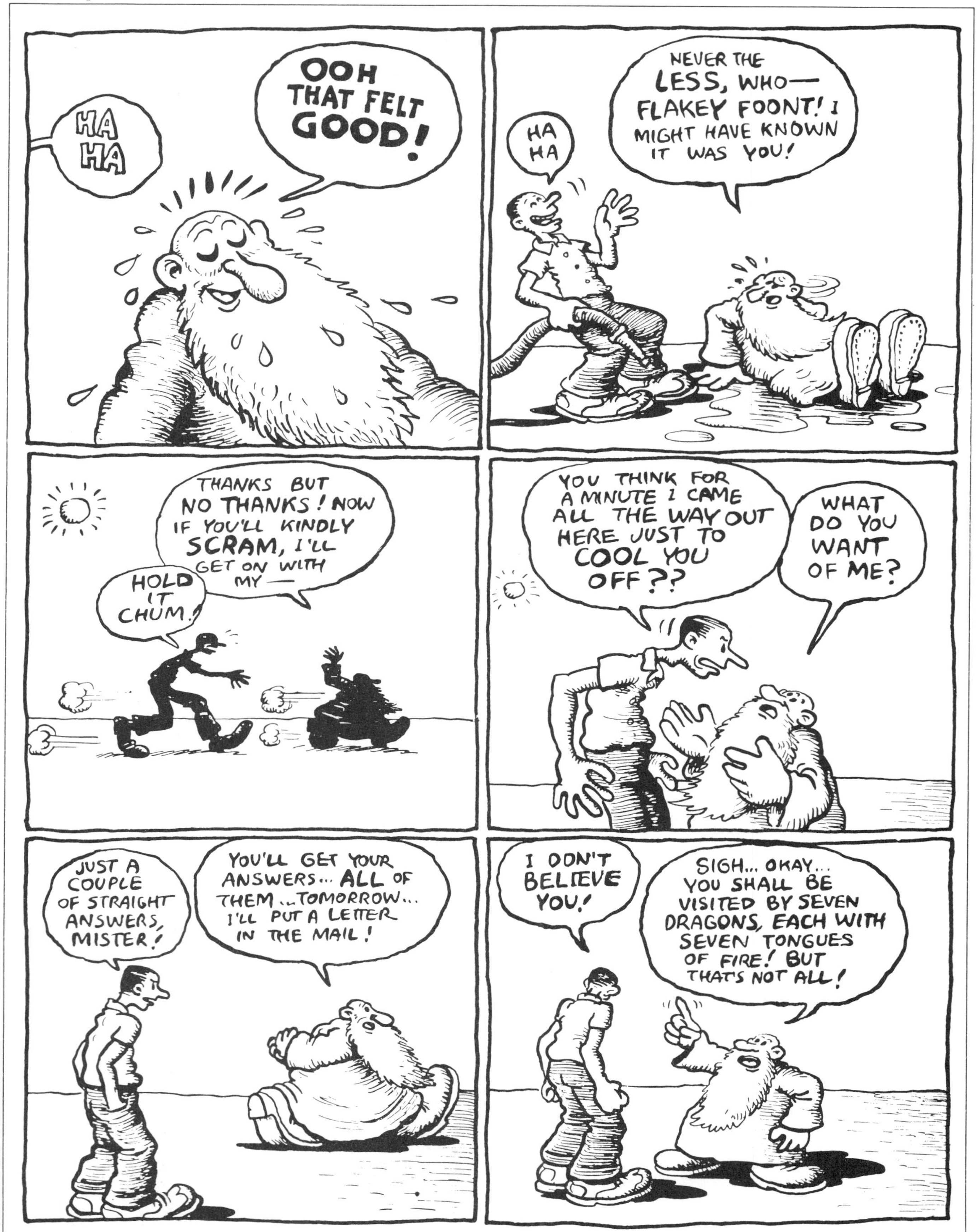
HA HA
OOH THAT FELT GOOD!
HA HA
NEVER THE LESS, WHO— FLAKEY FOONT! I MIGHT HAVE KNOWN IT WAS YOU!
THANKS BUT NO THANKS! NOW IF YOU'LL KINDLY SCRAM, I'LL GET ON WITH MY—
HOLD IT CHUM!
YOU THINK FOR A MINUTE I CAME ALL THE WAY OUT HERE JUST TO COOL YOU OFF??
WHAT DO YOU WANT OF ME?
JUST A COUPLE OF STRAIGHT ANSWERS, MISTER!
YOU'LL GET YOUR ANSWERS... ALL OF THEM...TOMORROW... I'LL PUT A LETTER IN THE MAIL!
I DON'T BELIEVE YOU!
SIGH... OKAY... YOU SHALL BE VISITED BY SEVEN DRAGONS, EACH WITH SEVEN TONGUES OF FIRE! BUT THAT'S NOT ALL!

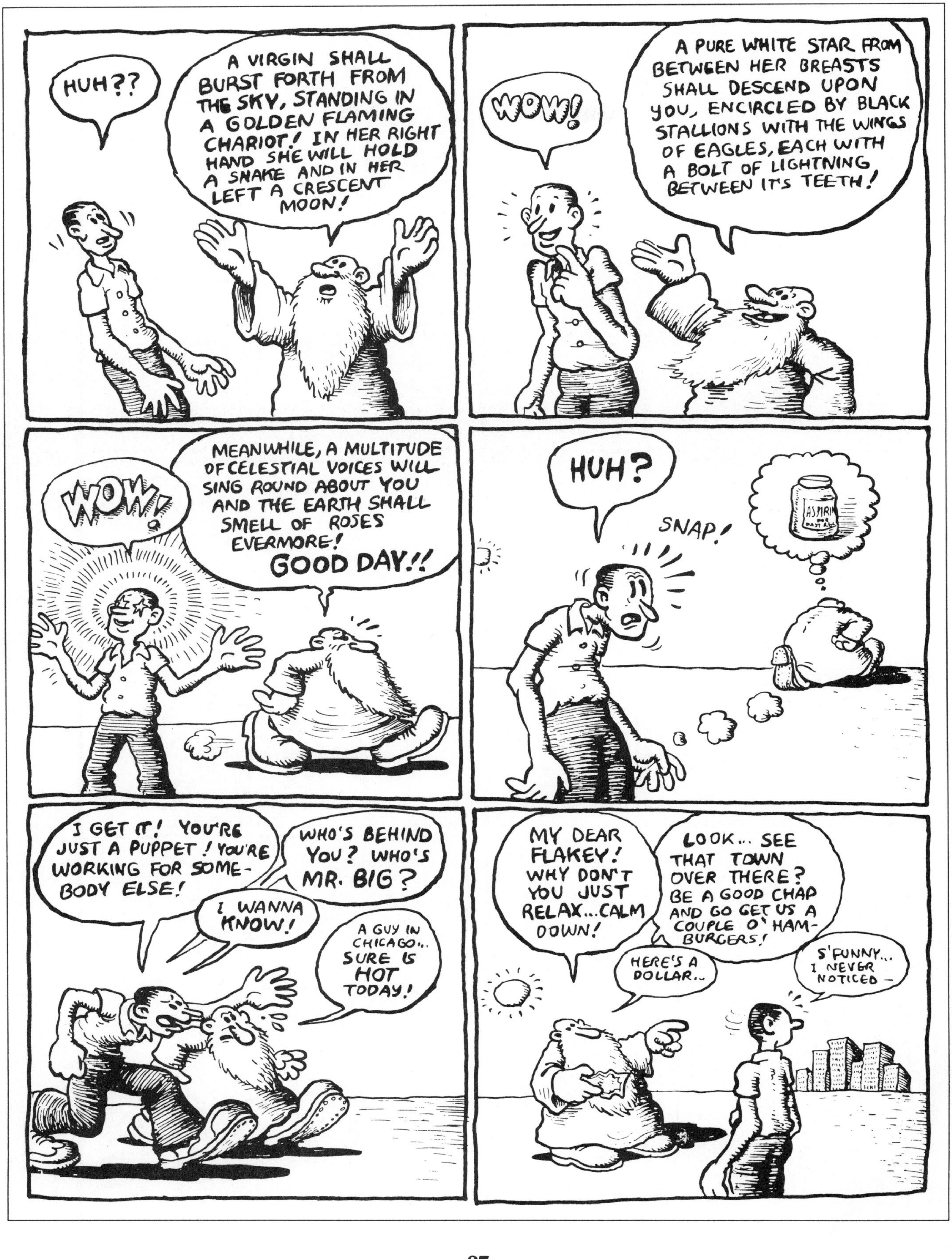
HUH??
A VIRGIN SHALL BURST FORTH FROM THE SKY, STANDING IN A GOLDEN FLAMING CHARIOT! IN HER RIGHT HAND SHE WILL HOLD A SNAKE AND IN HER LEFT A CRESCENT MOON!
WOW!
A PURE WHITE STAR FROM BETWEEN HER BREASTS SHALL DESCEND UPON YOU, ENCIRCLED BY BLACK STALLIONS WITH THE WINGS OF EAGLES, EACH WITH A BOLT OF LIGHTNING BETWEEN IT'S TEETH!
WOW!
MEANWHILE, A MULTITUDE OF CELESTIAL VOICES WILL SING ROUND ABOUT YOU AND THE EARTH SHALL SMELL OF ROSES EVERMORE! GOOD DAY!!
HUH?
SNAP!
ASPIRIN
I GET IT! YOU'RE JUST A PUPPET! YOU'RE WORKING FOR SOMEBODY ELSE!
WHO'S BEHIND YOU? WHO'S MR. BIG?
I WANNA KNOW!
A GUY IN CHICAGO.. SURE IS HOT TODAY!
MY DEAR FLAKEY! WHY DON'T YOU JUST RELAX...CALM DOWN!
LOOK... SEE THAT TOWN OVER THERE? BE A GOOD CHAP AND GO GET US A COUPLE O' HAMBURGERS!
HERE'S A DOLLAR...
S'FUNNY... I NEVER NOTICED —

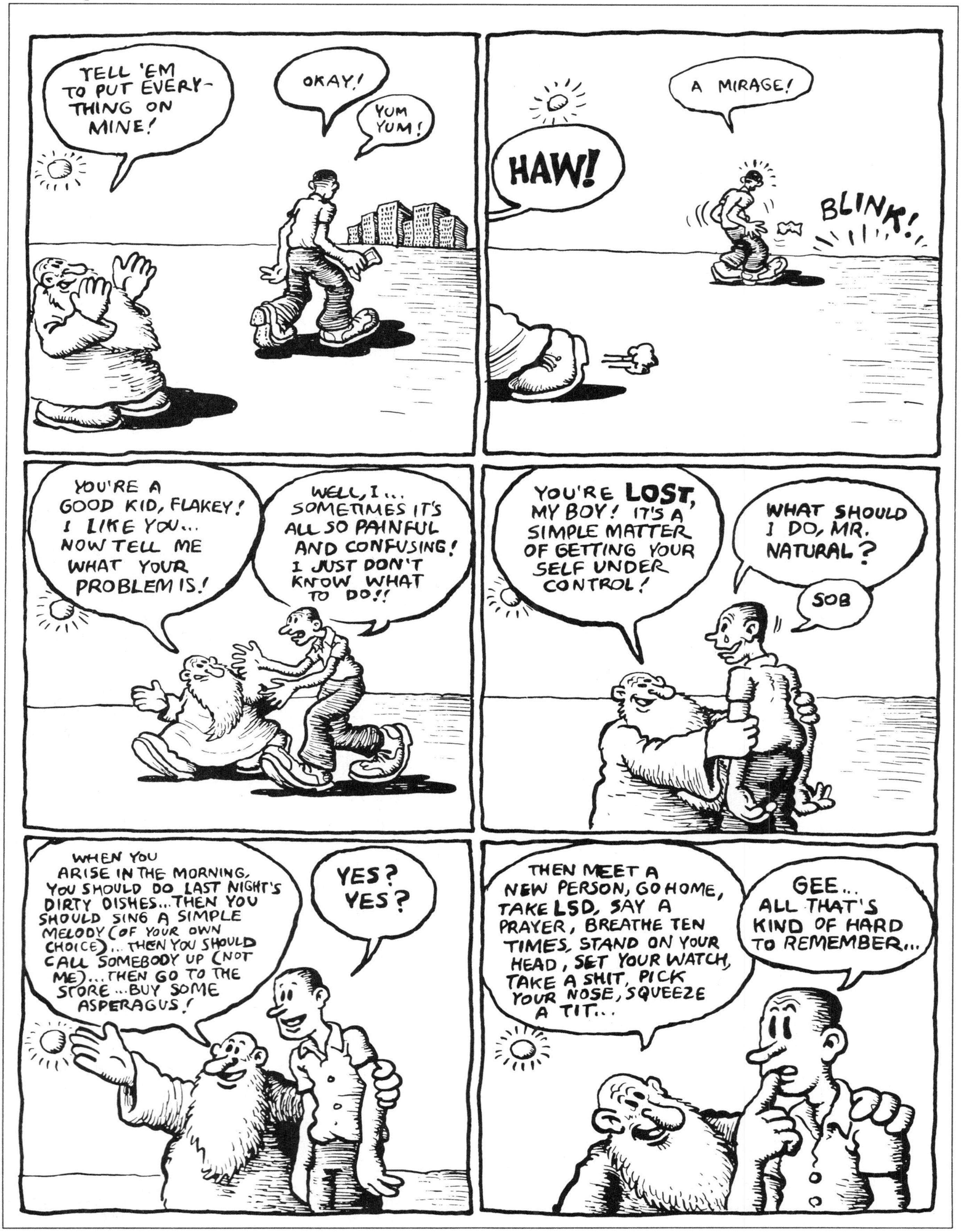
TELL 'EM TO PUT EVERY-THING ON MINE!
OKAY!
YUM YUM!
A MIRAGE!
HAW!
BLINK!
YOU'RE A GOOD KID, FLAKEY! I LIKE YOU... NOW TELL ME WHAT YOUR PROBLEM IS!
WELL, I... SOMETIMES IT'S ALL SO PAINFUL AND CONFUSING! I JUST DON'T KNOW WHAT TO DO!!
YOU'RE LOST, MY BOY! IT'S A SIMPLE MATTER OF GETTING YOUR SELF UNDER CONTROL!
WHAT SHOULD I DO, MR. NATURAL?
SOB
WHEN YOU ARISE IN THE MORNING, YOU SHOULD DO LAST NIGHT'S DIRTY DISHES... THEN YOU SHOULD SING A SIMPLE MELODY (OF YOUR OWN CHOICE)... THEN YOU SHOULD CALL SOMEBODY UP (NOT ME)... THEN GO TO THE STORE... BUY SOME ASPERAGUS!
YES? YES?
THEN MEET A NEW PERSON, GO HOME, TAKE LSD, SAY A PRAYER, BREATHE TEN TIMES, STAND ON YOUR HEAD, SET YOUR WATCH, TAKE A SHIT, PICK YOUR NOSE, SQUEEZE A TIT...
GEE... ALL THAT'S KIND OF HARD TO REMEMBER...

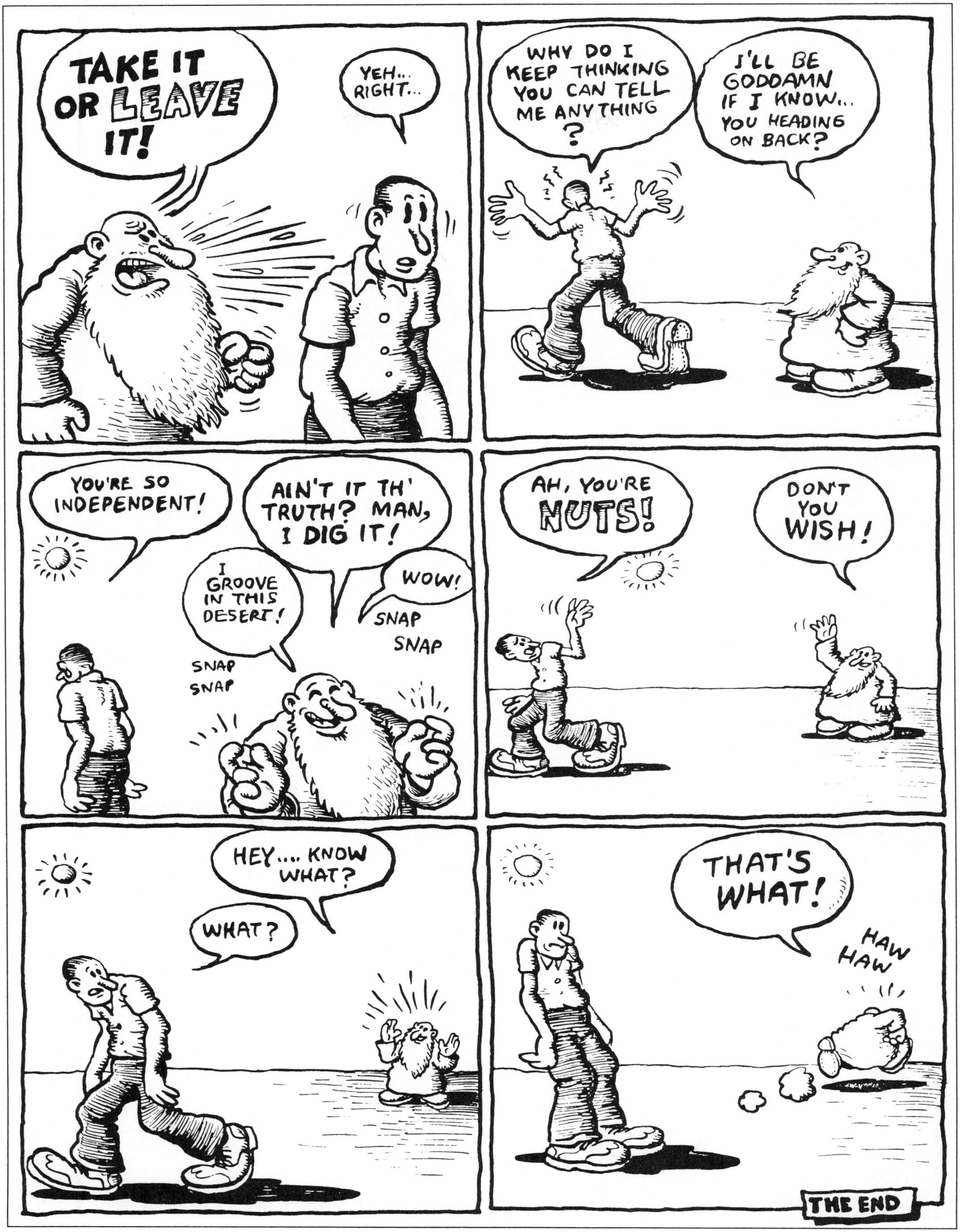
TAKE IT OR LEAVE IT!
YEH.. RIGHT...
WHY DO I KEEP THINKING YOU CAN TELL ME ANYTHING ?
I'LL BE GODDAMN IF I KNOW... YOU HEADING ON BACK?
YOU'RE SO INDEPENDENT!
AIN'T IT TH' TRUTH? MAN, I DIG IT!
I GROOVE IN THIS DESERT!
WOW!
SNAP SNAP
SNAP SNAP
AH, YOU'RE NUTS!
DON'T YOU WISH!
HEY.... KNOW WHAT?
WHAT?
THAT'S WHAT!
HAW HAW
THE END

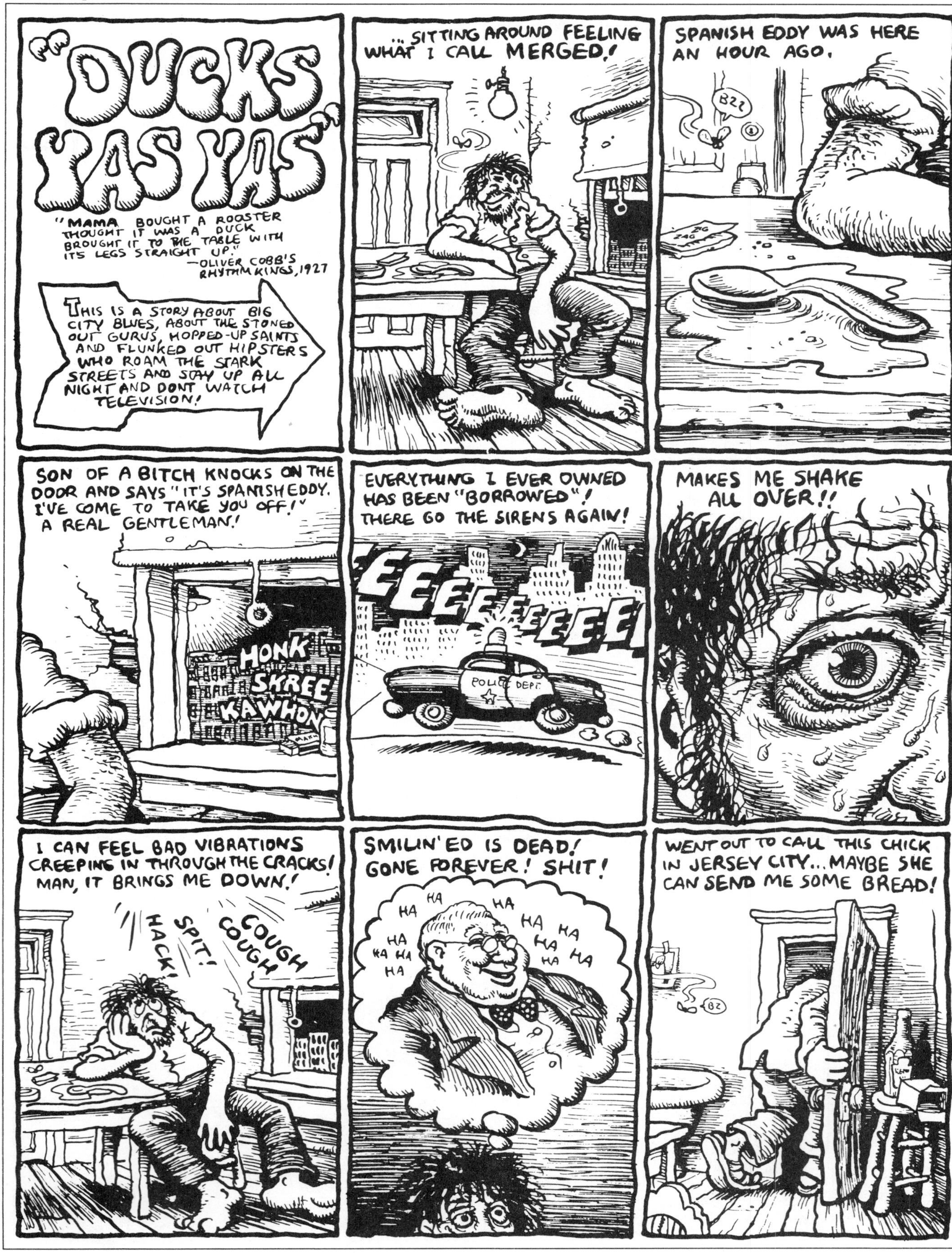
"DUCKS YAS YAS"
"MAMA BOUGHT A ROOSTER THOUGHT IT WAS A DUCK BROUGHT IT TO THE TABLE WITH ITS LEGS STRAIGHT UP."
—OLIVER COBB'S RHYTHM KINGS, 1927
THIS IS A STORY ABOUT BIG CITY BLUES, ABOUT THE STONED OUT GURUS, HOPPED-UP SAINTS AND FLUNKED OUT HIPSTERS WHO ROAM THE STARK STREETS AND STAY UP ALL NIGHT AND DONT WATCH TELEVISION!
... SITTING AROUND FEELING WHAT I CALL MERGED!
SPANISH EDDY WAS HERE AN HOUR AGO.
BZZ
SON OF A BITCH KNOCKS ON THE DOOR AND SAYS "IT'S SPANISH EDDY. I'VE COME TO TAKE YOU OFF!" A REAL GENTLEMAN!
HONK
SKREE
KAWHON
EVERYTHING I EVER OWNED HAS BEEN "BORROWED"! THERE GO THE SIRENS AGAIN!
EEEEEEEEEEE!
POLICE DEPT.
MAKES ME SHAKE ALL OVER!!
I CAN FEEL BAD VIBRATIONS CREEPING IN THROUGH THE CRACKS! MAN, IT BRINGS ME DOWN!
HACK!
SPIT!
COUGH COUGH
SMILIN' ED IS DEAD! GONE FOREVER! SHIT!
HA HA HA HA HA HA HA HA HA HA HA HA HA
WENT OUT TO CALL THIS CHICK IN JERSEY CITY... MAYBE SHE CAN SEND ME SOME BREAD!
BZ

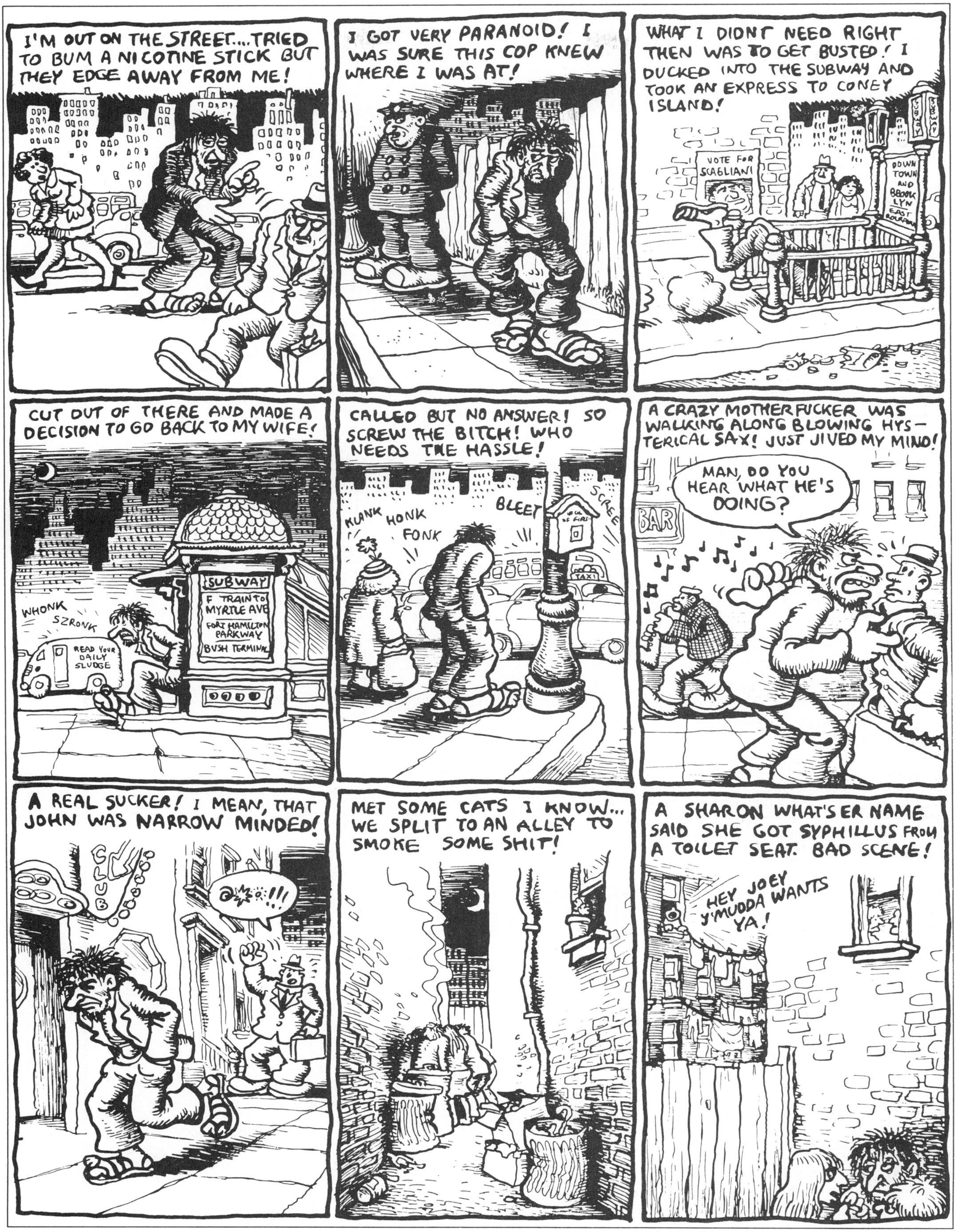
I'M OUT ON THE STREET....TRIED TO BUM A NICOTINE STICK BUT THEY EDGE AWAY FROM ME!
I GOT VERY PARANOID! I WAS SURE THIS COP KNEW WHERE I WAS AT!
WHAT I DIDN'T NEED RIGHT THEN WAS TO GET BUSTED! I DUCKED INTO THE SUBWAY AND TOOK AN EXPRESS TO CONEY ISLAND!
VOTE FOR SCAGLIANI
CUT OUT OF THERE AND MADE A DECISION TO GO BACK TO MY WIFE!
WHONK
SZRONK
READ YOUR DAILY SLUDGE
SUBWAY
F TRAIN TO MYRTLE AVE
FORT HAMILTON PARKWAY
BUSH TERMINAL
CALLED BUT NO ANSWER! SO SCREW THE BITCH! WHO NEEDS THE HASSLE!
KLANK
HONK
FONK
BLEET
SCREE
TAXI
A CRAZY MOTHERFUCKER WAS WALKING ALONG BLOWING HYSTERICAL SAX! JUST JIVED MY MIND!
BAR
MAN, DO YOU HEAR WHAT HE'S DOING?
A REAL SUCKER! I MEAN, THAT JOHN WAS NARROW MINDED!
CLUB
MET SOME CATS I KNOW... WE SPLIT TO AN ALLEY TO SMOKE SOME SHIT!
A SHARON WHAT'S ER NAME SAID SHE GOT SYPHILLUS FROM A TOILET SEAT. BAD SCENE!
HEY JOEY Y'MUDDA WANTS YA!

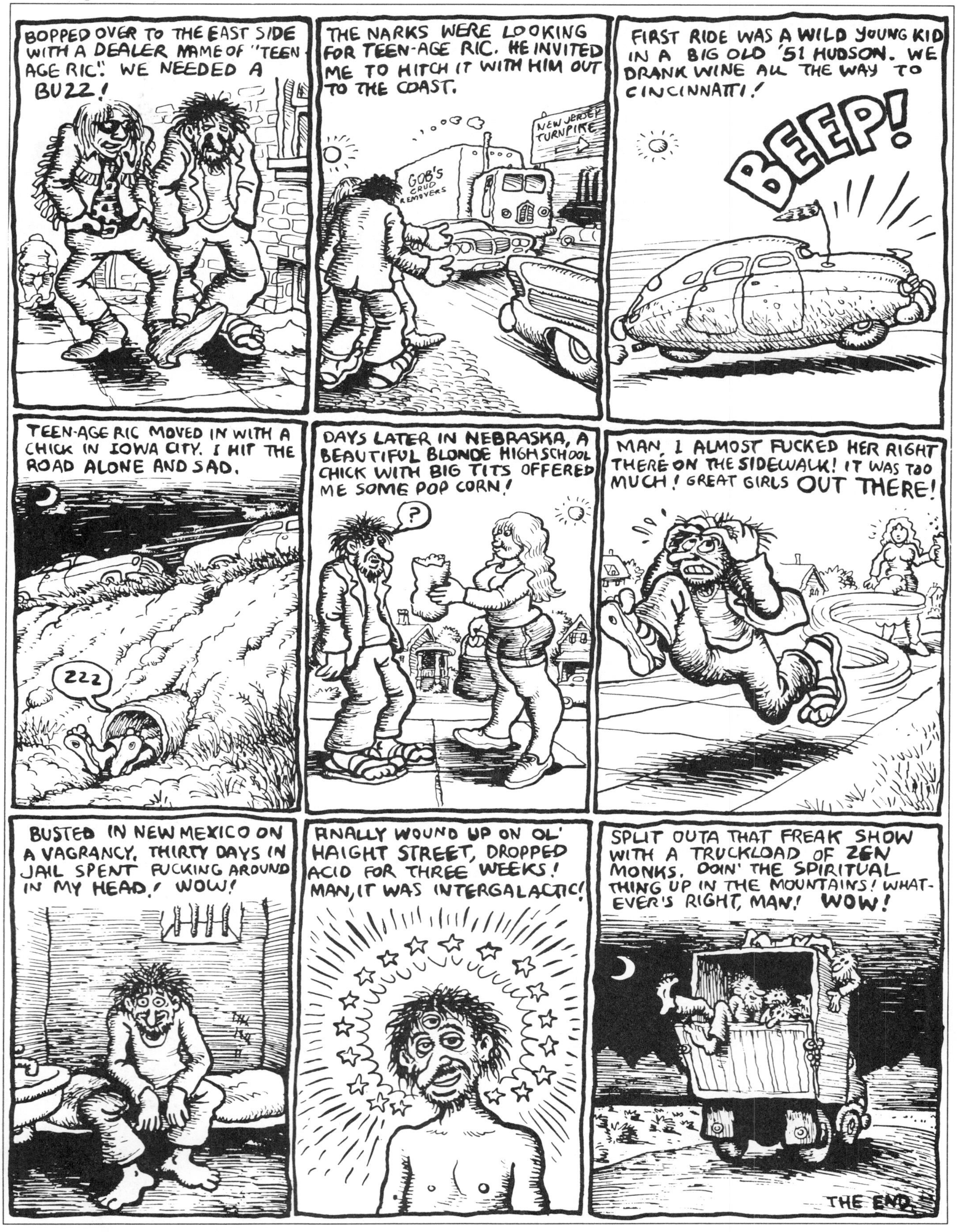
BOPPED OVER TO THE EAST SIDE WITH A DEALER NAME OF "TEEN AGE RIC". WE NEEDED A BUZZ!
THE NARKS WERE LOOKING FOR TEEN-AGE RIC. HE INVITED ME TO HITCH IT WITH HIM OUT TO THE COAST.
GOB'S CRUD REMOVERS
NEW JERSEY TURNPIKE
FIRST RIDE WAS A WILD YOUNG KID IN A BIG OLD '51 HUDSON. WE DRANK WINE ALL THE WAY TO CINCINNATTI!
BEEP!
TEEN-AGE RIC MOVED IN WITH A CHICK IN IOWA CITY. I HIT THE ROAD ALONE AND SAD.
ZZZ
DAYS LATER IN NEBRASKA, A BEAUTIFUL BLONDE HIGH SCHOOL CHICK WITH BIG TITS OFFERED ME SOME POP CORN!
?
MAN, I ALMOST FUCKED HER RIGHT THERE ON THE SIDEWALK! IT WAS TOO MUCH! GREAT GIRLS OUT THERE!
BUSTED IN NEW MEXICO ON A VAGRANCY, THIRTY DAYS IN JAIL SPENT FUCKING AROUND IN MY HEAD! WOW!
FINALLY WOUND UP ON OL' HAIGHT STREET, DROPPED ACID FOR THREE WEEKS! MAN, IT WAS INTERGALACTIC!
SPLIT OUTA THAT FREAK SHOW WITH A TRUCKLOAD OF ZEN MONKS. DOIN' THE SPIRITUAL THING UP IN THE MOUNTAINS! WHAT-EVER'S RIGHT, MAN! WOW!
THE END

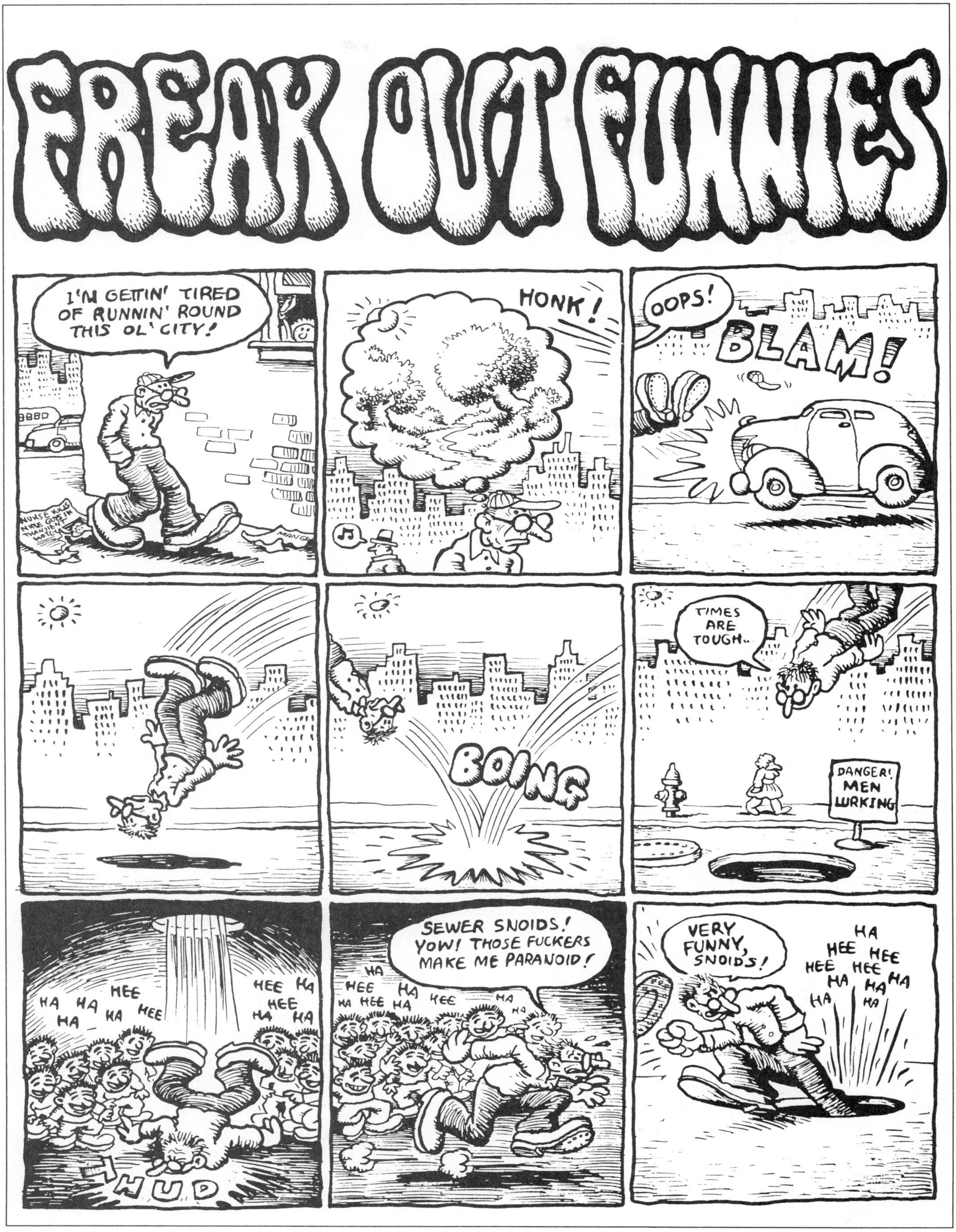
FREAK OUT FUNNIES
I'M GETTIN' TIRED OF RUNNIN' ROUND THIS OL' CITY!
HONK!
OOPS!
BLAM!
BOING
TIMES ARE TOUGH..
DANGER! MEN LURKING
HA HA HEE HA HA HEE
HEE HA HEE HA HA
THUD
SEWER SNOIDS! YOW! THOSE FUCKERS MAKE ME PARANOID!
HA HA HEE HA HA HEE HEE HA
VERY FUNNY, SNOIDS!
HA HEE HEE HEE HEE HA HA HA HA HA

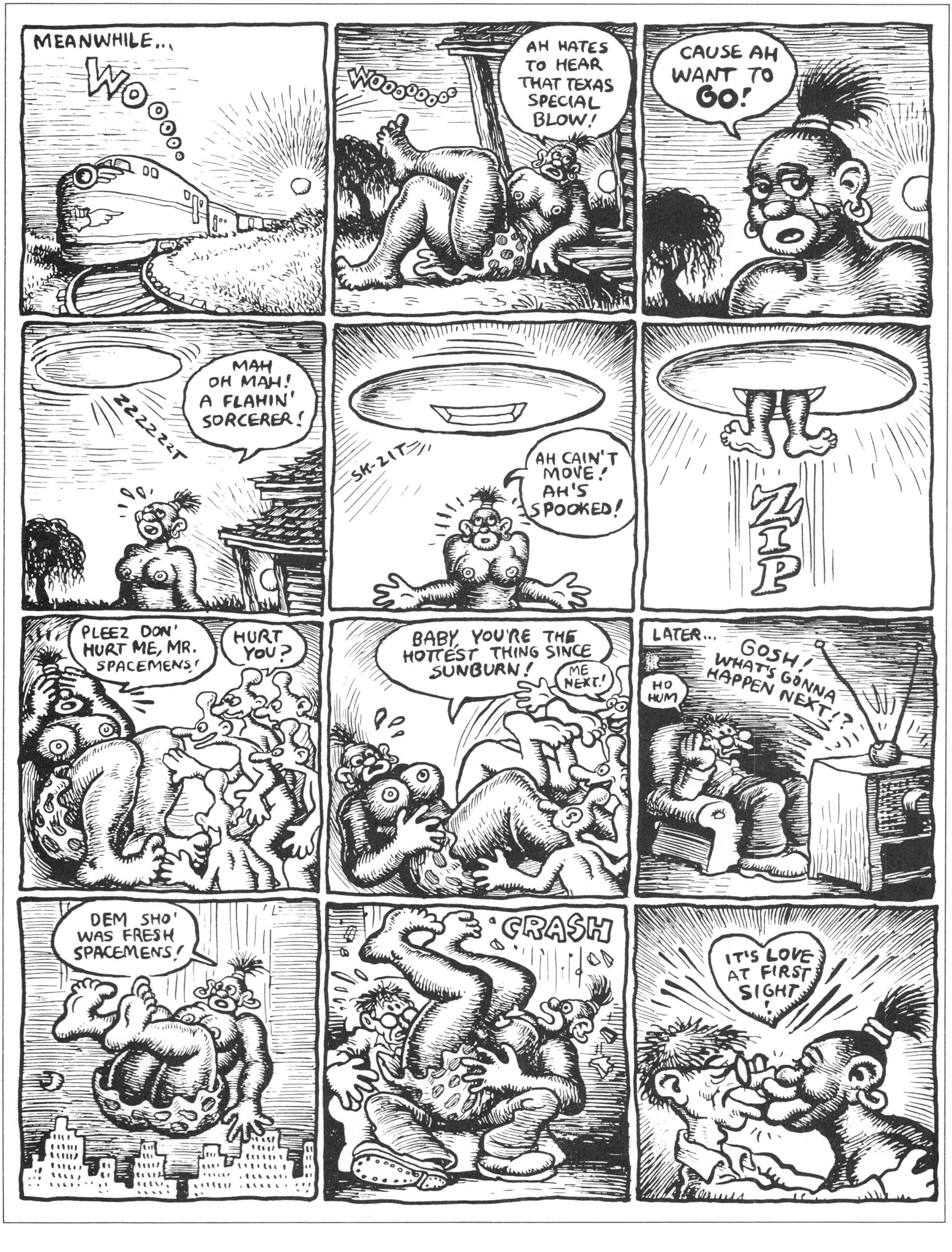
MEANWHILE...
WOOOOOO
WOOOOOOOOO
AH HATES TO HEAR THAT TEXAS SPECIAL BLOW!
CAUSE AH WANT TO GO!
ZZZZZZT
MAH OH MAH! A FLAHIN' SORCERER!
SK-ZIT
AH CAIN'T MOVE! AH'S SPOOKED!
ZIP
PLEEZ DON' HURT ME, MR. SPACEMENS!
HURT YOU?
BABY, YOU'RE THE HOTTEST THING SINCE SUNBURN!
ME NEXT!
LATER...
GOSH! WHAT'S GONNA HAPPEN NEXT!?
HO HUM
DEM SHO' WAS FRESH SPACEMENS!
CRASH
IT'S LOVE AT FIRST SIGHT!

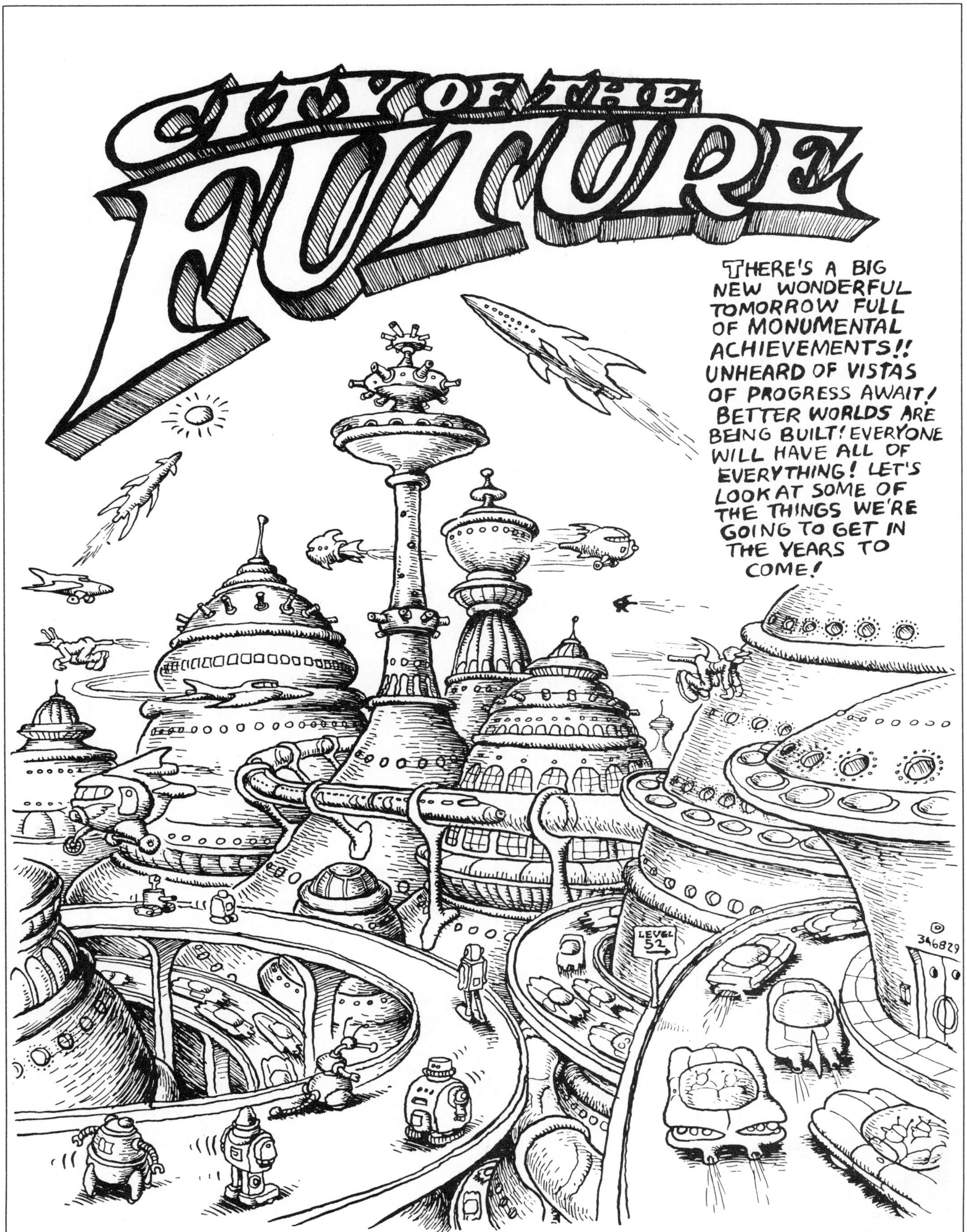
CITY OF THE FUTURE
THERE'S A BIG NEW WONDERFUL TOMORROW FULL OF MONUMENTAL ACHIEVEMENTS!! UNHEARD OF VISTAS OF PROGRESS AWAIT! BETTER WORLDS ARE BEING BUILT! EVERYONE WILL HAVE ALL OF EVERYTHING! LET'S LOOK AT SOME OF THE THINGS WE'RE GOING TO GET IN THE YEARS TO COME!
LEVEL 52
© 346829

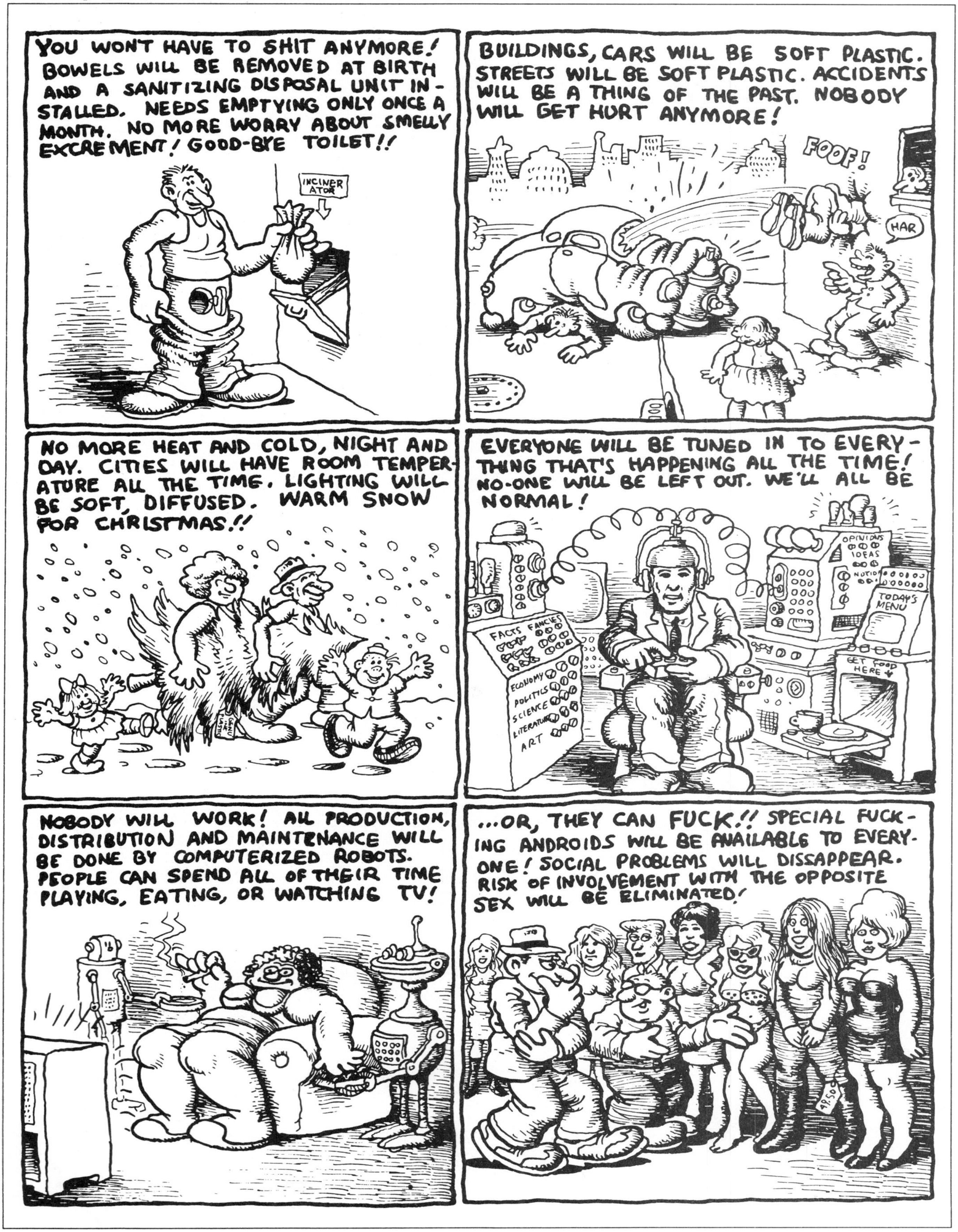
YOU WON'T HAVE TO SHIT ANYMORE! BOWELS WILL BE REMOVED AT BIRTH AND A SANITIZING DISPOSAL UNIT INSTALLED. NEEDS EMPTYING ONLY ONCE A MONTH. NO MORE WORRY ABOUT SMELLY EXCREMENT! GOOD-BYE TOILET!!
INCINERATOR
BUILDINGS, CARS WILL BE SOFT PLASTIC. STREETS WILL BE SOFT PLASTIC. ACCIDENTS WILL BE A THING OF THE PAST. NOBODY WILL GET HURT ANYMORE!
FOOF!
HAR
NO MORE HEAT AND COLD, NIGHT AND DAY. CITIES WILL HAVE ROOM TEMPERATURE ALL THE TIME. LIGHTING WILL BE SOFT, DIFFUSED. WARM SNOW FOR CHRISTMAS!!
EVERYONE WILL BE TUNED IN TO EVERYTHING THAT'S HAPPENING ALL THE TIME! NO-ONE WILL BE LEFT OUT. WE'LL ALL BE NORMAL!
OPINIONS
IDEAS
TODAY'S MENU
FACTS FANCIES
ECONOMY
POLITICS
SCIENCE
LITERATURE
ART
GET FOOD HERE
NOBODY WILL WORK! ALL PRODUCTION, DISTRIBUTION AND MAINTENANCE WILL BE DONE BY COMPUTERIZED ROBOTS. PEOPLE CAN SPEND ALL OF THEIR TIME PLAYING, EATING, OR WATCHING TV!
...OR, THEY CAN FUCK!! SPECIAL FUCKING ANDROIDS WILL BE AVAILABLE TO EVERYONE! SOCIAL PROBLEMS WILL DISSAPPEAR. RISK OF INVOLVEMENT WITH THE OPPOSITE SEX WILL BE ELIMINATED!
49.50

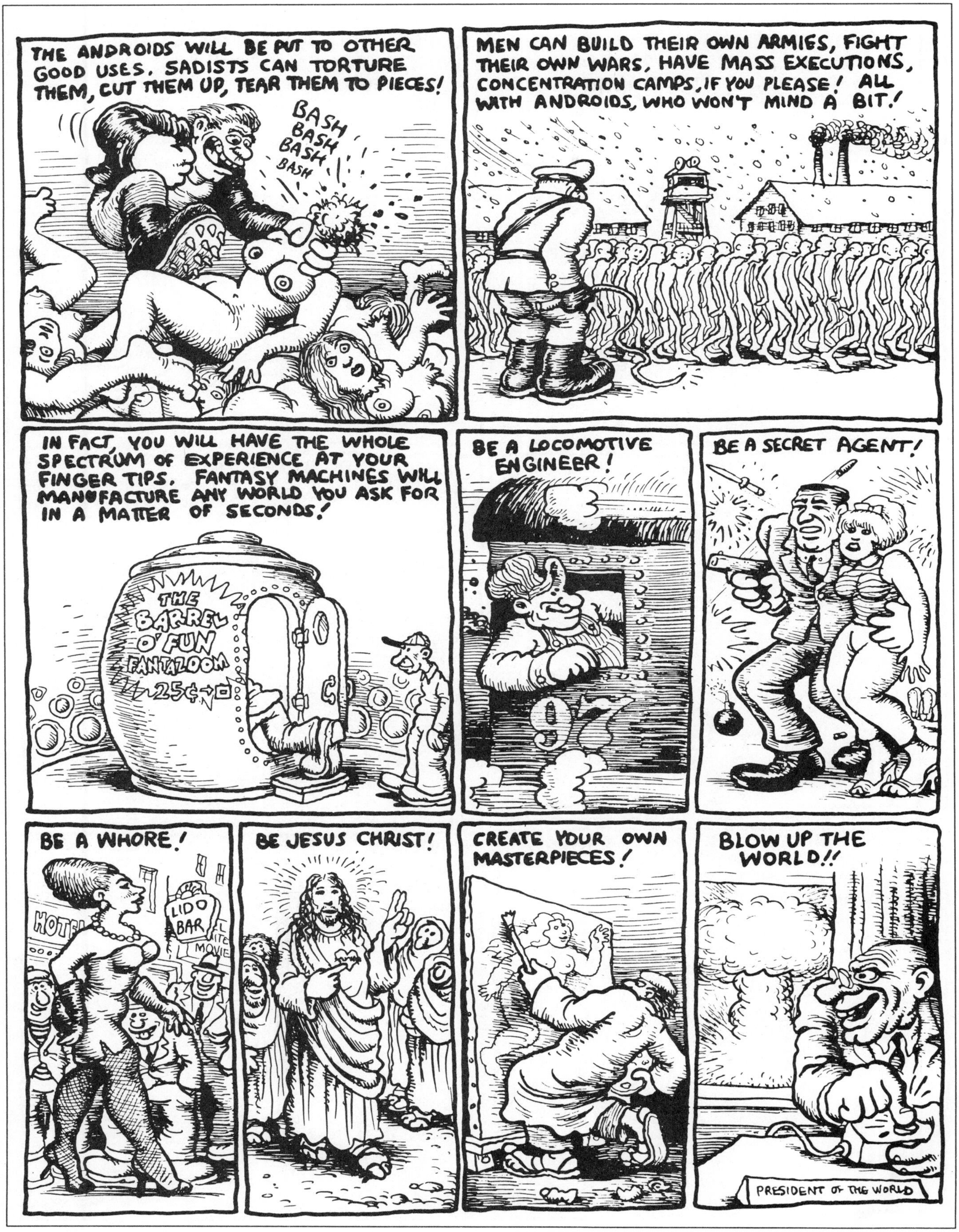
THE ANDROIDS WILL BE PUT TO OTHER GOOD USES. SADISTS CAN TORTURE THEM, CUT THEM UP, TEAR THEM TO PIECES!
BASH BASH BASH BASH
MEN CAN BUILD THEIR OWN ARMIES, FIGHT THEIR OWN WARS, HAVE MASS EXECUTIONS, CONCENTRATION CAMPS, IF YOU PLEASE! ALL WITH ANDROIDS, WHO WON'T MIND A BIT!
IN FACT, YOU WILL HAVE THE WHOLE SPECTRUM OF EXPERIENCE AT YOUR FINGER TIPS. FANTASY MACHINES WILL MANUFACTURE ANY WORLD YOU ASK FOR IN A MATTER OF SECONDS!
THE BARREL O' FUN FANTAZOOM 25¢
BE A LOCOMOTIVE ENGINEER!
97
BE A SECRET AGENT!
BE A WHORE!
HOTEL
LIDO BAR
MOVIE
BE JESUS CHRIST!
CREATE YOUR OWN MASTERPIECES!
BLOW UP THE WORLD!!
PRESIDENT OF THE WORLD

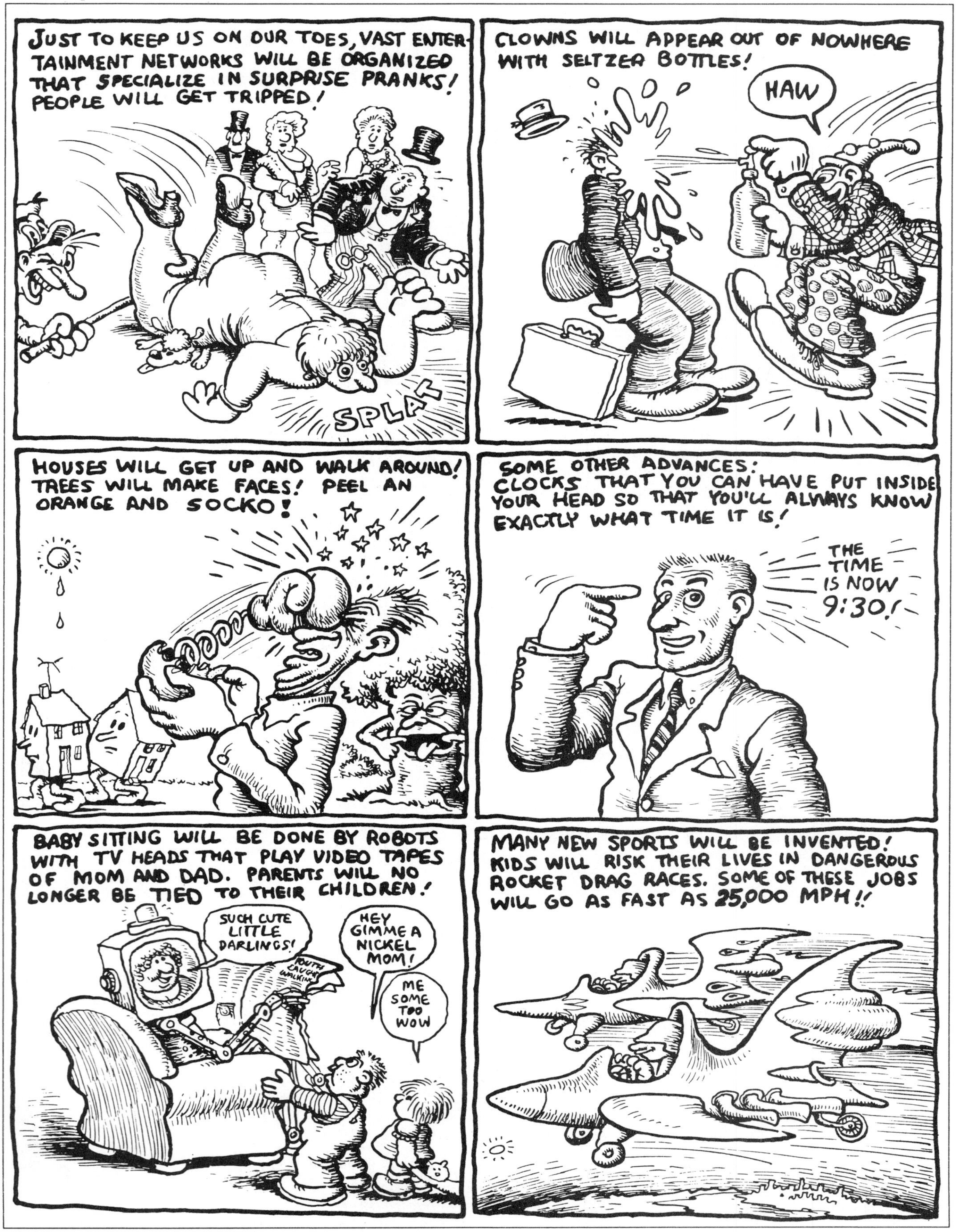
JUST TO KEEP US ON OUR TOES, VAST ENTERTAINMENT NETWORKS WILL BE ORGANIZED THAT SPECIALIZE IN SURPRISE PRANKS! PEOPLE WILL GET TRIPPED!
SPLAT
CLOWNS WILL APPEAR OUT OF NOWHERE WITH SELTZER BOTTLES!
HAW
HOUSES WILL GET UP AND WALK AROUND! TREES WILL MAKE FACES! PEEL AN ORANGE AND SOCKO!
SOME OTHER ADVANCES: CLOCKS THAT YOU CAN HAVE PUT INSIDE YOUR HEAD SO THAT YOU'LL ALWAYS KNOW EXACTLY WHAT TIME IT IS!
THE TIME IS NOW 9:30!
BABY SITTING WILL BE DONE BY ROBOTS WITH TV HEADS THAT PLAY VIDEO TAPES OF MOM AND DAD. PARENTS WILL NO LONGER BE TIED TO THEIR CHILDREN!
SUCH CUTE LITTLE DARLINGS!
HEY GIMME A NICKEL MOM!
ME SOME TOO WOW
MANY NEW SPORTS WILL BE INVENTED! KIDS WILL RISK THEIR LIVES IN DANGEROUS ROCKET DRAG RACES. SOME OF THESE JOBS WILL GO AS FAST AS 25,000 MPH!!

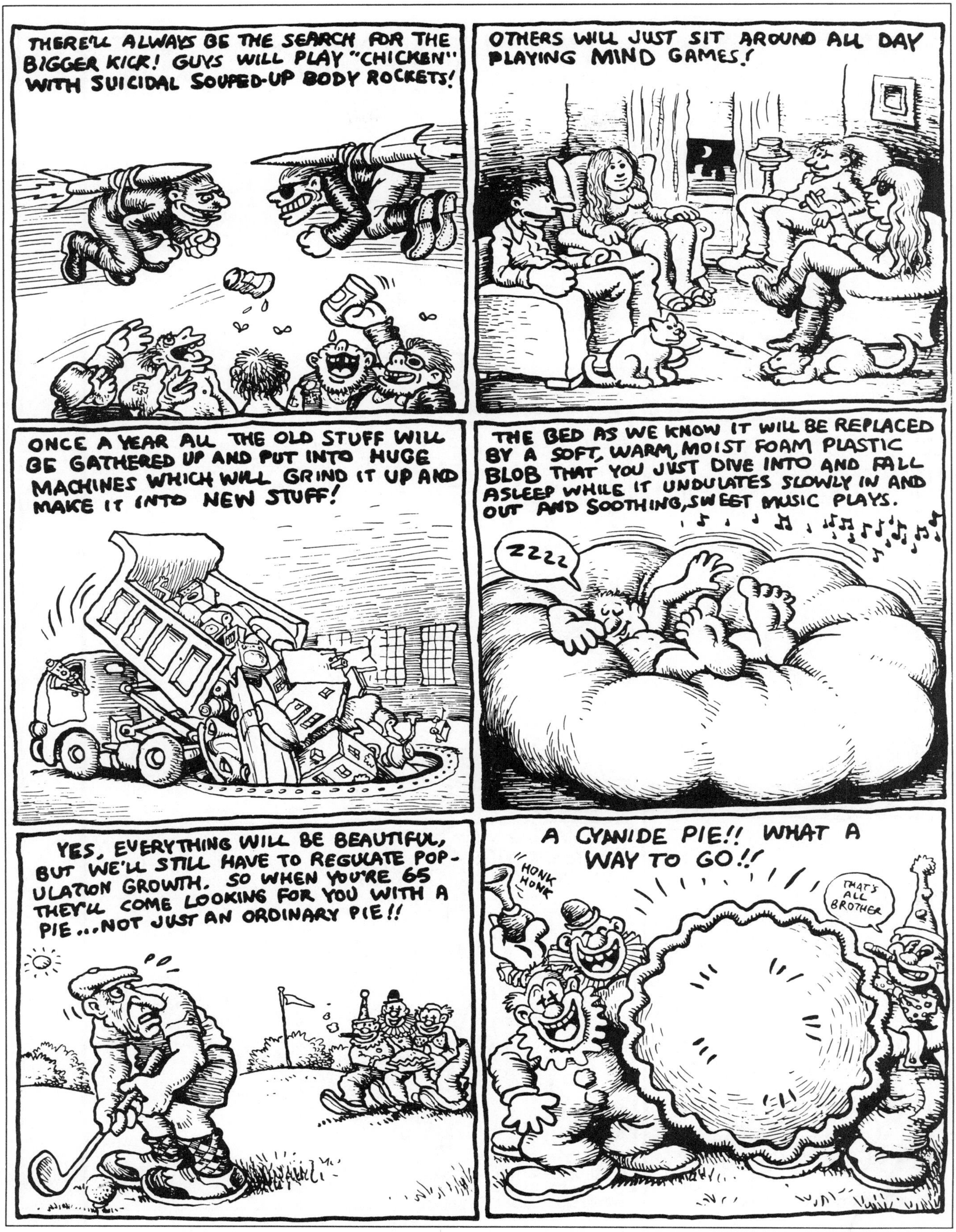
THERE'LL ALWAYS BE THE SEARCH FOR THE BIGGER KICK! GUYS WILL PLAY "CHICKEN" WITH SUICIDAL SOUPED-UP BODY ROCKETS!
OTHERS WILL JUST SIT AROUND ALL DAY PLAYING MIND GAMES!
ONCE A YEAR ALL THE OLD STUFF WILL BE GATHERED UP AND PUT INTO HUGE MACHINES WHICH WILL GRIND IT UP AND MAKE IT INTO NEW STUFF!
THE BED AS WE KNOW IT WILL BE REPLACED BY A SOFT, WARM, MOIST FOAM PLASTIC BLOB THAT YOU JUST DIVE INTO AND FALL ASLEEP WHILE IT UNDULATES SLOWLY IN AND OUT AND SOOTHING, SWEET MUSIC PLAYS.
ZZZZ
YES, EVERYTHING WILL BE BEAUTIFUL, BUT WE'LL STILL HAVE TO REGULATE POP-ULATION GROWTH. SO WHEN YOU'RE 65 THEY'LL COME LOOKING FOR YOU WITH A PIE... NOT JUST AN ORDINARY PIE!!
A CYANIDE PIE!! WHAT A WAY TO GO!!
HONK HONK
THAT'S ALL BROTHER

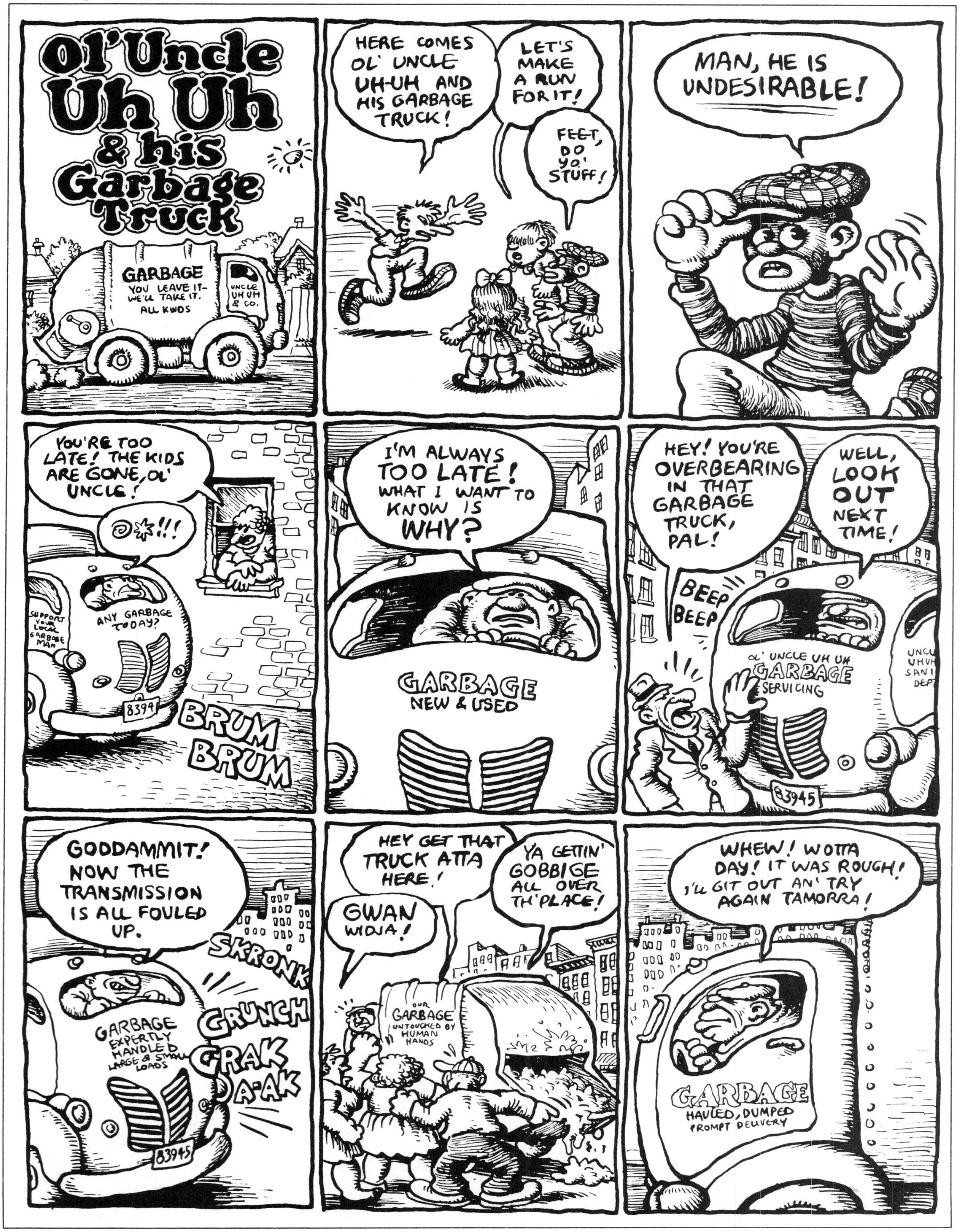
Ol' Uncle Uh Uh & his Garbage Truck
GARBAGE YOU LEAVE IT- WE'LL TAKE IT. ALL KINDS
UNCLE UH UH & CO.
HERE COMES OL' UNCLE UH-UH AND HIS GARBAGE TRUCK!
LET'S MAKE A RUN FOR IT!
FEET, DO YO' STUFF!
MAN, HE IS UNDESIRABLE!
YOU'RE TOO LATE! THE KIDS ARE GONE, OL' UNCLE!
@*!!!
SUPPORT YOUR LOCAL GARBAGE MAN
ANY GARBAGE TODAY?
8394
BRUM BRUM
I'M ALWAYS TOO LATE! WHAT I WANT TO KNOW IS WHY?
GARBAGE NEW & USED
HEY! YOU'RE OVERBEARING IN THAT GARBAGE TRUCK, PAL!
WELL, LOOK OUT NEXT TIME!
BEEP BEEP
OL' UNCLE UH UH GARBAGE SERVICING
83945
GODDAMMIT! NOW THE TRANSMISSION IS ALL FOULED UP.
SKRONK
GRUNCH
GRAK
A-AK
GARBAGE EXPERTLY HANDLED LARGE & SMALL LOADS
83945
HEY GET THAT TRUCK ATTA HERE!
YA GETTIN' GOBBIGE ALL OVER TH' PLACE!
GWAN WIDJA!
OUR GARBAGE UNTOUCHED BY HUMAN HANDS
WHEW! WOTTA DAY! IT WAS ROUGH! I'LL GIT OUT AN' TRY AGAIN TAMORRA!
GARBAGE HAULED, DUMPED PROMPT DELIVERY

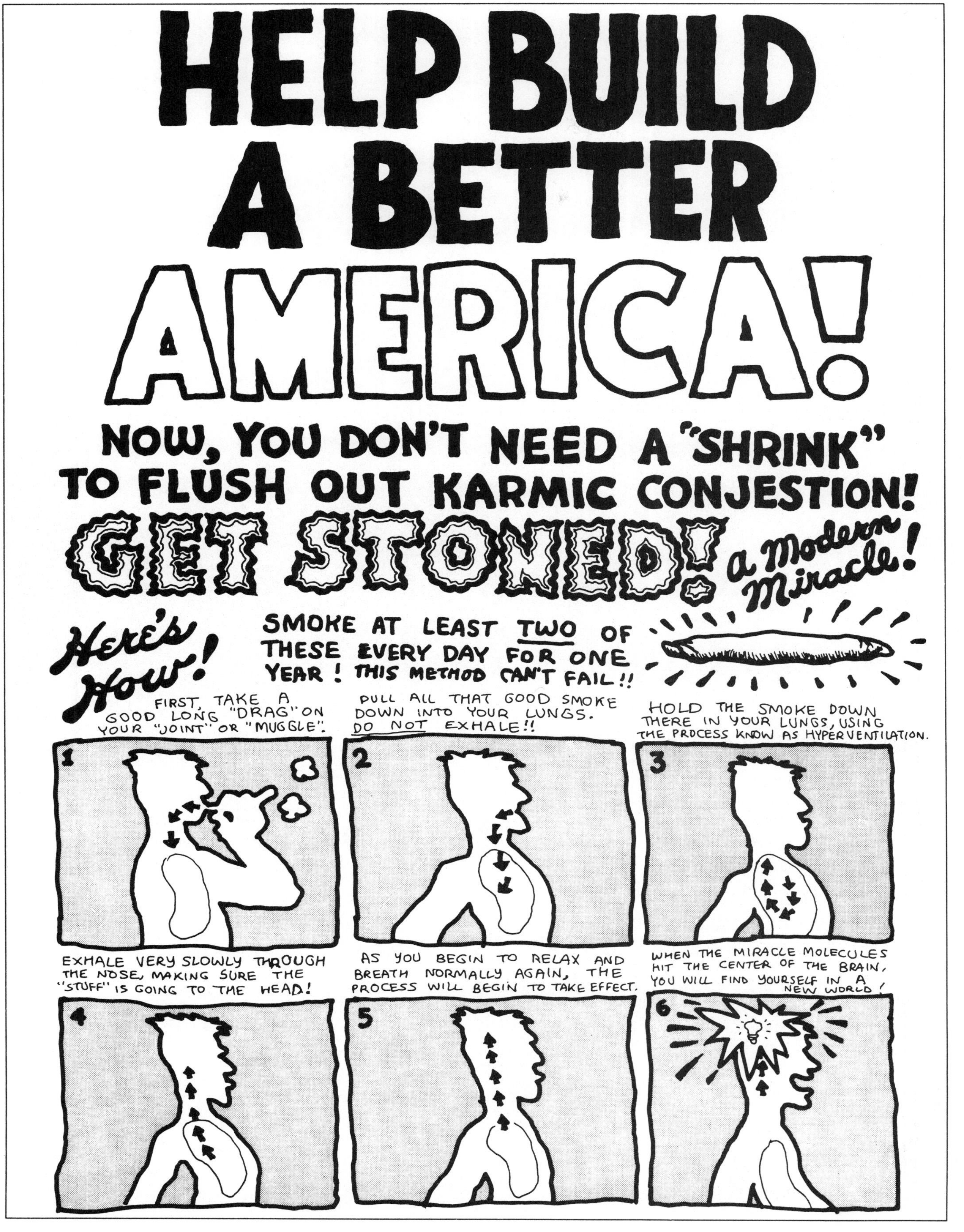
HELP BUILD A BETTER AMERICA!
NOW, YOU DON'T NEED A "SHRINK" TO FLUSH OUT KARMIC CONJESTION!
GET STONED!
a Modern Miracle!
Here's How!
SMOKE AT LEAST TWO OF THESE EVERY DAY FOR ONE YEAR! THIS METHOD CAN'T FAIL!!
FIRST, TAKE A GOOD LONG "DRAG" ON YOUR "JOINT" OR "MUGGLE".
1
PULL ALL THAT GOOD SMOKE DOWN INTO YOUR LUNGS. DO NOT EXHALE!!
2
HOLD THE SMOKE DOWN THERE IN YOUR LUNGS, USING THE PROCESS KNOW AS HYPERVENTILATION.
3
EXHALE VERY SLOWLY THROUGH THE NOSE, MAKING SURE THE "STUFF" IS GOING TO THE HEAD!
4
AS YOU BEGIN TO RELAX AND BREATH NORMALLY AGAIN, THE PROCESS WILL BEGIN TO TAKE EFFECT.
5
WHEN THE MIRACLE MOLECULES HIT THE CENTER OF THE BRAIN, YOU WILL FIND YOURSELF IN A NEW WORLD!
6

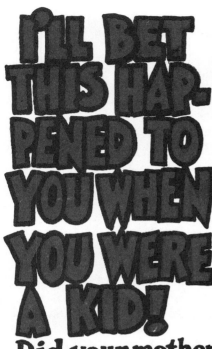

I'LL BET THIS HAPPENED TO YOU WHEN YOU WERE A KID!

I WANT YOU SHOULD STOP WASTING YOUR TIME READING THESE **CHEAP** COMIC BOOKS!

Did your mother ever tear up YOUR comic books? Did you ever recieve warnings about how comic books were going to RUIN your MIND? Were you given lectures about how comics were CHEAP TRASH put out by evil men?

Do you feel a spark of GUILT every time you pick up a comic book? Do you feel like you ought to be reading a good book instead? Let ZAP comics wisk away all such foolish notions! Takes only 15 minutes! Read ZAP comics!

— A MESSAGE FROM YOUR EDITOR, R. CRUMB

THIS AD IS NOT INTENDED FOR THOSE FORTUNATES AMONG US WHOSE PARENTS DIDN'T GIVE A SHIT IF THEY READ COMIC BOOKS.

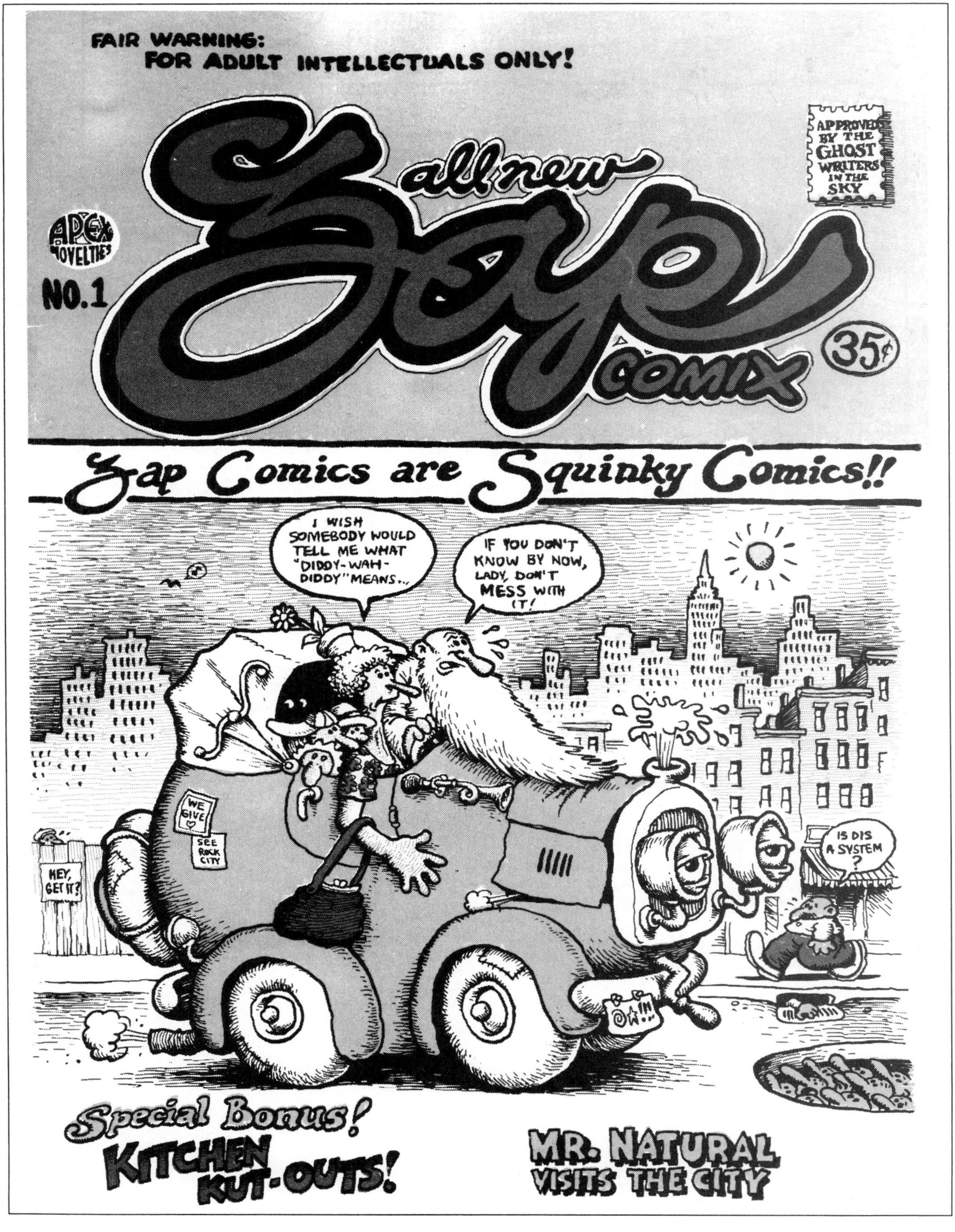
FAIR WARNING:
FOR ADULT INTELLECTUALS ONLY!
APPROVED BY THE GHOST WRITERS IN THE SKY
APEX NOVELTIES
NO. 1
all new Zap COMIX
35¢
Zap Comics are Squinky Comics!!
I WISH SOMEBODY WOULD TELL ME WHAT "DIDDY-WAH-DIDDY" MEANS...
IF YOU DON'T KNOW BY NOW, LADY, DON'T MESS WITH IT!
WE GIVE ♡
SEE ROCK CITY
HEY, GET IT?
IS DIS A SYSTEM ?
Special Bonus!
KITCHEN KUT-OUTS!
MR. NATURAL VISITS THE CITY

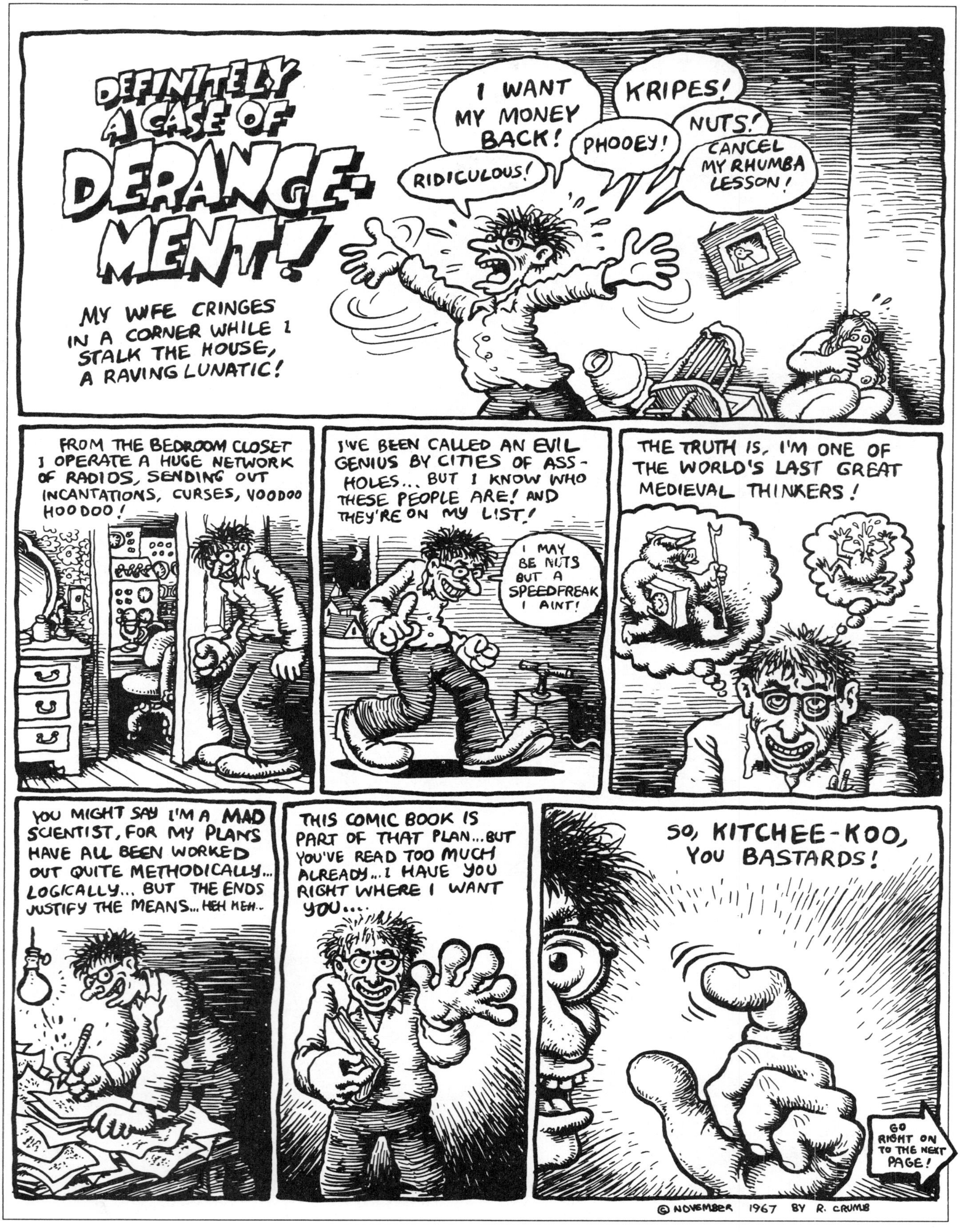
DEFINITELY A CASE OF DERANGE-MENT!
MY WIFE CRINGES IN A CORNER WHILE I STALK THE HOUSE, A RAVING LUNATIC!
I WANT MY MONEY BACK!
KRIPES!
NUTS!
PHOOEY!
CANCEL MY RHUMBA LESSON!
RIDICULOUS!
FROM THE BEDROOM CLOSET I OPERATE A HUGE NETWORK OF RADIOS, SENDING OUT INCANTATIONS, CURSES, VOODOO HOODOO!
I'VE BEEN CALLED AN EVIL GENIUS BY CITIES OF ASS-HOLES... BUT I KNOW WHO THESE PEOPLE ARE! AND THEY'RE ON MY LIST!
I MAY BE NUTS BUT A SPEEDFREAK I AINT!
THE TRUTH IS, I'M ONE OF THE WORLD'S LAST GREAT MEDIEVAL THINKERS!
YOU MIGHT SAY I'M A MAD SCIENTIST, FOR MY PLANS HAVE ALL BEEN WORKED OUT QUITE METHODICALLY... LOGICALLY... BUT THE ENDS JUSTIFY THE MEANS... HEH HEH...
THIS COMIC BOOK IS PART OF THAT PLAN... BUT YOU'VE READ TOO MUCH ALREADY... I HAVE YOU RIGHT WHERE I WANT YOU....
SO, KITCHEE-KOO, YOU BASTARDS!
GO RIGHT ON TO THE NEXT PAGE!
© NOVEMBER 1967 BY R. CRUMB

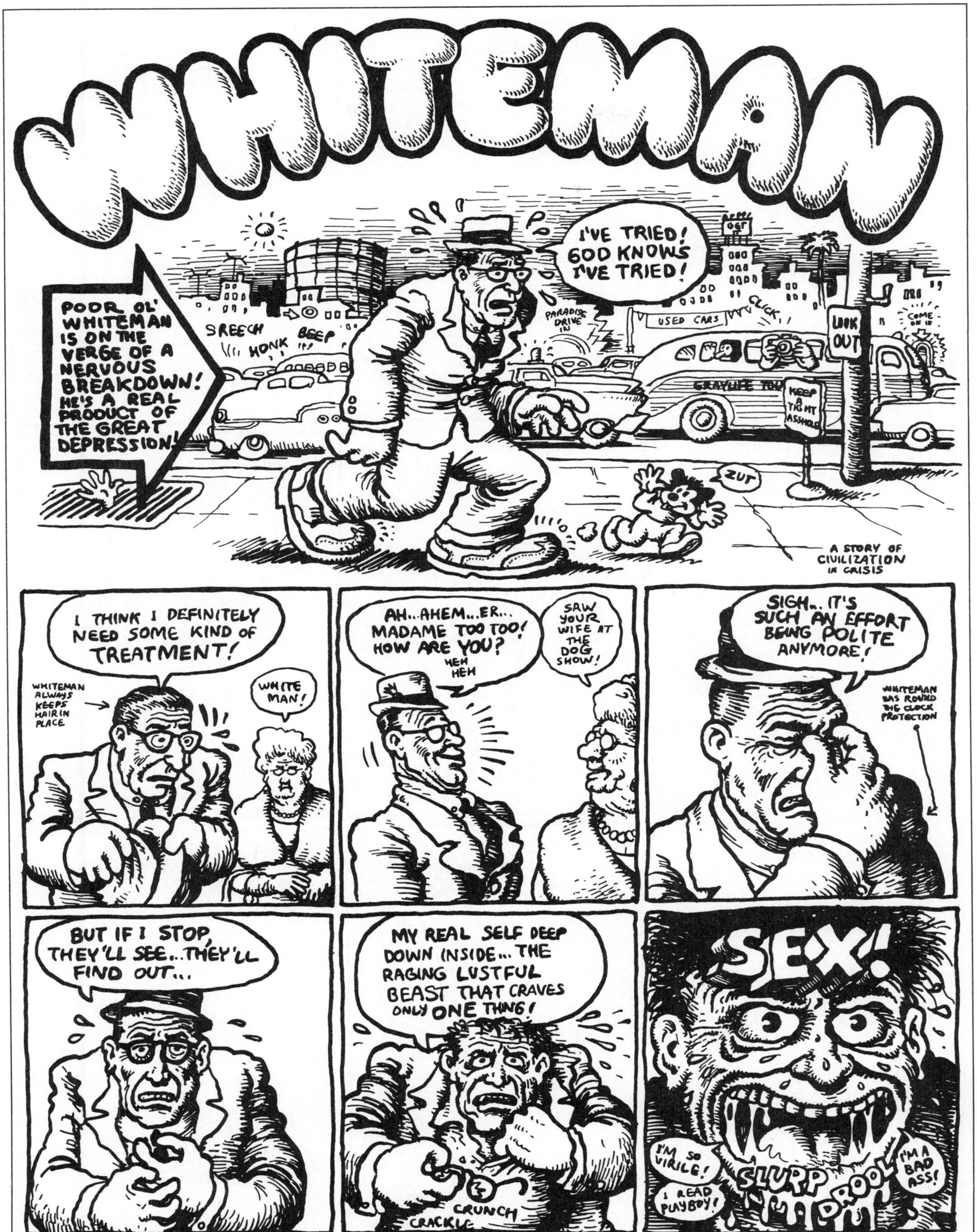
WHITEMAN
POOR OL' WHITEMAN IS ON THE VERGE OF A NERVOUS BREAKDOWN! HE'S A REAL PRODUCT OF THE GREAT DEPRESSION!
I'VE TRIED! GOD KNOWS I'VE TRIED!
SREECH
HONK
BEEP
PARADISE DRIVE IN
USED CARS
CLICK
LOOK OUT
COME ON IN
KEEP A TIGHT
ZUT
A STORY OF CIVILIZATION IN CRISIS
I THINK I DEFINITELY NEED SOME KIND OF TREATMENT!
WHITEMAN ALWAYS KEEPS HAIR IN PLACE
WHITE MAN!
AH...AHEM...ER.. MADAME TOO TOO! HOW ARE YOU?
HEH HEH
SAW YOUR WIFE AT THE DOG SHOW!
SIGH.. IT'S SUCH AN EFFORT BEING POLITE ANYMORE!
WHITEMAN HAS ROUND THE CLOCK PROTECTION
BUT IF I STOP, THEY'LL SEE...THEY'LL FIND OUT...
MY REAL SELF DEEP DOWN INSIDE... THE RAGING LUSTFUL BEAST THAT CRAVES ONLY ONE THING!
CRUNCH
CRACKLE
SEX!
I'M SO VIRILE!
I READ PLAYBOY!
SLURP
DROOL
I'M A BAD ASS!

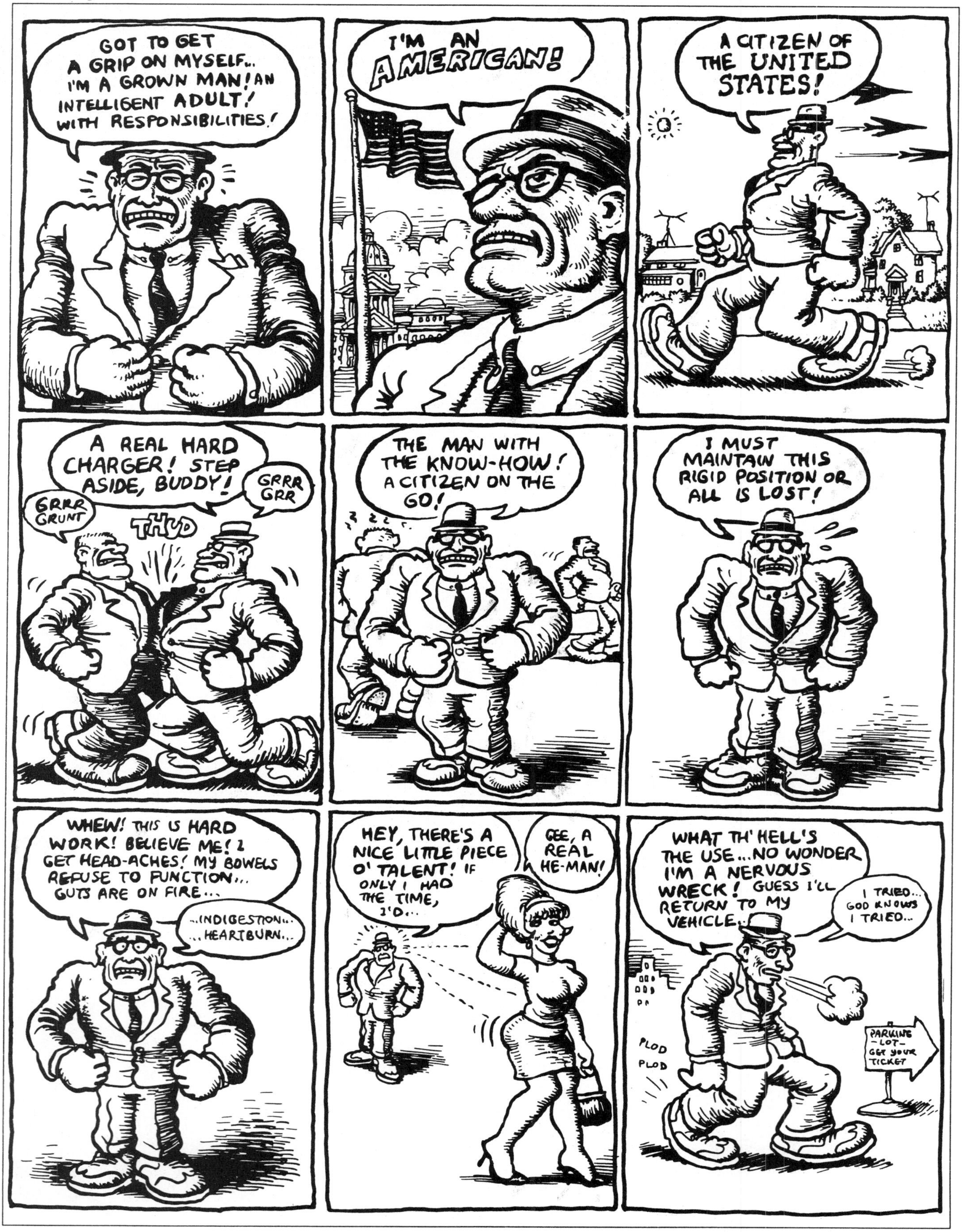
GOT TO GET A GRIP ON MYSELF.. I'M A GROWN MAN! AN INTELLIGENT ADULT! WITH RESPONSIBILITIES!
I'M AN AMERICAN!
A CITIZEN OF THE UNITED STATES!
A REAL HARD CHARGER! STEP ASIDE, BUDDY!
GRRR GRUNT
THUD
GRRR GRR
THE MAN WITH THE KNOW-HOW! A CITIZEN ON THE GO!
I MUST MAINTAIN THIS RIGID POSITION OR ALL IS LOST!
WHEW! THIS IS HARD WORK! BELIEVE ME! I GET HEAD-ACHES! MY BOWELS REFUSE TO FUNCTION... GUTS ARE ON FIRE...
...INDIGESTION... ...HEARTBURN...
HEY, THERE'S A NICE LITTLE PIECE O' TALENT! IF ONLY I HAD THE TIME, I'D...
GEE, A REAL HE-MAN!
WHAT TH' HELL'S THE USE... NO WONDER I'M A NERVOUS WRECK! GUESS I'LL RETURN TO MY VEHICLE...
I TRIED... GOD KNOWS I TRIED...
PLOD
PLOD
PARKING -LOT- GET YOUR TICKET

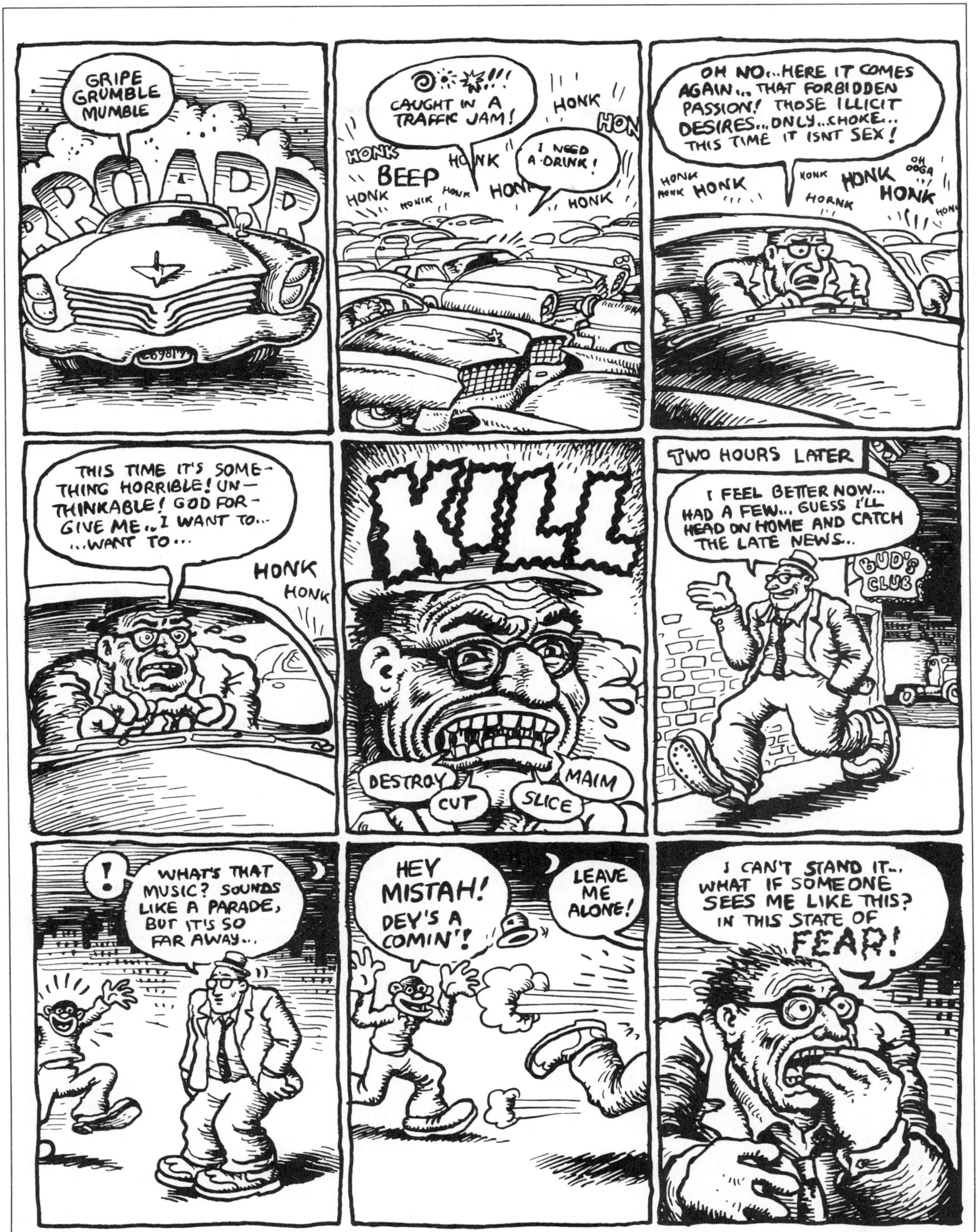
GRIPE GRUMBLE MUMBLE
ROARR
CAUGHT IN A TRAFFIC JAM!
HONK
HONK
BEEP
HONK
HONK
HONK
HONK
I NEED A DRINK!
HONK
OH NO...HERE IT COMES AGAIN... THAT FORBIDDEN PASSION! THOSE ILLICIT DESIRES...ONLY...CHOKE... THIS TIME IT ISNT SEX!
HONK HONK HONK
HONK
HONK
OH OOGA
HONK
HORNK
THIS TIME IT'S SOMETHING HORRIBLE! UNTHINKABLE! GOD FORGIVE ME..I WANT TO... ...WANT TO...
HONK
HONK
KILL
DESTROY
CUT
SLICE
MAIM
TWO HOURS LATER
I FEEL BETTER NOW... HAD A FEW... GUESS I'LL HEAD ON HOME AND CATCH THE LATE NEWS...
BUD'S CLUB
!
WHAT'S THAT MUSIC? SOUNDS LIKE A PARADE, BUT IT'S SO FAR AWAY...
HEY MISTAH! DEY'S A COMIN'!
LEAVE ME ALONE!
I CAN'T STAND IT... WHAT IF SOMEONE SEES ME LIKE THIS? IN THIS STATE OF FEAR!

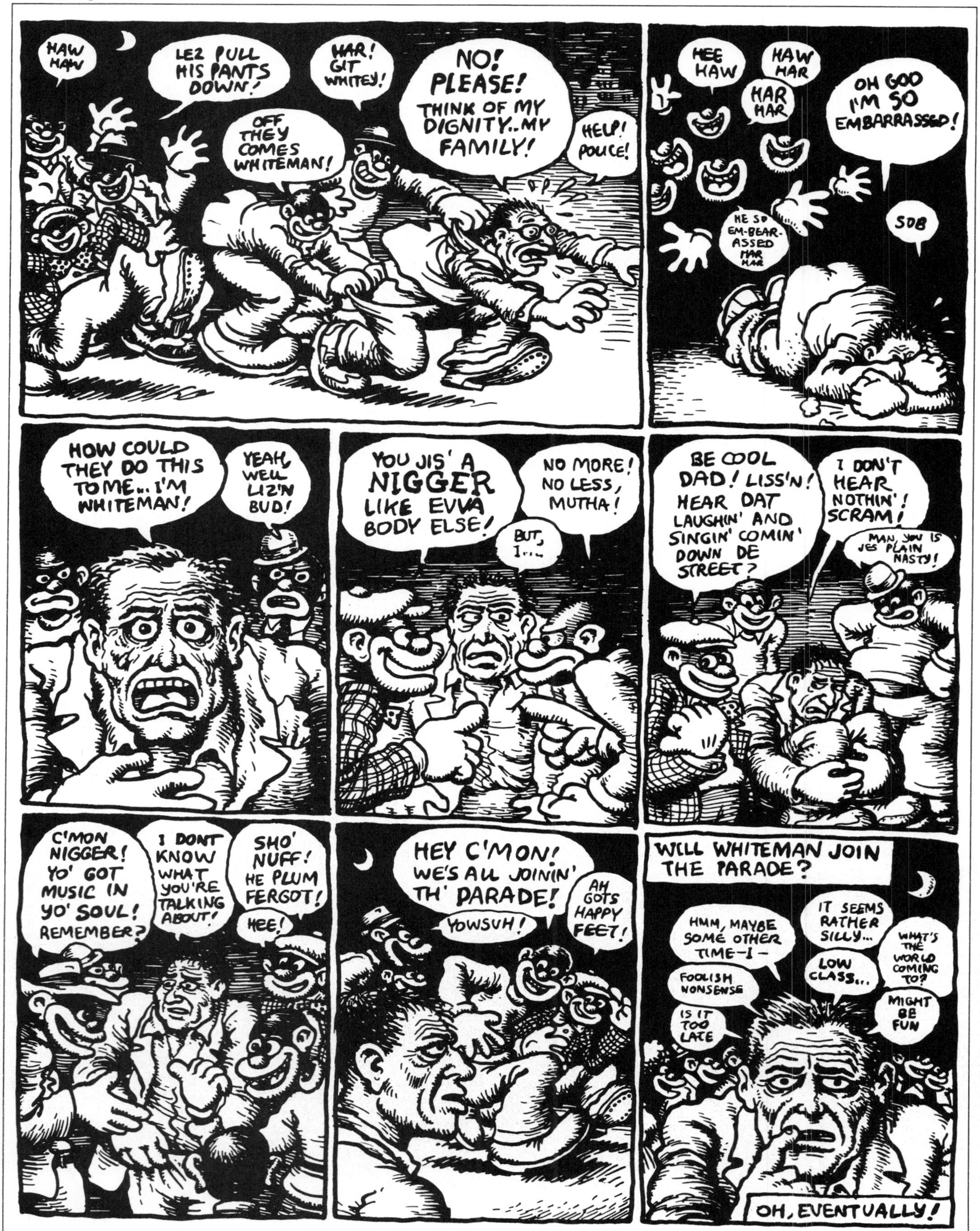
HAW HAW
LEZ PULL HIS PANTS DOWN!
HAR! GIT WHITEY!
NO! PLEASE! THINK OF MY DIGNITY..MY FAMILY!
OFF THEY COMES WHITEMAN!
HELP! POLICE!
HEE HAW
HAW HAR
HAR HAR
OH GOD I'M SO EMBARRASSED!
HE SO EM-BEAR-ASSED HAR HAR
SOB
HOW COULD THEY DO THIS TO ME.. I'M WHITEMAN!
YEAH, WELL LIZ'N BUD!
YOU JIS' A NIGGER LIKE EVVA BODY ELSE!
NO MORE! NO LESS, MUTHA!
BUT, I...
BE COOL DAD! LISS'N! HEAR DAT LAUGHIN' AND SINGIN' COMIN' DOWN DE STREET?
I DON'T HEAR NOTHIN'! SCRAM!
MAN, YOU IS JES PLAIN NASTY!
C'MON NIGGER! YO' GOT MUSIC IN YO' SOUL! REMEMBER?
I DONT KNOW WHAT YOU'RE TALKING ABOUT!
SHO' NUFF! HE PLUM FERGOT!
HEE!
HEY C'MON! WE'S ALL JOININ' TH' PARADE!
AH GOTS HAPPY FEET!
YOWSUH!
WILL WHITEMAN JOIN THE PARADE?
HMM, MAYBE SOME OTHER TIME—I—
IT SEEMS RATHER SILLY...
WHAT'S THE WORLD COMING TO?
FOOLISH NONSENSE
LOW CLASS...
IS IT TOO LATE
MIGHT BE FUN
OH, EVENTUALLY!

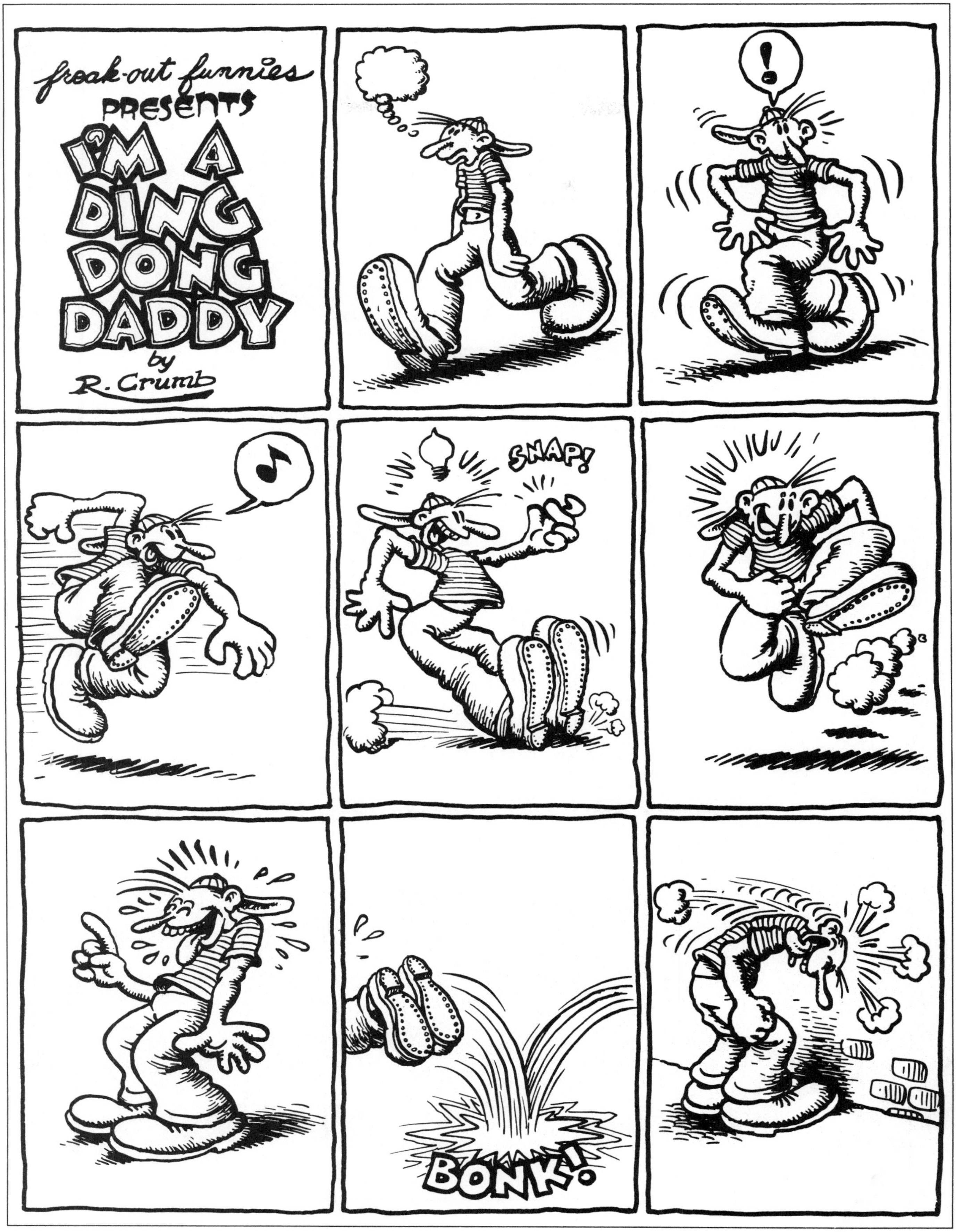
freak-out funnies
PRESENTS
I'M A DING DONG DADDY
by
R. Crumb
!
SNAP!
BONK!

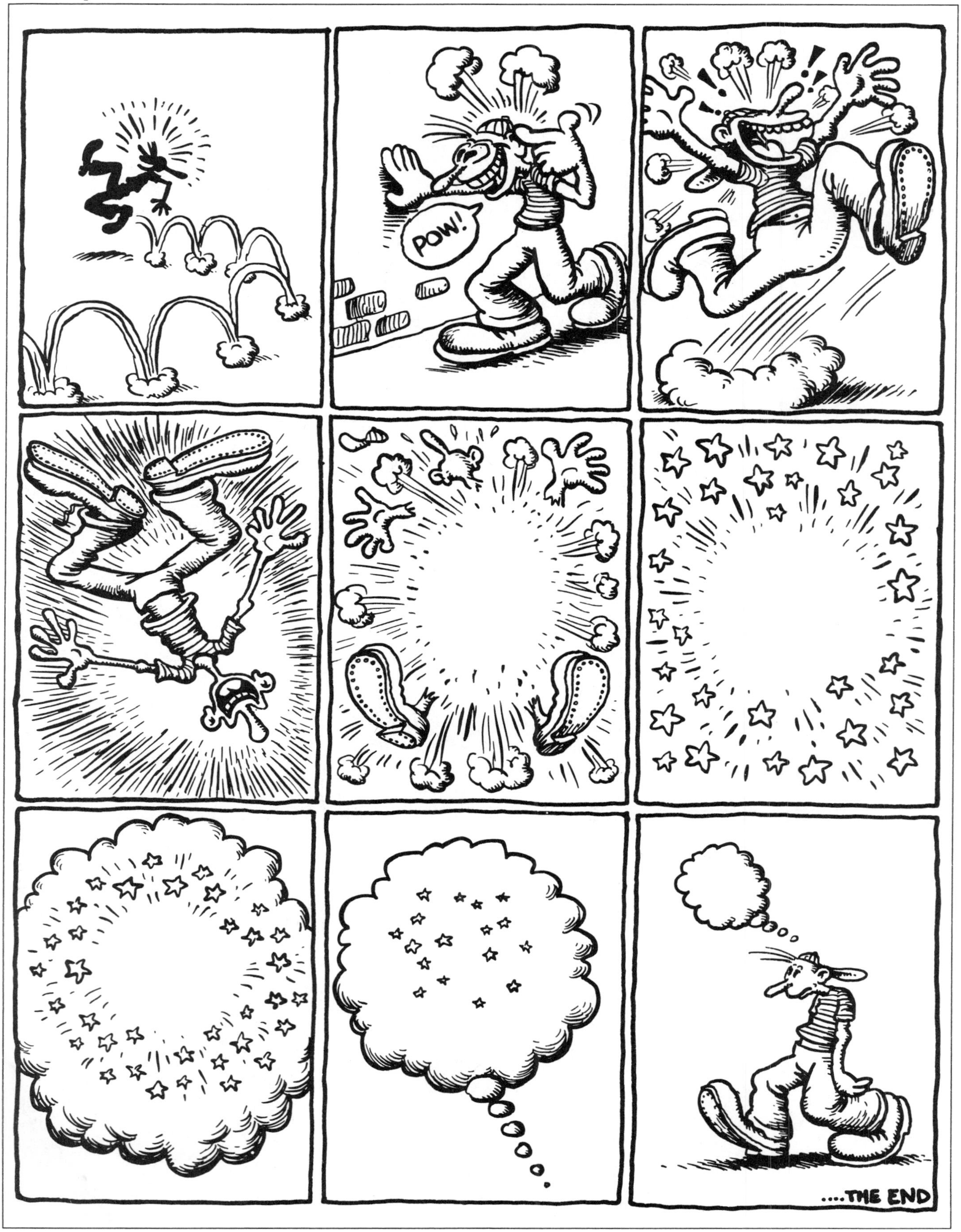
POW!
....THE END

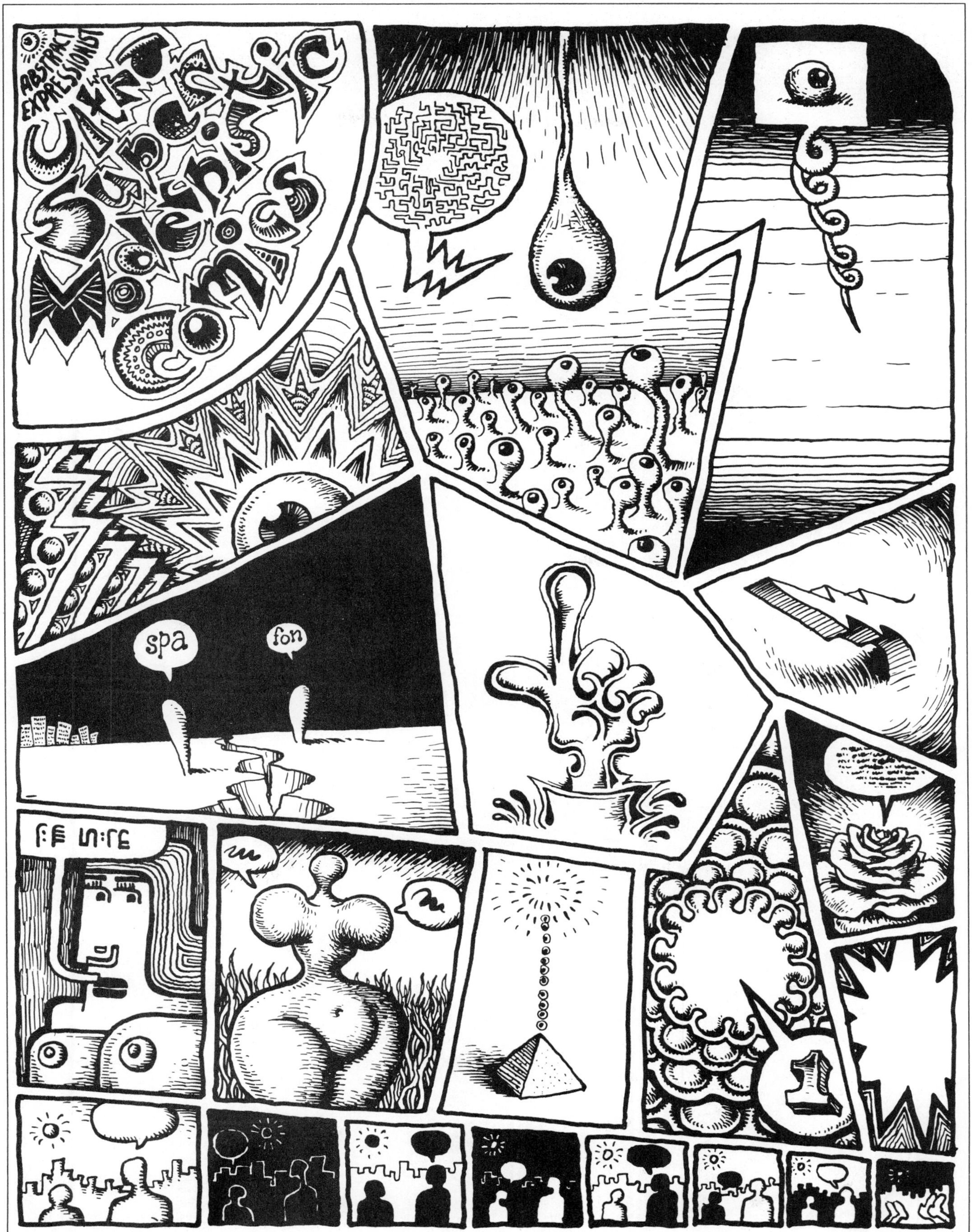
ABSTRACT EXPRESSIONIST
ULTRA SUPER MODERNISTIC COMICS
spa
fon

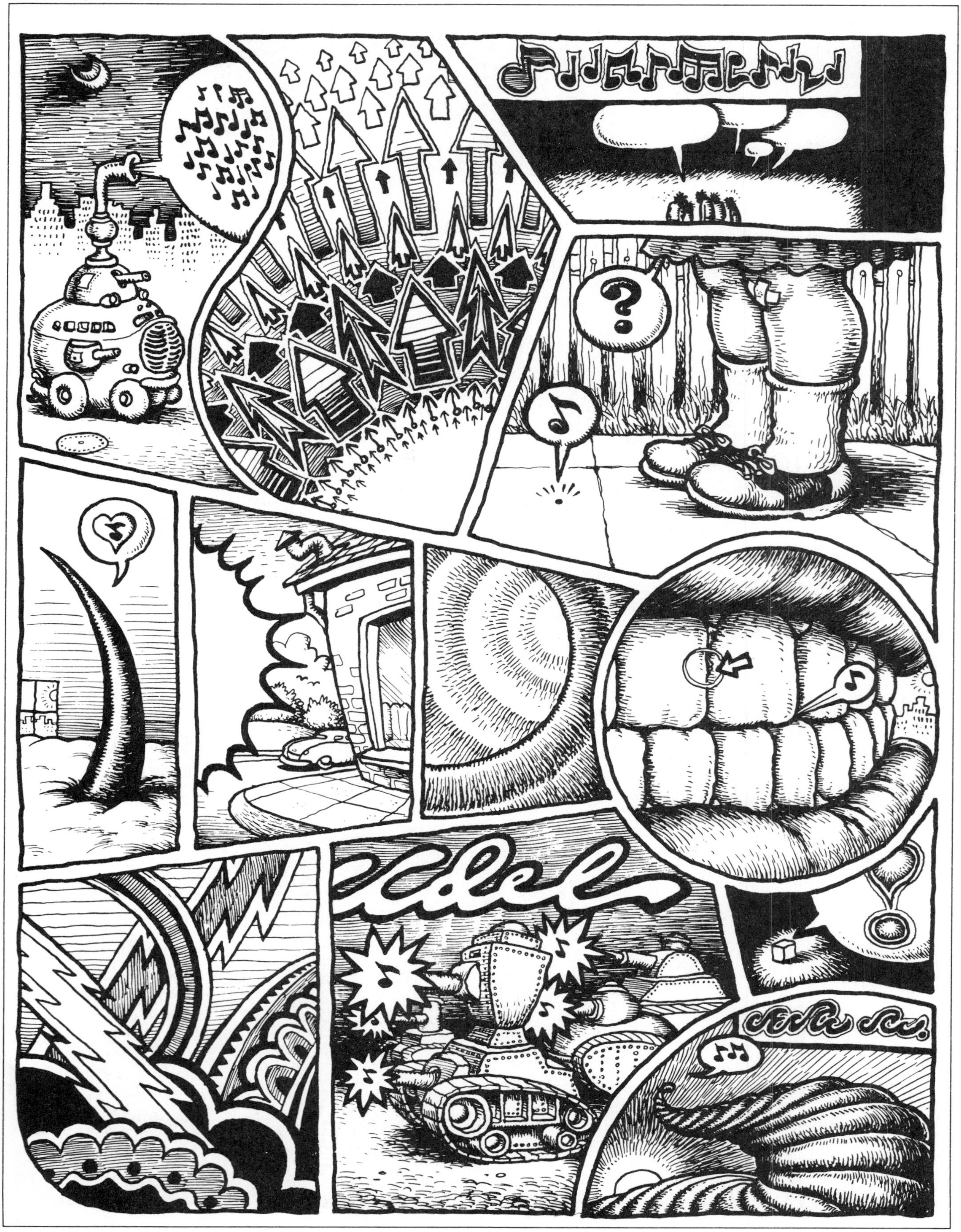

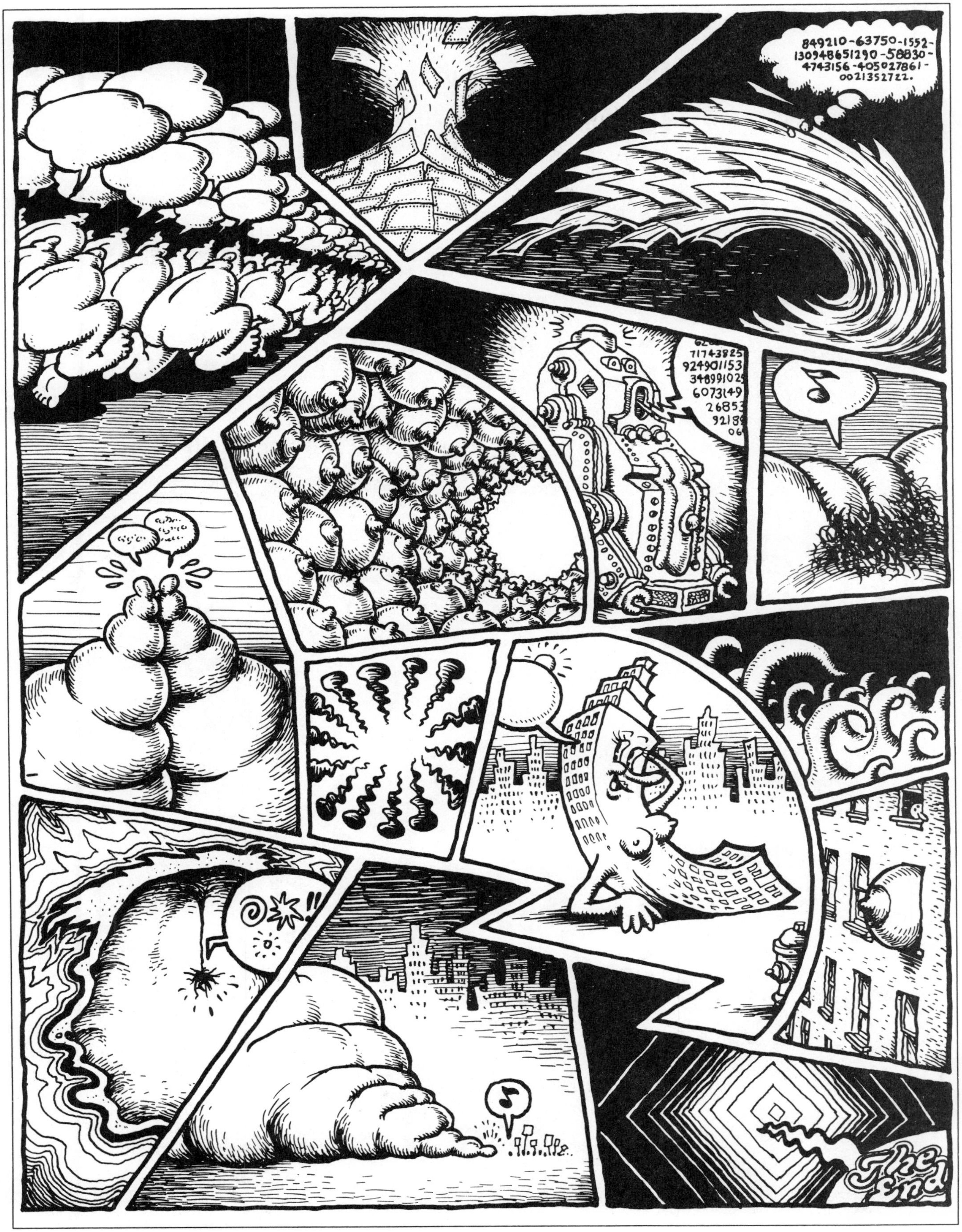
849210-63750-1552-
1309486512290-58830-
4743156-405027861-
0021352722.
71743825
924901153
34899102
6073149
26853
9218
06
The end

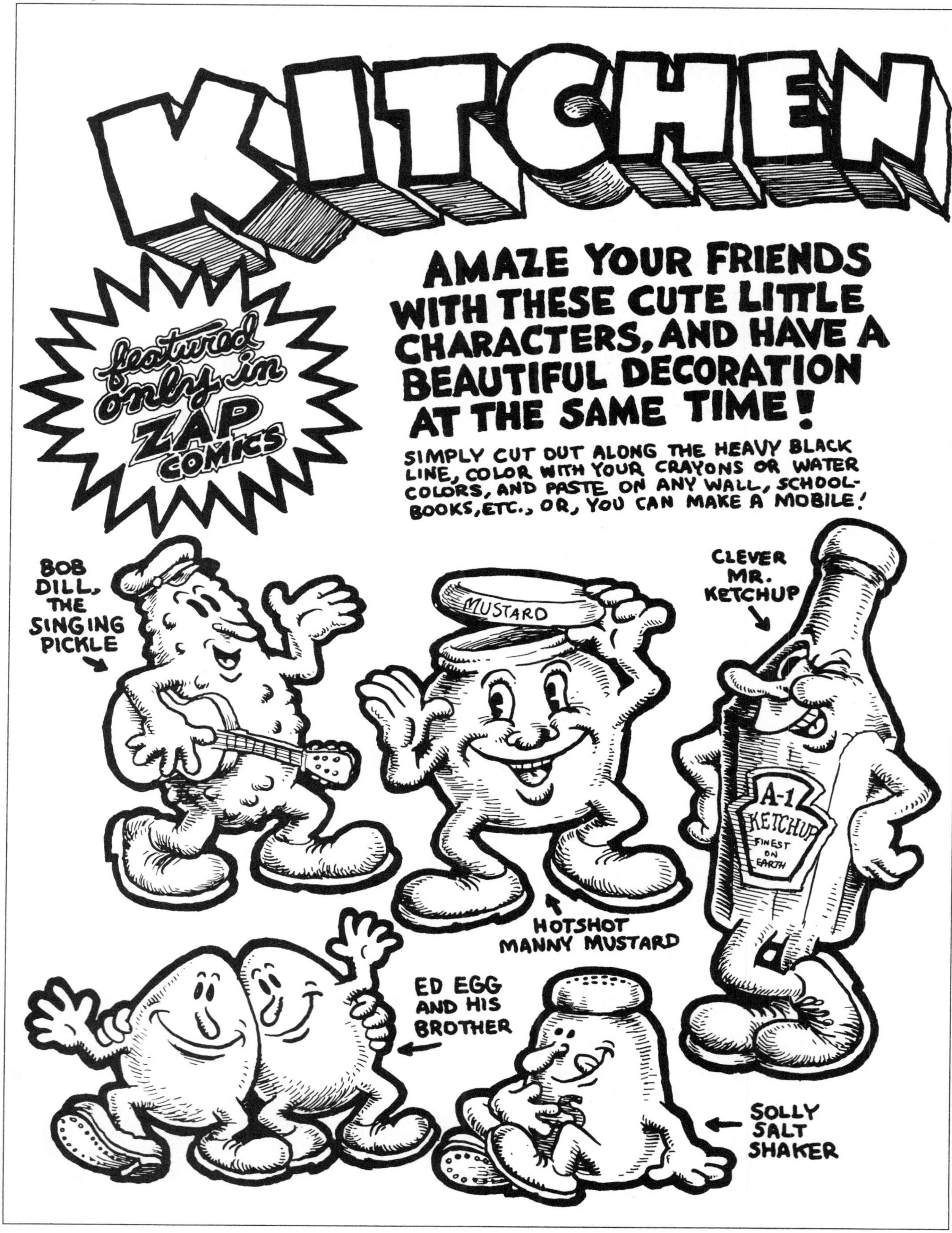
KITCHEN
featured only in ZAP COMICS
AMAZE YOUR FRIENDS WITH THESE CUTE LITTLE CHARACTERS, AND HAVE A BEAUTIFUL DECORATION AT THE SAME TIME!
SIMPLY CUT OUT ALONG THE HEAVY BLACK LINE, COLOR WITH YOUR CRAYONS OR WATER COLORS, AND PASTE ON ANY WALL, SCHOOL-BOOKS, ETC., OR, YOU CAN MAKE A MOBILE!
BOB DILL, THE SINGING PICKLE
MUSTARD
CLEVER MR. KETCHUP
A-1 KETCHUP FINEST ON EARTH
HOTSHOT MANNY MUSTARD
ED EGG AND HIS BROTHER
SOLLY SALT SHAKER

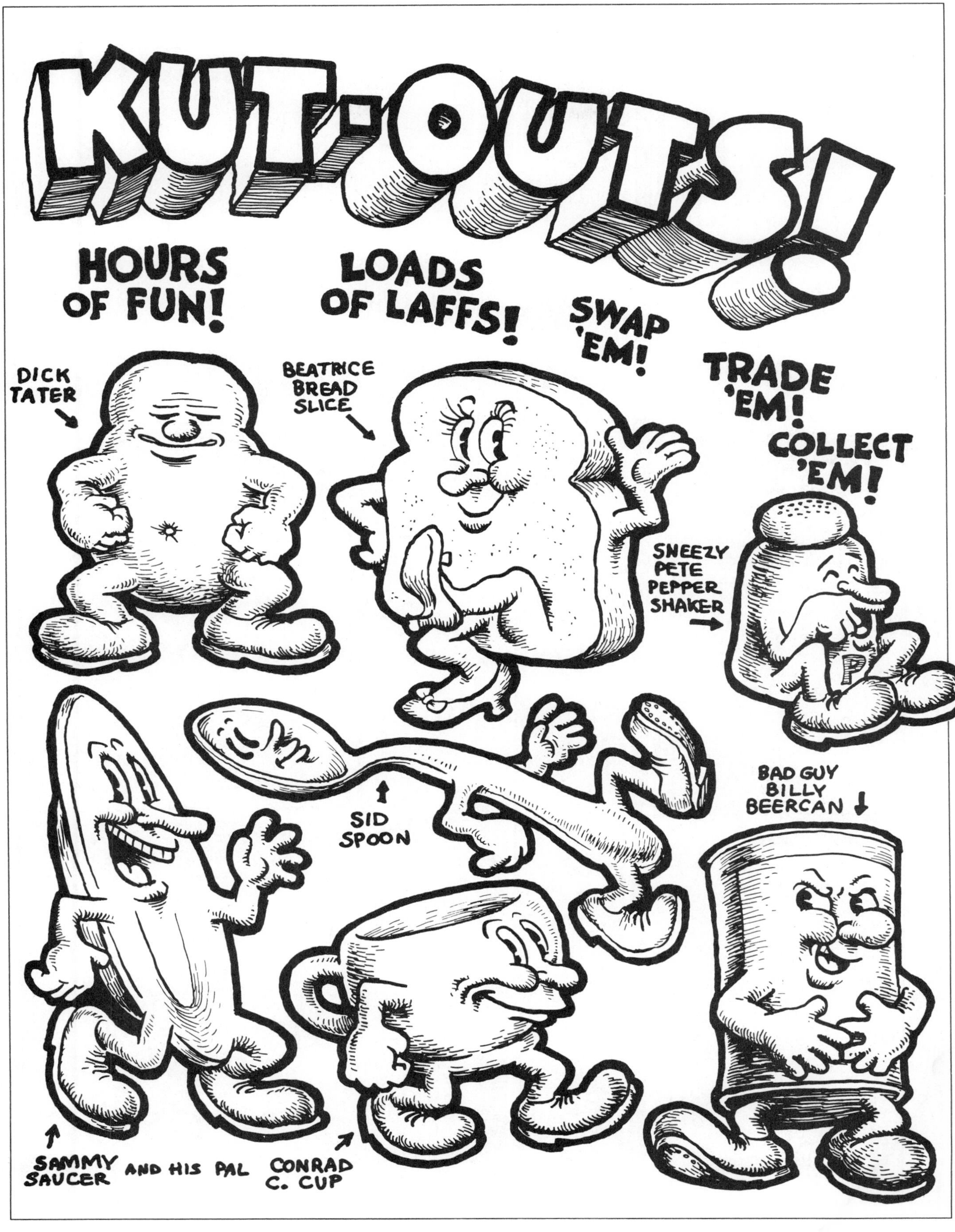
KUT-OUTS!
HOURS OF FUN!
LOADS OF LAFFS!
SWAP 'EM!
TRADE 'EM!
COLLECT 'EM!
DICK TATER
BEATRICE BREAD SLICE
SNEEZY PETE PEPPER SHAKER
SID SPOON
BAD GUY BILLY BEERCAN
SAMMY SAUCER AND HIS PAL CONRAD C. CUP

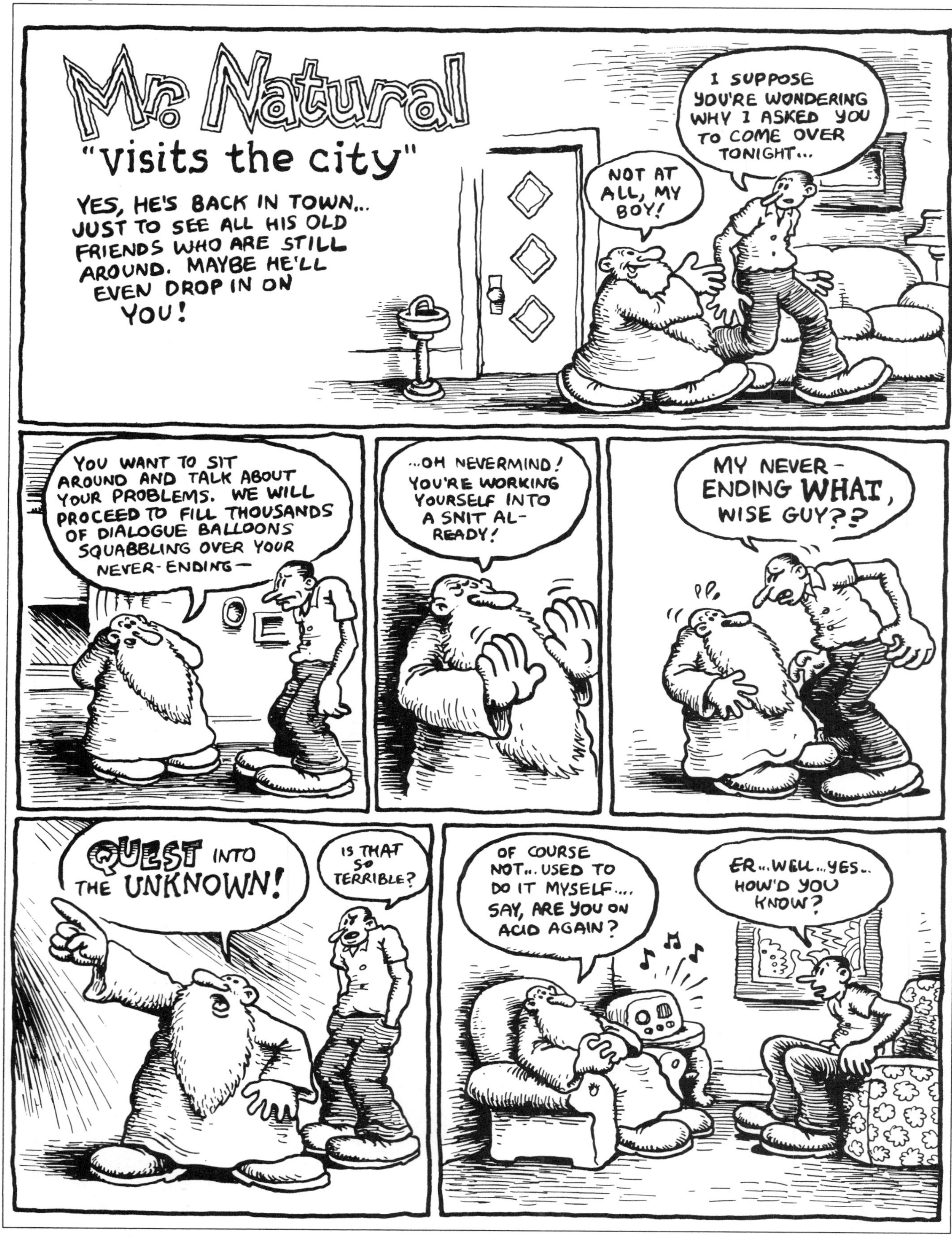
Mr. Natural
"visits the city"
YES, HE'S BACK IN TOWN... JUST TO SEE ALL HIS OLD FRIENDS WHO ARE STILL AROUND. MAYBE HE'LL EVEN DROP IN ON YOU!
I SUPPOSE YOU'RE WONDERING WHY I ASKED YOU TO COME OVER TONIGHT...
NOT AT ALL, MY BOY!
YOU WANT TO SIT AROUND AND TALK ABOUT YOUR PROBLEMS. WE WILL PROCEED TO FILL THOUSANDS OF DIALOGUE BALLOONS SQUABBLING OVER YOUR NEVER-ENDING—
...OH NEVERMIND! YOU'RE WORKING YOURSELF INTO A SNIT AL-READY!
MY NEVER-ENDING WHAT, WISE GUY??
QUEST INTO THE UNKNOWN!
IS THAT SO TERRIBLE?
OF COURSE NOT... USED TO DO IT MYSELF.... SAY, ARE YOU ON ACID AGAIN?
ER...WELL...YES.. HOW'D YOU KNOW?

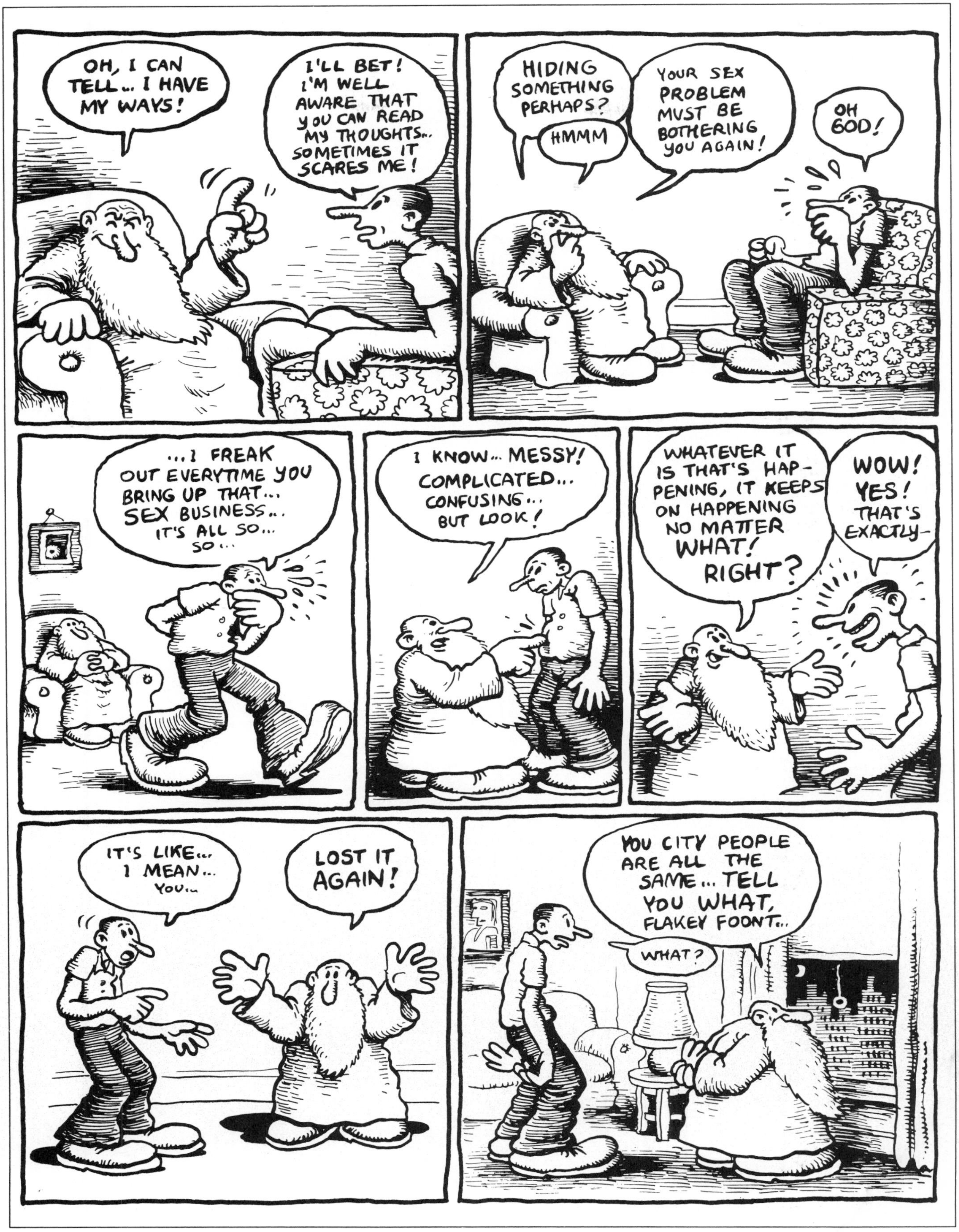

OH, I CAN TELL... I HAVE MY WAYS!
I'LL BET! I'M WELL AWARE THAT YOU CAN READ MY THOUGHTS... SOMETIMES IT SCARES ME!
HIDING SOMETHING PERHAPS?
HMMM
YOUR SEX PROBLEM MUST BE BOTHERING YOU AGAIN!
OH GOD!
...I FREAK OUT EVERYTIME YOU BRING UP THAT... SEX BUSINESS... IT'S ALL SO... SO...
I KNOW... MESSY! COMPLICATED... CONFUSING... BUT LOOK!
WHATEVER IT IS THAT'S HAP-PENING, IT KEEPS ON HAPPENING NO MATTER WHAT! RIGHT?
WOW! YES! THAT'S EXACTLY-
IT'S LIKE... I MEAN... YOU...
LOST IT AGAIN!
YOU CITY PEOPLE ARE ALL THE SAME... TELL YOU WHAT, FLAKEY FOONT...
WHAT?

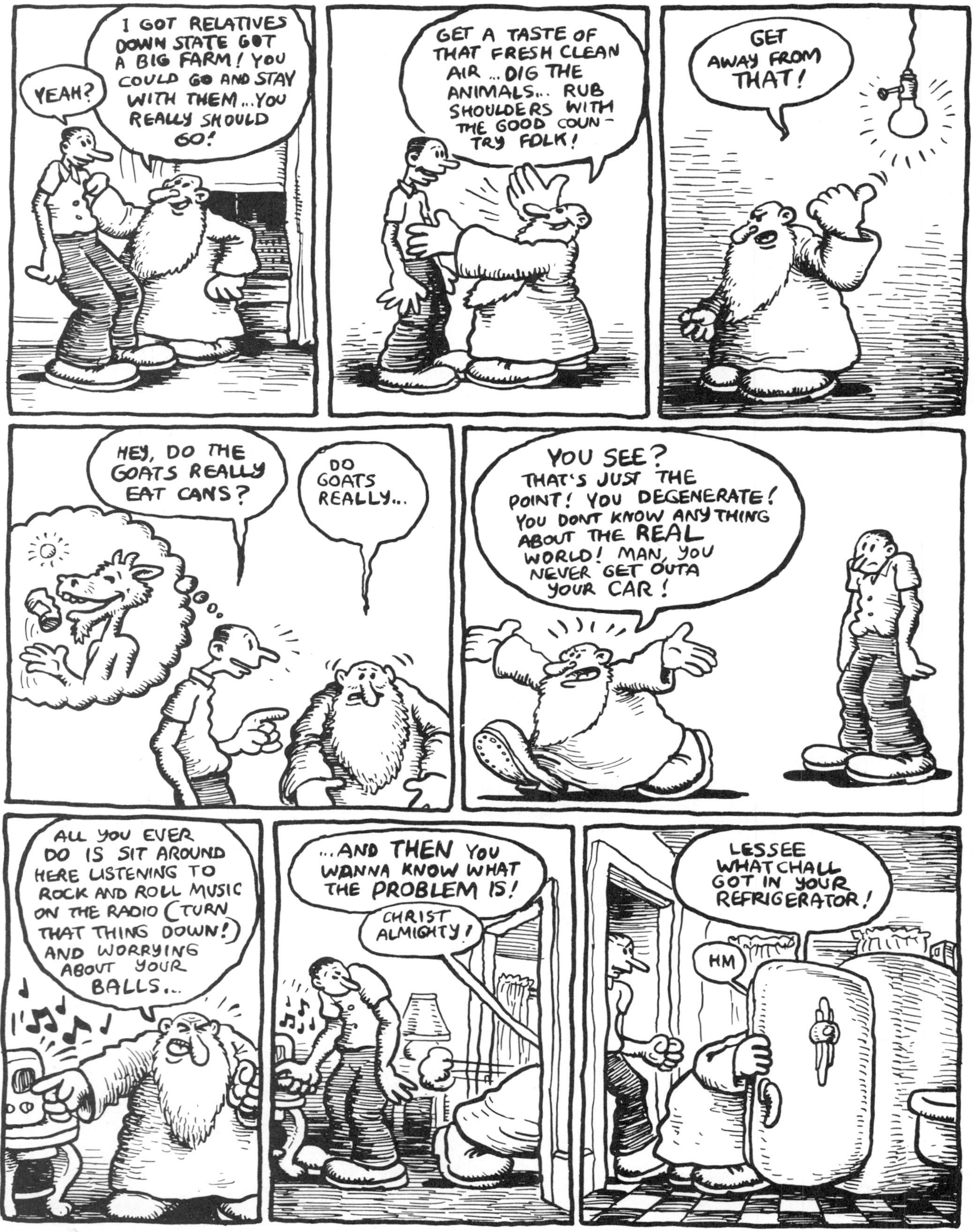
I GOT RELATIVES DOWN STATE GOT A BIG FARM! YOU COULD GO AND STAY WITH THEM...YOU REALLY SHOULD GO!
YEAH?
GET A TASTE OF THAT FRESH CLEAN AIR ...DIG THE ANIMALS... RUB SHOULDERS WITH THE GOOD COUNTRY FOLK!
GET AWAY FROM THAT!
HEY, DO THE GOATS REALLY EAT CANS?
DO GOATS REALLY...
YOU SEE? THAT'S JUST THE POINT! YOU DEGENERATE! YOU DONT KNOW ANYTHING ABOUT THE REAL WORLD! MAN, YOU NEVER GET OUTA YOUR CAR!
ALL YOU EVER DO IS SIT AROUND HERE LISTENING TO ROCK AND ROLL MUSIC ON THE RADIO (TURN THAT THING DOWN!) AND WORRYING ABOUT YOUR BALLS...
...AND THEN YOU WANNA KNOW WHAT THE PROBLEM IS!
CHRIST ALMIGHTY!
LESSEE WHATCHALL GOT IN YOUR REFRIGERATOR!
HM

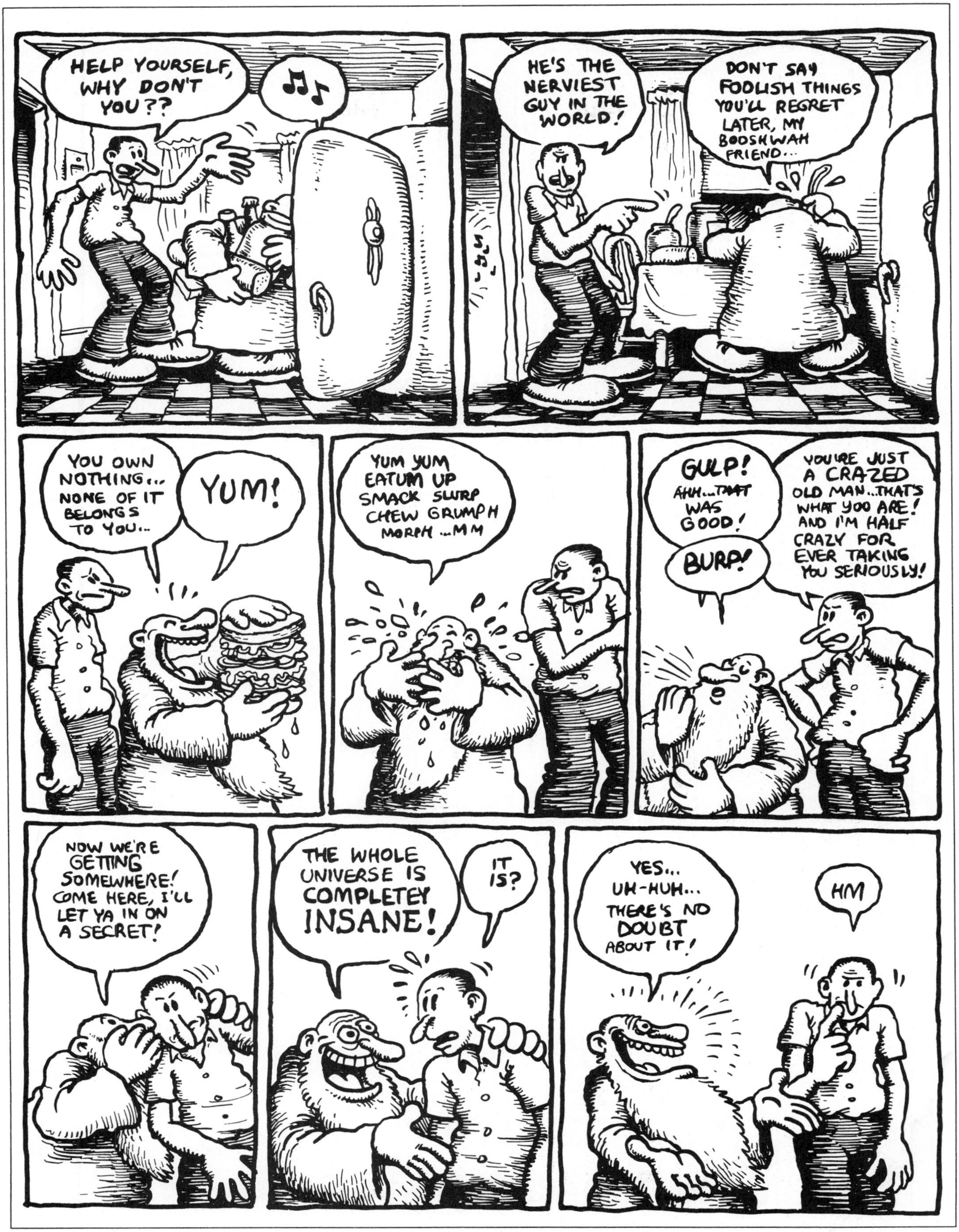
HELP YOURSELF, WHY DON'T YOU??
♫♪
HE'S THE NERVIEST GUY IN THE WORLD!
DON'T SAY FOOLISH THINGS YOU'LL REGRET LATER, MY BOOSHWAH FRIEND...
YOU OWN NOTHING... NONE OF IT BELONGS TO YOU...
YUM!
YUM YUM EATUM UP SMACK SLURP CHEW GRUMPH MORPH ...MM
GULP! AHH...THAT WAS GOOD!
BURP!
YOU'RE JUST A CRAZED OLD MAN...THAT'S WHAT YOO ARE! AND I'M HALF CRAZY FOR EVER TAKING YOU SERIOUSLY!
NOW WE'RE GETTING SOMEWHERE! COME HERE, I'LL LET YA IN ON A SECRET!
THE WHOLE UNIVERSE IS COMPLETEY INSANE!
IT IS?
YES... UH-HUH... THERE'S NO DOUBT ABOUT IT!
HM

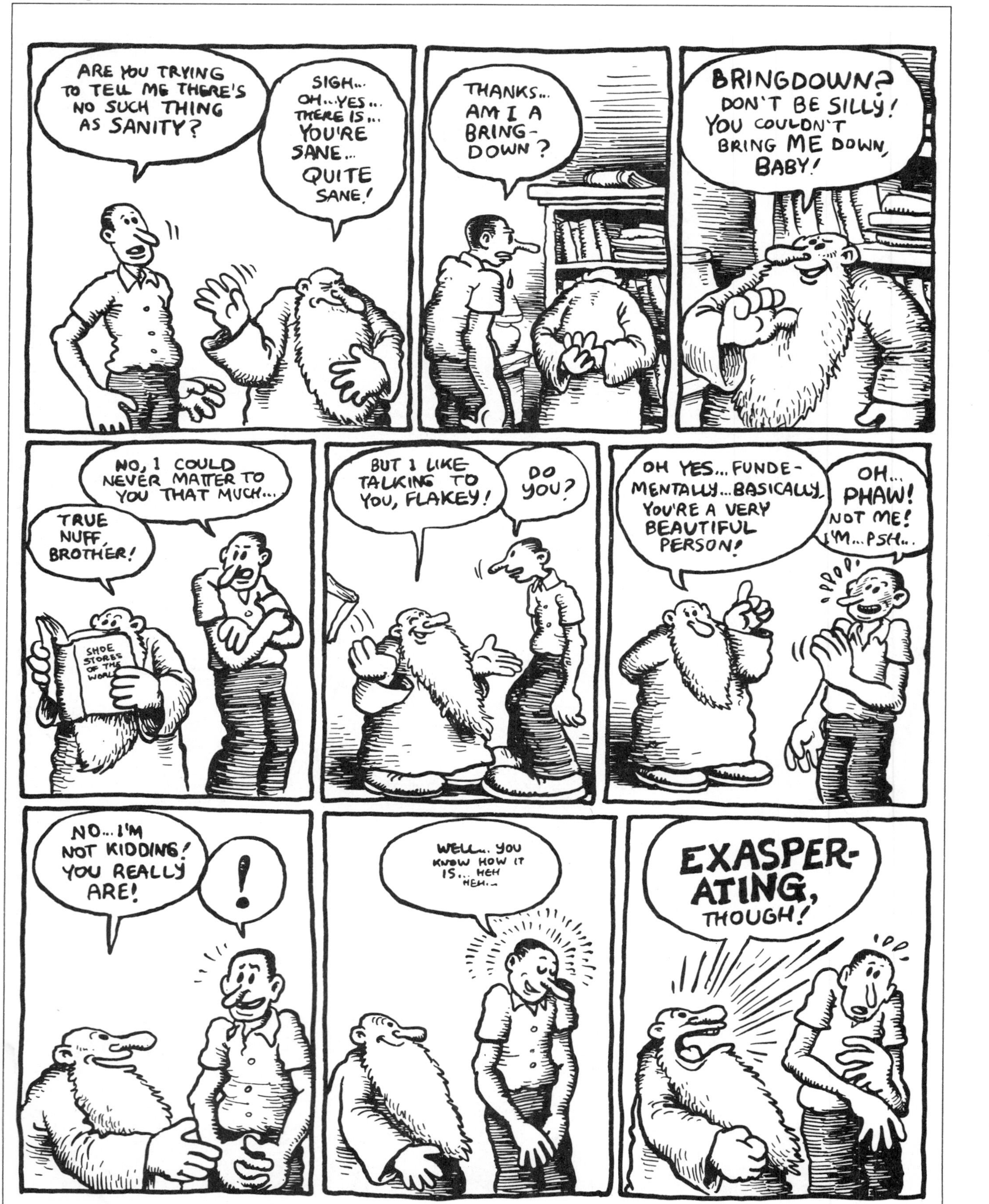
ARE YOU TRYING TO TELL ME THERE'S NO SUCH THING AS SANITY?
SIGH... OH...YES... THERE IS... YOU'RE SANE... QUITE SANE!
THANKS... AM I A BRING-DOWN?
BRINGDOWN? DON'T BE SILLY! YOU COULDN'T BRING ME DOWN, BABY!
NO, I COULD NEVER MATTER TO YOU THAT MUCH...
TRUE NUFF, BROTHER!
SHOE STORIES OF THE WORLD
BUT I LIKE TALKING TO YOU, FLAKEY!
DO YOU?
OH YES... FUNDE-MENTALLY... BASICALLY, YOU'RE A VERY BEAUTIFUL PERSON!
OH... PHAW! NOT ME! I'M... PSH...
NO... I'M NOT KIDDING! YOU REALLY ARE!
!
WELL... YOU KNOW HOW IT IS... HEH HEH...
EXASPER-ATING, THOUGH!

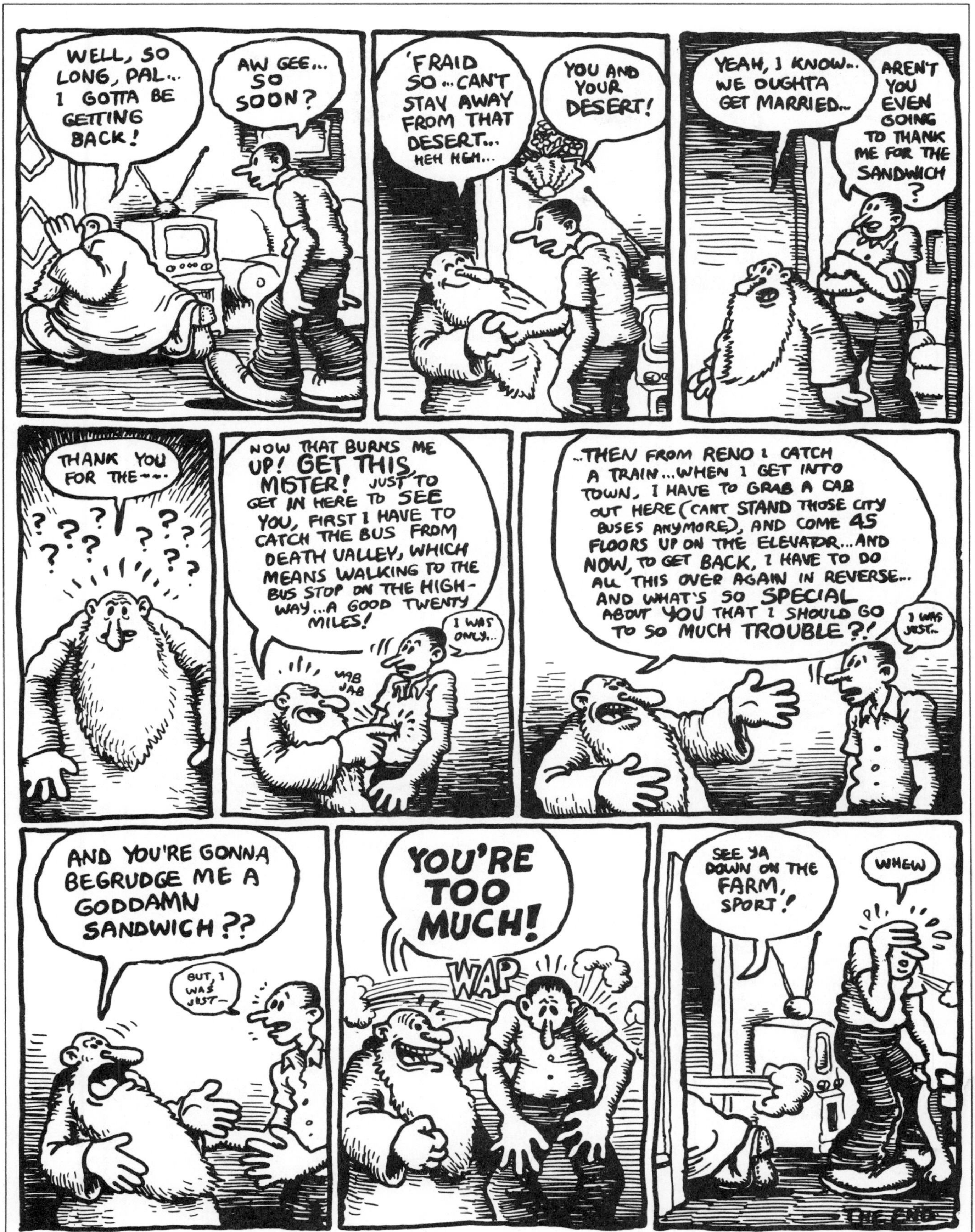
WELL, SO LONG, PAL.. I GOTTA BE GETTING BACK!
AW GEE... SO SOON?
'FRAID SO...CAN'T STAY AWAY FROM THAT DESERT... HEH HEH...
YOU AND YOUR DESERT!
YEAH, I KNOW.. WE OUGHTA GET MARRIED..
AREN'T YOU EVEN GOING TO THANK ME FOR THE SANDWICH?
THANK YOU FOR THE---
? ? ? ? ? ? ? ? ? ?
NOW THAT BURNS ME UP! GET THIS, MISTER! JUST TO GET IN HERE TO SEE YOU, FIRST I HAVE TO CATCH THE BUS FROM DEATH VALLEY, WHICH MEANS WALKING TO THE BUS STOP ON THE HIGH-WAY...A GOOD TWENTY MILES!
I WAS ONLY..
YAB JAB
..THEN FROM RENO I CATCH A TRAIN...WHEN I GET INTO TOWN, I HAVE TO GRAB A CAB OUT HERE (CANT STAND THOSE CITY BUSES ANYMORE), AND COME 45 FLOORS UP ON THE ELEVATOR...AND NOW, TO GET BACK, I HAVE TO DO ALL THIS OVER AGAIN IN REVERSE... AND WHAT'S SO SPECIAL ABOUT YOU THAT I SHOULD GO TO SO MUCH TROUBLE?!
I WAS JUST..
AND YOU'RE GONNA BEGRUDGE ME A GODDAMN SANDWICH??
BUT, I WAS JUST—
YOU'RE TOO MUCH!
WAP
SEE YA DOWN ON THE FARM, SPORT!
WHEW
THE END

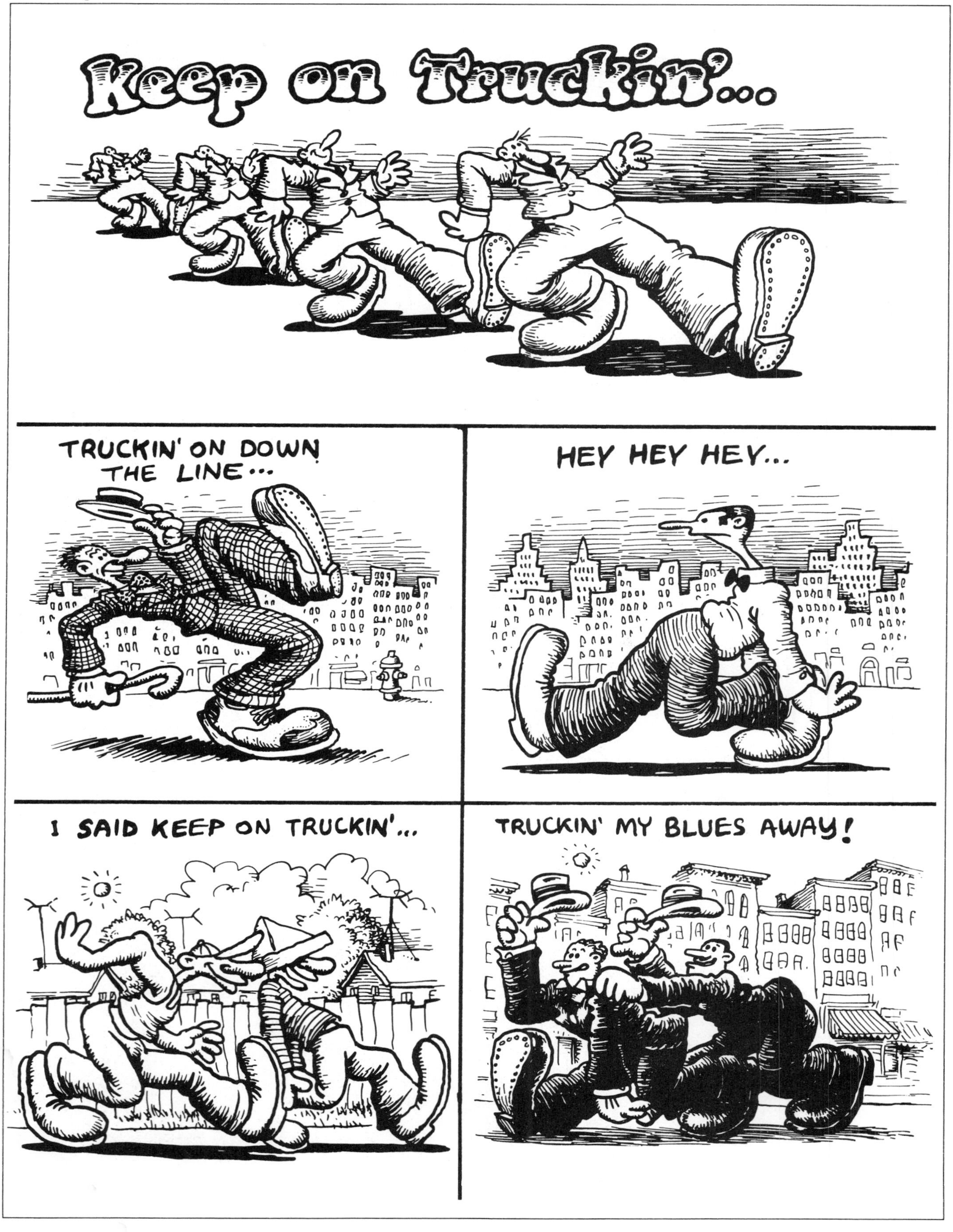
Keep on Truckin'...
TRUCKIN' ON DOWN THE LINE...
HEY HEY HEY...
I SAID KEEP ON TRUCKIN'...
TRUCKIN' MY BLUES AWAY!

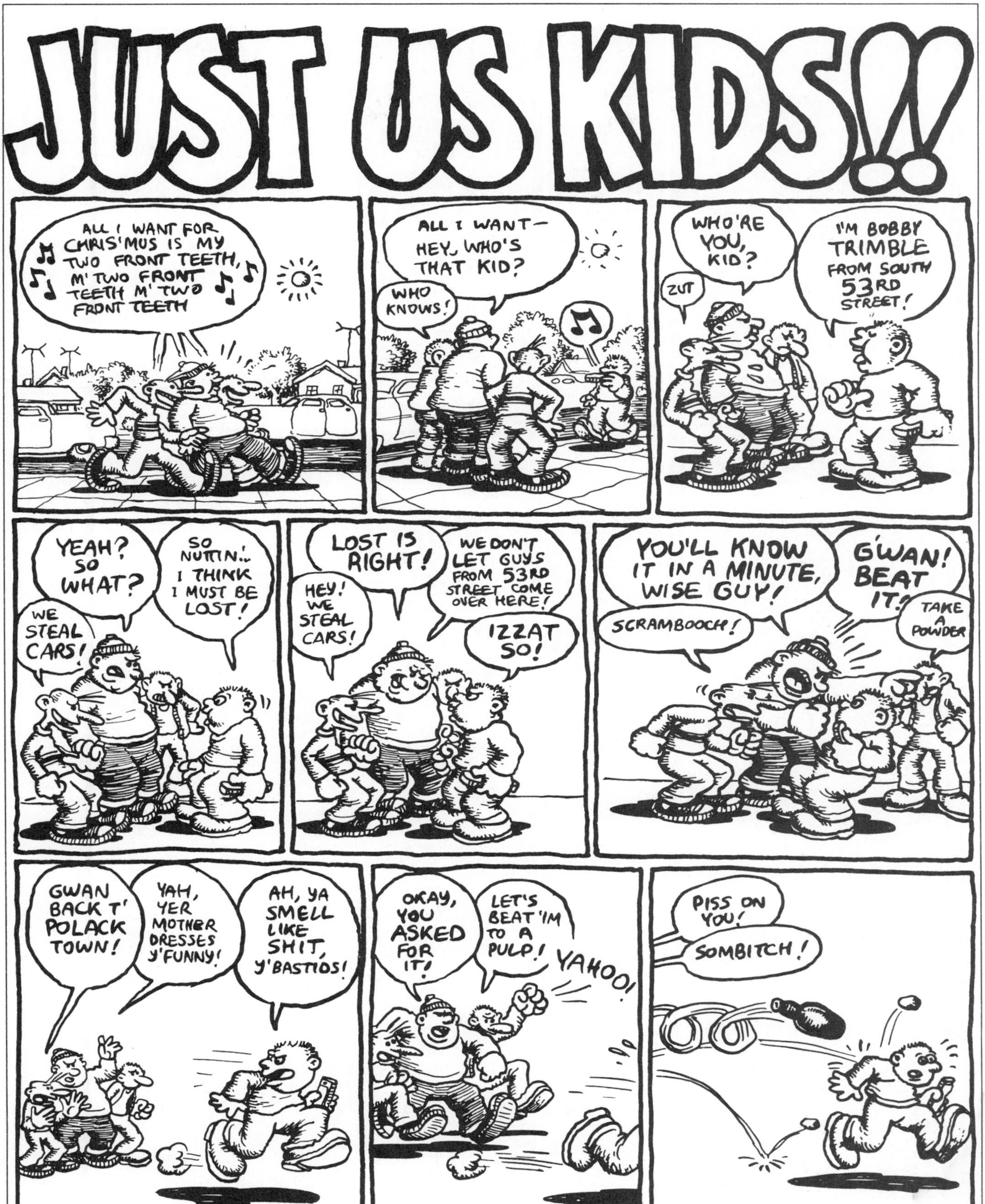
JUST US KIDS!!
ALL I WANT FOR CHRIS'MUS IS MY TWO FRONT TEETH, M' TWO FRONT TEETH M' TWO FRONT TEETH
ALL I WANT— HEY, WHO'S THAT KID?
WHO KNOWS!
WHO'RE YOU, KID?
ZUT
I'M BOBBY TRIMBLE FROM SOUTH 53RD STREET!
YEAH? SO WHAT?
SO NUTTIN'... I THINK I MUST BE LOST!
WE STEAL CARS!
LOST IS RIGHT!
WE DON'T LET GUYS FROM 53RD STREET COME OVER HERE!
HEY! WE STEAL CARS!
IZZAT SO!
YOU'LL KNOW IT IN A MINUTE, WISE GUY!
G'WAN! BEAT IT!
SCRAMBOOCH!
TAKE A POWDER
GWAN BACK T' POLACK TOWN!
YAH, YER MOTHER DRESSES Y'FUNNY!
AH, YA SMELL LIKE SHIT, Y'BASTIDS!
OKAY, YOU ASKED FOR IT!
LET'S BEAT 'IM TO A PULP!
YAHOO!
PISS ON YOU!
SOMBITCH!

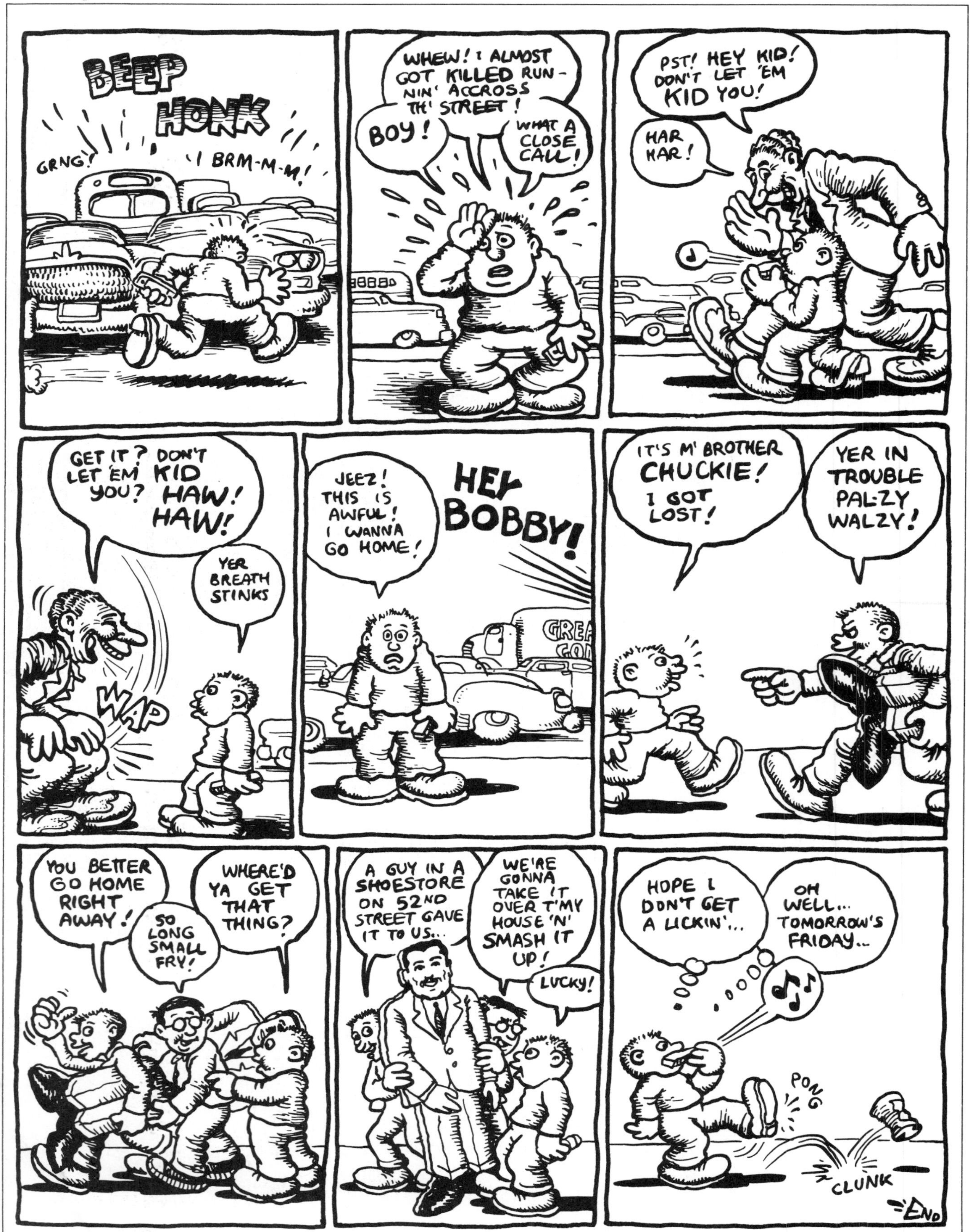
BEEP
HONK
GRNG!
BRM-M-M!
WHEW! I ALMOST GOT KILLED RUN-NIN' ACCROSS TH' STREET!
BOY!
WHAT A CLOSE CALL!
PST! HEY KID! DON'T LET 'EM KID YOU!
HAR HAR!
GET IT? DON'T LET 'EM KID YOU? HAW! HAW!
YER BREATH STINKS
WAP
JEEZ! THIS IS AWFUL! I WANNA GO HOME!
HEY BOBBY!
IT'S M' BROTHER CHUCKIE! I GOT LOST!
YER IN TROUBLE PAL-ZY WALZY!
YOU BETTER GO HOME RIGHT AWAY!
SO LONG SMALL FRY!
WHERE'D YA GET THAT THING?
A GUY IN A SHOESTORE ON 52ND STREET GAVE IT TO US...
WE'RE GONNA TAKE IT OVER T'MY HOUSE 'N' SMASH IT UP!
LUCKY!
HOPE I DON'T GET A LICKIN'...
OH WELL... TOMORROW'S FRIDAY...
PONG
CLUNK
END

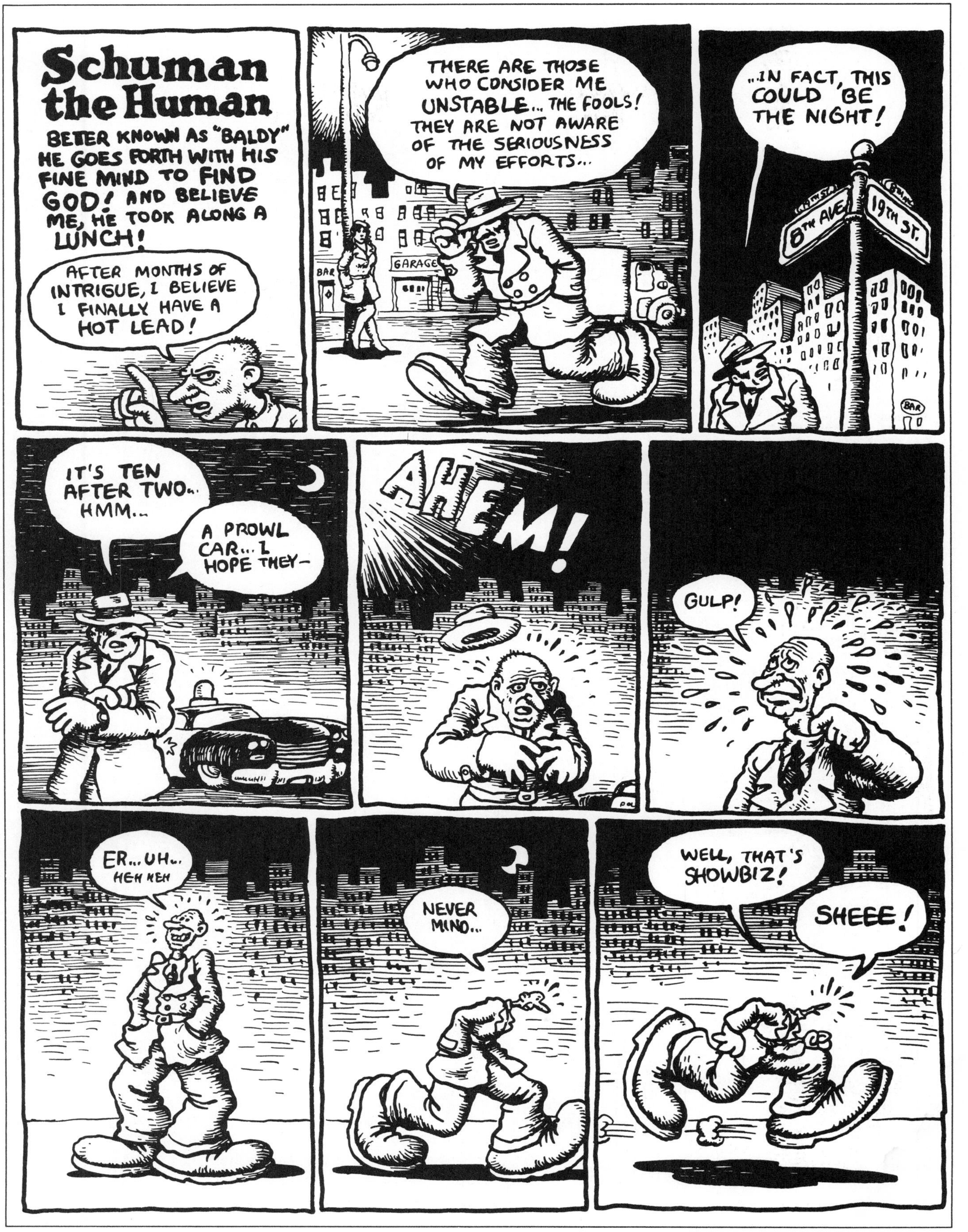
Schuman the Human
BETTER KNOWN AS "BALDY" HE GOES FORTH WITH HIS FINE MIND TO FIND GOD! AND BELIEVE ME, HE TOOK ALONG A LUNCH!
AFTER MONTHS OF INTRIGUE, I BELIEVE I FINALLY HAVE A HOT LEAD!
THERE ARE THOSE WHO CONSIDER ME UNSTABLE... THE FOOLS! THEY ARE NOT AWARE OF THE SERIOUSNESS OF MY EFFORTS...
GARAGE
BAR
...IN FACT, THIS COULD BE THE NIGHT!
8TH AVE
19TH ST.
BAR
IT'S TEN AFTER TWO.. HMM...
A PROWL CAR... I HOPE THEY-
AHEM!
GULP!
ER... UH.. HEH HEH
NEVER MIND...
WELL, THAT'S SHOWBIZ!
SHEEE!

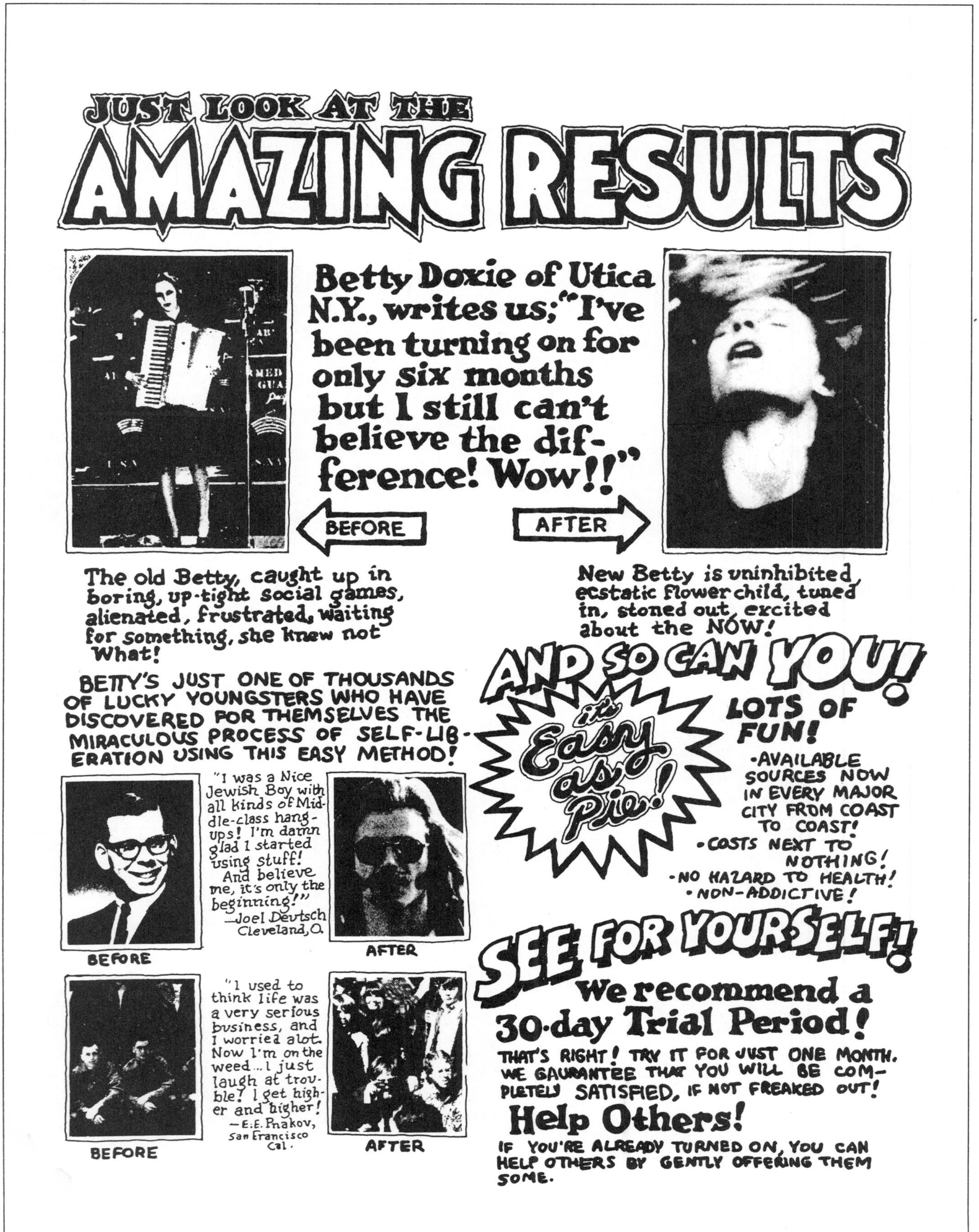

# JUST LOOK AT THE AMAZING RESULTS

Betty Doxie of Utica N.Y., writes us; "I've been turning on for only six months but I still can't believe the dif-ference! Wow!!"

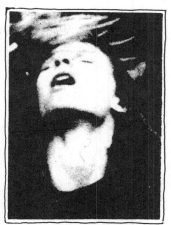

← BEFORE | AFTER →

The old Betty, caught up in boring, up-tight social games, alienated, frustrated, waiting for something, she knew not what!

New Betty is uninhibited, ecstatic flower child, tuned in, stoned out, excited about the NOW!

BETTY'S JUST ONE OF THOUSANDS OF LUCKY YOUNGSTERS WHO HAVE DISCOVERED FOR THEMSELVES THE MIRACULOUS PROCESS OF SELF-LIB-ERATION USING THIS EASY METHOD!

BEFORE

"I was a Nice Jewish Boy with all kinds of Mid-dle-class hang-ups! I'm damn glad I started using stuff!
And believe me, it's only the beginning!"
—Joel Deutsch Cleveland, O.

AFTER

BEFORE

"I used to think life was a very serious business, and I worried alot. Now I'm on the weed... I just laugh at trou-ble! I get high-er and higher!"
—E.E. Pnakov, San Francisco Cal.

AFTER

## AND SO CAN YOU!

it's Easy as Pie!

LOTS OF FUN!

• AVAILABLE SOURCES NOW IN EVERY MAJOR CITY FROM COAST TO COAST!
• COSTS NEXT TO NOTHING!
• NO HAZARD TO HEALTH!
• NON-ADDICTIVE!

## SEE FOR YOURSELF!

We recommend a 30-day Trial Period!

THAT'S RIGHT! TRY IT FOR JUST ONE MONTH. WE GAURANTEE THAT YOU WILL BE COM-PLETELY SATISFIED, IF NOT FREAKED OUT!

### Help Others!

IF YOU'RE ALREADY TURNED ON, YOU CAN HELP OTHERS BY GENTLY OFFERING THEM SOME.